Time-Steps of the Cosmic Horse

Time-Steps of the Cosmic Horse

The Contemplative Philosophy of the Great Forest (Bṛhadāraṇyaka) Upaniṣad

Debashish Banerji

Nalanda International
Los Angeles (USA)

DK PRINTWORLD
Publishers of Indian Traditions

Cataloging in Publication Data — DK

[Courtesy: D.K. Agencies (P) Ltd. <docinfo@dkagencies.com>]

Banerji, Debashish, author.

Time-steps of the cosmic horse : the contemplative philosophy of the great forest (Bṛhadāraṇyaka) Upaniṣad / Debashish Banerji.

pages cm

Includes bibliographical references and index.

ISBN 9788124612286 (HB)

1. Upanishads. Bṛhadāraṇyakopaniṣad – Criticism, interpretation, etc. I. Nalanda Consciousness Network (Los Angeles, Calif.), publisher. II. Title.

LCC BL1124.7.B756B36 2024 | DDC 294.59218 23

ISBN 978-81-246-1228-6
First published in India 2024

Published by:
Nalanda Consciousness Network
"Nalanda", 6418, Spring Park Avenue
Los Angeles, CA - 90056 (USA)
Phones: (310)-430-8057

and

D.K. Printworld (P) Ltd.
Regd. Office : "Vedaśrī", F-395, Sudarshan Park
ESI Hospital Metro Station, New Delhi - 110015
Phones : (011) 4172 2626, 98713 94815
e-mail : indology@dkprintworld.com
Web : www.dkprintworld.com

Printed by: D.K. Printworld(P) Ltd., New Delhi

To
the masters
of countercultural style

Preface

I CAME across Sri Aurobindo's translations and interpretations of the Upaniṣads in the 1970s, at a time when counterculture was "blowing in the wind" and the established and predictable answers to living had lost their taste. Not that these texts drew my attention sufficiently for me to delve into them at this time, but my contact with them was coloured by a freshness, not the deadweight of canonical literature. My own dissatisfaction with the expectations of life in which I found myself amplified by the mood of the time made me receptive to the creative power of Sri Aurobindo's translations and commentaries, even though I merely browsed these writings. The description of the sacrificial horse with which the *Bṛhadāraṇyaka Upaniṣad* begins made a particularly strong impact on me, a surreal and cosmic description that immediately expanded one's horizons. Within this remarkable description, there was a line that stopped the mind in its tracks with its unexpected implications: Time is the self of the horse sacrificial (*BU* I.1.1, in Aurobindo 2001: 268) – a line that left a seed waiting to germinate. To the static image of a cosmic Being it bestowed a soul of Becoming, the time-steps of freedom and unpredictable change. In retrospect I realized how fortuitous this was, since had I encountered instead the more common translation of this line by established scholars such as Radhakrishnan (1968: 149) or more recently, Olivelle, (1998: 37) "The year is the body of the sacrificial horse", the wooden animal would have never left its musty stable in my mind.

It was only after I came to Los Angeles at the end of the 1980s that the Upaniṣads beckoned to me again. The philosopher

Dr H. Maheswari from the Sri Aurobindo Ashram had come to visit the East-West Cultural Center and offered a retreat on Sri Aurobindo's interpretation of the *Īśa Upaniṣad*. In the very first of those sessions I re-experienced the shock I had experienced when I encountered the first stanza of the *Bṛhadāraṇyaka Upaniṣad*, a shock that had less to do with content than with style. To be presented with lines like

> One unmoving that is swifter than Mind. That the gods reach not, for It progresses ever in front. That, standing, passes beyond others as they run. In That the Master of Life establishes the Waters.
>
> That moves and That moves not; That is far and the same is near; That is within all this and That also is outside all this.
>
> – *ĪśaUp* 4-5, in Aurobindo 2001: 6-7

opened the doors on another dimension, it stunned the expected and brought close a profound presence. The noisy certitudes of thought were imperiously hushed by the entrance of something vast, like the being of Night dressed in countless stars. The mystery of the Upaniṣads was kindled in me once more, the seed that was sown in that early contact with the *Bṛhadāraṇyaka* had begun to sprout.

However, it was only after 2005 that I began a more systematic relation with these texts. For one, my teaching position at the University of Philosophical Research gave me the opportunity to spend more time with them as I taught a course in early Indian wisdom literature. But more importantly, this period coincided with an enhanced intuition of the relation of literary style with cultural history and, consequently, a growing sense of the historicity of the early Upaniṣads. Michel Foucault's epistemic understanding of history and the extension and application of these views to mystic literature by Michel de Certeau goaded me in this direction. I became increasingly aware of the countercultural concerns of the Upaniṣads, concerns that resonated profoundly with our own times. The more I thought of it, the more obvious were its signs, the sarcasm against casteism, ritualism, materialism, structuralism, monoculturalism; the value given to their opposites, pluralism, interpretation, direct experience, multiple modes of knowing, varieties of non-dualism. This semiology was the cunning style of language of the Upaniṣads, constituted by its literary choices, such as a flexible use of metaphor, paradox, polysemy, puns, puzzles, gnomic parables and an exploitation of the syntax-free property of Sanskrit to keep open a space of plurality. Above all this was an intangible diction that knocked on the doors of experience. I also became aware of the turn towards pre-Socratic philosophy in postmodern thought, starting with Heidegger's readings into early Greek thought, conducted through a profound contemplation of its language use and its literary devices, and saw clear parallels in Upaniṣadic thinking. I grew to appreciate the contemporary relevance of the *Īśa Upaniṣad* and along with it, its centrality in the problem of becoming which occupied Sri Aurobindo – a concern with radical pluralism understood as a contested separative ontology pitted against an even deeper concern with its opposite, the obliteration of pluralism in a monism of undifferentiated identity:

> Into a blind darkness they enter who follow after the Ignorance, they as if into a greater darkness who devote themselves to the Knowledge alone.
>
> Other, verily, it is said, is that which comes by the Knowledge, other that which comes by the Ignorance; this is the lore we have received from the wise who revealed That to our understanding.
>
> He who knows That as both in one, the Knowledge and the Ignorance, by the Ignorance crosses beyond death and by the Knowledge enjoys Immortality.
>
> – *ĪśaUp* 12-14, in Aurobindo 2001: 8-9

Knowledge, here *vidyā*, a transpersonal condition of undifferentiated unity, finds its cultural parallel in its symbolic translation as Veda, the canonical scripture, *Śabda-Brahman*. If the entry into a chaos of separative egos (*avidyā* – ignorance) was dangerous, the monocultural semantics of canonical scripture was even more dangerous, since it foreclosed interpretation and freedom of individual experience in the name of truth and hence constituted a fascism or totalitarianism of thought. Keeping pluralism open and fostering a culture of intimate relationship with truth required a style of thought that safeguarded openness through contemplative devices serving a paradoxical plane of becoming, That in which both knowledge and ignorance, absolute monism and radical pluralism were known as one. I began to value this style of thought as the revolutionary contribution of the Upaniṣads, a style of language at once poetic and philosophical, ambiguous and experiential. I realized, of course, that this was not the received understanding of the Upaniṣads, which the traditional Vedāntic commentators, starting with Śaṅkarācārya in the eighth century and perhaps from even earlier, from the *Brahmasūtra*, have considered indisputable revealed scripture, Śruti. It is this that has made the Upaniṣads today as canonical as the Veda, indeed more so in an interpretation of Vedānta, end of the Veda, as essence of the Veda. This convinced me even further of the constructed nature of our received history, its subjection to the politics of truth, active through all time. The contest between two forms of darkness, authoritarian monism and chaotic pluralism, whether seen as a cultural or psychological condition (or both), is equally a central problem of our times. My engagement with this problem of postmodernism side by side with the *Īśa Upaniṣad* as seen by Sri Aurobindo drove me to give a set of lectures which resulted in my book *Meditations on the Isha Upanishad* (2020).

Subsequent to this, this question of a praxis of open language as a style of thought, a noology, that operates as micropolitical strategy against cooptation by state or capital and forms the basis of an alternative nomadic and gnostic culture of plural approaches to and experiences of the absolute plane of immanence (*Brahman*), intensified with my encounter and engagement with the writings of Deleuze and Guattari (1986), particularly their conceptualization of minor literature through their study of Franz Kafka. This phase coincided with my move to the California Institute of Integral Studies in San Francisco in 2016. In 2018, I offered a course on the transformative themes and devices of the Upaniṣads, which allowed me further concentration on the Upaniṣads as a countercultural style of thought. The present meditations on the *Bṛhadāraṇyaka Upaniṣad* take their inception in these considerations. The excitement of these earliest texts where a space is being cleared for unmediated relationship and identity between the individual and the only thing that exists, one without a second (*ekamevādvitīyam brahma*), one and infinite at the same time, is palpable. The gap between the Real-Idea of Being and its multiple self-Becoming in freedom of relation is captured through a prismatic polygonality of traversal that allows multiple contemplations and connections, an alternative world of gnostic intimacy. The diverse world of power hierarchies is not substantial; something as insubstantial as breath or as fluid as fire is the self (*ātman*) of becoming that lives in us and mutates rhizomatically, shape-shifting into the constituents of this world. Knowing this puts us in contact with the self of all selves (*ātman*), the being of the becoming (*Brahman*). "Knowing", in this sense is the true Veda, a self-knowing that is our birthright since it is what knows itself as us. This contact with self-knowing is the mystic or gnostic hermeneutic circle of the Upaniṣad; indeed it *is* Upaniṣad, the secret knowledge, the one knowing which all is known, achieved and enjoyed – *yasmin vijñāte sarvam evaṁ vijñātaṁ bhavati* (*MuUp* I.3) – repeated infinitely in the relations of worlding, *ya evam veda*.

Earlier versions of some of these chapters were carried in

the house journal of the Sri Aurobindo Bhavan, Kolkata, *Śraddhā* and shared in contemplative retreats at the Sri Aurobindo Sadhana Peetham at Lodi, CA in 2019. I am grateful to the editor of *Śraddhā*, Arup Basu, to my students at CIIS and to friends gathering in contemplative fellowship at Lodi for their comments and contributions leading to this text. I am grateful to those who have spent time in one-on-one discussions with me after reading or listening to these chapters, such as Keka Chakraborty, Jonathan Kay, Amrita Banerji, Subhash Mutsuddi, Jim Ryan, Jim Page and Margaret Phanes. To the last also go my thanks for the custom-designed cover image for the book, *Warp and Hoof*.

Kolkata **Debashish Banerji**
30 August 2023

Contents

Abbreviations

AitUp	*Aitareya Upaniṣad*
BG	*Bhagavadgītā*
BU	*Bṛhadāraṇyaka Upaniṣad*
IU	*Īśa Upaniṣad*
KeU	*Kena Upaniṣad*
KU	*Kaṭha Upaniṣad*
MU	*Muṇḍaka Upaniṣad*
ṚV	*Ṛgveda*
TaittUp	*Taittirīya Upaniṣad*
VP	*Viṣṇu Purāṇa*

Introduction

Locating the Bṛhadāraṇyaka Upaniṣad

"GREAT Forest Upaniṣad" is a literal translation for the *Bṛhadāraṇyaka Upaniṣad*. More properly, it should be the Upaniṣad of the Great Forest, since *araṇya* is forest and *āraṇyaka* means "of the forest". Even more specifically, the Āraṇyakas are "forest texts", a class of Vedic literature originating from about the eighth century BCE and dealing with commentarial and contemplative considerations of the Vedas. The term *bṛhad*, meaning vast, is found in the Veda and treated as a synonym of *Brahman*, a term meaning the Divine Word in the Veda, but denoting absolute conscious reality (that which is everywhere, hence vast) in the Upaniṣads and appearing perhaps for the first time with this meaning in the *Bṛhadāraṇyaka Upaniṣad*. From this point of view, the *Bṛhadāraṇyaka Upaniṣad* can be translated as the Upaniṣad of the forest text pertaining to *Brahman*. *Upaniṣad* means literally "to sit near" though in the texts themselves, the term assumes several alternative meanings, such as "secret knowledge", "secret name" or "intimate relation"; thus, the *Bṛhadāraṇyaka Upaniṣad* could be thought of as the forest text of intimate relation with *Brahman* or the forest text of the secret knowledge of *Brahman*.

The *Bṛhadāraṇyaka Upaniṣad* is divided into six chapters (*adhyāyas*), which are grouped in three volumes (*kāṇḍas*) – Madhu Kāṇḍa (volume of honey), Muni Kāṇḍa (volume of the ascetic) and Khila Kāṇḍa (supplementary volume/appendix). Honey in the Veda (see *ṚV* I.90) and early Upaniṣads (*BU* II.5) is a synonym for bliss. The fifth section (*brāhmaṇa*) of the second *adhyāya* of the *Bṛhadāraṇyaka Upaniṣad* is a paean to bliss as the essence of macrocosmos and microcosmos, ending with the self (*ātman*) as the source of both. Muni Kāṇḍa, sometimes called Yājñavalkya Kāṇḍa, consists mostly of the interactions of Yājñavalkya with King Janaka and the advisors of his court, debating matters of conventional knowledge with unconventional twists, not without humour and sometimes with lethal consequences. The term *muni*, related to *mauna*, which means self-imposed silence, refers to one who practises asceticism. Both *madhu* and *muni* are terms related to the forest or wilderness and highlight the kinship of the Upaniṣad and its eponymous description to the forest. The Madhu Kāṇḍa consists of two Brāhmaṇas, the first set in cosmological space–time and the second set in a liminal space–time between domesticity and renunciation. The present text deals with the Madhu Kāṇḍa, which distills the mystic and contemplative philosophy of the Upaniṣad. The Muni Kāṇḍa, dealing with the colloquies of Yājñavalkya, is set in the courtly space–time of the polis, but as evident in the title, this is also a liminal courtly setting, visited by the figure of a *muni* who transits between and is equally at home in the court and the forest.

The Vedas (literally, Knowledge) are considered to be four in number, *Ṛg*, *Yajus*, *Sāma* and *Atharva* and each of these is divided into four classes of texts, the Saṁhitās, Brāhmaṇas, Āraṇyakas and Upaniṣads. The Saṁhitās constitute hymns or poems addressed to a variety of gods, the Brāhmaṇas include mythological passages and ritual instructions, the Āraṇyakas dwell on symbolic explanations and the Upaniṣads deal with proto-philosophical interpretations. Taken as a single body of Vedic literature, these divisions have been related to the four stages of Hindu life (*āśrama dharma*), the Saṁhitās meant for the student stage (*brahmacarya*), the Brāhmaṇas for the householder (*gṛhasthya*), the Āraṇyakas for those leaving social life (*saṁsāra*) to retreat to the forest (*vānaprastha*) and the Upaniṣads for renouncers of *saṁsāra* (*saṁnyāsa*).

This is how Vedic literature is understood by Hindus today, but such an understanding is historically constructed. All the texts mentioned have been codified at different times, the *Ṛgveda Saṁhitā* being the earliest, by modern reckoning, codified around 1700 BCE, the other Vedic Saṁhitās largely derived from the *Ṛgveda Saṁhitā* and thus, later, the *Atharvaveda* considered the latest, *c.*1200 BCE. The earliest Brāhmaṇas, such as the *Śatapatha Brāhmaṇa* originated around 900 BCE, with the Āraṇyakas and Upaniṣads shortly following. The *Bṛhadāraṇyaka Upaniṣad* and *Chāndogya Upaniṣad* are considered to be the earliest Upaniṣads, originating around the eighth-seventh century BCE. As they exist at present, there is no clear dividing line between the early Brāhmaṇas, Āraṇyakas and Upaniṣads. The *Śatapatha Brāhmaṇa*, which is associated with the "white" (organized) collection of the *Yajurveda*, contains the *Bṛhadāraṇyaka* as the eight chapters (*adhyāyas*) of its last book (*kāṇḍa*). Of the three *kāṇḍas* of the *Bṛhadāraṇyaka Upaniṣad*, each ends with a genealogy of teachers. A comparison of these genealogies also indicates the possibly independent diachronic existence of these texts and their retrospective suturing (see Bronkhorst 2007: 219-40).[1] Since there are two rescensions of the *Śatapatha Brāhmaṇa*, this is the fourteenth *kāṇḍa* of the Mādhyandina recension and the seventeenth *kāṇḍa* of the Kāṇva recension. Of these eight *adhyāyas*, the last six chapters constitute the *Bṛhadāraṇyaka Upaniṣad*. In other words, the *Bṛhadāraṇyaka Upaniṣad* is the last part of the Bṛhadāraṇyaka, which forms the last part of the *Śatapatha Brāhmaṇa*.

This conflation of texts points to the editorial extension of the *Śatapatha Brāhmaṇa* over a period, at a time when there may not have been a clear distinction between these bodies of texts. These texts also pre-date the *āśrama* system, particularly

---

[1] Here, Bronkhorst points to the differences in the lists of teachers to make his case for the historical eastward drift of Brāhmanism from the Kuru–Pāñcāla region to that of Kosala and Magadha.

the social institution of *vānaprastha*,[2] so to see the *Bṛhadāraṇyaka* as a text for Vedic *vānaprasthīs* and the *Bṛhadāraṇyaka Upaniṣad* as a text for *saṁnyāsīs* seems most improbable. By the eighth century BCE, the Vedas seem to have become the foundation for a ritually ordered symbolic society, particularly in the fertile regions of north-central India bounded by and surrounding the two rivers Gaṅgā and Yamunā, which took on the dominant clan names Kuru–Pāñcāla of central importance in the *Mahābhārata* (Bronkhorst 2007).[3] Whether for statecraft, domestic or individual activities, Vedic rituals mediated by brāhmaṇa priests were prescribed and considered binding in life and death. Under these circumstances, a counterculture seeking for freedom and unmediated access to truth through alternative understandings of reality and/or reinterpretations of Vedic texts is most likely to have developed. "Forest texts" (Āraṇyakas) or texts of contemplative insights belonging to "the outside" of the ritual system and a minor tradition of esoteric knowledge expressed for transmission in gnomic language (Upaniṣads) seem to be the literary products of this movement. The *bṛhadāraṇyaka* and the *Bṛhadāraṇyaka Upaniṣad* bear the signs of such a transition. They are both traditionally attributed to the Sage Yājñavalkya, who features prominently through his conversations in most sections of the *Upaniṣad*. The image we get of this person is that of a controversial wise man, priest

---

2 The *āśrama* system as we know it, as sequential stages of life, is attested to in the Dharmaśāstras, dating past the start of the first millennium. They are mentioned in the Dharmasūtras, which predate the Dharmaśāstras but there they are not spoken of as stages of life. Even these texts are no earlier than the fifth century BCE.

3 Though I do not agree with all the differentiating characteristics between social cultures of Kuru–Pañcāla and Kosala during the eighth century BCE he argues for, but his argument for a historical eastward drift is attested to by strong evidence of many sources.

or hermit, who challenges received wisdom, complicates the fixed numerologies of convention and renounces at will wives and property to retreat to the forest so as to turn his exclusive attention to union with absolute reality (*Brahman*).

The *Bṛhadāraṇyaka Upaniṣad* also features prominently the courtly caste of kṣatriyas as beings of wisdom, often with knowledge of *Brahman* not available to many brāhmaṇas, who are stuck in conventional or rote learning. Yājñavalkya's patron, the king, Janaka, is one of these kṣatriyas, an example of the Platonic philosopher-king. He is not the only example in this *Upaniṣad*. The *Chāndogya Upaniṣad*, which, along with the *Bṛhadāraṇyaka*, has the distinction of being one of the earliest Upaniṣads, includes examples not only of kṣatriya teachers of *Brahman* knowledge but of śūdras and animals. A bastard son of a servant girl is accepted as a student by a teacher of brāhmaṇas because he tells truth, revising the hereditary basis of brāhmaṇahood in the process. Many such examples throughout the Upaniṣads have resulted in a view that the Upaniṣads were reform literature composed by kṣatriyas seeking to overcome the priestly hegemony of the Brāhmaṇas and their subjection of truth to ritual. Among Indians, both Vivekananda and Sri Aurobindo held to this view. Among early Western Indologists, this view was argued and promoted by Richard von Garbe (1857–1927) and many others, following him. Contemporary scholars tend to attribute authorship of the Upaniṣads, like other ancillary Vedic literature, to brāhmaṇas. Whatever the case, these authors are unconventional and countercultural and their texts should be read as literature, not factual history. Of course, history leaves significant marks in fiction but these marks should be read more as strategic choices than as literal truths. Most of the *Bṛhadāraṇyaka Upaniṣad*, for example, is set in the region of Kosala, to the east of Kuru–Pāñcāla. These regions were not under the hegemony of Vedic society (Bronkhorst 2007) and, in my opinion, provide an appropriate fictional setting for an ideal state. In this state, the ruler is not bound by state rituals and is a seeker who brings together the wisdom of the state for public and personal contemplation. As mentioned earlier, he is a philosopher-king, but unlike the Platonic ideal, the kṣatriya knowledge-seeker is not self-contained and is rather in continuous dialogue with a mystical brāhmaṇa teacher, who himself transits between polis and wilderness, and values the knowledge of *Brahman* over all else.[4] He knows all the "correct" answers of convention but challenges them and handles them creatively in favour of personal *Brahman–ātman* identity realization.

Brahman and Ātman

Like the term *Brahman*, the *Bṛhadāraṇyaka Upaniṣad* is among the earliest texts to introduce the term *ātman*. Apropos the departure or distancing of the Upaniṣads from the ritually ordered social space of the Vedas, its most significant aspect is the conceptual creation of distance – the space of unmediated relationality. This is achieved exactly by the invention of the concepts of *Brahman* and *ātman* – *Brahman*, a principle and a Being, the only Being there is, one without a second (*ekamevādvitīyam*) and *ātman*, self, individual yet not separate from *Brahman*. The "distance" from the Knowledge (Veda), which subsumes all with its rules, with which there can be no relation, to the liminal relationality of sitting-near (Upaniṣad), is measurable by these concepts, which free the individual to relate to and experience identity with the infinite One. Experientially, the first of the

---

4 Bronkhorst points to different treatments in the priority of the teacher–student relation between Yājñavalkya and Janaka in *Śatapatha Brāhmaṇa* I.1.6.2, *Jaiminīya Brāhmaṇa* 1.22-25 and *Bṛhadāraṇyaka Upaniṣad* (*kāṇḍa* II) in 2007: 228-29. Bronkhorst uses these differences in priority (along with others) to argue for migration of Brāhmanism from West to East and for the incorporation of new ideas and power relations as a result. The specifics of these ideas and relations are not as convincing as the overall fact of migration.

two must be *ātman* (self), that must find its independence as individual before it can discover its Oneness. *Ātman* makes its appearance from the very first section (*brāhmaṇa*) of the first chapter (*adhyāya*) of the *Bṛhadāraṇyaka Upaniṣad*, but its proper introduction in terms of mystic philosophy comes to us in the fourth *adhyāya*, which begins with the world being a single Self (*Ātman*) shaped like a person (*Puruṣa*). It "looks around" and recognizes itself everywhere. Thus, self-consciousness is the first act of conscious Being. Consciousness, as the reflexivity (looking around) of being, is synonymous with self-awareness. What it asserts of the world at the start of the *adhyāya* is done in the image of the person, thus encouraging the replication of this "looking around" of consciousness in the individual, releasing the independence of the *ātman*. Yet this *ātman* is not the separative ego (*ahaṁkāra*), it is the Self of all selves. This equation is established in the 9th and 10th paras of the fourth *adhyāya*, where the term *Brahman* is now introduced for the first time. The *ātman* is the self-consciousness of *Brahman*. *Brahman*, when it is conscious of *ātman*, sees itself everywhere. It follows that the self of all things is the self of *Brahman*. To realize one's *ātman* is to realize *Brahman* as oneself. They say:

> Since men think that by the knowledge of *Brahman* they become all, what, pray, was it that *Brahman* knew by which It became all?
>
> *Brahman* indeed was this in the beginning. It knew its self (*ātman*) only as "I am *Brahman*" (*aham brahmāsmi*). Therefore, it became all. Whoever among the gods had this knowing, also became That. It is the same with the seers (*ṛṣis*), the same with humans .... – *BU* I.4.9-10

Reinterpreting the Veda

If this may be considered the central message or heart of the *Bṛhadāraṇyaka Upaniṣad* and indeed of all Upaniṣads, separating from the homogeneity of the social capture of the Vedas and setting up a new conceptual plane or plane of consistency for its metaphysics and praxis, the rest of the *Upaniṣad* may be considered an interpretive relationship with the Vedas in keeping with this plane and establishing its cosmology and axiology. In this respect, it is necessary to note that the *Ṛgveda Saṁhitā*, clearly the earliest layer of Vedic literature, has its own historicity. This is not merely a Western historical conjecture, but accepted in emic assumption, since the collection of hymns now known as the *Saṁhitā* is attributed to the editorial activity of Kṛṣṇa Dvaipāyana, the supposed author of the *Mahābhārata*, who is therefore also known as Veda Vyāsa. Further, there were a few different redactions of the collection, of which only one, attributed to Śākalya, exists for sure at present. This divides the text into ten *maṇḍala*s (volumes), each "coming through" a named seer (*ṛṣi*). Of these, modern dating considers *maṇḍala*s 2 to 7 to be the earliest and *maṇḍala* 10 to be the last. *Maṇḍala* 9 is made of hymns to Soma (elixir-god of strength, immortality and bliss). The earlier *maṇḍala*s are made of hymns to a variety of gods, often several to the same gods and often coupled or compounded as if acting together or as one and sometimes as synonyms of one another. In these hymns, the gods are adulated for their activities, which are often related to mythological legends in variant tellings.

By far the largest of these hymns are addressed to Indra, God of lightning and the next largest to Agni, God of fire. The first hymn in the entire collection is to Agni and the first hymns in each *maṇḍala* are addressed to Agni. The hymns to Agni call on this God to rise to the higher firmament and bring down the gods. In the ritual translation of the Veda, the Agni hymns correspond to the fire sacrifice (*homa*), central to all rituals, where the fire, fed with appropriate sacrificial materials, is invoked to call down the presence and benedictions of the gods appropriate to the function for which the ritual is conducted. In the hymns to Indra, we find the indications of legends relating to lighting up the darkness and doing battle with the demons of darkness, the Paṇis, Vṛtra or Vala, who hide the sun in the hill of darkness. The battles of Indra are often to release the sun from its concealment in the darkness, or to release the cows or the waters penned in the darkness (Aurobindo 1998: 138-58). The sun God is another object of adulation, though in a variety of names, Sūrya, Savitṛ, Mitra, Varuṇa, Aryaman, Bhaga, Pūṣaṇ, Aśvins, the dawn Goddess Uṣā, etc. It may be better to refer to them as divine solar functionaries, the Ādityas, sons of the celestial Goddess Aditi (ibid.: 490-99).

The traditional view, normalized by the fourteenth-century scholar, Sāyaṇācārya, as well as the modern Western view, following his lead, sees the Vedic hymns as functional elements within social rituals operationalizing symbolically their mythical content. This was most likely the case by the eighth century BCE, when the earliest Upaniṣads were being composed and certainly the case by the fifth century BCE, when the Buddha and Mahāvīra were teaching. However, this may not have been their only use earlier. Indeed, one may easily distinguish the lines of a larger philosophical cosmology in them, which might very well have lent itself to other uses. Sri Aurobindo (1872–1950) has parsed this cosmology, relating it to a probable layer of mystery initiations and/or individual psychospiritual praxis (Aurobindo 1998). Even from the brief outline of common features, one can discern an axiology of heaven and earth. Fire is earthly light and energy, illuminating the tracts immediately in front, whether of the individual or small collective. Lightning, hurled from the sky, illuminates larger tracts of earth from the cosmic vantage of the night. The sun dispels the darkness completely. These lead us to the three realms that form the media for these sources of illumination, the earth, the midworld and heaven, known respectively in the Veda as *pṛthvī*, *antarikṣa* and *dyauṣ*. This entire system, however, is subject to dualities, repeated days and nights, births and deaths, a geocentric perspective. Beyond the dualities lies the home of the solar gods of the eternity, the Ādityas, suns/sons of the Divine Mother, Aditi, sometimes figured as a Divine Cow. This home is Svar, the destination of the Vedic aspirant. Entering the realm of dualities, the sun is subject to the night and is stolen by the demons such as Vala, who hide it in the hill of darkness. Releasing the imprisoned sun and letting it return to its origin in Svar becomes the cosmological aim of the human, aided by gods such as Agni and Indra, along with their warriors. This heliocentric goal, however, is not exclusive of the geocentric one, as has been supposed in later schools of exclusive non-dualism, but to be known as the realm that becomes the geocentric and is always itself, one and free, even in and as the geocentric.

At the psychospiritual level, this cosmology and symbolism may be understood in a variety of ways. In one sense, it is the bridging of the three realms of earth, midworld and heaven by uniting the three sources of illumination related to these realms, fire, lightning and the sun, sometimes referred to as the three fires, *jaḍa agni* (material fire), *vaidyuta agni* (electric fire) and *saurya agni* (solar fire), thus building the "axis mundi", and reaching beyond the dualities to the home of Aditi, Svar.[5] To achieve this, the immanent solar powers hidden in the caves of the subconscient and inconscient would need to be released by invoking the power of Agni and Indra. These processes are expressed using a number of variant symbolic formulae and mythological schema. I have referred to the release of the sun or of cows or waters from the hill of darkness or from the rock. These are all symbols of the release of immanent solar powers – the sun, obviously, a vertical ascent to its origin, the waters and cows, horizontal distributions of solar power and wisdom respectively, since waters represent force and fluidity of movement, while cows, coding for light, represent spiritual

5 "To what gods shall the sacrifice be offered?" – see Aurobindo 2013: 26.

illumination. Another interesting myth related to the suns is that of Aditi giving birth to eight sons/suns. The first seven rise to the world of the gods, but the eighth (Mārtaṇḍa) is cast away to a mortal condition of repeated rebirths (*R̥V* X.72; Aurobindo 1998: 478). The implication here is that the eighth sun is the earth – Marta, in fact, is a name for Earth as also the place of Death (*mr̥tyu*), Mārtaṇḍa literally meaning "egg of Death" – subject to the dualities but potentially an immortal sun, meant to resume its place in heaven through the inner process of human transformation. Several of these themes appear in the first *adhyāya* of the *Br̥hadāraṇyaka Upaniṣad* – the order of perfection (*BU* I.1) and the fall to the realm of death or the dualities (*BU* I.2), the triple realm of the cosmos, ruled by the luminaries, sun, wind and fire (*BU* I.1-3, 5-6), the competition of the gods and the demons (*BU* I.3), the rise of the gods to a heavenly sphere above the dualities by the power of a psychic solar immanence (ibid.).

To the Vedic poets, the two primary animals of domestication, the cow and the horse, took on the highest significance, the cow as a symbol of Knowledge and the horse as a symbol of Power.[6] If Aditi the Mother of the solar gods is seen as a Cow, the Horse is related to war and sacrifice. In ritual terms, the Horse was associated with kingship and coronation, specifically the Aśvamedha sacrifice for establishing emperors (*cakravartins*).[7] It is this sacrificial Horse of the Aśvamedha ritual that starts in the first *adhyāya* of the *Br̥hadāraṇyaka Upaniṣad* and continues

---

6 "The vital powers are the motive forces that bear us on our journey and are therefore symbolized by the Horse. The herds are the illuminations that come to us from the supramental Truth, herding rays of the sun of Light." – Aurobindo 1998: 408, fn. 9

7 Sri Aurobindo gives the esoteric significance of the horse sacrifice: "The Horse sacrifice is the offering of the Life-power with all its impulses, desires, enjoyments to the divine existence." – 1998: 468, fn. 8

through the second. This is another reason supporting the argument that the *Bṛhadāraṇyaka Upaniṣad* was composed by kṣatriyas. Though the connection with kṣatriyas is likely, given the traditional understanding that the author was Yājñavalkya, it is equally likely that the *Upaniṣad* was written for kṣatriyas by one or more figure(s) like Yājñavalkya, who transited between polis and forest, and attempted to inspire a culture of unmediated *Brahman* realization among kṣatriyas. The kṣatriya teachers of *Brahman* and the philosopher-king Janaka could represent the ideal or alternative reality of such a culture.

The Puruṣa Sūkta

However, if this horse has anything to do with the ritual, it is so to reinvoke its esoteric cosmological and psychospiritual sense. To apprehend its image in its fullness one has to turn to the tenth and last *maṇḍala* of the *Ṛgveda Saṁhitā*. As mentioned, the tenth *maṇḍala* belonging to a later period, introduces new themes, symbols and forms of language. The hymn about Mārtaṇḍa, referred to before, for example, belongs to the tenth *maṇḍala*. By far the best known two hymns of the tenth *maṇḍala* are what have been called the Puruṣa Sūkta and the Nāsadīya Sūkta. The Puruṣa Sūkta (*ṚV* X.90) has gained notoriety as the origin of the hereditary and hierarchical Hindu caste system, in whose name flagrant inequalities were and continue to be practised in India. In fact, though the "castes" are named in this hymn, they are neither hereditary nor hierarchical. It is also difficult to be sure if they pertain to the social structure or the structure was a symbolical mapping based on them at a later time. According to Jamison and Brereton, contemporary translators of the *Ṛgveda Saṁhitā*, "the *varṇa* system seems to be embryonic in the *Ṛgveda* and, both then and later, a social ideal rather than a social reality"(2014: 57-58). Moreover, the naming of castes is but one aspect of this cosmogonic myth, according to which a multi-limbed "Person" (*Puruṣa*) is born as the cosmos and allows itself to be sacrificed by the gods, its parts making up the constituents of the cosmos:

> 1. *Puruṣa* (Person) has a thousand heads, a thousand eyes, a thousand feet. He fills the cosmos and extends beyond for a breadth of ten fingers.
>
> 2. *Puruṣa* himself is all this, whatever has been and whatever is to be. He is the lord of immortality and also that which grows and ascends by food.
>
> 3. All here is his greatness and *Puruṣa* is greater yet beyond all this. All universal beings make up a quarter of him; three quarters are the immortal in heaven.
>
> 4. With three quarters, *Puruṣa* has risen to the zenith and one quarter of him is here, manifest repeatedly, whence he has spread out everywhere, pervading that which eats and that which does not eat.
>
> 5. From him Virāj was born and from Virāj came *Puruṣa*, who, having been born, ranged beyond the earth ahead and behind.
>
> 6. Of the sacrifice which the gods performed, using *Puruṣa* as the offering, spring was the clarified butter (*ghṛta*), summer the fuel (wood), autumn the cooked offering.
>
> 7. They anointed *Puruṣa*, the sacrifice, born at the beginning, upon the sacred grass. By this the gods, *sādhya*s and sages sacrificed.
>
> 8. From that sacrifice in which everything was offered, clotted butter was obtained and they made it into beasts who live in the air, in the forest and in villages.
>
> 9. From that sacrifice in which everything was offered, the verses (*ṛk*) and the chants (*sāma*) were born, the metres (*chanda*) were born and the sacrificial formulae (*yaju*).
>
> 10. From it horses were born and those with two rows of teeth; cows were born from it and from it were born goats and sheep.
>
> 11. The *Puruṣa* that they divided up, into what parts did they think him up/imagine him? What became of his mouth,

what are his arms now called, what are his thighs and two feet called now?

12. His mouth became the *brāhmaṇaḥ*, his arms were made into the *rājanya* (ruling powers), his two thighs were the *vaiśyaḥ* (populace) and from his feet the *śūdraḥ* (workers) were born.

13. The moon was born from his mind; the sun was born from his eye. From his mouth came Indra and Agni and from his breath the wind (Vāyu) was born.

14. From his navel appeared the midworld (*antarikṣa*); from his head heaven (*dyauṣ*) came about. From his two feet the earth (*pṛthvī*), from his ears the directions (*diśaḥ*). Thus they imagined the worlds.

15. For this, seven were the enclosing fire-sticks and thrice seven *samit*-wood logs when the gods, spreading the sacrifice, bound down *Puruṣa* as the sacrificial beast.

16. By sacrifice the gods sacrificed to sacrifice; its *dharma*s became the first. By the glory of these (*dharma*s) the mighty ones reached the highest heaven where dwell the ancient *sādhya*s (aspirants, practitioners) and the gods.

– tr. Debashis Banerji

References to different aspects of this cosmogonic hymn can be found throughout the first chapter (*adhyāya*) of the *Bṛhadāraṇyaka Upaniṣad*. As with the overall theme of the Puruṣa Sūkta, the first *brāhmaṇa* of the *Bṛhadāraṇyaka Upaniṣad* is about cosmogenesis as a Sacrifice. In the Veda, the sacrifice is that of *Puruṣa*, what seems to be a hyper-anthropic Person. In fact, the only specifically anthropic sign about *Puruṣa* is the mention of "arms" (*bāhu*) implying a standing two-footed creature, rather than the forelegs and hindlegs (together generalized as limbs, *aṅga*) of a four-footed creature such as a horse, as in the *Bṛhadāraṇyaka Upaniṣad*. Features such as mouth, arms, thighs and feet are shared and the more anatomically concrete description of the Horse, could equally be that of an anthropic Person. A common spatial axiology connects the two – a vertical axis of earth (*pṛthvī*), midworld (*antarikṣa*) and heaven (*dyauṣ*), and a horizontal extension of the directions (*diśaḥ*) (*ṚV* X.90.13; *BU* I.1.1, I.2.3); the three Vedic gods Sun (Sūrya), Wind (Vāyu) and Fire (Agni) are related to the eye, breath and mouth respectively, of both (*ṚV* X.90.12; *BU* I.1.1). It is true that in the Vedic hymn, the Moon (Candra) is born from the Mind of *Puruṣa*, the Directions (Diśaḥ) from his ears and Indra coupled with Agni from his mouth; these correspondences are not found in *brāhmaṇa* 1 of the *Bṛhadāraṇyaka Upaniṣad*, but in *brāhmaṇa* 3, which deals with the struggle of the gods and the demons, in which the faculties are transformed to divinities, the divine origin of Mind is shown to be the Moon and that of hearing are the directions (*BU* I.3.15-16.).

In the Vedic hymn, the act of the sacrifice is conducted using ingredients that are equated to three seasons of the year. In a compressed equivalence, the *brāhmaṇa* 1 of the *Bṛhadāraṇyaka Upaniṣad* makes annular time (*saṁvatsara*) into the self (*ātman*) of the sacrificial Horse. In fact, this is the first use of the term *ātmā* in the *Upaniṣad*. Through this, the *Upaniṣad* highlights a central truth that it shares with the Vedic hymn, that this eternal image is a cosmic time-engine, a Being that includes the cosmos as a cyclical Becoming. This perennial and perpetual Becoming is its self (*ātmā*), by whose power it is eternally renewed. The propriety and audacity of the horse image is evident here, the time-steps of its galloping hooves being the eternally repeated rebirths of the sacrifice for the cosmos and all its creatures. *Brāhmaṇa* 2 of the *Bṛhadāraṇyaka Upaniṣad* elaborates this process further in its descriptions of the persistence and proliferation of the sacrificial horse in and through the eternal deaths and rebirths of all things; this is further developed in terms of the sacrificial process of birth and rebirth of all creatures in *brāhmaṇa* 4. In the Vedic case, this perpetual temporality is hinted at in the line:

> With three quarters *Puruṣa* has risen to the zenith and one quarter of him is here, manifest repeatedly, whence he has

> spread out everywhere, pervading that which eats and that which does not eat.

Here, it would seem that the Vedic hymn is more explicitly panentheistic, with the three eternally transcendent parts of *Puruṣa* (the spiritual triplicity sometimes called *tridhātu*, the "three elements" in the Veda and later known as Saccidānanda, Existence–Consciousness–Bliss) remaining unchanged while a quarter of it (the manifest world) undergoes repeated rebirth through living and non-living beings. But in *brāhmaṇa* 2 of the *Bṛhadāraṇyaka Upaniṣad* we are told "when the vital breaths leave the body, the mind remains in it" (*BU* I.2.6), indicating the inextricable spiritual component of physicality which returns in new bodies. In *brāhmaṇa*s 5 and 6, the "three parts" always unchanged above are identified and eulogized as the three gods Sūrya (Sun), Vāyu (Wind) and Agni (Fire), which are present together as the "singularities" of every individuation in the cosmos and constitute its secret trinitarian basis. Similarly, in the Vedic hymn, the "three parts above" are present equally below as the three seasons, birds, wild animals and men, the three Vedas and three kinds of domesticated animals, horses, cows and goats (*ṚV* X.90.8-10).

The Three

The cosmological equivalence of the three gods (Sun, Wind and Fire – macrocosmic) and the three faculties (sight, breath and speech – microcosmic) pervades the first chapter (*adhyāya*) of the *Bṛhadāraṇyaka Upaniṣad* and culminates with a statement of trinitarianism in the sixth and final section (*brāhmaṇa*). We also see a privileging of breath (*prāṇa*) in this section. This, again, is an indication of the relationship of this text with the kṣatriya, since the Wind God (Vāyu) and its microcosmic counterpart *prāṇa* (Life-force) represent the energetic element among the three sets of correspondences. Sun-sight, the element of Illumination and Wisdom, could be considered primary to the brāhmaṇa;

Wind-breath, element of Energy and Strength, primary to the kṣatriya, Fire-speech, element of Aspiration and Circulation, in its collective or universal aspect, primary to the vaiśya. Viś, having to do with universal pervasion and collectivity, the fire here indicates the aspiration of the universal or collective being, Viśva Nara. It is for this reason that fire in this aspect is known as Vaiśvānara. But this aspiration and preservation of the collective reality fragments further to the individual spark-soul, the fire burning in each particle of the dispersed sacrificial Body of the Real-Idea. This is the śūdra, the integral intensity in the radically decentralized fragment which gathers together to form the collective and stabilizes in Strength and Wisdom. *Brāhmaṇa* 2 of the *Bṛhadāraṇyaka Upaniṣad*, in its first three paras, develops this re-emergence of the sacrificed Horse through the work of Fire (Agni). Having re-established its image in the Becoming, Fire here divides itself into the other two functions/gods as thirds (*BU* I.2.3). It is clear here that what is being spoken of is not the separated God or function of fire but fire as a self-form (*ātma-rūpa*) of the sacrificed Being itself that becomes the three gods and three functions. It is hence the fourth, whose secret name (*upaniṣat*) is *ātman*. This immanent Self will later (by the time of the *Kaṭha Upaniṣad*) be differentiated by being called *antarātman*, the inner *ātman* (*KU* V.9). In the mystical terminology of Sri Aurobindo and the Mother, this is the psychic being or entity.

In the *brāhmaṇa* of the *Bṛhadāraṇyaka Upaniṣad*, which is about the battle of the gods and demons, the three functions, seeing, breathing and speaking, are unable by themselves to intone the *udgītha* (upward song), an epithet for the mystic syllable *oṁ*, by which they expect to outdo the corrupting influence of the demons. This, in fact, is one of the earliest references to this sound syllable, whose intoning is considered among the most powerful practices towards *Brahman* realization in the Upaniṣads. In each case, the demons corrupt the faculty with the dualities. It is only the mysterious "fourth" (here, in fact, the sixth, since the mind supervenes on its adjuncts, sight and hearing) that can overcome the demons and transform the faculties to their original godheads through the intoning of *oṁ*. This "stranger" is referred to as the "breath in the mouth"(*BU* I.3.7). In its descriptions, it is the essence of all the faculties that yet exists independent of them, not subject to the dualities, which is their limitation. One can see thus that though named a breath, this is equally the essence of the other faculties, speech and sight, and, indeed, hearing and mind as well. The utterance of the sacred/secret Word (*upaniṣat*) must be done not by any of the faculties but by uniting the breath, word and mind/sight in this element which is their essence. Again, though not named, this is the immanent Self (*antarātman*), psychic entity.

Finally, this trinity is re-invoked and breath (*prāṇa*) privileged at the end of the fifth *brāhmaṇa* and the short sixth and last *brāhmaṇa*, where speech and sight are exteriorized in their objects name (*nāma*) and form (*rūpa*) respectively. Breath (*prāṇa*) here is similarly exteriorized in "work" (*karma*) and equated to *ātman*. At the same time, all three are together declared to be the *ātman*, but name and form its appearances in the objective world (truth, *satyam*), concealing its immortal part (*amṛtam*), which is breath (*prāṇa*).

At the end of the fifth *brāhmaṇa*, we find an indication of esoteric praxis reduced to a simple act of breathing combined with focused psychic intent to immortality. Similarly, in the passages at the end of *brāhmaṇa* 3, the "breath in the mouth" is invoked in the act of chanting, with a pun on the word (*svara*), which means both perfection of note/tone and the "fourth" heliocentric world, which is the goal of the Vedic ascent. Relating chanting and "the word" (*mantra*) to the *brāhmaṇa* and practices of breath (*prāṇāyāma*) to the kṣatriya, these practices, in each case centred on the discovery of their essence as the *ātman*, address an esoteric goal of self-realization (*ātmabodha*) for both these sections of society, the basis for an ideal polis.

Numerology

The three parts above and one below of *Puruṣa*, composing Being and Becoming, or Spirit and Matter, comprise a numerology which is an equivalence of the one *Puruṣa*, the two realms of Being and Becoming, the "three parts" of eternity replicated above and below, in the "one part" of temporality, and the "above" and "below" together composing four parts. We see all these various numerologies equally at work in the first *adhyāya* of the *Bṛhadāraṇyaka Upaniṣad*, which, however privileges trinitarianism as a central handle for divinization. If three is the engine of individuation, four is the number of complete manifestation. The "one part" that "is here" and "becomes repeatedly" is the manifestation resulting from the time-engine of the sacrifice. This is reflected in the divisioning of the "body parts" of the anthropic image of *Puruṣa* to the functions related to the four castes in the Vedic hymn. These are related to the three parts above and the fourth "here" and are thus manifestations of mouth, arms, thighs and feet of *Puruṣa*. The mouth or head becomes the centre of knowledge (brāhmaṇa), the arms become the centre of power (*rājanya*), the thighs become the centre of universal exchange (vaiśya) (from *viś*, to extend) and the feet become the centre of infinite divisibility (śūdra). The *Bṛhadāraṇyaka Upaniṣad* turns to this discussion in *brāhmaṇa* 4. As mentioned before, whether the Vedic description is socially mapped to the castes or not at this time, or if so, how rigid this social division is, are debatable questions. Certainly by the time of the *Upaniṣad*, it seems to be more established socially. At the same time, as discussed above, the model being presented in the *Upaniṣad* is that of an alternative ideal, a state governed by a kṣatriya "philosopher-king" who is counselled by an unconventional brāhmaṇa, who is equally a *śramaṇa*, transiting between polis and wilderness. The relation between brāhmaṇa and kṣatriya in the discussion of the four castes in *brāhmaṇa* 4 sets up the context for the dialogues of the remaining *adhyāyas* and *brāhmaṇas*, which deal with the aforementioned state.

The discussion of *brāhmaṇa* 4 is initiated with an intertwined relationality between the brāhmaṇa and the kṣatriya (*BU* I.4.11), characteristic of the relation that is dramatized between Yājñavalkya and Janaka in *kāṇḍa* 2 of the *Bṛhadāraṇyaka Upaniṣad*. One could see this as a creative reading of the line from the Puruṣa Sūkta:

> From [*Puruṣa*] Virāj was born and from Virāj came *Puruṣa*, who, having been born, ranged beyond the earth ahead and behind.
> – *ṚV* X.90.5

This may be thought of as a description of the panentheistic reality of *Puruṣa* – transcendental Being of *Puruṣa* produces the space–time of the Becoming as Virāj and becomes immanent in it as *Puruṣa*. Virāj, related to the *rājanya* through the shared root *rāj* (to rule), is literally the Law which holds the becoming together (*dharma*). Though gendered feminine, it may also be considered the archetypal Being of the kṣatriyas who could be said to rule by its power. *Puruṣa* becomes immanent in its space–time but is actually its progenitor. The discussion of castes in *brāhmaṇa* 4 starts with *Brahman*, which being unproductive in isolation, manifests the ruling power (*kṣatra*). The *brāhmaṇa* goes on to enumerate the gods of the directions related to the ruling power and assert this power as the highest in the manifestation, one to which the brāhmaṇa must prostrate himself. It then immediately follows this by asserting that the brāhmaṇa is the womb of the *kṣatra* (*kṣatrasya yonir yad brahma*). Even if a king attains supremacy, he must resort to the brāhmaṇa as his source.

By itself, one may think of this as a form of mutual authorization by the primary priestly and warrior castes so as to stay in power and subjugate the rest of the population, as has been observed widely in world history. However, the *brāhmaṇa* goes on to speak of the incompleteness of the manifestation without the further development of the vaiśya and śūdra functions, equally necessary to the integral functioning of the body politic. It then decentres the "ruling power" from kṣatriya and brāhmaṇa, abstracting it in *dharma*, the law of unity holding together the becoming. This is available equally to all and any one may appeal to it equally. One may think of this as the abstract principle of the *kṣatra*, or Virāj of the Vedic hymn, the Being of Cosmic Law, the law by which the sacrifice (*yajña*) is upheld, which is spoken of in the last lines of the Vedic hymn:

> By sacrifice the gods sacrificed to sacrifice; its *dharma*s became the first. By the glory of these (*dharma*s) the mighty ones reached the highest heaven where dwell the ancient *sādhya*s (aspirants, practitioners) and the gods. – *R̥V* X.90.15

One must realize that this is not a "law-book" or mental code of conduct, it is a supramental Real-Idea of cosmic unity in Becoming with its immanent singularities that must be actualized dynamically in space and time. Finally, the *brāhmaṇa* indicates a second source of universal decentralized access to the Law. This is immanent to all beings as their very self, the *ātman (BU* I.4.15-16*).* Knowing the identity of *ātman* and *Brahman* is also to know the cosmic law, *dharma*, which holds together the world in its perpetual becoming, since it is the Self of *Brahman* that has become the selves of all its self-divisions down to its infinite self-distribution in Matter and as the śūdra.

A final point of comparison between the texts is with respect to "food" (*anna*). Social ritualization of Vedic hymns reduced them to material uses, such as wealth, nourishment, cattle and progeny. As if in response, the Upaniṣads often deal with food, partly in satire and partly with intent to illuminate a deeper understanding. In the Puruṣa Sūkta, food is mentioned in a more esoteric context: "He is the lord of immortality and also that which grows and ascends by food"(*R̥V* X.90.2). Food may be considered as all that can be "consumed"; in other words, the objects of the Subject, which refers to the cosmos as a Becoming that exists for the bliss of infinite experience, regenerating itself (manifest repeatedly) and expanding both horizontally ("spread out everywhere", variety) and vertically ("ascension", quality). In the *Bṛhadāraṇyaka Upaniṣad*, paras 4 and 5 of the second *brāhmaṇa* deal with Death as the maker and eater of food. The *Upaniṣad* equates this "eater" to Aditi, the Vedic mother of the gods through the use of a pun – *ad* is to eat and *iti* stands for whatever is available. The passage concludes esoterically by stating that one who knows (*ya evam veda*) this will become the master of food (i.e. the Experiencer or Subject, *Puruṣa*). This short foray is further expanded in *brāhmaṇa* 5, which is about qualities and quantities of food, contemplating the mystery of how when food is consumed continuously, it remains inexhaustible.

The Nāsadīya Sūkta

It is instructive also to consider the cosmogony of the first *adhyāya* of the *Bṛhadāraṇyaka Upaniṣad* against the other famous cosmogonic myth of the tenth *maṇḍala* of the *Ṛgveda*, the Nāsadīya Sūkta X.129. We may consider Wendy Doniger's translation:

> 1. There was neither non-existence nor existence then; there was neither the realm of space nor the sky which is beyond. What stirred? Where? In whose protection? Was there water, bottomlessly deep?
>
> 2. There was neither death nor immortality then. There was no distinguishing sign of night nor of day. That one breathed, windless, by its own impulse. Other than that there was nothing beyond.
>
> 3. Darkness was hidden by darkness in the beginning; with no distinguishing sign, all this was water. The Life-force that was covered with emptiness, that one arose through the power of heat.
>
> 4. Desire came upon that one in the beginning; that was the

> first seed of mind. Poets seeking in their heart with wisdom found the bond of existence in non-existence.
>
> 5. Their cord was extended across. Was there below? Was there above? There were seed-placers; there were powers. There was impulse beneath; there was giving-forth above.
>
> 6. Who really knows? Who will here proclaim it? Whence was it produced? Whence is this creation? The gods came afterwards, with the creation of this universe. Who then knows whence it has arisen?
>
> 7. Whence this creation has arisen – perhaps it formed itself, or perhaps it did not – the one who looks down on it, in the highest heaven, only he knows – or perhaps he does not know.
>
> – 2005: 25

This is a zero state prior to existence or non-existence, but it is not devoid of an unnameable One that lives without external input and can take shape by self-will (*tapas*). The emergence of cosmos from this state is attributed to the mysterious stirring of desire in it. The term *samavartata* used to describe the movement of desire (*R̥V* X.129.4) implies a rotation or "going around" – desire occasioned by traversing around that one in the beginning. The hymn is famous for its last line, which is taken to be a primordial agnosticism, though in fact it is more like an open question, relating to the epistemological category of "the unknowable" introduced by the Upaniṣads to describe the necessarily unmanifest aspect of radical infinity. The language of this hymn is quite unlike any other hymn of the *R̥gveda* and, if anything, is closer in spirit to the esoteric bareness of the Upaniṣads. Comparing to the first *adhyāya* of the *Br̥hadāraṇyaka Upaniṣad,* one can see strong similarities in *brāhmaṇa*s 2 and 4. *Brāhmaṇa* 2 begins with a zero state not unlike the Vedic hymn. But this is identified as "Death which is Hunger" in which the thought to be embodied arises. The process that ensues, re-establishes the horse of the first *brāhmaṇa*. It is not difficult to suppose from this that what *brāhmaṇa* 2 represents is the aftermath of the horse's sacrifice and its reconstitution and regeneration from within that Death. Such an understanding may very well also apply to the Nāsadīya Sūkta, describing a state such as that following the sacrifice of *Puruṣa*, the ensuing Absence and ghostly memory of Origin resulting from the sacrifice, arising as desire. A similar process is described in *brāhmaṇa* 4 of the *Bṛhadāraṇyaka Upaniṣad*, where the primordial Self (*ātman*) "looks around" (*so 'nuvīkṣya*), starting a process that leads to the desire for companionship. The "looking around", similar to the "round" self-traversal of desire in "that One" of the Vedic hymn, is an act of self-consciousness (*ātma-cetanā*), a reflexivity which activates a duality of Being and Consciousness in the One. Such a duality is also a relationality awaking to the "desire" for companionship. Both *brāhmaṇa*s, 2 and 4, explore in their own ways the question with which the Nāsadīya Sūkta ends – whence has this creation arisen – perhaps it formed itself, perhaps it did not? – not as a question with a single answer but as an invitation to experiment and experience in unique ways. It also provides an answer to the question – not a propositional answer but a genetic answer – the reflexivity of *Brahman*'s consciousness of self (*ātman*) is the paradoxical image of the origin point of cosmos, a Big Bang of self-discovery and contemplation that haunts the self-becoming of every being in/and its univocal Self-Becoming.

Vedānta and Vedāntins

Running through this interpretation of the *Bṛhadāraṇyaka Upaniṣad* is the historical conjecture that the Upaniṣads represent a revision of the ideas of the Veda through the foregrounding of unmediated relationality between individual and absolute conscious being and becoming. This is announced eponymously in its self-identification as *upaniṣad* (sitting-close) in contradistinction to Veda (knowledge), through the revision of the term *Brahman* to mean absolute reality and through the invention of the term *ātman*, meaning Self, declared in its identity with *Brahman*. The central message is one of the self of each individual being a self-presentation of absolute Being in its self-becoming. In its origins, this is likely to have been a minor movement, both in terms of the size of population affected and in the sense of minor literature as defined by Deleuze and Guattari (2009), that is a cultural expression designed to resist and escape the hegemonic capture of the state apparatus. The importance of the politics of language to this cultural milieu can be understood by analogy to our time, when the word "science", literally meaning knowledge, has totalized the entire field of knowing, both in content and method. The term *veda* applied to the Saṁhitās and ritual texts (Brāhmaṇas) structuring and defining Vedic society and also meaning "knowledge" should be seen as playing a very similar, if not identical, role to the society named after it by the eighth century BCE. It defines a social ontology determined by a certain epistemology which is its scriptural bedrock translated into static form through the assignment of hereditary and hierarchic symbolic roles and dynamic form through operational ritual conventions among these roles. Within this society, a literary movement naming itself *Upaniṣad* and extending a teaching of universal fundamental identity with conscious truth is clearly revolutionary.

However, as social historians of religion in India have noted, the period from second century BCE to fifth century CE saw the consolidation of practices and teachings forming what has been called "the Hindu synthesis" (Hiltebeitel 2007: 12). The teaching of radical plurality and absolute oneness of the Upaniṣads seems to have played a considerable part in the formation of this complex synthesis that reached its fulfilment with the writing of the Purāṇas and Tantras, and the development of temple culture in India. By around the fourth century CE, this role of the Upaniṣads seems to have been recognized by the compilation of its principal teachings in the *Brahmasūtra*, which also came to be called the *Vedāntasūtra*, thus designating the Upaniṣads as Vedānta, literally "end of the Veda". In the same sense of the politics of language mentioned above, the use of the term *vedānta* was clearly a move to bring the Upaniṣads into alignment with the Veda as canonical literature to be taken as revealed scripture (Śruti), nullifying its attempt to establish critical distance from the social authority of the Veda.

From this time, the Upaniṣads have been considered as part of the Veda. In the eighth century, Śaṅkarācārya presented interpretations of the some Upaniṣads as logical arguments for exclusive monism (Kevalādvaita Vedānta). In doing this, he pressed the identification of "the end of the Veda" further by reading it as "the essence of the Veda". He also established the convention for logical interpretation of the Upaniṣads, the *Brahmasūtra* and the *Bhagavadgītā* (*prasthāna traya*) for establishing new metaphysical viewpoints (*darśana*). Since the *Brahmasūtra* is entirely based on the Upaniṣads and the *Bhagavadgītā* is substantially based on the ideas of the Upaniṣads (in its later textual form it identifies itself as text for knowledge of *Brahman* (*brahma-vidyā*) and an Upaniṣad) the schools of philosophy (*darśana*) which developed from these commentaries are all interpretations of the ideas of the Upaniṣads presenting a logical viewpoint on reality. They thus name themselves as different schools of Vedānta, their founder-teachers (*ācārya*s) known as Vedāntins. The principal schools of Vedānta include Śaṅkarācārya's Advaita Vedānta (exclusive non-dualism), Rāmānuja's Viśiṣṭādvaita Vedānta (qualified non-dualism), Nimbārka's Dvaitādvaita Vedānta (dualistic non-dualism), Madhvācārya's Tattvavāda or Dvaita Vedānta (dualism), Vallabhācārya's Śuddhādvaita Vedānta and Caitanya's Acintya Bhedābheda Vedānta (unthinkable difference in unity). Several of these lineages have interpreted the *Bṛhadāraṇyaka Upaniṣad*, each to support its viewpoint. In comparing these with the original and each other, one often finds selective omissions and contorted interpretations to fit the text to the metaphysical scheme of the Vedāntic school.

For example, though the term *ātman* is introduced in the very first section (*brāhmaṇa*) of the first chapter (*adhyāya*) of the *Bṛhadāraṇyaka Upaniṣad* and the term *Brahman* is introduced in the fourth *brāhmaṇa*, in Śaṅkarācārya's commentaries supporting transcendental monism or exclusive non-dualism (Kevalādvaita Vedānta), neither of these instances qualifies for what he considers *Brahman* as primary unconditional Reality or Truth. The image of the horse in the first *brāhmaṇa* or the cosmic foundation of Death which is Hunger in the second *brāhmaṇa* or the mentions of *Ātman* and *Brahman* that we encounter in the fourth *brāhmaṇa* are all taken to be the conditioned cosmic reality, Virāj or Hiraṇyagarbha, seen ultimately as a product of Māyā and hence unreal. The *Bṛhadāraṇyaka Upaniṣad* itself does not make this distinction; if anything, all these are equally real forms of *Brahman* to it. According to Rāmānuja's qualified non-dualist (Viśiṣṭādvaita Vedānta) position, the cosmic aspect of reality, such as the horse in *brāhmaṇa* 1 or Death as the creator in *brāhmaṇa* 2, could easily be seen as real forms or aspects of *Brahman*, but he does not mention them; he makes a single reference only to the fourth *brāhmaṇa* to support his theistic interpretation of *Brahman* as Viṣṇu or Nārāyaṇa.

Sri Aurobindo (1872–1950) is a modern *yogī* and philosopher, who has engaged with several of the Upaniṣads, presented his philosophical and praxeological vision in texts such as *The Life Divine* (2005) and *Synthesis of Yoga* (1999). He has early translations of several of the major Upaniṣads including the first two *brāhmaṇa*s of the *Bṛhadāraṇyaka Upaniṣad*, incomplete commentaries on some, including the *Bṛhadāraṇyaka* and complete commentaries on two, the *Īśa Upaniṣad* and *Kena Upaniṣad*. The *Īśa Upaniṣad* particularly occupied his interest over a long period; he wrote a number of commentaries on it and based his philosophical magnum opus *The Life Divine* partly on its central vision. This vision, as he saw it, may be summarized as defining a goal of becoming as identification in consciousness (*yoga*) with a plane in which absolute monism and infinite pluralism coexist without erasing or subordinating the other. Attainment of this plane of consciousness, which he identified as *vijñāna* in the Upaniṣads, became the central teaching of Sri Aurobindo's *yoga*. Since he sometimes expressed his philosophy in terms taken from the Upaniṣads, the scholar Haridas Chaudhuri has designated it as a Vedānta and named it Pūrṇādvaita Vedānta (integral non-dualism) or Vijñāna Vedānta (supramental non-dualism). From this viewpoint, *Brahman* is absolute and presents itself as relative but remains absolute in each and all of its self-presentations and relations.

In my approach to the first *adhyāya* of the *Bṛhadāraṇyaka Upaniṣad*, I have avoided the ideological straitjacket of the traditional Vedāntins. In reading the text on its own terms, without privileging any aspect or category over others unless explicitly so expressed, I have found a deeper consonance in it with the vision of Sri Aurobindo, an integralism of being and its multiple self-becomings. A good example of the difference this implies in interpretation may be seen in *Bṛhadāraṇyaka Upaniṣad* I.3.22, which ends with the words: *aśnute sāmnaḥ sāyujyaṁ salokatāṁ jayatiya evametatsāma veda.* This is a complex sentence which lends itself to a variety of interpretations and, hence, translations. There is some punning with the words *sāman* and *veda* here. Of course, the *Sāmaveda* is one of the four canonical scriptures of the Veda. It is made up of hymns to be chanted. The entire passage in which this sentence occurs complicates the ritual understanding of the Veda. This paragraph and several of its neighbours seems to be about the correct prescriptions for chanting the *Sāmaveda*; at the same time, they deliberately mystify what this may mean by using terms like *sama* and *veda* in alternative and more primordial ways. *Sama*, for example, more primordially means "equal" or "same" (the latter similarity in sound due to the same Indo-European origin), while *veda*, as we have seen means "knowledge". Without going into the details of the passage (which I do when dealing with it in Chapter 2) the sentence in question can be translated ritually as:

> He who knows the *Sāmaveda* to be such attains union or lives in the same world with the *Sāmaveda*.

This, in fact, is how Radhakrishnan (1968: 161) translates it. It would mean that perfection in chanting the *Sāmaveda* would lead to identification with its magical power in oral performance or, as a "next best", residence in proximity (in the same world) with it. But paying heed to the passage in which it is situated, a translation which illuminates this context much better would be "He who knows the same enjoys union with it and lives in the same world with the same". *Sāyujya* (union with) and *sālokya* (dwelling in the same world with) become in fact terms with extensive historical mileage for the schools of Vedānta as privileged forms of liberation (*mukti*), differentiating their goals of becoming. For Advaita Vedānta, *sāyujya* is the authentic liberation, *sālokya* could be a preparatory state, ultimately unreal. For Viśiṣṭādvaita and other Vaiṣṇava Vedāntas, *sālokya* is clearly superior to *sāyujya*. From either of these perspectives, the sentence from the *Bṛhadāraṇyaka Upaniṣad* presents two distinct alternatives, an "or" with one seen as the goal and the other as the "second best". However, the sentence does not give any indication of hierarchy in these goals, speaking of them side by side in the same breath, a conjunction. If we see this from the perspective of Sri Aurobindo's integral non-dualism according to which *Brahman* is absolute and presents itself as relative but remains absolute in each and all of its self-presentations and relations (i.e. its world), absolute *Brahman* is the same everywhere even in its relational "unequal" appearances. One who knows this One truth (*ya evam etatsāma veda*) of the Being and infinite self-Becoming(s) of the One, realizes oneness with this absolute truth (*sāyujya*) and enjoys the infinite relations that come from residing with it in its world (*sālokya*). It is this "having one's cake and eating it too" that I see as the mystical message of this passage.

This raises the larger question of absolute meaning vs interpretation. The academic legacy of the Enlightenment is the evidentiary search for absolute meaning which is tantamount to a politics of hair splitting in the name of a logical truth which must abide by the law of the excluded middle. I hold that the hermeneutic search for an absolute truth through academic method is spurious and hides the fascist aim of subjecting infinite and essential mutiplicity to an exclusive interpretation. Instead, I take a position which affirms a plurality of interpretations for any object of inquiry based on goals of becoming. From this point of view, the interpretations of all the Vedāntins may be said to have relative merit, so long as they do not claim a hegemonic right over others and relativize their claims to their own goals of becoming. The difficulty arises from the fact that each of these schools bases the authenticity of its goal as being identical to that of the Upaniṣads, since they hold the Upaniṣads as scriptural (*Śabda-Brahman*). This is a tautology and clearly illegitimate as a hermeneutic principle. One may bring a specific goal of becoming into one's engagement with a text, which will inflect the interests, emphases and eventual vision of the interpretation, but one must engage with the text as a whole in all its parts. This demands a coherent and complete approach to the Upaniṣads engaged with. To be adequate and coherent interpretations, each of these should take into account the totality of the existing text and its contexts, and uncover a virtual structure of sense in the text based on this. There is always an inevitable ambiguity to read a text and its contexts in various ways; each such reading is legitimate as a relative reading that serves a goal of individual and social becoming subjectively engaged with them. Each such reading, if in engagement with the known totality of the text and its contexts, extends a virtuality in terms of a coherent set of probabilities in consonance with what exists as material evidence and what is subjectively relevant to the goal of becoming of the interpreter. The totality of a text refers here to the relations between words, stanzas/paragraphs and sections in a particular text.[8] The totality of contexts includes the relation of any particular text to a larger class of texts to which it belongs as well as the synchronic and diachronic cultural historicity of the class of texts. In the case of the first *adhyāya* of the *Bṛhadāraṇyaka Upaniṣad,* this means that the interpretation should engage with all the words and their internal relations to the units they compose as well as the material evidence forming the cultural situatedness of the text. This hermeneutics of immanence is what I have followed in this work. It rests on a close reading of the text along with an interpretation of the cultural history of the work and the spatio-temporal meanings this makes possible, in engagement with a paradoxical goal of becoming towards a plane in which absolute monism and radical pluralism coexist as one without erasing or subordinating another.

Translation

In attempting a commentary in English of this ancient Sanskrit text, the question of translation faces us before all else. All translation is approximate and hence all translation is creative and interpretive. Moreover, there is a history of translation which leaves its own continuing legacy forming the cultural historicity of any attempt to interpret and comment on a text in another language.

The discovery of the Upaniṣads in the West is part of the

---

8 This exclusive hermeneutics of the text is what had been privileged in the literary movement originating in the US of the mid-twentieth century known as New Criticism. Instead, a focus on the text which relates it to cultural and intellectual history has been the aim of New Historicism. What I call here the "hermeneutics of immanence" combines these two.

initiation of Indology in the early nineteenth century. The earliest nineteenth century translation by Abraham Hyacinthe Anquetil-Duperron (1731–1805) was made in French and Latin from a version of a Persian translation of a collection of the Upaniṣads. Early English language translations also come from this time period. Some of these translators include Henry Thomas Colebrooke (1765–1837) and Rammohun Roy (1772–1833). A more systematic effort to translate the principal Upaniṣads was undertaken around the turn of the nineteenth and twentieth centuries by scholars such as Max Müller (1823–1900) (*Twelve Principal Upaniṣads*), Paul Deussen (1845–1919) (*Sixty Upaniṣads*) and Robert Ernest Hume (1877–1948) (*Thirteen Principal Upaniṣads*). The two more recent attempts at translating the principal Upaniṣads into English are those by S. Radhakrishnan (1888–1975) and Patrick Olivelle (1942–). Radhakrishnan's *The Principal Upaniṣads* (1968)is a translation of thirteen principal Upaniṣads published in 1953 and carrying an extensive introduction, the original text in Roman transliteration, English stanza by stanza translation and comparative notes. Patrick Olivelle published translations of thirty-two Upaniṣads in two volumes titled *Upaniṣads* in 1996. The first of these volumes contains the translations to twelve principal Upaniṣads along with an introduction and notes appended to the end of the text. In 1998, Olivelle published *The Early Upaniṣads*, which is largely a republication of volume one of *The Upaniṣads* with the addition of the Sanskrit text. Apart from these more systematic modern attempts, there have been a number of partial translations. As mentioned earlier, Sri Aurobindo has translated fully and commented extensively on the *Īśa Upaniṣad* and *Kena Upaniṣad*. He has also translated but not commented or left incomplete commentaries on a number of Upaniṣads such as the *Aitareya*, *Taittirīya*, *Kaṭha*, *Praśna*, *Muṇḍaka* and *Māṇḍūkya*. With regard to the *Bṛhadāraṇyaka Upaniṣad*, around 1912, he translated the first two *brāhmaṇa*s of the first *adhyāya* and left some incomplete notes.

For the present text, I have consulted the translations of Radhakrishnan, Olivelle and where available, Sri Aurobindo. The historicity of these texts encapsulates for me an engagement with past translations as well, which their authors refer to explicitly or implicitly. However, I have found inadequacies with all these translations for my purpose of close reading, due to which I made my own translation of the first *adhyāya* of the *Bṛhadāraṇyaka Upaniṣad*. Each chapter of this book, dealing with a section (*brāhmaṇa*) of the first chapter (*adhyāya*) of the *Bṛhadāraṇyaka Upaniṣad*, starts with a translation of that *brāhmaṇa* which is referred to in the contemplation of the text, while the entire text, transliteration and translation, is carried in an Appendix at the end. As mentioned, all translations are creative and interpretive; the question is what ideas, principles and/or politics do they serve? As also mentioned, all interpretations carry conscious or unconscious metaphysical assumptions. In translating as in interpreting a text, we may start with an openness to its assumptions, but we bring our own into engagement with it. If we are conscious of this engagement, our interpretations are dialogic and open a space of différance, as the philosopher Jacques Derrida would say. This, in my opinion, is the liminal space of relationality that the Upaniṣads encourage eponymously an intimacy of sitting-near; this is also the space of the vast forest that this particular *Upaniṣad* encourages also eponymously as in pun. In the famous colloquy of Yājñavalkya and Maitreyī that occurs in *adhyāya*s two (*BU* II.4) and four (*BU* IV.5) (not covered in this book), the praxis for knowing the *ātman* is given as *manana śravaṇa darśana nididhyāsana* (hearing, seeing, thinking and coming into union in consciousness). This may also be considered *upaniṣad*, in the sense of "secret teaching", the hidden key to the study of the text itself. It refers to a method which is not one of a hermeneutics of "explanation" or "commentary" but one of contemplation leading to identity with a plane of existence that is extensive and includes connections, disjunctions and conjunctions. It is in this spirit that I have called my approach to the first *adhyāya* of the *Bṛhadāraṇyaka Upaniṣad* "meditations to the mystic philosophy of the *Bṛhadāraṇyaka Upaniṣad*".

Literal-minded translations foreclose this space of contemplation. In the case of the modern translations, I have referred to Radhakrishnan is more explicit about his philosophical assumptions and his philological conjectures. He is also well known as a philosopher, who has left us an extensive elaboration of his metaphysical views. His views rest on Śaṅkara's Advaita Vedānta, though inflected with important modern modifications. In his notes, he often acknowledges the metaphysical sources of his interpretations. Olivelle does not claim to be a philosopher and brings more of a surface philological conjecture to his interpretations. This has its advantages and shortcomings. While it seems to be more metaphysically open to the text, it is not absent from assumptions, which often betray unclear mixtures of materialism and idealism. In both cases, the mysticism of subjective experience, which the Upaniṣads as a whole have served to facilitate for spiritual aspirants through the centuries in India, receives little to no acknowledgement. In the case of Sri Aurobindo, who is a *yogī*-philosopher, it is this mystical import of the Upaniṣads that is its primary meaning and purpose. However, his translations are poetic expressions of the original in English and though they address the semantics and syntactics of the text without omission, they often deviate from the literal movement of the text that is important to its detailed contemplation.

An example that will illustrate the differences in approach between these translations can be seen in the first *adhyāya* in the description of the horse, where we have the phrase *saṁvatsara ātmā aśvasya medhyasya*. It is noteworthy that, here in this initiating paragraph of the *Upaniṣad*, this is the very first mention of the term *ātman*, perhaps the very first mention ever of this term, that is central to all Upaniṣads. Radhakrishnan translates this, "the year is the body of the sacrificial horse" (Radhakrishnan 1968: 149); Olivelle translates it, "the body (*ātman*) of the sacrificial horse is the year" (1998: 37); Sri Aurobindo translates it, "Time is the self of the horse sacrificial" (2001: 268). Why, when *ātman* has such a well-established meaning as self, do both Radhakrishnan and Olivelle translate it as body? Radhakrishnan justifies his translation of *ātman* as body by appealing to Śaṅkara's statement *śarīram cātmā* in his commentary of this passage. This is clearly ideologically aimed at reducing the horse to a phenomenon and its self as a phenomenal, hence unreal, self. Olivelle follows Radhakrishnan but does not identify the source of his authority, anonymizing it to tradition sans reason, while also pointing to the more established meaning of the word:

> In these documents, the term most frequently used with reference to a living, breathing body is *ātman*, a term liable to misunderstanding and mistranslating because it can also mean the spiritual self or the inmost core of a human being, besides functioning as a mere reflexive pronoun. The body which is the object of investigation, moreover, is primarily the male body. – Olivelle 1998: 22

Sri Aurobindo assumes the common meaning and provides a footnote to his use of "time" as translation for *saṁvatsara*: "Time is that which upholds existence in material space & is the soul of it" (2001; 268 fn. 4). In this case, year is the more commonly accepted meaning of the term *saṁvatsara*, it is also in keeping with the ritual significance of the peregrinations of the sacrificial horse of the Aśvamedha. However, if we relate the text to the interpretation of its cultural history as a distancing from ritual understanding and an invocation of subjective and mystical meanings, it would be more appropriate to consider *saṁvatsara* as an annular time unit. Even more primordially time itself can be understood as a discrete unit underlying experience with a repeated structure of a beginning, middle and end or the functional cycle of creation, preservation and destruction. At the cosmological plane what is the cycle of solar revolution becomes at the psychological plane the essence of cyclical becoming, the time-steps of the cosmic horse. This eternal return of infinite Being as Becoming is the self (*ātman*) of the cosmic "eternal event" figured as the Real-Idea of the horse of the sacrifice compelled to appear and disappear as the cosmos and seeded with the will to freedom and immortality in each of its parts or portions. As it is this contemplative possibility that I have pursued in my text, I have translated *saṁvatsara* as annular time, attempting thus to bridge the material literalism of "year" with the subjective mysticism of "Time".

The Image of the Horse
Adhyāya I: Brāhmaṇas 1 and 2

Brāhmaṇa One

1. *Oṁ*, Dawn is the head of the sacrificial horse, the sun its eye, the wind its life-breath, its open mouth the Vaiśvānara fire, cyclical Time is the Self of the sacrificial horse. Heaven its back, the intermediate region its belly, the earth its hoof, the four directions its sides, the intermediate directions its ribs, the seasons its limbs, the months and half-months its joints, days and nights its feet, the stars its bones, the clouds its flesh. Its half-digested food is the sand, the rivers its blood-vessels, its liver and lungs the mountains, medicinal plants and vegetation its hair. Its forepart is the rising sun and its hind part the setting sun. When it stretches lightning flashes, when it shakes its body then it thunders, when it urinates then it rains and its neighing is indeed the Word.

2. Day was the glory that was born in front of the horse (as it ran). Its womb is the eastern ocean. Night was the glory that was born behind it. Its womb is the other ocean. These are the glories that came into being on either end of the horse. As *haya* it carried the gods, as *vājī* the *gandharva*s, as *arvan*, the *asura*s, as *aśva*, humans. The sea is its brother and the sea its womb.

Brāhmaṇa Two

1. Nothing whatever existed here in the beginning. By Death all this was covered-by hunger; hunger, verily, is Death. That created Mind, (thus thinking) "let me have a Self". He moved about worshipping. From his worshipping, water was produced. "Indeed, while worshipping, bliss came into being," (Death thought); that indeed is the fiery solar essence. Thus bliss, indeed, is born to him who knows the fiery solar essence.

2. Water, indeed, is solar fire. That which was foam of water compacted; that became the earth. On that he toiled. From the concentrated energy of his exhausting labour, the essence of heat emerged. That was fire.

3. He divided himself into three: the Sun one-third and the Wind one-third. This is that Life-force divided threefold. His head is the east and His arms are that (the north-east) and that (the south-east). His rear is the west and His hip-bones are that (the north-west) and that (the south-west). His sides are the south and the north, the heaven is his back, the intermediate region his belly and this (earth) is his chest. Thus he stands firm on water. He who knows this stands firm wherever he goes.

4. He desired: "Let a second self (*ātman*) be born of Me", and He, Death that is Hunger, brought about the intercourse of mind with speech. What was the seed there became the year (cyclical Time). Prior to that there had been no year. He (Death) bore him in himself for as long as a year and after that time projected him. Then, when he was born, Death opened his mouth to devour him. He cried "Bhān!" and that, indeed, became speech.

5. He thought: "If I kill him, I shall have but little food"; therefore, through that speech and that self he brought forth all this, whatever there is: the Ṛks, the Yajus, the Sāmans, the meters, the sacrifices, men and animals. Whatever He created that he resolved to eat. Verily, because he eats everything, therefore (he is) the essence of Aditi. He who knows this essence of Aditi becomes the eater of everything and everything becomes his food.

6. He desired: "Let me sacrifice again with a greater sacrifice". He laboured and gathered heat through austerity. From him thus full of exertion and heated, his glory and virtue came forth. The Life-forces indeed are glory and virtue. When the *prāṇas* go forth, the body begins to swell, but even so the mind is set in the body.

7. He desired: "Let this (body) of Mine be fit for a sacrifice and let Me have a self through this." Because the body swelled, therefore it came to be called horse. And because it became fit for sacrifice, therefore, the Horse sacrifice came to be known as Aśvamedha. He who knows this verily knows the Horse-sacrifice. Letting it remain free, he reflected. At the end of a year he sacrificed it to himself and dispatched the other animals to the gods. Therefore, priests even now sacrifice to Prajāpati the sanctified (horse) dedicated to all the gods. Verily, that (sun) which radiates heat is the Horse sacrifice. His self is the year (cyclical time). This fire is the *arka* (solar essence), whose selves are these worlds. So these two, fire and the sun, are the *arka* and the Aśvamedha (Horse sacrifice). These two, again, become the same God, Death. He who knows this conquers further death; Death cannot overcome him; death becomes his self; and he becomes one with these deities.

I

THE Upaniṣads are today known as Vedānta or end of the Veda and are classified in relation to the Vedas, i.e. the major Upaniṣads are each connected to one of the Vedas. The term Vedānta is most certainly a later classification;[1] even later we find the division of Indian wisdom texts to what are called Śruti and Smṛti or what is heard and what is remembered, respectively. Śruti has come to mean that which is revealed and hence sacred in a canonized understanding. The Vedas and Upaniṣads are given that distinction; for some, this is extended to the *Gītā*. As revealed literature, there is another term used for the Veda – *apauruṣeya*.[2] *Apauruṣeya* could be translated as impersonal.

---

1 Possibly fourth century CE with the finalization of the *Brahmasūtra* (aka *Vedāntasūtra*).

2 The early two groups of practitioners based on the Veda, known as the Mīmāṁsakas and Vedāntins, took different approaches to the term *apauruṣeya*. For the ritually based Mīmāṁsakas (*karma-kāṇḍa*), the literal text of the Veda is the eternal body →

Puruṣa is person, hence *apauruṣeya*, impersonal; that is, no person is involved in producing these texts. At the same time, each hymn of the Veda is attributed to a *ṛṣi* (seer). *Ṛṣi*s are also called poets (*kaviḥ*). From this viewpoint, the Veda are poetic creations. At the same time, they are considered *apauruṣeya* impersonal and unauthored. Thought of psychologically, all poetry is of this nature, poets are conscious of being channels of an articulation that they can't entirely claim as their own. Vedic hymns may thus be thought of as poetical creations in the highest sense, literature channelled by pure conduits that received the sight (*ṛṣi*) and the word (*kaviḥ*) of the hymn; and they announced the creation of the cosmos by the power of the word. In other words the poet of the Veda allowed the impersonal secrets of cosmic creation to be voiced through him or her – this is the self-understanding of the Veda. We may think of this as the height and power of poetry that is given by the *ṛṣi*s, who are considered partly human and partly non-human.

The Vedic *ṛṣi*s belong to families, each of which is considered the source of one of the ten volumes (*maṇḍala*) of the *Ṛgveda*. At the same time, the Veda themselves refer to a class of *ṛṣi*s that are considered ancestors or forefathers, the *pitṛ*. This is an anterior memory, a remembrance of something from the distant past, the forefathers, sometimes identified as seven original seers (*saptarṣi*) and often referred to as the Āṅgirasa seers. A large numbers of Vedic hymns are attributed to the Āṅgirasas. The Āṅgirasas are given legendary status in the Veda. They are the ones who broke the dark places with their words and released the Sun,[3] they are

← of truth (*śabda pramāṇa*), while the Vedāntins, particularly the later Vedāntins from *c*. eighth century, reduced the Veda to the "end of the Veda" (Vedānta), i.e. the Upaniṣads, and took the semantics of the Upaniṣads to be equivalent to truth-evidence of the Veda (*śabda pramāṇa*).

3 E.g. *ṚV* I.62.5, II.15.8, II.23.18, III.31.7. More examples may be found in Sri Aurobindo's *Hymns to the Mystic Fire* (2013). For a →

spoken of as gods. Āṅgirasas are embodiments of the solar fire (*saurya agni*). Even today, we can find the word *aṅgāra* in use; it refers to glowing embers that burn within the ash when a fire dies and which may be used to light another fire. The Āṅgirasas are embodiments of fiery substances that never die out, who can always be invoked to start the next fire. We will have the occasion to consider the Āṅgirasas in our dwelling on the first sections of the *Bṛhadāraṇyaka Upaniṣad*.

This is the sense in which the Veda are considered Śruti (impersonal heard or revealed literature). But the Upaniṣads are also classed as Śruti in our present understanding. This understanding is historically established. We can question this understanding by the fact that early Indian literature identified itself eponymously, in its name. The revealed status of the Veda is announced in its name, which literally means knowledge. *Upaniṣad*, on the other hand, if we consider it by name, means to sit near (*upa* – close, *ni* – down, *ṣad* – sit). It is thus intimate literature, a literature of the liminal zone between oneness and twoness. This is how the Upaniṣad announced itself, not as revealed knowledge (Śruti), Veda, but as relational knowledge. Generally, it is taken to mean that the Upaniṣads refer to themselves as literature belonging to intimate circles of teachers and students, what has been called the *guru–śiṣya paramparā*; in other words, students at an *āśrama* (secluded residence), which is usually the family home of the teacher (*gurukula*), sit together and learn from the teacher. Thus, the name Upaniṣad marks the intimacy of that learning space, not a space of the urban institution; the space of a minor literature. But this meaning has also the esoteric aspect of a sitting-close to or an intimacy with truth. It is not the knowledge, Veda, but a sitting-close to knowledge (Upaniṣad). It is a literature expressed in intimate relation with knowledge, so close there is an indeterminate

---

← contextual treatment of the Āṅgirasas, see chapters XIV-XVI of Sri Aurobindo's *Secret of the Veda* (1998).

dividing line between it and knowledge. The fifth *brāhmaṇa* of the first *adhyāya* of *Bṛhadāraṇyaka Upaniṣad* I.5.23 indicates this mystic status by referring to its twofold goal as *sāyujya* and *sālokya* (union and nearness). The category of the intimate is not a divisible category, it is a liminal or threshold category, marking the hazy boundary between the one and the two.

This is what makes it accessible to us even today because it is available to our contemplation. Veda, the knowledge, keeps itself deliberately outside the scope of our contemplation; we cannot come close to it, we have to either be one with it in ritual performance or we are outside it. If we consider the Veda to be composed in a time-window between 2000 BCE and 1500 BCE – by 1200 BCE we begin seeing the development of ancillary literatures – e.g. the Brāhmaṇas, related to the ritual use of the Veda. These rituals could be of various kinds – some for the state, some for the clan or the family. The anointing of a king, for example, would be a ritual of the state. This is a large-scale sacrifice (*yajña*) conducted over many days. If we look at Sri Aurobindo's interpretation of the Veda, he sees these rituals as dramatizations of internal processes. It is these internal processes that were the foundation of the Vedic hymns as experienced by the *ṛṣis* who developed the ability to channel the word body of those experiences.

The Eternal Event and the Fall

The notion of the word body (*vāṅmaya śarīra*) is central to this literature; it relates to the Idea. The Idea is at the foundation of the Western philosophical and mystical traditions, though over time, it has lost importance in the Indian tradition. It is central to Plato, for example, for whom, there is an ideal world, a world of ideas that is the basis of the forms and laws underlying our world. However, a sense of imperfection and incompletion haunts our world, so one may say these Ideas are not perfectly manifest in our world. Plato tries to account for the gap between the perfect ideas and the imperfect expressions of those ideas here by borrowing the Orphic–Pythagorean idea of a fall. The notion of a fall is a myth found in many cultures. It follows the intuition that something is not right with us, but this is because we have fallen from a state where all is perfect. The most well-known version of this is the Abrahamic myth of the Fall of Adam and Eve from the Garden of Eden. The Veda also contains a myth of a Fall. This is implied in the Ṛgvedic hymn of the sacrifice of *Puruṣa* (*ṚV* X:90), which we will consider later in this chapter.

In the *Phaedrus*, Plato's account of the Fall relates to souls that have fallen due to the inability to control desire (*Phaedrus* 246c). They consequently enter into a cycle of many rebirths before they can regrow their wings and ascend to their heavenly origin (ibid. 247e-249d). This myth is very similar to a section of the *Kaṭha Upaniṣad*, except that the *Kaṭha* does not contain any explicit mention of Ideas or a fall.[4] In Plato's case, it is the philosophers who return fastest to the origin, since they retain the memory of the Ideas (*Phaedrus* 248e). This is Plato's theory of anamnesis, which he develops with greater clarity in the *Meno* and *Phaedo*.

According to Plato, the Ideas are intuited by us in our geometry and our philosophies; it is the hazy foundations of the ideals by which we try to structure our lives and build our laws. As principles or Forms, such Ideas include the Beautiful, the True and the Good, with the last being given the highest position. Sri Aurobindo starts his *The Life Divine* (2005) by talking about such ideals as God, Truth, Freedom and Immortality, which return repeatedly after every obscuration – the eternal return of the Ideas. These are static Ideas; but there is another way in which we can think of Ideas. This is as Real-Ideas of cosmic

---

4 Though *Kaṭha Upaniṣad* I.3.7-9 does not mention a fall of souls from an origin in heaven, it resembles Plato's account also with respect to reincarnation in earthly rounds or freedom from such reincarnations.

becoming.[5] Such Ideas exist as eternal Events. An eternal Event sounds like a paradox, events occur in time, while eternity knows no time. So an eternal Event is a bridge between eternity and Time, in fact, it is the origin of Time, a recurring image which structures Time. It may thus also be called a Time-Image or Time Crystal.[6] This is an image or idea that encapsulates the properties of eternity as an exploration in time. An Idea that gives birth to an eternal exploration is an eternal event. It resides in eternity but it lends itself to perennial exploration. Time-images can be of many kinds. They can be given as narratives or stories or they can be given as images. Sri Aurobindo's *Savitri* begins with the intimation of such an eternal Event in the symbolic form of a dawn – "across the path of the divine Event" (1997, vols 21-22: I.1). Its perpetual recurrence as Time-Image is referred to in a few lines – e.g. "the brief perpetual sign recurred above" (ibid.: I.3). This is what makes this dawn a symbol Dawn. Another Time-Image we can think of is Sri Aurobindo's symbol, which is a very ancient and the most simple Tāntric symbol. In the Western tradition, it has been called The Seal of Solomon, made of two intersecting triangles. This symbol represents an event in eternity; it is static, at the same time dynamic. It is static because it has a fixed image; it is dynamic because it has a structure coding for a perennial eternity of descents and ascents. Something is descending continuously without end and to respond to it something ascends continuously. It is a reciprocal system that is inexhaustible; coming from the inexhaustible

---

5 "Real-Idea" is a term taken from Sri Aurobindo's *The Life Divine* (2005: 125): "It is conscious Reality throwing itself into mutable forms of its own imperishable and immutable substance. The world is therefore not a figment of conception in the universal Mind, but a conscious birth of that which is beyond Mind into forms of itself."

6 I have adapted the ideas of Time-Image and Time Crystal from Gilles Deleuze 2005: 66-94.

and reaching out for the inexhaustible. This is what makes it an eternal event. Radical infinity lends itself to a structure to become a recurrent bound infinity at the foundation of a cosmos. One may experience such things – one must go beyond the duality of being and becoming to touch these images. They come from what Sri Aurobindo calls Supermind. Supermind is the home of events in eternity or Time-Images that are at the head of time.

The *Bṛhadāraṇyaka Upaniṣad* begins with a such an image of time. Traditionally, it is not thought of in this way, because an emphasis on the meaninglessness of the world and the need to escape it has developed in the Indian tradition. If it becomes our concern to jump into pure Being, we are not interested in what bridges Being and Becoming, in the image of time. On the other hand, if we only concern ourselves with the laws of the world, we search empirically for a single structure yet always end up with an unexplainable remainder. Or we try to fit the existent into the nearest approximate mould, distorting, excluding or exterminating what refuses to fit. We cannot build that structure with the mind. The hubris of the world-spanning modern knowledge academy is a continuation of this attempt to find a single picture by which we can explain the world. All our knowledge academies are part of this one epistemological project – How can we piece together all our specialized understanding to come up with a single picture of the world, a systems theory of everything? This is why the philosopher Martin Heidegger (1977: 115-54) has called the modern age the age of the world picture. It is a search for the Time-Image. Yet this search is not new. It is a displacement of Platonic foundations and even prior to Plato, the pre-Socratic search for the Logos. But the Logos is not accessible to the human mind because the human mind is a trader in finite logic. The Logos belongs to the logic of the Infinite. To the mind, One and Infinity are incompatibles, but to Supermind, it is its natural law. The images of Supermind are One and Infinite at the same time, as we saw with the Time-Image of the double triangle. It is only if the human mind can ascend to Supermind that we can catch these ideas or rather be caught by them. Rising to this level and being made a mouthpiece for the Idea, i.e. the *ṛṣi*. It is what makes the *ṛṣi* like us and unlike us. The *ṛṣi* is like us because each of us has the potential to be a *ṛṣi*. Every act of writing poetry brings us a step towards the *ṛṣi* because the poet is a trans-personal channel; s/he is partly here and partly not here. Something speaks through the poet which is not the limited agency of the human. But to what extent can this channel be made conscious to allow the highest Vision to manifest through one? That is the *yoga* of the Word, the *yoga* of poetry that all these texts that we call Śruti are about. The Veda is Śruti in this sense and the Upaniṣad sits close to Śruti, it exists in a liminal zone which aspires to the condition of the Śruti.

The Horse

The opening chapter (*adhyāya*) of the *Bṛhadāraṇyaka Upaniṣad* begins with two sections (*brāhmaṇa*s) that describe the cosmic horse meant for a sacrifice. This sacrifice refers us to a Vedic ritual, the Aśvamedha, conducted by kings preparing to become emperors (*cakravartin*s) (literally, turners of the wheel). The very meaning of *cakravartin* connects us to the solar symbology of this ritual and of the horse. The *cakravartin* is he who turns the wheel, in other words, a replica of the sun, in whose orbit, all things revolve.[7] The earth's revolution takes a year, the period

[7] In a related but slightly different meaning, a *cakravartin* is "one whose wheels move without obstruction", referring to the movement of the chariot. The movement of the horse through neighbouring kingdoms is related to this. The image of the wheel moving unobstructed over space is also a Vedic description of the Sun. See, for example, the hymn to Uṣā (*ṚV* III.61.3): *samānamarthaṁ caraṇīyamānā cakramiva navyasyā vavṛtsva* (Do thou move over them like a wheel, Oh new Day! travelling over an equal field). – Translated and commented on in Sri Aurobindo 1998, vol. 15: 293

of the horse's meanderings through neighbouring kingdoms. The kingdoms thus visited come under the orbit of the emperor conducting the sacrifice. At the end of the year, the horse is killed (sacrificed) and its meat eaten, internalizing the power of the Source for the spatial and temporal order of the territory covered by it.

The *Bṛhadāraṇyaka Upaniṣad* refers to this sacrifice in its opening with a Horse, whose description is that of the cosmos, in terms of space, time and the powers of agency (gods) within it. These gods are first described as the properties of the head of the horse – Sun (Sūrya) as the eye (sight), Wind (Vāyu) as the breath and Fire (Agni) as the mouth (speech):

> 1. *Oṁ*, Dawn is the head of the sacrificial horse, the sun its eye, the wind its life-breath (*prāṇaḥ*), its open mouth the Vaiśvānara fire.

These are also the principal gods to be invoked as agents helping the *yogī* – fire through the power of aspiration (externally the fire ritual), wind through the power of controlling and directing energy (*prāṇāyāma*) and the sun through the power of gnosis, an intrinsic knowledge that is the goal of the Vedic journey and that is invoked in the Gāyatrī (*ṚV* III.62.10). These three can also be seen as the beings behind Knowledge (sun/eye), Power (wind/breath) and Will-to-union (mouth or word/Fire). Fire is often equated with the Word of the *mantra*, particularly the Vedic hymn (*ṛk*) or the *oṁ* (*udgītha*, the ascending song). The term Vaiśvānara is used for fire here. Sri Aurobindo translates this portion "his wide open mouth is Fire, the master might universal, …" (2001, vol. 18: 268-71). Vaiśvānara is literally that which is descended from the universal (*viśva*) human (*nara*). It is a meaning reminiscent of the sacrifice of *Puruṣa*, the Universal Man formed by the proper joint functioning of the fragmented portions of *Puruṣa*. This functioning or individuation is a universal aspiration for Oneness which holds together the parts.

Hence, the Word of the cosmic Being is the universal Will to Oneness.

Being and Becoming

Space and Time are then described in an interwoven fashion:

> … [C]yclical Time (*saṁvatsara*, the year) is the Self (*ātmā*) of the sacrificial horse. Heaven its back, the intermediate region its belly, the earth its hoof, the four directions its sides, the intermediate directions its ribs, the seasons its limbs, the months and half-months its joints, days and nights its feet, the stars its bones, the clouds its flesh. Its half-digested food is the sand, the rivers its blood-vessels, its liver and lungs the mountains, medicinal plants and vegetation its hair. Its forepart is the rising sun and its hind part the setting sun. When it stretches lightning flashes, when it shakes its body then it thunders, when it urinates then it rains and its neighing is indeed the Word (*vāk*).

If we untangle these dimensions, we can see that Space has two planes or dimensions, a vertical one, the axis of heaven (*dyauṣ*) and earth (*pṛthvī*) connected by the midworld (*antarikṣa*); and a horizontal one, made up of eight directions.[8] These are both Vedic divisions. The horizontal plane of the earth is described as the internal organs of the horse, in terms of watery (rivers), semi-solid (sand), aspirant material (hills) and vegetal (plants and herbs of healing) substances. Time is delineated by the year (assumed as in the Veda to have a dark half and a luminous half), itself divided into months, fortnights, and days and nights. Time is given as the self (*ātman*) of the horse, in other words its subjective truth. Finally, four functions, which bridge the higher and lower regions of the vertical axis, are enumerated, in terms of external activities of the horse – these are lightning, thunder, rain and speech. Like the Vedic gods earlier mentioned, these functions are to be thought of as powers to be harnessed in

---

[8] Made more explicit in *Bṛhadāraṇyaka Upaniṣad* I.2.3.

yoga – śaktis (goddesses, gendered feminine), in the convention of presences as masculine and powers as feminine, established by the Veda. In Vedic terms, thunder and lightning would be Inspiration and Revelation respectively, represented as powers or instruments of Indra, the goddesses Sarasvatī and Ilā (Aurobindo 1998, vol. 15: 96). Rain is the descending power of solar (Gnostic) knowledge and the Word (often equated with Fire) is the traveller of the worlds, capable of both ascending and descending the planes of existence (unlike the other three, which only descend – though the rain eventually ascends also, but only by the power of the deity behind it, the Sun).

After giving us this description, the next section of this *brāhmaṇa* establishes the priority of manifest Space and Time:

> 2. Day was the glory that was born in front of the horse (as it ran). Its womb is the eastern ocean. Night was the glory that was born behind it. Its womb is the other ocean. These are the glories that came into being on either end of the horse ....

Time (day and night) is born afterwards; in other words, follows the spatial establishment, though it is the soul of the cosmic Being. It is another way of establishing the priority of Being over Becoming, the heliocentric order of eternity over the geocentric order of temporality, based on the succession of days and nights or births and deaths. The Vedic hymns represent these two views of reality, the solar (heliocentric) world of Aditi and the Ādityas and the earthly (geocentric) world of humans and earth-creatures (Aurobindo 1998, vol. 15: 289). The heliocentric world is of oneness which sees all in its own light, while the geocentric world is one of dualities and separateness, which moves through successions of appearance and disappearance. The horse as the heliocentric view of the cosmos, stands eternally in Space, with all movement experienced within it cyclically, internal to its reality. But its movement through the year belongs to the order of Time or Becoming, the succession of the dualities and, thus, a geocentric view.

Its sacrifice is what marks the descent from Being to Becoming, from the heliocentric to the properly geocentric. Thus, the Sacrifice may be seen as an event in eternity similar to the repeated rising and setting of the sun, a symbolic or archetypal event, which inaugurates Time or Becoming, since it is the Sacrifice of Being to Becoming. Such an Event in eternity is the very meaning or the Self (*ātman*) of Time. Or reversing this equation, we may say Time is the Self of the Sacrificial Horse because in its sacrifice, Time is born and all things temporal are marked by its perpetual sacrifice.

Finally, we are given four names of the Horse, forms by which it is known by different creatures for whom it is the vehicle:

> As *haya* it carried the gods, as *vājī* the *gandharva*s, as *arvan*, the *asura*s, as *aśva*, humans. The sea is its brother and the sea its womb.

These are four being-types which belong to the Becoming and which bear, in their own way, the Sacrifice of the Horse as the form of their Becoming – i.e. the Sacrificial Horse, in its four forms, bears them. The four creatures are gods, *gandharva*s, *asura*s and humans, and may be related to the quadripartite divisioning of Space, gods of the Heaven world, *gandharva*s of the midworlds, humans of the mortal world and *asura*s of the world of Darkness. The names of these forms of the Horse are significant and related to the four kinds of beings, *haya* related to delight, characteristic of the gods; *vāji* related to occult richness, characteristic of the *gandharva*s; *arvan* related to strength, characteristic of the *asura*s and *aśva*, related to force, but also to an alchemical power of rebirth (as we will see in *brāhmaṇa* two), characteristic of the human (Aurobindo 2001, vol. 18: 283-86).

Death

After these two paragraphs of the first *brāhmaṇa*, presenting an integral Space-Time-Image, we move to a new *brāhmaṇa*, in which it seems as if we are beginning with a new idea, that of a Non-Being, Death or Absence, which yet is constituted by Hunger:

> Nothing whatever existed here in the beginning. By Death all this was covered-by hunger (*aśanāyayā*); hunger, verily, is Death. That created Mind, (thus thinking) "let me have a Self (*ātman*)".

Hunger implies a Memory of Plenitude, from which there has been a separation and, hence, this Death always already implies its opposite, a Being, a Presence, a Birth and a Wholeness, hidden within it, but forgotten in a kind of amnesia. As we read the rest of this *brāhmaṇa*, we realize that it is linked to the first *brāhmaṇa* and is indeed the evolutionary Becoming of the Sacrificial Horse, leading to its Sacrifice and its consequences. We also realize that from a heliocentric view, we have abruptly moved to a geocentric view, a discontinuous jump to an ontology of Becoming, from *nivṛtti* (Night-of-Being) to *pravṛtti* (Day-of-Becoming).[9]

Finally, we realize that this *brāhmaṇa* sets out to answer three questions, which are existential needs of the human, addressed in the Vedas through the ritual of the Aśvamedha. We may formulate these questions as – the question of habitation, the question of food and the question of death. The Aśvamedha sacrifice establishes the *cakravartin* and his territory, and the partaking of its meat makes immanent to the king and kingdom the power of the Solar Divinity incarnated in the horse, to establish order, providing a place and hence a habitation to its citizens, providing well-being and relational experiences and hence food (substance), and providing the seed of divine order, which will remain alive through the darkness of inevitable night/death, leading to a rebirth and another Aśvamedha sacrifice. The *Upaniṣad* speaks in the most physical terms,

---

9 The Day-of-Becoming is actually a successive Night-and-Day-of-Becoming. Elsewhere, I have referred to the originary womb of Becoming as the Night of Becoming.

following the materialist doublespeak of the Veda and may be said to follow a geocentric phenomenology of the body/earth in dealing with an integral reality, inclusive of the four realms, physical, vital, mental and supramental.

Thus, the beginning of this second *brāhmaṇa* may be seen as the literal sacrifice of the heliocentric Horse presented to us in the first *brāhmaṇa*, its sacrifice as Conscious Being into its opposite, loss of Consciousness-of-Being, Night, Absence, Death, which is also Time, Becoming, the order of duality, the geocentric order. It is also the Sacrifice of its absolute (indivisible, though differentiable) Unity-of-Being into an infinite dispersion, the Ocean of Chaos in place of the Unity-Order of a heliocentric Cosmos, with only a Hunger of Absence as the individuating factor representing a Memory or invisible axis of continuity with its solar origin.

Building the Virtual Image

This Hunger thus moves towards a gathering of the dispersion and a reaching out towards the Plenitude of the heliocentric Origin. Yet, this is a manner of speaking in the mode of Time. An unbridgeable Mystery marks the shift from heliocentric Being to geocentric Becoming. From the viewpoint of the first, where there is no Time, there is the eternity-image of the Sacrifice of Being, which inaugurates an ontology of beginningless and endless Time, the Time-dimension. This image has implicit in it a structure of forgetting-and-remembering. As a form of experience it means a succession of time-quanta, units of experience marked by beginnings, persistences and ends, appearances of order and disappearances into chaos and death. Every creature of the cosmos is a being experiencing the becoming in terms of repeated different time-quanta of experience. This is also why Time is the Self or Subject, subjective experiencer of the Horse. To each such time-unit is also a memory of a beginning of Wholeness, the heliocentric Origin and a hunger to recover That. This is the meaning of Work and the ground for the felicity (*kaṁ*) that comes from this knowledge of the truth of work as a substantiation of the original plenum:

> He moved about (*acarat*) worshipping (*arcan*). From his worshipping (*arcata*), water (*āpo*) was produced. "Indeed, while worshipping, bliss (*kaṁ*) came into being", (Death thought); that indeed is the fiery solar essence (*arkasya arkatvam*). Thus bliss, indeed, is born to him who knows (*ya evam veda*) the fiery solar essence (*arkasya arkatvam*).

Yet such a recovery can never be a return, because the static heliocentric Origin belongs to another dimension, entering which one loses temporality. The lost beginning is actually not a beginning, since the Time-dimension has no beginning, but a Real-Idea of Being as Becoming. Knowing this, one becomes the Being of Becoming in-the-becoming. This is the conquest of death which is the ultimate answer of these *brāhmaṇa*s. The *Upaniṣad* emphasizes that the experience has a physically embodied aspect to it, which is why it states its metaphysics in terms of a phenomenology of the body. It is also important to note the phrase *ya evam veda* (who indeed knows). This phrase is repeated like a refrain from verse to verse throughout the *adhyāya*. Its inclusion of the word *veda* should tip us off to its intentional revisioning of this term. "Knowing" here is not scriptural knowledge but self-evident knowledge of the Subject of the becoming. "Who indeed knows" is an invitation to identity with this being of the becoming who knows because he/she/they/it is.

Thus the beginning of the second *brāhmaṇa* may be thought of as a description of the Horse's loss of consciousness and integrity due to the Sacrifice. It seems to be a beginning of all things, but is always a middle which remembers an aporetic never-beginning beginning. It is a Death and a Dispersion which carries in itself the memory of a prior Wholeness, in the form of a Hunger. It is this Hunger, *aśanāyā* (related to *aśva*, the horse) that is the recaller and worker referred to in the passages of this *brāhmaṇa*.

This portion also bears comparison with the first canto, The Symbol Dawn, of Sri Aurobindo's *Savitri*. As the Night begins to awake, Sri Aurobindo introduces the lines:

Then something in the inscrutable Darkness stirred.
A nameless movement, an unthought Idea
Insistent, dissatisfied, without an aim,
Something that wished, but knew not how to be,
Teased the Inconscience to wake Ignorance.

– 1997: 1-2

Within the Death, the loss of Consciousness, there is the stirring of a memory. This memory awakens ignorance. Ignorance is a forgetfulness that yet moves towards the fullness of remembrance; it is an evolutionary condition. Similarly in the *Bṛhadāraṇyaka*, we find that Hunger arises from Death. Death is Inconscience, in itself there is no Hunger; but the stirring of the memory of its origin, awakes Ignorance from it in the form of Hunger, product of Deprivation, stirred to work by the memory of its Fullness.

The first product of its recall is the awakening of the Mind.[10] Mind is conceptual space, it is formless consciousness groping to create forms that will fill its emptiness and recover its original Wholeness. One may say conceptual space is already a substance, a space of unmanifest dark matter, the unexpressed waters of the Veda, *apraketam śalilam* (*ṚV* X.129.3). The gathering and concentration of this is the work of the mind, which first produces manifest and objectified substance in the liquid state (water). To express this action of mind and its result, the words *arca*, *cara* and *arka* are used repeatedly. Sri Aurobindo translates *arcā* as work (2001, vol. 18: 269), Olivelle translates it as liturgical

---

10 That created Mind, and he said, Let me have substance (*BU* I.2.2).

recitation (1998: 37), Radhakrishnan as worship (*arcanā*) (1968: 151). The root of the word is related to the *mantras* of the *Ṛgveda* (*ṛg* or *ṛk* is the Vedic hymn). The essence of this is the word of invocation or aspiration, often equated with fire (*agni*). We saw this in the relating of fire with the mouth; we find this relation commonly in a variety of places in the Upaniṣads. *Cara* means to move, the mind moves worshipping or mobilizing the word of aspiration calling out to a transcendental horizon of Wholeness to activate its immanence within it. But in this context, the use of this word achieves more than its cognitive meaning. Associated with *arca*, the phonemic sound-value of *acara* amplifies the *ṛc* sound. Sri Aurobindo translates *arka* as action or activity but *arka* can mean light, fire and/or sun and also amplifies the sound-value *ṛk* or *ṛc*. This collision of the consonants *ṛ* and *c* or *k* produces an impression of friction, an energism conducive to the production of fire. Thus, though not explicitly manifest, the work of the mind in seeking to fill its sense of hunger produces a vibration which could be thought of as the subjective phenomenology of fire, an upward-rising force of aspiration or invocation.

In the process of this action of aspirant energy, felicity, joy or bliss (*kaṁ*) is born. The para then talks of the essence of *arka* (*arkasya arkatvam*, the *arka*-ness of *arka*) as being joy or bliss. Whether we translate *arka* as fire or light, it is the solar essence present within the becoming and mobilized by mind in its seeking, that is referred to here. Bliss is the essence of the solar divinity, here activated in the work of invocation/aspiration, since that is the solar essence in the becoming. This passage highlights the intrinsic divinity and bliss of works done in a gathered aspiration for wholing.[11]

---

[11] As he worked the waters were born and he said, Felicity was born to me as I worked. This verily is the activity in action. Therefore, felicity cometh to him who thus knoweth this soul of activity in action (*BU* I.2.1).

This leads to a further concentration of substance, resulting in the production of material earth as the solidified froth of the water:

> 2. Water, indeed, is solar fire (*arka*). That which was foam of water compacted; that became the earth. On that he toiled. From the concentrated energy of his exhausting labour, the essence of heat emerged. That was fire (*agni*).

Death further toils or labours in matter and thus labouring and heated to exhaustion point, the essence of its energy emerges as fire. *Tapta* and *tejas* are the terms related to heat and fiery light used here. The very beginning of the para asserts water to be *arka*, solar essence, fire. The essence of this fire is present in the Hunger, which is Death. Hence, following the style of the *Upaniṣad*, we may say Death is itself, in its self/*ātman* nothing other than *arka* (solar essence, Fire). Indeed, this is what will be asserted towards the end of the *Upaniṣad*. It is also the very meaning of the Aśvamedha Sacrifice, the creation of a Night of Becoming with the sun-seed in its heart. This is also Vedic Mārtaṇḍa, the Dead Egg or Egg of Death of Aditi, her eighth son who is born downward but is in its self, a Sun, the solar essence, that seeks re-manifestation.[12]

> 3. He divided Himself into three: the Sun (Āditya) one-third and the Wind (Vāyu) one-third. This is that Life-force (*prāṇa*) divided threefold. His head is the east and his arms are that

---

[12] 8. Eight are the Sons of Aditi who from her body sprang to life. With seven she went to meet the gods she cast Mārtaṇḍa far away.

9. So with her Seven Sons Aditi went forth to meet the earlier age.

She brought Mārtaṇḍa thitherward to spring to life and die again – *R̥V* X.72.8-9, tr. Ralph T.H. Griffith, as in https://www.sacred-texts.com/hin/rigveda/rv10072.htm (last accessed on 16 February 2020)

> (the north-east) and that (the south-east). His rear is the west and his hip-bones are that (the north-west) and that (the south-west). His sides are the south and the north, the heaven (*dyauḥ*) is his back, the intermediate region (*antar̥ikṣaḥ*) his belly and this (earth) is his chest. Thus he stands firm on water. He who knows this (*ya evam veda*) stands firm wherever he goes.

The Veda refers to Fire as a god that includes all the gods. Repeatedly, from the very first hymn of the *R̥gveda*, Agni, God of Fire, is invoked as the seer-priest of the Vedic sacrifice, a god who will bring all the gods. Here, Fire divides itself into the three primary gods that constituted the head of the Time-Image of the Horse. With the emergence of Fire (Agni), these three Vedic deities of the three realms of heaven, midworld and earth, i.e. Sun (Āditya), Wind (Vāyu) and Fire (Agni), take their places as lords of their respective domains, forming the vertical axis linking the heliocentric to the geocentric. These domains themselves become membered as the cosmic organization of Space in terms of directions within the Becoming. These conditions of consciousness, their laws and their mutual relations form the foundation of cosmic existence and hence the steady footing of the cosmic horse. The one who knows this becomes well established and has, as it were, a habitation. This answers the first of the three existential needs which form the *Upaniṣad*'s focus of attention, i.e. knowing the virtual image of the Being of the Becoming is the meaning of stability in the Becoming.

The Becoming

As with the Upaniṣadic relationship in priority between Being and Becoming, within the Becoming, it is the conditions of experience, the ordering of cosmic Space, which comes before the cycles of cosmic Time. Such a priority can be questioned. In the Śākta Tantra, Becoming has been privileged over Being; in the Upaniṣads, Becoming is certainly not irrelevant, but Being is privileged over Becoming. If the possibility of a cosmos arises from a Night of Becoming (which may be also called the Night of Time, Kālarātri, such a possibility lies latent within the substantial conditions of experience, which must first evolve. This is the Being of the Becoming, the Horse of the Sacrifice established as spatial order and reconstituted as virtual Image or Real-Idea within the Becoming.

To release cosmos, its latency must take objective shape within this substantial order. Such an objective shape, however, is not a specific object; it is a diagram of relations, an abstract machine representing the matrix of an infinity of objects bound by its idea-relations, the transcendental conditions of cosmos. The urge to instantiation (or actualization) of this virtual image arises when the Hunger of Inconscience and Fragmentation which has laboured to gather and invoke its lost substantiality, so as to fill its Lack, reaches a point of desiring individuation:

> 4. He desired: "Let a second self (*ātman*) be born of Me", and He, Death that is Hunger (*aśanāyā mṛtyu*), brought about the intercourse (*mithuna*) of mind (*manaḥ*) with speech (*vācam*). What was the seed there became the year (*saṁvatsara*, cyclical Time). Prior to that there had been no year. He (Death) bore him in himself for as long as a year and after that time projected him. Then, when he was born, Death opened His mouth to devour him (*abhivyādadād*). He cried "Bhān!" (*bhān akarot*) and that, indeed, became speech (*vāg*).

First the image of the Horse, second the loss of the Horse – the relation between Being and non-Being and the return of Being within non-Being. Then, the relation of the whole duality of Being and non-Being with a new law – the law of Becoming. This is shown by the fact that the horse that re-emerged now emerges fully in time. The *Bṛhadāraṇyaka* (and following it, several of the early Upaniṣads) often uses language to refer to material realities, following its perception of the materialistic turn in contemporaneous Vedic symbolism. There is undoubtedly some irony in this, a form of Upaniṣadic humour. At the same time, through this symbolism, new profundities are introduced. For example, it refers to Matter as Food (*anna*) and deals almost obsessively with this idea through acts related to food, such as eating. Vedic rituals at the level of the family, for example, were performed for the attainment of food and children, and at the level of the State for abundance and prosperity in agriculture. Referring to this materialism, facts of food and sex are oft repeated in the *Bṛhadāraṇyaka* and made into symbols of irony while at the same time coding for a deeper level of truth. So, in the case of the re-emergence of the Horse, after the appearance of Mind, we find that it has sexual intercourse (*maithuna*) with the Word.

This implies the expansion or proliferation into Language of the mentality of Hunger. The Language of Hunger is the conceptual space of Hunger, the problematics of Hunger, its space of Becoming (the birth of Time). Hunger expands into all its shades and manifestations in the cosmos, along with a question in its heart – How may I find to a condition in which there is no Hunger? The innumerable ways in which this question may be answered occupies the conceptual-space of Hunger. This conceptual-space is our cosmos. One may sense the ironic and materially concrete mode of reference as this is equally an ontological and existential Hunger. This is very much in character of the dark humour of Yājñavalkya, if he is the author of the *Bṛhadāraṇyaka*. Yājñavalkya expresses dark irony about Vedic society which has begun construing reality as merely Matter, reduced to Food and its desire, Hunger. It is all about food and sex – this is how he approaches it. At the same time, this material reduction is the grim reality which besets the victims of such a society. The polysemy of the material realities of food and sex in the early *Upaniṣad*s thus bears important consideration.

The stanza represents a stage in cosmogenesis which may be likened to the mirror stage in Lacanian psychology, when a child begins to be conscious of itself as an individual with a boundary and morphological and functional parts (Lacan

2001, chap. 1: 1-8). This self-consciousness is an imaginative self-exteriorization, a doubling of the self, forming an interiority and exteriority. In the Night of Becoming, this figures itself as a wish for a second self (*dvitīyo ma ātmā jāyeteti*).

The mirror phase is also an inauguration leading to the conditions of language, the power to differentiate and relate to other individuals with their boundaries and properties organized around a social order (ibid., chap. 3: 33-124, chap. 8: 311-22). The intrinsic property of Mind is this differentiation, but it needs the power of language to manifest or objectify this potential. Thus, the mirror phase coincides with the process leading to the child's awakening to its immersion in a world of language. In the *Upaniṣad*, Death uses Mind to mate with Speech. Speech (Vāk), a Vedic deity, appears in this *brāhmaṇa* for the first time. Prior to this, its appearance has been prepared in *brāhmaṇa* 1, where the heliocentric Horse's sound has been equated with Speech. In the appearance of properties due to the toil of Death in the Night of Becoming, this is a new appearance. Elsewhere in the Upaniṣads, Fire, Agni, is often equated with the Word, Vāk, particularly the Word of the Vedic *mantra*. We have seen a glimpse of this in this *Upaniṣad* in the play with the sounds related to the Vedic stanza (*r̥c*) and the solar essence (*arka*). Thus, the manifest emergence of Fire also makes possible the emergence of Speech. However, we may also think of Speech as a transcendental deity who is invoked by the Fire from its heliocentric origin for the purposes of this stage of the Becoming. Following the material phenomenology of the body, this meeting/mating of Mind and Word is spoken of as a sex act, producing a seed or embryo which gestates for a year.

The year is a cyclic unit of Time. We are told that there was no year before this, though it was latent in the Night of Becoming. Thus, this birth of the possibility of a cosmos, the individuation process, is also the birth of the time-quantum of Becoming, a unit of experience bounded by a birth and a death.

As discussed earlier, the Vedic year was figured as a six-month night and a six-month day. Within this there are other fractal subdivisions of alternate polarities. This gestation marks the origin of cosmic time and a leaping forth of the Horse into the Day-of-Becoming, which is really a perpetual succession of the days and nights of Becoming. Thus, this gestation period may be called the Night of the Cosmos. What emerges from this is not the cosmos but the conceptual-space of the cosmos, the Egg or Image of Cosmic Space–Time, spawning the instances of an evolutionary exploration of Absence/Hunger and its ideas of fulfilment.

Death and Reproduction

Hunger, which has exteriorized this Image could reabsorb it, a form of autophagy or corpophagy. Upon the exteriorization of this double, Death opens its mouth (*abhivyādadād*) in a moment of indecision of whether to fill its Hunger with this self-exteriorized food:

> Death opened His mouth to devour him (*abhivyādadād*). He cried "Bhān!" (*bhān akarot*) and that, indeed, became speech (*vāg*).

But the food has a life of its own, constituted by the transcendental Word, which, as it were, slips out of the jaws of Death, with the cry Bhāṇ. Like *ṛc*, this sound must be thought of as a *bīja*, a māntric vibration of powerful expulsion, the escape of cosmic Life from Death. The sound syllable *bha* is related to being, *bhā* is to shine or bring into presence. It is also related to the word, for language is known as *bhāṣā*, since it brings into existence. The nasal sound *ṇ* at the end forcefully expels in an exteriorization, thus brings into cosmic existence. Once again, the materialist phenomenology envisions this integral phenomenon in material terms, but we may extend food and eating to mean power of experience.

> 5. He thought: "If I kill him, I shall have but little food (*annam*)"; therefore through that speech (*vāc*) and that self (*ātmā*) He brought forth all this, whatever there is: the Ṛks, the Yajus, the Sāmans, the meters, the sacrifices, men and animals. Whatever He created that He resolved to eat (*tad attum*). Verily, because He eats (*atti*) everything, therefore (He is) the essence (*aditer adititvam*) of Aditi. He who knows this (*ya evam veda*) essence of Aditi (*aditer adititvam*) becomes the eater (*āttā*) of everything and everything becomes his food.

Death at this point holds back, since reabsorption of the possibility-space would result in the cessation of experience and a return to an Inconscience marked by Lack. The escape of the power of cosmic Becoming makes possible an infinite cosmos marked by the manifestation of the idea-space of Hunger, a cosmos of infinite individuals reproducing perpetually and evolutionarily the time-quantum of becoming marked by death and reaching for immortality. This is cosmogenesis expressing through a fractal and evolutionary will-to-individuation. Death proceeds to actualize the infinite possibilities of this space through the instrumentation of the word with the agency of the self (*ātman*). Thus, it becomes the self of infinite creatures, or in other words, replicates itself in them. The *Upaniṣad* then says that Death resolves to eat all these creatures, bringing us back to the materiality of Hunger and its seeking for food.

This is a continuation of the dark humour, an extended reflection in a materialist vein, to mimic the materiality into which the Vedic corpus has sunk and the material needs it serves. In being the self of the creatures, it has already eaten them, for they have no existence outside it. In this way, it also experiences its own infinity and hence loses the edge to its Hunger. The mystic satire expresses its genius when it equates this indivisibility with eating in the word Aditi. The use of this word invokes the esoteric symbolism of the Veda, the Plenum,

Source and Essence of the heliocentric realm, from whom all suns are born (the Sun from which we kindle all our suns) and from whom Mārtaṇḍa (Dead Egg) has descended into materiality (*R̥V* X.72.8-9, see above). This descent, indeed, is no other than the Sacrifice of the Horse, from the eternal Day of heliocentric Being to the cosmic Night-and-Day of geocentric material becoming. And Hunger is a fact of material becoming, being in essence a separation from the only thing there is.

The paradox involved in thinking this is the discontinuity from Being to Becoming. Of course, to the only thing there is, there can be no other, hence no separation. This is Aditi (literally undivided), the solar Cow or Mother of the gods of the Veda, the heliocentric consciousness. Yet, the ontology of separation can be an experience within the only one there is. Because it is the only one, it is the absolute one, hence also the infinite one; and the radical infinity of the absolute one includes its infinite otherness to itself. Hence, the experience of the separated one is an experience of the only one. Only, while for the only one it is an experience, for the separate one it is the only experience. This experience of Separation from the only one is the cause of Hunger or Lack or Incompleteness.

This is the geocentric and material realm of food (*anna*). If it were to see that its only experience is *an* experience of the only one, it would lose its Hunger and become the only-one-being-the-separate-one. This is the experience of Aditi, the only one, the indivisible one. Division within it is also an experience of its infinity. Thus, it bridges the heliocentric and geocentric realms, the realm of the experience of the solar Goddess and the realm of the experience of Death, Hunger and eating. It has become Death and Death is, in reality, Aditi in the form of Death, the Dead Egg (Mārtaṇḍa). Through its brilliant phonemic word play, the *Upaniṣad* equates these two functional realms in the word Aditi, the indivisible one and the one that eats or devours all, Death.[13] This is the immortality towards which the *Upaniṣad* moves, but it does so through stages – the knowledge of habitation, the knowledge of food, the knowledge of rebirth and, finally, the knowledge of immortality. In this section, it is the knowledge of food, the object of material hunger and its equation with Aditi that is accomplished. The Aditi-ness of Aditi, or the essence of Aditi is asserted in terms of eating – that for which all exists as food. He who knows this becomes master of food; all is food for his eating, for all things are but the only one in its experience of itself as fragmentation, change, death, exchange, transformation and conservation, in other words, the self-experience of the One's infinity in/as time, space and quality.

Death and Rebirth

But the Dark Horse has not exhausted its full capacity of individuation with the cyclic cosmos. It wants a fuller individuation to overcome its originary Hunger. So, in a complete repeat of the toil and heat production at the beginning of the *brāhmaṇa*, Death labours and concentrates its energies to ignition and exhaustion point and expends all of its energy, which emerges from it as *yaśaḥ* and *vīryam* (glory and vitality) a sublimation of libido:

> 6. He desired: "Let me sacrifice again with a greater sacrifice." He laboured (*aśrāmyat*) and gathered heat through austerity (*tapo atapyat*). From him thus full of exertion and heated, his glory (*yaśaḥ*) and virtue (*vīryam*) came forth. The Life-forces (*prāṇas*) indeed are glory and virtue. When the *prāṇas* go forth, the body begins to swell (*śvayitum*), but even so the mind is set in the body.

---

13 Sri Aurobindo translates Aditi here as substance or that which can be destroyed but the reference to the Vedic Goddess is unmistakable. Such word-play with Aditi also repeats in other Upaniṣads (e.g. the *Kaṭha Upaniṣad*).

These qualities, or rather the consciousness having these qualities, are equated with the life-breath (*prāṇa*). When the life-breaths leave, the radiance and vitality also leave and the body begins inevitably to swell (*śvayitum*). Death initiates this further Sacrifice in itsef and in all its creatures, labouring in intensity to the point of the departure of the heat, strength and life.

But glory and vitality, which are carried by the life-breaths, also have the fiery and luminous element within them. This is *agni*, fire, which is *arka*, the solar essence that we have encountered before. It is the divinity of Death. When the life-breaths leave carrying this with them, the body begins to swell or rot. However, the original Mind of Night, which was the first thing to awake in the Night of Becoming, remains focused on the idea of being embodied, as the condition for the perpetual repetition of the Image of the Sacrifice within the Becoming. It wishes for a body that can be sacrificed, i.e. a living body. Thus, Mind here plays the role of a disembodied self, which seeks to be an embodied self. What has gone out are the Life-force and the solar essence, which may be called the soul of the Night/Horse. Upon being invoked, they reanimate Matter and the corpse becomes a living Horse.

Symbolically, this return to life, this rebirth, is effected for all the creatures which Death has become, since it has exteriorized or bestowed upon them its innermost reality, its soul. In this way, its eating is not merely a transmutation of Substance, but the condition for a perpetual rebirth of all the creatures in the Image of the Horse Sacrifice. Sri Aurobindo has a sentence in *The Synthesis of Yoga*: To be perpetually reborn is the condition of a material immortality (1999, vols 23-24: 5). This is how Aditi maintains its indivisibility even in the eating of Death, not only through the transformation of substantial exchange but through the persistence of reality in each fragment of the Sacrifice through the rebirth of its essence.

What makes this persistence possible is the vital current or life-breath (*prāṇa*). Leaving the body, it makes the body swell and entering it, it swells in the body. This is also a covert reference to the Veda, where the Lord of Life is named Mātariśvan, He who swells in the Mother/Matter.[14] Continuing the word-play we have encountered earlier, the phonetic root for swelling *śva* is identifiable with the Horse (*aśva*). We see here that the Sacrificial Horse is none other than the Master of Life, who carries the solar essence (*arka*) from its heliocentric origin, Aditi, to the geocentric Night of Matter, which is Death and propels it into a Becoming through perpetual rebirth in the Image of the Sacrifice. The *Upaniṣad* thus equates the Horse Sacrifice with the fact of rebirth of all individuals and asserts this to be the true meaning of the Horse Sacrifice, known to its knowers. Such a knowledge would be the knowledge of the persistence of the soul, one's temporal immortality through the successive time-quanta of Becoming.

The *Upaniṣad* then takes us through the cycle of one such time-quantum, the day-and-night of a year, at the end of which the Horse is sacrificed:

> 7. He desired: "Let this (body) of Mine be fit for a sacrifice and let Me have a self (*ātman*) through this." Because the body swelled (*aśvat*), therefore it came to be called horse (*aśva*). And because it became fit for sacrifice (*medhya*), therefore the Horse Sacrifice came to be known as Aśvamedha. He who knows this verily knows the Horse Sacrifice. Letting it remain free, he reflected. At the end of a year he sacrificed it to himself and dispatched the other animals to the gods. Therefore priests even now sacrifice to Prajāpati the sanctified (horse) dedicated to all the gods. Verily, that (sun) which radiates heat (*tapati*) is the Horse Sacrifice. His self (*ātman*) is the year (cyclical time). This fire (*agni*) is the *arka* (solar essence), whose selves are these worlds (*loka*s). So these two, fire and the sun, are the *arka* and the Aśvamedha (Horse Sacrifice). These two, again,

14 See Sri Aurobindo's commentary of the *Īśa Upaniṣad* (2003, vol. 17: 10, 27-28, 45, 78) and Banerji 2020: 49-64.

> become the same God, Death. He who knows this (*ya evam veda*) conquers further death; death cannot overcome him; death becomes his self; and he becomes one with these deities.

Death, whose solar essence is in the Horse, sacrifices it to itself, i.e. the original Time-Image at the heart of Becoming. Other animals – i.e. the variations and instances of the abstract machine of Becoming – are sacrificed to the gods. Though all creatures carry the solar essence within them, the souls of other animals remain under the compulsion of the cosmic conditions ruled by the gods. The term used for these creatures is *paśu*, literally those who are bound.[15] The Horse as the symbol of Divine Life is the soul of the Becoming, hence, the universal soul of originary Death, superior to the cosmic conditions, though obeying them.[16] Death, in this status is equated to Prajāpati, the Creator or Lord of all Creatures. The father/lord (*pati*) of all those who are compelled to birth (the preposition *pra* applied to the phoneme *ja*, to be born) is Prajāpati. Sacrificing to Prajāpati, one automatically sacrifices to all the gods.

Horse, Fire and the Sun

This equation of Death and the Lord of all Creatures becomes the trigger for pushing back to the heliocentric origin of the Horse Sacrifice – That which is the Aśvamedha, that is the Sun source of heat (*tapati*):

> That which is the Aśvamedha that is the Sun (*tapati*); the year is its self. This Fire (Agni) is the Sun (*arka*); these worlds (*loka*s) are its selves. So these two are together, the fire and the Aśvamedha (*arkāśvamedhasau*). Again they become one God; Death too. He [who knows this] is victorious over re-death, Death cannot take this one for itself. Death becomes this one's self; and he becomes one with the gods.

15 From *pāśa*, knot of bondage.

16 A later Upaniṣad, the *Aitareya*, reserves this privilege for the human.

The Sun is itself now asserted to be the Horse Sacrifice. The property of the Sun by which it is named here is its power of producing heat by concentration (*tapas*). Relating back to the heliocentric description of the Sacrificial Horse in the first *brāhmaṇa*, its body or self is again asserted to be the year or cyclic time-quantum, unit of Becoming within Being. The solar essence (*arka*) which has descended into the Becoming is asserted to be the same as Fire (*Agni*) of Aspiration in all things. Hence, all the worlds belong to it, since it resides as essence at the centre of all things. These two, the Sacrificial Horse (or the Sun in relation to the Becoming) and the Fire are asserted as the two principal realities and/or gods. Then they are equated and identified, as they are also identified with Death. Death is nothing but the Sacrifice of the Sacrificial Horse, the descent of the Sun into the Night for the sake of the Day-and-Night cycle of Becoming. Even in Death, at its heart, the solar essence (*arka*), burns as the Fire (*Agni*) whose heat (*tapas*) gathers the dispersion of the Night of Matter and causes it to seek the realization of its heliocentric origin through repeated deaths and births, evolving individuations of the One. Even through this process, it is only the only One. He who knows this overcomes death because s/he becomes Death, in other words, the Being of Death, the Sacrifical Horse in its origin, Aditi, the heliocentric Origin, who even in becoming Death, separation and disappearance, remains the immortal indivisible One.

Gods, Demons and Immortality

Adhyāya I: Brāhmaṇa 3

1. Two were the classes descending from the Lord of Creatures (Prajāpati): the gods (*deva*s) and the demons (*asura*s). Of these, the gods were the younger and the demons the elder. They struggled with one another for mastery of these worlds. The gods said, let us overcome the demons at the sacrifice by means of the Udgītha (the ascending song, the *oṁ*).

2. They said to the organ of speech: "Chant the Udgītha (ascending song) for us". "So be it", said speech and ascended singing for them. Whatever enjoyment belongs to speech, it brought to the gods, whatever blessing is in speech, it brought for itself (*ātman*). They (the *asura*s) knew that through this singer they (the *deva*s) will overcome us. They rushed at it and pierced it with evil. That evil which consists in improper speech, that is that evil.

3. Then they said to the life-breath (*prāṇa*): "Chant the Udgītha (ascending song) for us". "So be it", said the life-breath and ascended singing for them. Whatever enjoyment belongs to the life-breath, it brought to the gods, whatever blessing is in smell, it brought for itself (*ātman*). They (the *asura*s) knew that through this singer they (the *deva*s) will overcome us. They rushed at it and pierced it with evil. That evil which consists in improper smell, that is that evil.

4. Then they said to the eye: "Chant the Udgītha (ascending song) for us". "So be it", said the eye and ascended singing for them. Whatever enjoyment belongs to the eye, it brought to the gods, whatever blessing is in sight, it brought for itself (*ātman*). They (the *asura*s) knew that through this singer they (the *deva*s) will overcome us. They rushed at it and pierced it with evil. That evil which consists in improper seeing, that is that evil.

5. Then they said to the ear: "Chant the Udgītha (ascending song) for us". "So be it", said the ear and ascended singing

for them. Whatever enjoyment belongs to the ear, it brought to the gods, whatever blessing is in hearing, it brought for itself (*ātman*). They (the *asuras*) knew that through this singer they (the *devas*) will overcome us. They rushed at it and pierced it with evil. That evil which consists in improper hearing, that is that evil.

6. Then they said to the mind: "Chant the Udgītha (ascending song) for us". "So be it", said the mind and ascended singing for them. Whatever enjoyment belongs to the mind, it brought to the gods, whatever blessing is in thought, it brought for itself (*ātman*). They (the *asuras*) knew that through this singer they (the *devas*) will overcome us. They rushed at it and pierced it with evil. That evil which consists in improper thinking, that is that evil.

7. Then they said to the vital breath in the mouth: "Chant the Udgītha (ascending song) for us". "So be it", said the vital breath and ascended singing for them. They (the *asuras*) knew that through this singer they (the *devas*) will overcome us. They rushed at it, intending to pierce it with evil. But as a clod of earth, striking against a rock is scattered, even so they were scattered in all directions and destroyed. Thereupon the gods became established in their true selves and the demons perished. He who knows this becomes his true self and his spiteful kinsman perishes.

8. Then the organs said: "Where is that which joined us to our true selves?" After deliberation they discovered that it was here, within the mouth (*asye*). Hence the vital breath (*prāṇa*) is called *ayāsya* and also, because it is the essence (*rasa*) of the limbs (*aṅga*) of the body, *aṅgirasa*.

9. That deity is called *dūr*, because death is far (*dūr*) from it. From him who knows this, death is far away.

10. Verily that divinity took away the evil of these gods, even death and carried it to where the end of the quarters is. There it deposited their evils. Therefore let no one visit persons (of that region), or travel to the country beyond the border, lest he should meet there with evil, with death.

11. That divinity, after removed the evil, the death of the gods, carried them beyond death.

12. Indeed it transported Speech first. When (Speech) was freed from Death it became fire. That fire, having transcended Death, shines beyond its reach.

13. Then it carried the life-breaths. When that was freed from Death it became Wind (Vāyu). That Wind, having transcended Death, blows beyond its reach.

14. Then it carried the Eye. When that was freed from death it became the sun (Sūrya). That sun, having transcended death, shines beyond its reach.

15. Then it carried the Ear. When it was freed from Death, it became the quarters (Diśaḥ). Those quarters, having transcended Death, remain beyond its reach.

16. Then it carried the Mind. When the mind was freed from Death it became the moon (Candra). That moon, having transcended death, shines beyond its reach. Thus, verily, that divinity carries beyond death him who knows this.

17. Next it (the breath in the mouth) obtained food for itself by singing. For whatever food is eaten, is eaten by that (the vital breath) alone. In it (the vital breath) is established.

18. These gods said: "Indeed, just this much is all the food there is and you have obtained for yourself by singing. Now let us have a share of this food." "Then sit around facing me." "So be it." They sat down around it on all sides. That is why whatever food one eats through it satisfies also these others. So do his relatives gather around him who knows this; he becomes their supporter, the foremost among them and their leader; an eater of food and their lord. Whoever, among his kinsmen, desires to be a rival of the man who has this knowledge will be unable to support his own dependents. On the other hand, he who follows him (the knower of the vital breath) and who, following him, desires to support his dependents, indeed, is able to do so.

19. It is Ayāsya Aṅgirasa, for it is the essence (*rasa*) of the limbs (*aṅga*). Indeed, this life-breath (*prāṇa*) is the essence of the limbs, yes indeed this life-breath (*prāṇa*) is the essence of the limbs. From whichever limb this life-breath departs, that limb is sure to wither; for it is the very essence of the limbs.

20. And it is also Bṛhaspati. Speech is Bṛhatī and this is its lord (*pati*). Therefore it is called Bṛhaspati.

21. And it is also Brahmaṇaspati. Speech is *Brahman* and this is its lord (*pati*). Therefore it is called Brahmanaspati.

22. And this also is Sāman (equal). Speech is verily Sāman. It is she (*sā*) and he (*ama*). That is the equality (*sāmatvam*) of the Equal (*sāman*). Or because it is equal (*sama*) to a white ant, equal to a mosquito, equal to an elephant, equal to these three worlds, or even equal to all others; therefore it is indeed the Equal (*sama*). He who knows this Sāma enjoys union with it and lives in the same world with the Sāman.

23. And it is also the ascending song, Udgītha. The life-breath is verily ascension (*ut*), for by the life-breath all this is upheld (*uttabdham*). Speech is *gīthā* (song). And ascending (*ut*) song (*gīthā*) is therefore Udgītha.

24. As to this there also Brahmadatta Caikitāneya, while drinking the King elixir [Soma], said: "May this King strike off my head if I say that the Aṅgirasa Ayāsya sang the Udgītha by any other means, for by Speech and the Life-breath alone did he sing it".

25. He who knows the wealth of this Sāman obtains wealth. Tone (*svara*), indeed, is its wealth (*sva*). Therefore let one who is going to perform the sacrificial work as a priest desire that his voice may be rich in tone and let him perform the sacrifice with that voice rich in tone. Therefore people desire a priest with a rich tone at a sacrifice, like one who has wealth. He who thus knows thus the wealth of the Sāman obtains wealth.

26. He who knows the gold (*suvarṇa*) of the Sāman obtains gold. Tone (*svara*) is verily its gold (*suvarṇa*). He who thus knows what is the gold of the Sāman obtains gold.

27. He who knows the support of the Sāman obtains a foundation. Speech verily is its support. For, supported in speech, the life-breath is transformed into a song. Some, however, say food (*anna*) is the support.

28. Next follows the repetition (*abhyāroha*) only of the purificatory hymns (*pavamāna*). The priest called *prastotṛ* indeed chants the *sāman*; while he chants it, let the sacrificer recite these [*Yajur* verses]: "Lead me from the unreal to the real. From darkness lead me to light. From death lead me to immortality." When he says: "Lead me from the unreal to the real", "the unreal" means death and the "real", immortality; so it says, "From death lead me to immortality", that is to say, "Make me immortal". When it says: "From darkness lead me to light", "darkness" means death and "light", immortality; so it says: "From death lead me to immortality", that is to say, "Make me immortal". "From death lead me to immortality", there is nothing that is hidden here. Whatever the other hymns by them one should obtain food for one's self. Therefore in them he should ask a boon (*varam*) – anything he desires. Whatever objects this singer of the ascending word (*udgātṛ*), endowed with such knowledge, desires for himself or for the sacrifice (*yajamāna*), that he obtains. This, indeed, is world conquering. He who thus knows the *sāman*, for him there is no fear of being without a world.

I

THE second *brāhmaṇa* of the first *adhyāya* of the *Bṛhadāraṇyaka Upaniṣad* ends with the parable of the population of the field of cosmic Becoming as the result of the sex act of the mind of Death-Hunger with Speech. This multiplied dispersion should be understood as the population of the conceptual-space of Hunger, which is Death, thus marked by an escape from Death and a capture by Death. There is a shock value to this imagery and a puzzling character to it. Indeed, the puzzling question will be brought to the fore later more explicitly in the fifth *brāhmaṇa* – how is it that this Eater eats whatever emerges yet never exhausts its food? Whatever comes into existence is its own infinite, since It is the infinite that is manifesting in all things that manifest. Each emergence is a bound infinity and a self-presentation of radical infinity. One human implies the birth of infinite humans; we know today that even a couple is not required for the replication of a species; a single instance, even a single cell, any cell will do for cloning the whole individual. Whatever emerges into existence escapes from the jaws of Death and proliferates into its infinity. All these infinite instances are marked by Death but they all re-emerge and escape back into Life – inexhaustibly, though always different, never the same. So this Birth from the copulation of Death's Mind and the Word is an eternal Event which is a sign of Being-and-non-Being within the Becoming. This play between Being and non-Being structures the entire cosmos and its creatures.

To summarize the first two *brāhmaṇas*, the Horse of the Being, through Sacrifice, became the Horse of the non-Being and the Horse of the non-Being, through the successions of Hunger, Work, Mind and Language, becomes the Horse of the Becoming. We see the dualities that have pursued us to this point – the duality of Being and non-Being and the duality, not only of Being and Becoming but of Being-and-non-Being with Becoming. Becoming is marked in every step by the coexisting duality of Being-and-non-Being. Being in Becoming is Life; non-Being in Becoming is Death. Everything goes through successions of living and dying in its Becoming. Thus, the Horse sacrifice is shown as going from Being to non-Being and from non-Being to Becoming, the Becoming then shown as a process that leads to another death and a rebirth. We are taken in these two *brāhmaṇas* through transformations that show us the different lives of the Horse – the Horse as a permanent Being, the horse as a Being that emerges in non-Being, the Horse that is the virtual Becoming, the Horse that is the (repeated) rebirth of the Horse of the Becoming. So, in the first two *brāhmaṇas* of the *Bṛhadāraṇyaka Upaniṣad*, we are given Genesis in a cosmic Time-Image that encounters the major dualities of creation. This processual axiology continues through further dualities in the third *brāhmaṇa*.

II

The new cosmogonic duality presented in the third *brāhmaṇa* is the opposition between the gods and the demons:

> 1. There were two classes of the descendants of Prajāpati, the gods (*deva*s) and the demons (*asura*s). Of these the gods were the younger and the demons were the elder ones. They were struggling with each other for these worlds. The gods said, come, let us overcome the demons at the Sacrifice through the *udgītha*.

The battle between the gods and the demons (*deva* and *asura*) refer back to the Veda. Just as a state ritual, that of establishing a "solar" emperor (*cakravartin*) is given an esoteric and cosmogonic significance in the first two *brāhmaṇa*s of the first *adhyāya*, the third *brāhmaṇa* parallels other rituals of the Veda, meant to protect the state by putting the demons to flight and clearing a space for the manifestation of the gods. If we think of the fossilization of Vedic society by the time of the Upaniṣads, such rituals had become routine and were conducted with the intention of material prosperity, such as agricultural abundance. A state ritual of this kind conducted by a brāhmaṇa for a kṣatriya king is the conventional social model against which an esoteric and cosmogonic version of the ritual is presented in this *brāhmaṇa*.

Deva and Asura

Deva and *asura* are solar names. *Deva* is derived from *div*, from which, by Indo-European kinship, we get "Divine". It is also present in *dīp* (lamp) or "Divālī" (festival of Lights). *Div* is derived from Dyauṣ or heaven, the firmament of light, hence *deva* is a being of light. This is related to the solar cosmology of the Veda. The Sun is called *sūrya*, also derived from *svar* (heaven). "Sura", related to *sūrya* is a word for the gods of the Veda. In *Īśa Upaniṣad* 3, one finds the term *asūrya* (sunless), in the phrase *asūrya loka* (sunless worlds). Sunless worlds are worlds distant from the Sun in our solar system. They are caught by the gravitation of the Sun, yet try to escape this gravitation. They belong to the system but they have a force against the system. The sunless worlds are dark; the word *asura* may be seen as related to *asūrya* – sunless, though in early Vedic use, *asura* is a name signifying divine power. Thus, *deva* and *sura* are light beings, *asura* are their contraries – the ones that are lightless. Sri Aurobindo also indicates the earlier etymology for *asura* because in the Veda the Sun God himself is the first *asura*.[1] *Asura* there means Being of Power from *asu* (power); Sri Aurobindo translates *asura* as "mighty Lord" in this context (1998, vol. 15: 427, fn. 2; 523, fn. 5). This root is present in *aśva*, the Horse of the Sacrifice we have encountered in the first two *brāhmaṇa*s, an image of the Divine Force of the solar Origin (Aurobindo 2001, vol. 18: 277). Thus, we can see the two meanings of *asura* that relate to the two realms that are implied in this cosmology. In the heliocentric solar realm, it is the Sun but in the geocentric realm it is the will to darkness, against the Sun. This parallels the Vedic image of Death, Yama who is the son of Vivasvān, another name for the Sun God.

Thus, *deva*s and *asura*s may be thought of as archetypes but they are also faculties that exist in evolving entities. In the Upaniṣads the gods are often spoken of as human faculties, housed in the human, yet they have an existence of their own. Some modern thinkers, such as Henri Bergson, or following him Gilles Deleuze, believe that our faculties evolve independent of the specific beings to which they belong. This is the reason

---

1 This usage coincides with the Zoroastrian supreme God, Ahura Mazda, due to shared early Indo-Iranian roots.

why Bergson says that the eye evolves similarly along different evolutionary phylae and under different conditions (1998: 54-88). It is as if these faculties evolve themselves utilizing creatures as conditions of their evolution. This is similar to the Upaniṣads' view of the matter. These faculties of seeing, hearing, etc. are the gods that have fallen into a medium of non-Being, with a memory of their integral origin (see *AitUp* II.1-4). They thus seek evolution and integration. They do so by housing themselves in creatures. We take our faculties for granted; they give us knowledge. But if we think of each one separately, it is a marvel how they work together, in an integrated fashion to give us a single understanding of reality. Even the two eyes give us separate overlapping images which we integrate to obtain a single image with depth that we take to be the real nature of space. Thus, there is an integrating function that makes these faculties into a single system; just as the horse was a single system. In the evolution the work is ongoing to re-create the image of the Eternal Event that has entered Time.

The Upaniṣads are related in these matters. For example, the *Aitareya Upaniṣad* (chap. I) gives us a Time-Image of the *Puruṣa* just like the Horse in the *Bṛhadāraṇyaka*. *Puruṣa* may be translated as Person; we are not told that it is a human but we could think of it as a proto-human or even a post-human. It emerges from the Ocean by the power of concentration of the Self (*ātman*) and once it emerges, its faculties begin to open; and the opening of each faculty gives rise to the virtual possibility space of that faculty. In the next section, the gods who are the rulers of these faculties, fall separately into the Inconscient Ocean and begin looking for a home that is adequate to them so as to reconstitute the integral image from which they fell. When they find the human they leap into it. Then the *Ātman* (Self) also enters the human. That Self is the nucleus and secret integrator, the hidden integer or "I" that holds together the operation and evolution of the faculties.

The *Bṛhadāraṇyaka Upaniṣad* may be said to provide the model on which other Upaniṣads like the *Aitareya* build their images of the gods and their evolution/integration. There, we first have the image of the Horse with its faculties, which are described in terms of the gods:

> Dawn is the head of the sacrificial horse, the sun its eye, the wind its life-breath (*prāṇaḥ*), its open mouth the Vaiśvānara fire ....

Dawn (Uṣā), Sun (Sūrya), Wind (Vāyu), Fire (Agni) – these are the gods, given as the head organs of the Horse. Or more properly, Dawn is the God represented by the head of the Horse, with the other gods, Sun, Wind and Fire as its parts. In a vertical dimension, as in the divisions of an axis mundi, these gods represent a hierarchy – Dawn representing the Supermind, with Sun as the heaven world, Wind as the life world and Fire burning as the self of the earth world. The sacrifice of the Horse is its self-subjection to its opposite, the subjection of Being to non-Being which is the Eternal Event that forms the Time-Image of Becoming. For this, the Will to non-Being must first arise within Being for it to be subject to non-Being. This non-Being forms a deep amnesia in which the gods disappear. The creatures of the Will to non-Being are the *asura*s; therefore, the *asura*s precede the *deva*s. This is why we have the convention of older and younger as given in the *Bṛhadāraṇyaka* – the *asura*s were the elder, the gods the younger. The *deva*s emerge once Being starts arising out of non-Being. We saw this happening in the Horse sacrifice because once the inner remembrance began the work of regenerating the image of the Horse within the non-Being, the gods began arising. It generated Fire, it generated the Wind, it generated the Sun and then it generated the rest of the organs – these are the gods. They came after the subjection of Being to non-Being and represent the Will-to-Being emerging after the Will-to-non-Being; hence, the *asura*s are older and the gods younger.

Once the gods appear within the contested realm of Being-and-non-Being or Being-in-non-Being, there is the struggle. Will the cosmos endure in its existence and evolve or will it drop into extinction, into the Death of non-Being out of which it arose? So at the outset we are brought face to face with the precarious existence of the cosmos, its foundational relativity. This struggle of Being to emerge into existence and endure against the forces constantly attempting to obliterate it, is the essence of cosmic Work, the foundation of work as struggle, the very mark of cosmic existence. This is also the first form of evolution, the evolution of power, the Will-to-Power. Is consciousness powerful enough to stand against the will to dissolution? This is an active will to destroy, the will to annihilate. This is what makes it "evil", evil is the impersonal Will-to-non-Being, the will to remain Ignorant.

The Mother says that the most interesting thing about our creation are the properties of Freedom and Joy.[2] Freedom is granted even before consciousness is. This is why those who wish to remain unconscious are given the freedom to stay so. This is the freedom at the base of our cosmos. It allows the cosmos to have relativity and choice, which become the basis of struggle. This struggle is the journey of the *deva*s and *asura*s. The *deva*s and *asura*s in their struggle against each other further an aspect of the journey. In the fourth *brāhmaṇa*, we are introduced to another aspect of the journey, which is yet another duality, that of polarity of productive opposites, or complements, as we know it in the cosmos. The duality of *deva*s and *asura*s does not appear to be a productive polarity on the surface, where it is a mutual repulsion. But at a deeper level, this opposition is the basis of an evolutionary journey. Much later, in the Purāṇas, this is brought out more explicitly in the image of the churning of the ocean for the purpose of raising the pitcher of

---

2 The Mother, *Questions and Answers 1957-1958*, 16 October 1957, *CWM* 9, p. 207.

Immortality (*amṛta*) (see *VP*, chap. IX). The gods and demons must participate together for this churning. The churning at first raises destructive poisons, but later it raises new gifts from underwater. In the third *brāhmaṇa* of the *Bṛhadāraṇyaka*, the contest between the gods and demons is not explicitly productive, but even before this *brāhmaṇa*, the contest is active in the production of fire. This is at the heart of the Upaniṣadic journey. We saw this in the second *brāhmaṇa* in the work that coded for the production of fire in the sounds of its words. We noted that the repetition of the *ṛc/ṛk* sound was also a covert churning, not a churning of the waters, but a churning of the amnesia of Death, as by a kindling stick. The journey began by the production of memory, from which came Fire. In the Veda, the God of Fire, Agni, is often called Jātaveda, the knower of births (*ṚV* III.26.7, V.4.11). In the Mother's and Sri Aurobindo's language, this would be the psychic memory, the true memory of persistence in each being.[3] The source of this memory is the power of the Sun itself hidden in the heart of the non-Being as Fire. It is friction that produces fire. The ancients made fire by churning a kindling rod. They twirled a stick on a base of tinders so that the friction produced fire. In an esoteric fashion the dynamic opposition between the gods and the demons serves as the churning. This journey happens in the macrocosm and in the microcosm. It is a struggle within and without that produces the fire of the soul that will call out to its heliocentric origin, so as to build the axis mundi that connects the individual to its source.[4] So, even in the duality, it knows the unity. The goal of

---

3 For example, "Psychic memories possess a very special character, they have a wonderful intensity. ... They are unforgettable moments of life when the consciousness is intense, luminous, strong, active, powerful and sometimes turning-points in life that have changed the direction of one's life." – The Mother, *Bulletin* 41, November 1967, quoted and discussed further in *The Mother, Words of the Mother, CWM*, 15: 126.

4 See hymns to Skambha in *Atharvaveda* X.7, X.8.

the Upaniṣads, as brought out explicitly in the *Īśa Upaniṣad* 14, is knowing the Two together as One.

The Udgītha

The *deva*s and *asura*s struggle with each other for the mastery of the worlds and the *deva*s are interested in annihilating the *asura*s so that they can establish a heavenly state in the contested cosmos:

> *Hantāsuram*, let us annihilate the *asura*s in this fire sacrifice by the power of *mantra*.

The *mantra* by which this will be effected is the *udgītha*. Literally, *udgītha* (the upward rising song), *ud* (to ascend), *gīta* (song), hence the song that calls upwards, an invocation to the Sun! In Vedic chanting, it was the second and main step in the chanting of the *Sāmaveda*. At the same time, *udgītha* is commonly understood to mean the monosyllabic *mantra oṁ*. Hence, the gods (*deva*s), who are beings of Light, solar beings possess this powerful *mantra*, this anti-gravitational or negentropic Word with which they will destroy the beings that pull towards the Black Hole of non-Being.

For this, they approach the first of the gods, Speech (*Vāk*) and ask it to chant the *udgītha* for them:

> 2. They said to the organ of speech: "Chant the Udgītha (ascending song) for us". "So be it", said speech and ascended singing for them. Whatever enjoyment belongs to speech, it brought to the gods, whatever blessing is in speech, it brought for itself (*ātman*). They (*asura*s) knew that through this singer they (*deva*s) will overcome us. They rushed at it and pierced it with evil. That evil which consists in improper speech, that is that evil.

The God of Speech is summoned to utter the fire word, the word that rises up. It utters that and the good that comes of speech goes to all the gods. But that which is well said is retained by Speech.

This is an example of what the contemporary philosopher Gilbert Simondon calls trans-individuation. Trans-individuation occurs when individuals compose a social unit which is more than a conglomerate of individuals and an individual itself, a trans-individual.[5] In a trans-individual, each individual is more than a part of the trans-individual, it identifies with the whole. Thus, what it does is for the benefit of the whole and it is aware of that. Each individual is the collective and what it does brings the good of the collective; the whole and all its parts are nourished by it. At the same time, what is brought down answers the specific call of the invoker, which is nourished in a special way by it. We are being told here that the gods compose an integral unit through the emergence of a hidden common potential that belongs to each of them, a whole in this process of uniting against the demons and invoking a destructive power against them. Each God is incapable of doing it by itself. They are in the process of forming a composite body; each one, in turn, is called to offer itself as the soul of this body. We are similarly made to cycle through the other gods – the Life-breath, the Eye, the Ear and the Mind. Beings will now be related to the senses, we have the Word and we have the different senses. For example, breath is connected to the nose and becomes subject to evil in the form of bad smells. Each sense becomes infected by duality – good and bad words, good and bad smells, good and bad sight, good and bad hearing, good and bad thoughts.

---

5 Simondon discusses this over-compensation of elements in a composite in many places, concerning individuation and trans-individuation. See, for example, his description of the invention of the Guimbal turbine in his *Mode of Existence of Technical Objects* as discussed in Arne De Boever, Alex Murray and Jon Roffe, "'Technical Mentality' Revisited: Brian Massumi on Gilbert Simondon", in *Gilbert Simondon: Being and Technology*, ed. Arne De Boever, Alex Murray, Jon Roffe and Ashley Woodward, 2012, pp. 24-30.

Each sense is invoked to utter the secret Word and brings some good to the whole; but it is not sufficient.

To speak the *oṁ* is understandable, but to breathe, see, hear and think the *oṁ*? One of the revisions of Vedic practice introduced by the Upaniṣads pertains to the *mantra*. Whereas the Vedic *mantra* was the Ṛgvedic hymn that had become rote repetition by priests in rituals, the Upaniṣads developed a new conception of the *mantra*. One of its manifestations could be a seed-syllable, later popularized in Tantra as the *bīja*. For the Upaniṣads the quintessential *bīja* was *oṁ*. *Oṁ* was *Śabda-Brahman* or *Brahman* in the form of sound; yet blind repetition of the syllable was discouraged. In its place, an integral participation of the faculties was enjoined. At a later stage, there arose an Upaniṣad of the *oṁ*, the *Māṇḍūkya Upaniṣad*, which gave ideational content to the *oṁ*. One could focus one's mind on this content as one recited it. In this parable of the gods and demons, something of this kind is intended. Recitation of the *oṁ* includes a breathing rhythm, a visualization practice, a hearing and a mental concentration on the Idea. As the *oṁ* is recited, each of these components can take the foreground and become the leader of the practice.

We may also take the word *udgītha* in its literal meaning. After all, its equation with the seed syllable *oṁ* is something established by the *Upaniṣad*, but it literally means "the upward rising song". It is thus a power of ascension, an ideal focus which each of the senses can interpret differently, making it an instrument of *yoga*. Recalling the image of the solar sacrificial Horse described in the first *brāhmaṇa*, we can see how these faculties together reconstruct the Horse's head. Each of the faculties is a representative of a god and can be made into a channel for *yoga*. There is a *yoga* of speech, a *yoga* of sight, a *yoga* of hearing, a *yoga* of thought-contemplation. Later specializations in *yoga* have taken each of these and made fields of *yoga* from them – *prāṇāyāma* as the *yoga* of the breath (*nāda-yoga*) and *saṅgīta-yoga* (*yoga* of sound), *śilpa-yoga* (*yoga* of art), or *dhyāna-yoga* (*yoga* of visualization), *jñāna-yoga* (*yoga* of the mind).

Of these, the sight and the hearing are the two primary senses in the thought of the Veda. Sight and Hearing are related to the two primary self-presentations of the Divine in Supermind; they are the goddesses Ilā and Sarasvatī (Aurobindo 1998, vol. 18: 96). According to Sri Aurobindo, these are the goddesses, respectively, of Revelation and Inspiration. Ilā visions the divine, its vision is not a representational vision, but a self-presentational vision. In other words, it is the basis of *darśana* – seeing of the revealed body of God. Sarasvatī gives the word of the *mantra*; the sound body of God. Thus, these two are related to the Yogic powers of inner sight, which is guided by and aspires to union with Ilā (Goddess of Revelation); and inner hearing, the faculty for receiving the sound body of the Divine, Vāk which aspires to union with Sarasvatī (Goddess of the Word). These are themselves powers of Indra (God of the Mind). It is interesting to see that eyes and ears are not subsumed by the mind here, but given independent status. The Mind is often treated as the sixth sense. Later, Indian psychology, as for example, the school of Sāṁkhya, which is dealt with in *Sāṁkhya Kārikā* 21-38, differentiates mind and its phenomenological apparatus in a way more familiar to our present understanding – the senses are here subsumed by the Mind, which itself is differentiated in terms of a sense mind (*manas*), an ego (*ahaṁkāra*) and an intelligence (*buddhi*). But in the *Upaniṣad*, the mind (*manaḥ*) is put at the same level as the senses, since they are interested in recognizing the heterogeneity of the faculties and allowing each of them to find their independent connections to the Divine, while also collaborating to find an integration. So, it goes through the faculties, asking each one of these separately to lead the way, but none of them is adequate. The *Upaniṣad* says – all these organs were found incapable of chanting the *udgītha* as they have contracted evil on account of their attachment to doing well.

The Breath in the Mouth

After all the mental faculties are found incapable of chanting the *udgītha*, they approached "the life-breath in the mouth" – in Sanskrit, *atha hemam āsanyam prāṇam ūchuḥ; hemam* is mouth; *āsanyam* like *āsana*, seated; *prāṇam*, vital energy – they ask this vital energy seated in the mouth to recite the *udgītha*. Here is something mysterious and esoteric; what is the vital energy seated in the mouth? It is something hidden, secret, that belongs to the interior, not something seen or known from the outside. It is a *prāṇaḥ* (vital energy), at the same time residing in the mouth it is related to the word and to the element of fire as per the original description of the Horse in *Bṛhadāraṇyaka Upaniṣad* I.1.1. This mysterious "breath in the mouth" chants for them:

> 7. Then they said to the vital breath in the mouth: "Chant the Udgītha (ascending song) for us". "So be it", said the vital breath and ascended singing for them. They (*asuras*) knew that through this singer they (*devas*) will overcome us. They rushed at it, intending to pierce it with evil. But as a clod of earth, striking against a rock is scattered, even so they were scattered in all directions and destroyed. Thereupon the gods became established in their true selves and the demons perished. He who knows this (*ya evam veda*) becomes his true self and his spiteful kinsman perishes.

What is this secret breath in the mouth? The "secret breath" is the psychic element. If one were to use the Christian terminology, one could call it "the holy ghost", *pneuma* in Greek or *spiritus* in Latin. Here the psychic vitality is being foregrounded. The psychic element is the Divine element behind all the gods. It knows them in essence and includes in itself corresponding properties of all the gods – it is a psychic flame, Agni, a psychic breath, Vāyu and a psychic word (Vāk), all these are integrated within it. Hence, when it utters the *udgītha,* it integrates the gods and builds the vertical axis between heaven and earth, the heliocentric and geocentric realms. The *Upaniṣad* remains esoteric about how it does this and does not give us an explicit practice. This may be because the text is backgrounded by an oral tradition, which is restricted to initiates, but it is also because the hearer is encouraged to find his/her own practice, in keeping with the contemplative freedom being promoted by the Upaniṣads. Fire, wind and the word – we saw how these three are representatives of the Divine in the three regions of Matter, Life and Mind respectively. They are united in the psychic. Moreover, of these it is the fire, Agni, which includes the other two and is the most essential immanent psychic element. We recollect that in the original image of the Horse, it was fire, Agni, that is the God related to the mouth.

When we think about Ilā and Sarasvatī, the Vedic supramental goddesses of Revelation and Inspiration, we can see how they operate together on the other planes. They are present, for instance, as powers in Overmind, symbolized in the thunderbolt of Indra, which is both thunder and lightning. Lightning flashes and reveals the terrain in the darkness. It is related to the faculty of Sight and carries its message prior to thunder, which brings the sound body of Truth to our hearing, directing our action in Will. Fire is similar in that it includes the two elements of Light and Heat, Wisdom and Power fused in one. The psychic fire that is being called the "breath in the mouth" is this combined word and its force! One is vital and other is mental; we are reminded once again of the two original Vedic animals – the Cow and the Horse. It is the braiding of the two in the psychic fire, that alone is adequate to defeat the demons.

The word is the intelligent component, the breath is the energetic component. Each word has a sound image that propagates vibrations when we intone it. This is the basis of the *mantra* because these vibrations act directly on the subtle centres (*cakras*) of the body, while the word meaning acts on our understanding. The senses, having failed to overcome the demons and, in fact, having become infected with their shadow realities, called to the invisible breath in the mouth, the hidden immanence of the Origin. They cannot see it, yet they intuit it and invoke it. Having exhausted their resources, they invoke the hidden breath in the mouth – and the magic happens. The demons rush at it to infect it but are shattered to pieces and destroyed. The faculties that invoked it are taken aback, surprised by this result. As we have seen, the "breath in the mouth" is the secret essence of each sense; yet, it is separate from them and at their origin. Hence, they are surprised that this something, which seemed to be a part of each of them, "stuck to them" or "attached to them" (*āsakteti*) has acted and succeeded when they could not; it appeared from a secret immanent source and has disappeared to its secrecy:

> 8. Then the organs said: "Where is that which stuck to us?" After deliberation they discovered that it was here, within the mouth (*asye*). Hence the vital breath (*prāṇa*) is called *ayāsya* and also, because it is the essence (*rasa*) of the limbs (*aṅga*) of the body, *aṅgirasa*.

They locate it within and identify its name as Ayāsya Aṅgirasa. Here, all of a sudden we find the incursion of a Vedic Aṅgirasa Ṛṣi; at the same time, the term *aṅgirasa* is given an unconventional etymological derivation – *aṅga* means limb or body part and *rasa* is sap, emotion or essence, hence essence of the limbs.

Ayāsya Aṅgirasa

Who is this secret being? We have encountered the Aṅgirasa Ṛṣi of the Vedas. They are the ancestors; etymologically, they are embers that remain smouldering even when the fire has died. This particular Aṅgirasa has the name Ayāsya. This Aṅgirasa Ṛṣi Ayāsya is invoked in specific hymns of the *Ṛgveda* that have to do with a ritual that takes ten months (1998, vol. 15: 159-86). In these rituals, there are nine *ṛṣi*s known as the Navagva. *Gva* refers to cows, in other words, they who have nine cows. But *go* from which *gva* is derived, also means light. Sri Aurobindo discusses these *ṛṣi*s and their nine month ritual in *The Secret of the Veda* (pt. I, chap. XVII). He refers to the *ṛṣi*s as they of the nine cows or the nine-rayed ones. They conduct the sacrifice for nine months but find it too difficult to complete the tenth month; the level of difficulty escalates beyond their capacity, in a way reminiscent of the gods in the *Bṛhadāraṇyaka*. Suddenly, there appears into their mix another Aṅgirasa, Ayāsya; he is characterized as one in possession of the seven words. With these seven words he can have dominion over the realm of Svar, which is what the Navagva need to complete their sacrifice. He joins them and they complete the 10th month, accomplishing the goal of the sacrifice, which is the attainment of the world of Svar. Here is what Sri Aurobindo says:

> [T]hese seem to have been two different powers of Aṅgirasahood and in that case the Navagvas themselves might well become Dashagvas by extending the period of the sacrifice to 10 months instead of 9. The expression in the hymn *daśa māso ataran* indicates that there was some difficulty in getting through the full period of ten months. It is during this period apparently that the sons of darkness had the power to assail the sacrifice; for it is indicated that it is only by the confirming of the thought which conquers Svar – the solar world, that the *ṛṣi*s are able to get to the ten months, but this thought once found they become assured of the protection of the gods and pass beyond the assault of the evil, the harms of the Panis and Vṛtras. This Svar-conquering thought is certainly the same as that seven-headed thought which was born from the truth and discovered by the Ayāsya, the companion of the Navagvas; for by it, we are told, Ayāsya becoming universal, embracing the birth in all the worlds, brought into being a fourth world, a fourfold world which must be the supramental beyond the

> three lower sessions – Dyauṣ, Antarikṣa and Pr̥thvī, that wide world which according to Kaṇva, son of Ghora, men reach or create by crossing beyond the two Rodasi after killing Vr̥tra. This fourth world must be therefore Svar. The seven-headed thought of Ayāsya enables him to become *viśvajanya* which means probably that he occupies or possesses all the worlds or births of the soul or else that he becomes universal, identifying himself with all beings born – and to manifest or give being to a certain fourth world (Svar) .... – 1998, vol. 15: 176

Thus, we see that this is the seeking for the Supermind. The gods and the demons belong to the cosmic planes; these are the three planes or Pr̥thvī, Antarikṣa and Dyauṣ, or Matter, Life and Mind. Beyond them is the fourth word of Svar or Supermind. These three lower worlds are infected with duality, they are the geocentric realms. They are occupied by the gods and the demons. But to be free of duality, to overcome the demons, the gods need to get to the fourth solar or heliocentric world. For this, their own power is insufficient, they need something more, an integral power. The first access to the integral on the earth is the psychic being. The psychic is the element that is the secret in every God as its divine essence, yet separate and greater than all the gods. It is the immanent divinity of the system.

We explored the probable Vedic etymology of Aṅgirasa, relating it to unextinguished embers that can relight a fire once it has died. In the Upaniṣads, we find a very different etymology. This, again, is a common Upaniṣadic device. They use off-beat etymology, partly to break our habits of thinking, partly to open up new understandings and partly as a form of humour, encouraging creative originality. It is also in character with Yājñavalkya, if we think of him as the writer of the *Br̥hadāraṇyaka*. Aṅgirasa is broken up into *aṅga* (limb or portion) and *rasa* ("taste", "quality of affect" or "essence"). In this way, Aṅgirasa is the essence or secret quality of every limb or faculty; he is called Aṅgirasa Ayāsya for he is the essence (*rasa*) of the faculties (*aṅga*). This may be compared to *arkasya arkatvam*, the solar essence of the fire, the sun descended into the Night, which we encountered before. The *Upaniṣad* continues:

> 9. That divinity verily is *dūr* by name because death is far (*dūra*) from it; for him who knows this (*ya evam veda*) death is far off.

Immediately after telling us how this mysterious Aṅgirasa is the essence of all the faculties, intimately part of our existence, we are told that it is called *dūr* (the distant). This juxtaposition to describe the immanent divine element continues to be used in later Upaniṣads. By the time of the *Īśa*, it has become a statement of paradox to be contemplated:

> *tad ejati tannaijati tad dūre tad u antike* ।
> *tad antarasya sarvasya tadu sarvasyāsya bāhyataḥ* ॥

> *That moves and that does not move, that is far and that is intimate. That is within all things and that is outside of all things.*

Immortality

We saw how the conception of Space was created in the second *brāhmaṇa* through the mating of the Mind of Hunger with the Word. This is the Space of Death, of non-Being or Lack, expanding to fill itself. It is structured by the opposite forces of the Will-to-Death and the Will-to-Immortality. These are the *deva*s and the *asura*s. When the *deva*s, by the power of the Divine immanent within the non-Being, discover psychic Immortality, they create a new Space, the Space of the gods, or the enduring Space of Cosmic manifestation. This is not a Space of realized Immortality but a Space of bounded Immortality. This means that Immortality manifests under bounded conditions of repetition. Sri Aurobindo says in the *Synthesis of Yoga*, "To be perpetually reborn is the condition of a material immortality". This is a bounded immortality in which the forces of non-Being, the *asura*s, remain to contest Consciousness at the individual level, but cannot force the precariousness of the cosmic manifestation.

The psychic being is the reincarnating element in us; it is thus untouched by death. Those who discover the psychic being maintain their consciousness through death and between lives. The *Upaniṣad* continues to describe this consequence of the victory of the Divine at the cosmic level:

> 10. Verily that divinity took away the evil of these gods, even death and carried it to where the end of the quarters is. There it deposited their evils. Therefore let no one visit persons (of that region), or travel to the country beyond the border, lest he should meet there with evil, with death.

Just as we have the Sun with its power of gravitation, so the planets that are farthest from it, at the extreme orbit, get no light; this may be considered the bounded Space of the stable cosmic manifestation. Ayāsya stakes out a cosmic territory for the *deva*s to manifest securely. Outside this bound, there is again the danger zone of precarious dualities. These are the "sunless worlds" of the *Īśa Upaniṣad*. In discussing Ayāsya's contribution in the Vedic legend, Sri Aurobindo wrote about Ayāsya becoming universal. If our first access to the power of the integral is the psychic being, the second access to the integral is the universal or cosmic being. The first victory of Ayāsya is at the level of the individual; it creates an ambit or orbit of secure individuation. But in contesting the powers of non-Being, it grows universal, creating a wide secure space for cosmic manifestation. But at the peripheries of this bounded Space, the *asura*s continue to exist, hence one is cautioned not to go to the "end of the quarters lest one meet there with evil, with death". The closer one keeps one's consciousness to the centre of the psychic Fire, the Hearth of solar aspiration, one travels the sunlit path; the further one goes from this, one enters the no man's land and the dark domains of the demons.

But having created this Space for the gods, Ayāsya takes a further step. We are told that he takes the gods beyond death:

> 11. That divinity, after he removed the evil, the death of the gods, carried them beyond death.

We must understand this crossing in terms of the evolution following the sacrifice of the Horse. All of these gods are modes of the Divine's self-perception. These modes of self-perception, having fallen into the Inconscient, evolve laterally across the manifestation, striving to become the most adequate possibilities of organs for the experience of the Divine. This lateral evolution converges towards an integration in a being so as to function together in a plural reconstruction, held together by the Āṅgirasa Ayāsya, the *rasa* or hidden spirit of the integral experience of the organs or the spark of God in the Immanence. Ayāsya builds the invisible orbit of the geocentric cosmos, so as to give it Space to manifest; then it crosses over from the geocentric to the heliocentric world, the Supermind. The geocentric encompasses the three Vedic realms of Pṛthvī, Antarikṣa and Dyauṣ, or Earth, Life-World and Mind-World. It crosses the intermediate zone of Darkness beyond these to the solar zone of the Supermind, where the gods find their origins.

This is the third crossing, from the cosmic to the supramental. It carries Speech across first and when freed from death Speech becomes Fire. Let us recollect that Ayāsya as the breath in the mouth unites the elements of psychic Matter, Life and Mind – i.e. Fire, Wind and Speech. In chanting the *udgītha*, it is Speech that is the first of its powers that makes the crossing. In the reconstruction of the head of the Horse, it is the Horse's mouth from which Fire came, so in its crossing over to its heliocentric origin, it finds its identity with the solar Fire (*saurya Agni*). Similarly, the other faculties also cross over to discover their heliocentric doubles. The breath, Vāyu crosses over next and finds its supramental double, the Divine Life-force, the solar Wind. Third, Sight crosses over and finds its solar double as the Sun, as the eyes of the horse were suns, symbolizing solar Sight. Next, Hearing crosses over and recognizes its solar origin as the Directions, or solar Space. This is the third kind of Space, Supramental Space, the Space of unbounded Immortality, that can take the forms or Real-Idea of cosmic bounded Immortalities. We encountered first the Space of Hunger which was the Space of mortality, then the Space of cosmos, which was the space of bounded Immortality and now we encounter the origin of these spaces, the Space of Supermind, which is the Space of unbounded Immortality. Finally, Mind crosses over and discovers its supramental double in the Moon. This seems to be another deviation from the symbolic conventions of the Veda, for which it is the Sun which is the integral Supermind. Instead, the sun has here been shown as the supramental double of the eye, hence restricted to the power of Divine Sight (*darśana*). In the early Upaniṣads, the Mind is not seen so much as an integrator of the senses as an independent faculty at the same level as the senses, a faculty of reason and conception. Hence, one may think of its heliocentric double as the supramental Reason, or comprehensive conceptive organ of the Real-Idea. Within the geocentric Night, it is a refracted surrogate of the Sun.

Return to Matter and Integration

This ascension and victory of the gods is followed by a return to Matter. The "breath in the mouth" now takes possession of material existence:

> 17. Then it (the breath) chanted food for itself (obtained food by chanting). For whatever food is eaten is eaten by him alone. In it (breath) is established.

It is the psychic being in us which experiences. The *Bṛhadāraṇyaka* returns to its satirized rendition of the Vedic ritual with its reduction of experience to material experience and further to food, by making this the goal of the psychic spirit in its return to earthly existence. But by food and eating we must understand all embodied experiences. That which eats is that which experiences. The one experience inside us is not the experience of the senses, not even the mind; there is something behind the mind that experiences and carries the experiences from life to life; that is the psychic being; this is the true experiencer in us. Once the psychic comes to the front in the material existence, the other faculties feel the need to be partners in its experience, since it now knows its integrative power:

> 18. These gods said: "Indeed, just this much is all the food there is and you have obtained for yourself by singing. Now let us have a share of this food." He said, then sit around facing me or enter into me. So be it. They sat around, entered into him, on all sides. Therefore whatever food one eats by this breath they are satisfied by it. So do his relations come to him who know this (*ya evam veda*); he becomes the supporter of this people; their chief, their foremost leader and eater of food and their lord. Whoever among these people desires to be the equal of him, who has this knowledge is not able to support his own dependents; but whoever follows him and whoever following him desires to support his dependents, he indeed will be able to support his dependents.

This is the integration of the faculties around the psychic being. This is the culmination of psychic individuation, the psychicization of the faculties and the emergence of the psychic being as the central Person. The gods become One due to the evolving element in the human. Each of them independently realizes the psychic as its essence. This psychological integration also has a social dimension to it. In the image of the people gathering around the leader, we can recognize the idea behind the word *upaniṣad* – to sit near. It points to an alternative model of the polis, made up of circles of realized *yogī*s with their close-knit communities, forming *gurukula*s (families of initiates); the *yogī* extending his knowledge of identity to those who gather around him.

The next few stanzas eulogize the psychic entity or spirit, in turn as the psychic *prāṇa* (life-breath), which is the essence of all the faculties and the psychic Idea or the Word. In the latter sense, it is equated successively with the Vedic gods Bṛhaspati and Brahmaṇaspati. The etymological connection with these two gods is made in the verses of the *Upaniṣad* itself – both *Bṛhatī* and *brahma* being equated with *Vāk* (the Word) with *pati* (Lord), both these gods thus refer to the Lord of the Word. In his translation and commentary of the Hymn to Bṛhaspati of the *Ṛgveda*, Sri Aurobindo indicates a subtle difference between the two – *Bṛhaspati* more related to the power of the Word and *brahma* to the soul intuition or Idea behind the Word (1998, vol. 15: 315-25). We must also remember the Aṅgirasa, whose etymology the *Upaniṣad* draws on to establish the identity of Ayāsya as the secret life-breath, which is the essence of all the faculties, is more commonly relatable to the fiery ember. The three fused elements of the psychic entity, Fire, Wind and Word, which mark the presence of the Divine in the three realms of Matter, Life and Mind, are thus again invoked.

This relation of the secret psychic entity to the Word fused with the spiritual life-breath, making it the adequate chanter of the *udgītha*, also connects it to the *Sāmaveda*, which is the Veda of chanting. At this point (stanza 22) the *Upaniṣad* continues its comic-profound creative etymology by pointing to two meanings of *sāma* – the combination of "he" and "she" (*sā* = she, *ama* = he) and "equal" (*sāmam* = equal).

> 22. And this also is Sāman, the Equal. Speech is verily Sāman. It is she (*sa*) and he (*ama*). That is the equality (*samatvam*) of the Equal (*sāman*). Or because it is equal (*sama*) to a white ant, equal to a mosquito, equal to an elephant, equal to these three worlds, or even equal to all others; therefore it is indeed the Equal (*sāma*). He who knows this (*ya evam veda*) Sāma enjoys union with it and lives in the same world with the Sāman.

As the equality and union of the "she" and the "he", the psychic being is the androgyne. We see this in a variety of traditions; in modern times, it is an important element in the psychology of C.G. Jung: it is the case also in the Gnostic traditions and the alchemical traditions where arriving at the androgynous unity is referred to as syzygy (1968: 11-22). In Sri Aurobindo, this union is one way of understanding the integral. The integral consciousness belongs to Supermind, in which the polarities of Being and Consciousness-Force are paradoxically one and separate at the same time. In the cosmic manifestation, they separate to become soul and nature. Soul, the origin of Person (*Puruṣa*), is conventionally gendered male, while Nature (*Prakṛti*) is conventionally gendered female. In the evolution of soul, we arrive at the psychic being, which is the first level of integration of the two. The psychic being is the first access to the union between *Puruṣa* and *Prakṛti* – the androgynous unity. The cosmic being is the second and the Supermind is the origin. We saw these three steps earlier in terms of the relation of the gods and demons (*deva*s and *asura*s) – the first step integrated the gods and defeated the demons at the individual level, the second step created the universal orbit and pushed the demons to its edge; the third step made the gods immortal by entry into the Supermind or Svar and discovery of their identity with their supramental doubles. Here, we are shown another potency of the psychic being – as a uniter of the polarity which has been sundered in the geocentric realm of the dualities. This reference is also a foretaste of the fourth and next *brāhmaṇa*.

This is followed by another aspect of the psychic equated with the *Sāmaveda* that plays on the fact that one meaning of *sāma* or *samam* is "equal". The psychic element in us is the same substance in all beings, though manifest uniquely in each. The recognition of this identity behind all diversity is heightened through this meaning and brought graphically into our contemplation through enumeration of a variety of creatures, from the very small to the very large and finally to everything – a white ant, a mosquito, an elephant, these three worlds and everything – to which it is equal. It ends the stanza by saying

"He who knows the Sāma (Equal) to be such, attains union with it or lives in the same world with it". There is a monistic way and a theistic way of understanding this goal of realization. That which is equal to everything is the equal to sign, it is the equal one, *Samam Brahman*, the being of equality. This would be the monistic realization. At the same time, to "live in the same world" is understood in later theistic interpretations as *sālokya*, residing in the same ontological state as the Supreme Being. The psychic is a spark or breath of the Divine Being, hence of the same ontological state in relational nearness. Oneness and nearness at the same time – is this not the very condition described by the word *upaniṣad* – a liminal nearness, to live in union with the Truth and to live in the same world with the Truth. Schools like Vaiṣṇavism and Tantra which do not want to obliterate the relational self, highlight this kind of approach. The famous Tāntric devotional mystic Rāmprasād Sen, when told he could become one with the Divine said – "Why would I want to become sugar? I want to taste sugar". This is the Bliss of relation with the Divine. This is why this section of the *Upaniṣad* is called Madhu Kāṇḍa (chapter of honey).

What was initially invoked as "the breath in the mouth" and succeeded in chanting the *udgītha*, the ascending song, so as to win the victory for the *deva*s against the *asura*s is now recognized as the Divine Word, at first as Vāk, then the *Sāmaveda* and finally as the *udgītha* itself. Indeed, it is only the *udgītha* that can perfectly manifest itself and the psychic element is seen to be the immanent Word in each being:

> 23. And it is also the ascending song, *udgītha*. The life-breath is verily ascension (*ut*), for by the life-breath all this is upheld (*uttabdham*). Speech is *gīthā* (song). And ascending (*ut*) song (*gīthā*) is therefore Udgītha.

We saw this etymology at the very beginning of our consideration, *udgītha* means the ascending song – *ud* is to rise and *gīta* is song, the invocation to the supreme, the Word that reaches the Divine.

Esoteric and Exoteric

I have mentioned how this esoteric parable of the struggle between the gods and demons parallels, dramatizes and internalizes the Vedic state ritual for clearing a sacred space for the gods to manifest for the prosperity and abundance of the state. The parable hints at this in various places before this, prominently for example, when the "breath in the mouth" after obtaining the victory for the gods, begins chanting for food. The state rituals were conducted for the court by brāhmaṇa priests, often singing hymns of the *Sāmaveda*. The Upaniṣadic parable transposes this ritual into psychological space by substituting the faculties in place of the gods and the psychic element in place of the priest. The word which would bring the victory is made the *udgītha*, literally ascending song, understood in the Upaniṣads to be the sound syllable *oṁ* and behind it, the psychic aspiration. In this last section of the third *brāhmaṇa*, the mysterious psychic element is equated with the *Sāmaveda* and the *udgītha*, thereby bringing us back to the state ritual. As discussed earlier, part of the subtext of the *Bṛhadāraṇyaka Upaniṣad* is to hint at the conditions for an ideal state. It will do this in the second *kāṇḍa* through the dealings between the countercultural brāhmaṇa Yājñavalkya and his unconventional courtly patron, the King Janaka. In the first *kāṇḍa*, the state ritual and its courtly setting is invoked in this section of the third *brāhmaṇa*. The priest is introduced in the next stanza in the guise of a character Brahmadatta Caikitāneya. He is also given a countercultural flavour. While "drinking king" (*rājānam*, taken to be Soma, but also indicating an unconventional relationship with royalty), he announces that Aṅgirasa Ayāsya chanted the *udgītha* by means of the breath and the word. He makes this announcement like a show-off taking an oath of certitude, saying "May the king strike off my head if I say that Āṅgirasa Ayāsya chanted the *udgītha* by any means other than the word and the breath".

> 24. As to this there also Brahmadatta Caikitāneya, while drinking the King elixir [*Soma*], said: "May this King strike off my head if I say that the Aṅgirasa Ayāsya sang the Udgītha by any other means, for by Speech and the Life-breath alone did he sing it."

Striking off or bursting of the head is an event that happens on a number of occasions in the *Bṛhadāraṇyaka Upaniṣad*. At one level, it reminds us of capital punishment, perhaps an index of the draconian oppression of the state which the *Upaniṣad* refers to through dark humour, but also a startling doublespeak for the limits of reason. This affirmation indicates that ideal priests in ideal kingdoms need to follow the esoteric process of making the psychic element the leader of their faculties and invoking the hymns of the *Sāmaveda* using the psychic aspiration.

The next stanza tells us that the wealth of the *Sāmaveda* is the perfection of its notes.

> 25. He who knows (*ya evam veda*) the wealth of this Sāman obtains wealth. Tone (*svara*), indeed, is its wealth (*sva*).

The reference to wealth, in the doublespeak of the Upaniṣads, is an ironic indicator of the obsession with material riches in social Vedic ritualism. The word used for musical note is *svar*; this is the same word that refers to the supramental world that Ayāsya achieved in the Vedic Aṅgirasa hymns (Aurobindo 1998, vol. 15: 176). The basis of *saṅgīta-yoga* (*yoga* of music), coming down orally from antiquity is the purity of the musical note; each note, sung perfectly, is supposed to bring union with one aspect of the Divine. But Svar also means Supermind. The pun here is that the true wealth obtained by the proper invocation of the *Sāmaveda* is the Supermind. At a more fundamental level, the true wealth of the Supermind (Svar) is obtained through the perfection of equality (*samatā*) as later enunciated in the definition of *yoga* in the *Gītā*: *samatvam yoga ucchaye* (II.48), equality is called *yoga* and referring to the undifferentiated equal One that has become each thing in the relational universe through an unequal distribution of forces. This proper invocation is achieved through the purity of the notes, as manifest through the psychic aspiration. This lesson is enjoined on would-be priests of the ritual (*ṛtvij*):

> Therefore one who is about to perform the duties of a *ṛtvij* priest desires to have a rich *svar* in his voice.

There were four types of priests in Vedic rituals. The general name for these priests was *ṛtvik*. Of these, the one who sang the hymns of the *Sāmaveda* was the *udgātṛ* (singer of the ascending word). In a simplified way, the *Upaniṣad* is saying that only the priest who sings with soul can achieve the true wealth of the ritual. Of course, we must understand this in its profoundest sense – to sing with soul is to be a fully psychicized personality and the true wealth of the ritual is the achievement of the supramental world.

The semantic fusion of the esoteric and exoteric forms of the ritual is achieved in the next stanza:

> 26. He who knows (*ya evam veda*) what is the gold of this Sāman obtains gold (*suvarṇa*). The note (*svara*) verily is its gold (*suvarṇa*). He who thus knows the gold (*suvarṇa*) of the Sāman obtains gold (*suvarṇa*).

At the mundane level, it means if we perform the ritual with the proper intonation of the *Sāmaveda*, we will achieve the material riches (gold) that we seek. But this is a joke. Below this it means, if we know that the true wealth of *Brahman* (*Sāman* = *Samam Brahman*, the One *Brahman*) is the achievement of the Supermind (Svar), we will achieve the Supermind. Svar is the Supermind and gold (Suvarṇa) as a metal is a symbol of the Supermind, as we find also in alchemy. Suvarṇa also evokes another resonance, its literal disjunction (*su* + *varṇa*) means "good colour" or "good caste", "good breed". I see this as a dig at the hereditary essentialism of the caste system. The achievement of the Supermind (Svara) is also the nullification of all caste in the attainment of the glorious or golden body of the supramental physicality.

This is followed with a statement of the three levels of the Ignorance, Matter, Life and Mind, symbolized here by food, vital breath and the word. The word is supported by the vital breath and the food so as to achieve its ascent to the Supermind. We had encountered the fusion of these principles in the psychic being. The secret Divine presence burning in Matter is Fire, Agni. This is also the central principle of the psychic, here kept secret. Instead, the representation of Matter by Food (*anna*) is a pervasive convention, though one cannot help but suspect that it is another ironic reference to the materialistic goals of Vedic rituals.

> 27. He who knows (*ya evam veda*) the support of this Sāman is indeed supported; speech verily is its support – *vāgevapratiṣṭhā* – speech verily is its support for when supported on such the vital breath chants, but some said it is supported on food.

The *brāhmaṇa* ends with an invocation of a very famous and oft-repeated *mantra* of the Upaniṣads:

> 28. Now next the repetition (*abhyāroha*) only of the purificatory hymns (*pavamāna*), verily, the *prastotṛ* priest indeed chants the *sāman*; and while he recites it, let the sacrificer recite these three *Yajur* verse:
>
> *aasatomā sadgamaya tamaso mā jyotirgamaya mṛtyor mā amṛta-mgamaya*
>
> From the unreal lead me to the real; from darkness lead me to light; from death lead me to immortality. …

The three verses are all shown to be movements from the conditions of Ignorance to Immortality. This is what the contest between the gods and the *asura*s was really about. Each of the statements in the stanza is reduced to a single opposition and a single achievement – from Death to Immortality. We have seen the opposition of the gods and demons in this *brāhmaṇa* formed part of the emergence of cosmos from the Divine sacrifice. The Sacrifice itself set up the condition of non-Being and the Force of non-Being, against which the emerging consciousness of the reconstitution of the Horse must struggle. We have also seen how the gods occupy the head faculties of the Horse. This struggle, in itself, is the struggle of the *deva*s and *asura*s referred to in this *brāhmaṇa*. We have also seen how in the esoteric meaning of the ritual, it is by invoking the immanent psychic element that the *asura*s were defeated and immortality was obtained for the gods. This concluding stanza clarifies this central meaning of the third *brāhmaṇa*. It is not about clearing a space for material abundance for the kingdom, it is about the evolution of Consciousness, the self-oblivion of Spirit, its subjection to Death and its emergence against the Forces of non-Being by the power of immanent Divinity in it to establish itself in a material, vital and mental manifestation in time and space in its Divine Immortality.

The three qualities by which this Divine condition is identified, Truth, Light and Immortality, are the triple Divine, sometimes called *sat–cit–ānanda* (Existence, Consciousness, Bliss) and otherwise *satyam, jñānam, anantam* (Truth, Knowledge, Infinity) in the Upaniṣads (see *TaittUp* II.1). Immortality is Infinity manifest in Time. This is the attainment of the supramental Truth, Knowledge and Power, and the establishment of these properties on earth. That is the world conquering that this last stanza refers to. The world conquering is much more than the establishment of property and/or prosperity in the nation, it is an ontological transformation of the world from a world of Death to a supramental world of Immortality. It is achieved by the bringing of the psychic to the front, the lighting of the psychic aspiration in each of the faculties and in their integration around the psychic, to form an engine (*yantra*) to reach the Supermind and then to repossess Matter in a supramental Form. This concludes the third *brāhmaṇa* of the first *adhyāya* of the Madhu Kāṇḍa of the *Bṛhadāraṇyaka Upaniṣad*.

Self and Self-Becoming

Adhyāya I: Brāhmaṇa 4

1. In the beginning, this universe was *Ātman* alone, in the shape of Person (*Puruṣa*). It looked around and saw nothing other than Itself. He first said *so 'ham asmi* (I am He). Therefore, arose the name I (*aham*). Hence, even now, when a person is addressed, he first says: "It is I" and then says whatever other name he may have. And because It burnt (*auṣaṭ*) all evils, before It, therefore, It is called *Puruṣa* (Person). He who knows this verily burns up him who/what wishes to be ahead of him.

2. He was afraid. Therefore, one who is alone is afraid. He thought: "There is none other than I, of what am I afraid?" Thereupon, His fears were gone; for what was there to fear? Assuredly, it is from a second that fear arises.

3. He indeed had no delight. Therefore, when alone a person has no delight. He desired a second. He became the size of a man and woman in close embrace. He divided this self into two. From that division arose husband (*pati*) and wife (*patnī*). Therefore, as Yājñavalkya said, this (body) is one half of a split pea. Thus, this space is indeed filled by the wife. He united with her. From that human beings were born.

4. She thought: "How can he unite with me after having produced me from himself? Well, let me hide myself." She became a cow, the other became a bull and was united with her; from that cows were born. The one became a mare, the other a stallion; the one became a she-ass, the other a he-ass and was united with her; from that one-hoofed animals were born. The one became a she-goat, the other a he-goat; the one became an ewe, the other became a ram and was united with her; from that goats and sheep were born. Thus, indeed, he produced everything that exists in pairs, down to the ants.

5. He knew: "Indeed, I am the creation, for I produced all this." Therefore, He became the creation. He who knows this becomes this creation.

6. Then he rubbed back and forth thus and produced fire from the vagina, the mouth and the hands. Therefore, both the hands and mouth are hairless inside as the vagina is hairless inside. When they say "Sacrifice to him", "Sacrifice to that one", these are all his manifestations: he himself is all the gods. Now, whatever is liquid, He produced from semen; and that is Soma. This whole (world) is just food and the eater of food. Soma is food; and fire, the eater of food. This is the highest creation of Brahmā, that He created the gods, who are superior to Him. This is the highest creation because He, although mortal Himself, manifested the immortal. He who knows this truly becomes a creator in this highest creation.

7. Now, all this universe was then undifferentiated. It became differentiated by name and form: it was known by such and such a name and such and such a form. Thus, to this day, this universe is differentiated by name and form; so it is said: "He has such a name and such a form". This Self has entered into these bodies up to the very tips of the nails, as a razor lies hidden in its case, or as fire, which sustains the world, lies hidden in its source. People do not see the Self, for when viewed in parts, It is incomplete: when breathing, It is called the vital breath (*prāṇa*); when speaking, the organ of speech; when seeing, the eye; when hearing, the ear; when thinking, the mind. These are merely Its names according to Its functions. He who meditates on one or another of Its aspects does not know, for It is then incomplete: the Self is separated from Its totality by being associated with a single characteristic. The Self alone is to be meditated upon, for in It all these become unified. Of all these, this Self alone should be known, for in it all these become one. This Self is the foot-trace of all this, for by it one knows all this, just as by its footprints one can find again (a lost cow). He who knows this obtains fame and association with dear ones.

8. This Self is dearer than a son, dearer than wealth, dearer than everything else, because It is innermost. If one holding the Self dear were to say to a person who speaks of anything

other than the Self as dear, that he, the latter, will lose what he holds dear – and the former is certainly competent to do so – it will indeed come true. One should meditate upon the Self alone as dear. He who meditates upon the Self alone as dear – what he holds dear will not perish.

9. They say: "Since men think that by the Knowledge of *Brahman* they become all, what, pray, was it that *Brahman* knew by which It became all?"

10. *Brahman* indeed was this in the beginning. It knew itself only as "I am *Brahman*". Therefore, it became all. Whoever among the gods had this knowing, also became That. It is the same with the seers (*ṛṣi*s), the same with men. The seer Vāmadeva, having realized this self as That, came to know: "I was Manu and the sun". And to this day, whoever in a like manner knows the self as "I am *Brahman*", becomes all this universe. Even the gods cannot prevent his becoming this, for he has become their Self. Now, if a man worships another deity, thinking: "He is one and I am another", he does not know. He is like an animal to the gods. As many animals serve a man, so does each man serve the gods. Even if one animal is taken away, it causes anguish to the owner; how much more so when many are taken away! Therefore, it is not pleasing to the gods that men should know this.

11. In the beginning this was indeed *Brahman*, one only without a second. He, being one, did not flourish. He projected, further, an excellent form, the *kṣatra* power, even those who are *kṣatra*s (rulers) among the gods: Indra, Varuṇa, Soma (Moon), Rudra, Parjanya, Yama, Mṛtyu (Death) and Īśāna. Therefore, there is none higher than the kṣatriyas. Thus at the Rājasūya sacrifice, the brāhmaṇa sits below and worships the kṣatriya. He confers that glory on kṣatriyahood alone. But brāhmaṇahood is nevertheless the source of kṣatriyahood. Therefore, even though the king is exalted in the sacrifice, at the end of it he resorts to brāhmaṇahood as his source. He who slights a brāhmaṇa strikes at his own source. He becomes more evil, as one who slights his superior.

12. Yet He did not flourish. He projected the Viś (the commonalty) – those classes of gods who are designated in groups: the Vasus, Rudras, Ādityas, Viśvedevas and Maruts.

13. Still He did not flourish. He projected the śūdra order as Pūṣaṇ. This earth is Verily Pūṣaṇ (the nourisher); for it nourishes all that exists.

14. Yet He did not flourish. He projected, further, that excellent form, *dharma*. This *dharma* is the controller of the kṣatriya. Therefore, there is nothing higher than *dharma*. So even a weak man hopes to defeat a stronger man through *dharma*, as one does with the help of a king. Verily, that which is *dharma* is truth. Thus, if a man speaks the truth, they say he speaks what is just and if he speaks what is just, they say he speaks the truth; for, justice alone is both these.

15. So these, the brāhmaṇa, the kṣatriya, the vaiśya and the śūdra. Among the gods *Brahman* became fire and among men he became the brāhmaṇa. He became a kṣatriya through kṣatriya power, a vaiśya through vaiśya power and a śūdra through śūdra power. Therefore, by fire, people desire the world of the gods and (a place) among men (in the power of) a brāhmaṇa. For *Brahman* existed (predominantly) in these two forms. Now, if a man departs from this world without realizing his own World, It, being unknown, does not protect him – as the Vedas, unrecited, or as a deed unaccomplished, do not protect him. Nay, even if one who does not know It should perform here on earth a great many meritorious acts, those acts will in the end surely perish for him. One should meditate only upon the World of the Self (*ātman*). He who meditates upon the Self (*Ātman*) as the world – his work does not perish; for, from this very Self (*Ātman*), he creates whatever he desires.

16. Now, this self is the world of all beings. Insofar as he offers oblations in the fire and performs sacrifices, he becomes the world of the gods. Insofar as he studies the Vedas, he becomes the world of the *ṛṣis*. Insofar as he makes offerings to the forefathers and desires offspring, he becomes the world of the

forefathers. Insofar as he gives shelter and food to humans, he becomes the world of humans. Insofar as he gives fodder and water to the animals, he becomes the world of the animals. Insofar as beasts and birds and even ants find a living in his home, he becomes their world. Just as one wishes no injury to one's body, so do all beings wish no injury to him who has this knowledge. All this, indeed, has been known and well investigated.

17. In the beginning this was just the self, one only. He desired: "Let me have a wife, so that I may be born as the child; and let me have wealth, so that I may perform rites." This much, indeed, is the range of desire; even if one wishes, one cannot get more than this. Therefore, to this day, a man who is single desires: "Let me have a wife, so that I may be born as the child; and let me have wealth, so that I may perform rites". So long as he does not obtain each one of these, he thinks he is incomplete. Now, his completeness: The mind is his self, speech his wife, the vital breath his child, the eye his human wealth, for he finds it with the eye; the ear his divine wealth, for he hears it with the ear; the body his instrument of rites, for he performs rites through the body. So, this sacrifice has five factors – the animals have five factors, men have five factors and all this that exists has five factors. He who knows this obtains all this.

IN THE first four *brāhmaṇa*s of the first *adhyāya* of the *Bṛhadāraṇyaka Upaniṣad*, we find repeated expressions of Creation. Each of these is expressed in a different image. In the second *brāhmaṇa*, we encountered the struggle to be born from a zero condition of consciousness, which has to draw on the faint recollection, as of a ghost, of a repressed knowledge of absolute Being. The phenomenology of Time must assume an origin point, an ever-receding "beginning of Time" at which this repression occurred. This violence done by self on self is the "wounding" without which there would be no evolution of consciousness-power (*cit-tapas*). This Real-Idea of Time as a static image of self-forgetting initiates the work of remembering, an eternally deferred self-discovery in the form of an evolution of the power of consciousness, pressing on the closed door of amnesia, as if to break it and recover the origin. This reverse concentration to the forgetting, which may be called the Sacrifice of the *Puruṣa* or the Involution, is given in the *Bṛhadāraṇyaka Upaniṣad* as the Sacrifice of the Divine Horse, a non-anthropic metaphor, conducive to kings (kṣatriyas) engaging in the Aśvamedha *yajña*. The cosmos is figured as a Horse, which, in its origin, is a reference to the Vedic Sun God traversing its infinite cosmic extension at once, its vehicle the Divine Chariot drawn by the Divine Horse (Aśva). The Sacrifice of the Aśva is its plunge into the Darkness which is the inverse of the Sunworld, an alternate image for Mārtaṇḍa, the eighth Sun which is the Egg of Death, as also the seemingly Dead Egg. Just as this Dead Egg yearns to release Life and Mind and the Egg of Death yearns to be the Sun of Immortality, the Sacrificed Horse exists to multiply the image of its wholeness in the play of Multiplicity and Consciousness, to reconstitute the integral perfection as the creative expression of collective play.

But the idea of collective play must be understood equally as work, the work of remembering, of the intuition of the "open whole".[1] This is what makes Deleuze and Guattari posit desire at the foundation of production, so that all eros is productive in the sense of work, the work of reconstitution.[2] This reconstitution or remembering, for them, is not Freud's "work of mourning", a

---

[1] The integral becoming in which the infinite Whole is always present, yet always manifesting what has never been manifest. See Gilles Deleuze 1990: 105-07.

[2] According to Deleuze and Guattari, absence or lack is not the "cause" of desire but the "result" of the investment of desire in an ideal or problem of becoming (a form of contemplation). Desire in this view is a productive expression of the plenitude of being. See the section "A Materialist Psychiatry" in Deleuze and Guattari 2009: 22-28.

coming-to-terms with the past. It is an acknowledgement of the immanence of the Whole even in the process of its reconstitution. The *Bṛhadāraṇyaka* follows a similar course, the Absence of the Death or Sacrifice of the Horse is a creative remembrance in which the different kinds and degrees of consciousness-power presage the reconstitution of the Horse as an enduring image. Thus, the work of consciousness is a work of wholing and a work of survival, a negentropic drive towards Immortality.

During this work, it is Wind, Fire and Word that are the principal powers of consciousness involved, the three Vedic gods. It is Death or the symbol of non-Being from which they emerge. As the elements begin conjuring the image of the lost cosmos, it gives birth to Mind, with self-awareness and the extension of Idea–Space. Rising from a state of Death, at first it is the Mind of Death. But Death, by this time, is not really Death, it is Death that is Hunger. Death that is Hunger is a Death that lives; the Mind of Death that is Hunger is the Idea–Space of Hunger, all the kinds and degrees of Hunger reaching for an overcoming of Hunger, in other words, for Wholeness. The copulation of Hunger and Speech brought about by Mind implies this Idea–Space reaching to the horizon of the integral image. The birth of a "second" within this is an entry of the self into the Idea–Space of Hunger. Hunger attempts to consume this but it "slips" out, with the sound syllable "Bhāṇ". Moreover, Hunger, by an act of calculative reason, thinks it is better to let it multiply, so its "food" will be enhanced. But this birth of Life, accompanied by the Word, is also an interior negentropic individuation. This multiplication of individuations, each constituted by Wind, Fire and the Word is the evolution from Untruth to Truth, from Darkness to Light, from Death to Immortality of the cosmic ontology of Death that is Hunger releasing a plural potential for its self-overcoming.

The third *brāhmaṇa* introduces us to a new narrative of Creation, not the One that loses itself to become Zero, which it makes the condition for the re-emergence of the One in multiplied form, but the dialectic of antagonistic duality. In the first two *brāhmaṇa*s, this was implicit in the will to forgetting and the will to remembering. These Wills are now embodied by the gods and demons. It is their antagonism that extends a vertical axis infinitely in both directions, setting up a scale of consciousness. The gods look for a God-power to overcome the demons. The gods select successive powers, some of which we have encountered in the earlier *brāhmaṇa*s – speech, breath, seeing, hearing and thinking (mind). Each of these powers is infected by the demon, so that they cannot be successful in overcoming the will to forgetting, i.e. manifest forms of negentropic survival. Finally, it is only "the breath in the mouth" that the demons cannot infect and which is successful in routing the demons. This "breath in the mouth" is the secret union of Fire, Wind and the Word – i.e. the psychic integrity that speaks the true *mantra*.

Brāhmaṇa 4 introduces the theme of Creation for a third time, but here it is in terms of a complementary duality, that of gendered polarity and union (*mithuna*). Thus, if the third *brāhmaṇa* was about the enduring survival of the Creation, the fourth *brāhmaṇa* is about the extension and multiplication of the Creation. Like the second *brāhmaṇa*, it begins with the forgetting, the Absence of Involution contingent on the Sacrifice. What is hidden in this forgetting is the power of experiencing.

> 1. In the beginning, this universe was *Ātman* alone, in the shape of Person (*Puruṣa*). It looked around and saw nothing other than Itself. He first said *so 'ham asmi* (I am He). Therefore, arose the name I (*aham*). Hence, even now, when a person is addressed, he first says: "It is I", and then says whatever other name he may have. And because It burnt (*auṣaṭ*) all evils, before It, therefore, It is called *Puruṣa* (Person). He who knows this verily burns up him who/what wishes to be ahead of him.

We are made aware at the inception of the *brāhmaṇa* of the equivalence of the Horse with the *Puruṣa*; the Sacrifice of the

Horse is nothing other than the Sacrifice of the *Puruṣa* in the *Ṛgveda*. The *Puruṣa* is the Person, the Experiencer. The essence of the Experiencer is its self-consciousness. This is *Ātman*. Self-consciousness is self-evident, it is the Subject without Object. Its mode of Knowledge is known as *jñāna*. But the Subject can also objectify itself and specialize itself. This is *vijñāna*.[3] Self-consciousness is then the consciousness of experience between Subject and Object, both of which are Self, Self as Subject and Self as Object. This is Person or Experiencer experiencing itself with the essence of Sense, an operation of pure Knowledge that traverses itself at infinite speed. In other words, it traverses infinite distance at once. Thus, the self-objectification of *Ātman* as *Puruṣa* (Experiencer) produces itself as infinite Space in an act of experience or Knowledge. In the Sacrifice of *Puruṣa*, it is the self-consciousness of *Puruṣa*, its *jñāna* of *ātman*, which is obscured. In its re-emergence, it is its power of objective experience (*vijñāna*) that acts and gives evidence of its essence as *jñāna* of *Ātman*.

The operation of *vijñāna* is the traversal of Distance and the recognition of itself everywhere. It is also the intuition of Duality, of Subject and Object. Hence, the starting verse of the *brāhmaṇa* begins with the operation of *vijñāna* (looking around) and finding the Self everywhere. "Looking around" is the act of self-traversal. It is the movement of Consciousness (*cit*) in Being (*sat*). Arising from the Sacrifice of *Puruṣa* and the obscuration of self-consciousness (*ātman*), it is of the nature of a "sudden Enlightenment", repossessing the consciousness of its extent as an infinite Oneness in the instantaneous act of "looking around". Thus, the operation of *vijñāna* is an instantaneous reflexivity in which at once, the Person, *Puruṣa*, recognizes itself as Experiencer, recognizes the extent of its Self in experience and recognizes its essence as self-illuminating Self (*Ātman*) and Source of self-evident Knowledge (*jñāna*). Extent implies

---

3 See the distinction of *jñāna* and *vijñāna* in the *Bhagavadgītā*, chap. VII (*Jñāna-Vijñāna-Yoga*).

measure and objective knowledge implies duality. Hence, *Puruṣa* is *Ātman* inhabiting an infinite world of measure in a mode of duality through the operation of reflexive Knowledge (*vijñāna*).

The first verse recognizes these elements in saying that in the beginning there was nothing but *Ātman*, which wore the form of *Puruṣa*. *Ātman* as *Puruṣa* looks around and sees none other than itself everywhere. With this it also awakes to its essence as Self. Thus, its first action of self-experience is to affirm its self-existence throughout its extent measured by its reflexive self-consciousness. One of the "great sayings" (*mahāvākyas*), of the Upaniṣads is used to make this affirmation – *so 'ham asmi* (I am That). This is the assertion of an identity mediating a duality, that of Subject and Object, necessary to the self-experience of Self (*Ātman*) as Person or Experiencer (*Puruṣa*). This affirmation marks the phenomenology of *Puruṣa*'s spatial self-extension; in other words, those that exist within the cosmos made possible by *Puruṣa*'s reflexive self-regard know themselves first and primordially by the self-evidence of this affirmation, which is the recognition of the *ātman* existing as *Puruṣa* or *Ātman*'s *jñāna* extending itself as *Puruṣa*'s *vijñāna*. The *Upaniṣad* draws attention to this existential phenomenology by pointing to the original self-recognition of *Puruṣa* as cause for the primordial self-evident identity of all beings:

> Hence, even now, when a person is addressed, he first says: "It is I" and then says whatever other name he may have.

The verse follows this assertion with a creative etymology of the word *Puruṣa* indicating the primordiality and primacy of its self-knowledge, replicable in all beings, with the result of freedom from *pāpa* (sin/evil) and absolute power over all obscuration or impersonation:

> Because ahead of/before all that there is, it burnt all evil, it is *Puruṣa*. He who knows this burns him/that which wishes to (be)come ahead/before it.

The measuring of self as space of being by reflexivity of self-knowledge emerges from an original Nescience, the result of the Sacrifice of *Puruṣa*. It needs recognition that "original" here implicates time, but temporality is paradoxical, in the sense that the Sacrifice precedes the Nescience and the Nescience precedes the emergence of Being in a Becoming that replicates the Sacrifice. It points to the Being of Time as a circularity of coexistence of Non-Being and Being, or as a dimension of Being using non-Being to (perpetually) Become. This Becoming is a perpetual remembrance of a Death/Rebirth aporia, the Fire (Agni Jātaveda, knower of births) born from the collision of opposites, the remembrance of an Eternal Event or Image of Time. The *Puruṣa* of Becoming is Being whose self-experience is this remembrance. It wakes from Sleep or flashes forth illumining the Forgetting completely, seeing itself everywhere. This is why the Veda images it as the Sun God whose light is not a partial illumination of the Night like that of earthly fire, lightning or the stars; it is an extermination of Darkness. Flashing across its Negation, it traverses its infinity at once and sees Oneness everywhere (see *IśaUp* 6-8, 16). The creative etymology of *Puruṣa* refers to this when it speaks of burning up the evil in front. Evil (*pāpa*) refers to the self-obscuration, the Negation of Self represented by the Sacrifice. The rebirth of *Puruṣa* founds the spatial identity of a cosmic Becoming which replicates itself in degrees of temporality in its multiple becomings. Hence, each of these becomings carries this foundation at its origin. Knowing it (*ye evam veda*) it experiences the clearing of the path of *Puruṣa*'s self-traversal, burning up that/he which/who wishes to come in front of it, in other words, the obscuration of the Forgetting, Inconscience or Ignorance.

The Act that is laid by this verse is then focused in slow motion in the following verses to outline the Becoming of the cosmos.

> 2. He was afraid. Therefore, one who is alone is afraid. He thought: "There is none other than I, of what am I afraid?" Thereupon, His fears were gone; for what was there to fear? Assuredly, it is from a second that fear arises.

We saw the introduction of an original ontological duality, the Death/Rebirth aporia which became replicated as the phenomenological duality of Subject and Object in the *Puruṣa*. Confronting the original duality implies an awakening to the presence of the Other prior to eradicating it and recognizing itself everywhere. The Shadow of this confrontation is the fear of the Other. Since the Other is the Negation of the Self, the phenomenology of this Fear is accompanied with Loneliness. Loneliness is a finitude that senses its isolation in a relative existence with its Other. Fear arises due to the uncertainty of intent in the Other. The awaking of the sense of the Other brings with it this Shadow before its overcoming and eradication by the recognition of its absolute self-existence, the presence of Oneness everywhere. We are reminded here of the well-known lines from *Īśa Upaniṣad* 6-7:

> 6. But he who sees everywhere the Self in all existences and all existences in the Self, shrinks not thereafter from aught.
>
> 7. He in whom it is the Self-Being that has become all existences that are Becomings, for he has the perfect knowledge, how shall he be deluded, whence shall he have grief who sees everywhere oneness? – tr. Aurobindo 2003, vol. 17: 7

But perceiving itself everywhere does not put an end to Loneliness. It is the original duality of Being and non-Being that made *Puruṣa* "look around" and see that it was everywhere. "Looking around" and "seeing", in other words, the operation of *jñāna* as *vijñāna* inaugurates *Puruṣa* as the Subject and Object of itself and hence displaces the ontological and external duality into a phenomenological and internal duality. *Puruṣa* can "no longer" be one even when it sees oneness everywhere, since it is aware of itself as the Two-in-One. Having known its internal duality, the One cannot return to its oneness without the simultaneous knowledge of its twoness. Of course, the One can be one and two at the same time (which, after all, is one way to understand the liminality of "sitting near" – *upaniṣad*), but within its twoness, its oneness cannot operate as an undivided whole without "forgetting" it duality. This is the persistence of the shadow of Loneliness, which colours the intrinsic Delight of Being (*ānanda*). If the undivided One knew *ānanda* as the Bliss of Self-Absorption and the Sacrificed One experienced the Absence of this Bliss, the waking to Itself inaugurates the Bliss of Relation. In a return to Self-Absorption, there is an erasure of the Bliss of Relation. Once known under the shadow of Loneliness, the Bliss of Relation, to experience itself in its fullness needs necessarily to maximize the separation of the duality into two independent relational infinities.

> 3. He indeed had no delight. Therefore, when alone a person has no delight. He desired a second. He became the size of a man and woman in close embrace. He divided this self into two. From that division arose husband (*pati*) and wife (*patnī*). Therefore, as Yājñavalkya said, this (body) is one half of a split pea. Thus, this space is indeed filled by the wife. He united with her. From that human beings were born.

This may be considered a dimensional displacement of the instantaneous self-regard of Being, its *vijñāna*, where the consciousness of "looking around" detaches itself and becomes an independent immanence experiencing the reflexivity in graded spatial and temporal degrees as a manifestation or Becoming of relationality. The initiation of this self-division is referred to in the *Upaniṣad* as a "splitting apart". The complete division of a subject–object relation creates an ontology of poles in which each pole is subject and object of its other. This implies a materialization for full objectivity housing a vitalization and mentalization for degrees and kinds of subjectivity. This manner of polarized division is referred to as a man and woman in close embrace that splits apart like a pea pod, releasing its two halves, that then function as husband and wife. The sexed polarity of husband and wife grounds the division of subject and object in a physical life form. The text invokes Yājñavalkya, who is either the seer of the *Upaniṣad* or the head of the *gurukula* of its production, referring to him as saying that "this", meaning the objective physical form, is one half of a split pea. The space within, in other words, subjective space, is filled with the woman. The verse continues by saying, "He came to union with her. From that human beings were born", referring both to the externalized sexual process of reproduction as well as the androgynous composition of the human soul.

> 4. She thought: "How can he unite with me after having produced me from himself? Well, let me hide myself." She became a cow, the other became a bull and was united with her; from that cows were born. The one became a mare, the other a stallion; the one became a she-ass, the other a he-ass and was united with her; from that one-hoofed animals were born. The one became a she-goat, the other a he-goat; the one became an ewe, the other became a ram and was united with her; from that goats and sheep were born. Thus, indeed, he produced everything that exists in pairs, down to the ants.

The next verse exacerbates the paradox of separation. The One became two by "othering" itself. It remains itself but separates its reflexive double that assumes independence. At the same time, it carries the intuition of its origin and its oneness. This paradox is referred to severally in early Vedic texts, as for example, through the myth of Brahmā having sex with his daughter.[4] Here too, the conjunction of the One with its separated reflexive Other, leads to a third Shadow, that of Shame in the separated Other, here referred to as the female or wife. Phenomenologically, this

[4] This myth is repeated in several texts – e.g. the *Śiva Purāṇa* and *Jñāna Saṁhita* 49.65-80.

third Shadow is related to the completion of separation, which implies the ontology of Mind. Mind is characterized by the logic of non-contradiction and the excluded middle, which means that an entity cannot be one and two at the same time. The paradoxicality of the One that can be Two-in-itself is denied by the ontology of Mind, which by this process, separates reality into discrete strata or dimensions. Ontologically, this division is the foundation of what will be known in later Upaniṣads as *avidyā* (Ignorance). The separated Other carries the intuition of its oneness with its relational partner, an intuition that awakes the knowledge of the Falsehood of Twoness so as to engineer an externalized Oneness, as in sexual union at its most separated state of consciousness, its physicality.

We can see this phenomenology of the Shadow of Shame arising from the ontology of Mind in several mythical narratives. For example, in the Biblical narrative of the Fall, the Shame of Adam and Eve upon eating of the Fruit of Good and Evil pertains to the same ontological shift, from a condition of being differentiated but not divided in consciousness to one of being separated with a remembrance of Oneness, so that the experience of assuming separation and the endeavour to regain oneness through sexual union of exclusives is intuited as a Falsehood awaking Shame. In the verse from the *Bṛhadāraṇyaka*, this Shame of assuming separation motivates a flight and pursuit into deeper distances from the origin and deeper levels of Forgetting to escape from the paradoxical Memory of being Two and One at the same time. The *Upaniṣad* describes this in terms of a downward involution along a line of life, from the human successively to the cow, the horse, the ass, the goat, the sheep and so on to the ant. Each such manifestation of polarity and its ability to reproduce itself should be understood as a relative space–time experience of the absolute flash of self-knowledge (*vijñāna*) at the awakening from the Sacrifice, the "looking around" of *Puruṣa* to see itself everywhere. We spoke about the impulse of Measure in such an awakening. In the manifestation of separated relations, a relational Measure operates simultaneously over the absolute self-knowledge, slowing down its infinite velocity into degrees of durational experience and reducing its infinite distance into grades of space experience, along an infinite gradient of discrete relationality coexisting in/as bounded space–time infinities. This is the virtual space of cosmos generated simultaneously with the absolute Time-Image of self-experience. The absolute reflexive knowledge of *vijñāna* may be called the Divine *māyā*, the absolute Measurer, while its relational operation is the Mental or Cosmic *māyā*, the discrete and relative Measurer. Divine *māyā* characterizes *vidyā*, while Cosmic *māyā* characterizes *avidyā*.

> 5. He knew: "Indeed, I am the creation, for I produced all this." Therefore, He became the creation. He who knows this (*ya evam veda*) becomes this creation.

In the following short verse, this graded and phased virtual space of relational cosmic Becoming is seen from the viewpoint of *Puruṣa*, who is possessor of both the operations of *vijñāna*, that of the Divine *māyā* and the Cosmic or Overmind *māyā*, and not bound by the latter, like the creatures of the relative and relational cosmos. Hence, it views this cosmos as itself in the form of a multiply infinite self-knowledge. The verse ends with the assertion "Who knows this himself becomes this creation", implying the absolute and integral identity of the One, the All and the Each. Each one is none other than the entire Creation because he/she is the One who has become the Creation and each one in it by the operation of its *vijñāna*. Therefore, each one can know itself as the entire self-knowledge of the *Puruṣa*.

> 6. Then he rubbed back and forth thus and produced fire from the vagina, the mouth and the hands. Therefore, both the hands and mouth are hairless inside as the vagina is hairless inside. When they say "Sacrifice to him", "Sacrifice to that one", these are all his manifestations: he himself is all the gods. Now, whatever is liquid, He produced from semen;

> and that is Soma. This whole (world) is just food and the eater of food. Soma is food; and fire, the eater of food. This is the highest creation of Brahmā, that He created the gods, who are superior to Him. This is the highest creation because He, although mortal Himself, manifested the immortal. He who knows this (*ya evam veda*) truly becomes a creator in this highest creation.

The virtual space–time of the cosmos now actualizes itself in the form of a reverse Sacrifice, the extension of the self-knowing of *vijñāna* in every dual form of space–time experience as the materialized will to the reconstitution of *Puruṣa*. This is an evolutionary will to self-knowledge in each form, knowing itself as the immortal and integral *Puruṣa* in itself, in the cosmos and in all others. Arising from the law of separated duality and finite space–time experience the principles of Will-to-self-exceeding and Delight of experience are born in each as the condition of Sacrifice operating in and as their lives. These are figured as the two Vedic gods, Agni and Soma respectively, as related in the Vedic sacrifice (*yajña*) of the oblation of Soma into Agni. The verse presents this in a complex and mystic expression in which *Puruṣa* "rubs back and forth" to produce fire or Agni in three locations, the vagina, the hands and the mouth. In a graphic simultaneity, rubbing back and forth evokes three simultaneous images, that of the sex act, that of kindling fire by twirling the kindling stick and that of the rubbing of lips and tongue to produce words. A similarity is asserted of these three locations in the hairlessness of all their interiors. This enigmatic statement connects us back to the beginnings of this *brāhmaṇa* when we were given the etymology of *Puruṣa* as he who burns what is in front, in the extension of self-knowledge as it "looks around" and sees itself everywhere. The hairlessness is a sign of the "clearing" of the space of Self in each of these locations, making for a recognition of the Will to immortality and oneness of the Self.

The verse similarly attributes Soma to semen which is asserted as the producer of all things moist. The entire cosmos is said to replicate the sacrifice of the oblation of Soma in Agni, translating this to the most basic material terms of food, as we earlier saw in this *Upaniṣad* – Soma is food and Agni is the eater of food. In the most general sense, this means that cosmic experience, whether that of the maintenance of physical individuality through the act of eating, or experiencing the world subjectively through all our interactions, is the experience of a form of delight which is offered for the purposes of self-exceeding in the ascent of individuation towards identity with and reconstitution of the integrality of *Puruṣa*.

The sacrifice of Soma and Agni conducted at the three sites of the sex organs, the hands and the mouth pertains to the libidinal economy of the psyche in its individuation and self-transcendence.[5] At the level of the sex centre, in the act of sex there is a certain reintegration of polarity and realization of self-exceeding in the immortality of species replication. In terms of individual experience, the reintegration of polarity is brief, but the result in the union of genetic materials carries forward in new life forms. This process leads to a self-exceeding in immortality, not of the individual but of the species. Sigmund Freud has pointed to the sublimation of libido in the works of civilization (1953-74: 90). At the level of the hands, Fire is the primordial will to technology, expanding the clearing for humanity to survive and driving the engines of civilization so as to realize the immortality of the species in the works of culture (Stiegler 2011: 90). The Greeks saw the gift of fire for human flourishing and connecting with Nature as a possession of the gods, stolen for humankind by the titan Prometheus. The contemporary philosopher Bernard Stiegler writes of the Nietzschean will-to-power towards the overhuman as "the will to overmortality"

[5] My use of "libidinal economy" here follows Bernard Stiegler. See, for example, Stiegler 2011: 152-55.

(2009: 48-49, 54). Drawing on another philosopher, Gilbert Simondon, he sees libidinal sublimation in technology serving the purposes of individuation at the individual and collective levels. The Fire may be stolen in egoic profit making by the interests of global capital, but its right use in the formation of civilization is towards self-exceeding in the overcoming of Death, both for the collective and the individual. The Sacrifice of Soma in Agni at this level is the sublimation of the will to enjoyment towards the works of culture and education that support individual and collective (trans-)individuation towards a reconstitution of integrality.

In Indian *yoga*, the sublimation of the libido at the individual level is an alchemical transformation of the raw sexual energy, *reta*s, to a higher qualitative mode *ojas*, which supports the vitality and raises it towards a divine functioning. At a higher pitch of its working, it becomes a luminosity, *tejas* and *jyoti*, of the nature of solar fire (*saurya agni*, *arka*) itself (Aurobindo 2003, vol. I: 372-75). The vision and inspiration it brings guide the *yogī* towards crossing the boundary of the Overmind *māyā* and connecting with the Divine *māyā*. At the site of the mouth, it becomes the source of the *mantra* of the creative Divine Word that inaugurates a Divine Life for the individual and the collective. The oblation of Soma in Agni, seen in *yoga*, would lead to this divinization. At the level of the sex organs, it would be a sublimation of the physical libido into the higher vital libido, from *retas* to *ojas*. At the level of the hands, it would be a sublimation of the higher vital libido to the mental libido, from *ojas* to *tejas*, externally expressed as the works of fire or technics and at the level of the mouth it would be a sublimation of the mental libido towards the cosmic and transcendental source of the libido, from *tejas* to *jyoti*, externally expressed as the power of the Word, the Divine *mantra*. Here, Soma would reveal itself to be a form of Agni and reveal both to be self-forms of the supramental Sun God (Sūrya).

It is this reverse Sacrifice reconstituting the *Puruṣa* in each individual that is meant by this verse. Hence, it revises the misconception of the Vedic sacrifice as a seeking for boons from the gods to assert that this process gives birth to the gods, that the gods are not outside the human but found within the human in its transformative journey. The verse calls this creation of *Brahman* the highest creation since in it the mortals have been enabled to give birth to the immortals.

We may pause here to consider the stages of the creation as outlined in this mythos, starting from a zero moment after the Sacrifice of the *Puruṣa* and proceeding from the reflexive self-possession of *vijñāna* through successive Shadow manifestations marked by Fear, Loneliness, Lack of Delight and Shame. Kashmir Śaivism conserves this cosmogonic structure in its adaptation of Sāṁkhya *tattva*s that may be fruitfully compared to these stages to illuminate them (Lakshmanjoo 2015: 1-10). According to this, the "descent" from a transcendental unitary consciousness (*parā*) to a divided relative one (*aparā*) is accomplished through five stages in the status of relationship between Śiva and Śakti. In the highest Supreme stage, Śiva (Nāda Tattva), Śiva and Śakti, the I and the That (*aham* and *idam*) are undifferentiated and One. In the next stage, Śakti (Bindu Tattva), the One is aware of itself as its Consciousness. This may be thought of as the stage of *Puruṣa* "looking around" and finding itself everywhere. In an inverse sense, it generates the Shadow of Fear in the consciousness of an Other. The third stage is one of interchangeability, Śiva can take its position as Śiva or Śakti, Subject or Consciousness; it recognizes a duality within itself, both sides of which are equal locations of Self. In an inverse sense, it generates the Shadow of Loneliness in the consciousness of a loss of either status of Being. The fourth stage is one of a duality of possession, where Śiva possesses its Śakti, Consciousness is recognized as the Consciousness of *Puruṣa*. Bliss of relationship is recognized and its lack is realized as a lack of the Delight of Relationship. In the fifth stage, Śiva and Śakti separate into *Puruṣa* and *Prakṛti*, and become independent of each other for the independent Bliss of Relation. Consciousness experiences a sense of exile and the Falsehood of Separation, resulting in the Shame of a false reconstruction of Unity, motiving a reverse evolution towards the reconstitution of the One through Identity in Relation.

These first six verses conclude the cosmogonic section of this *brāhmaṇa*. The following verses reflect on the process and consequences, demonstrating the identity and equivalence of Self (*Ātman*) and the cosmos and opening the ways for this identity to be experienced in the bliss of relation within the separated and fragmented world. Verse 7, for example, returns us to a synoptic view of the process of cosmic creation – *Ātman* as *Puruṣa*'s reflexive self-regard and the division of its internal duality creating the virtual (subtle physical) cosmos of creatures with their names and forms.

> 7. Now, all this universe was then undifferentiated. It became differentiated by name and form: it was known by such and such a name and such and such a form. Thus, to this day this universe is differentiated by name and form; so it is said: "He has such a name and such a form". This Self has entered into these bodies up to the very tips of the nails, as a razor lies hidden in its case, or as fire, which sustains the world, lies hidden in its source. People do not see the Self, for when viewed in parts, It is incomplete: when breathing, It is called the vital breath (*prāṇa*); when speaking, the organ of speech; when seeing, the eye; when hearing, the ear; when thinking, the mind. These are merely Its names according to Its functions. He who meditates on one or another of Its aspects does not know, for It is then incomplete: the Self is separated from Its totality by being associated with a single characteristic. The Self alone is to be meditated upon, for in It all these become unified. Of all these, this Self alone should be known, for in it all these become one. This Self is the foot-trace of all this, for by it one knows all this, just as by its footprints

> one can find again (a lost cow). He who knows this (*ya evam veda*) obtains fame and association with dear ones.

We saw this process at the penultimate stage of Separation. The verse asserts that *Puruṣa* is in possession of all these names and forms and is present in its entirety in each of them, though hidden, unknown and seemingly fragmented. Not only is it present in its entirety in each name and form, it is present in its entirety in each of its functions. Here, we are introduced to the principal functions maintaining the creature in the cosmos, each of which is a god. We were introduced to these functions as gods at the very start of the *Upaniṣad*, in the description of the Sacrificial Horse. The functions are breathing, speaking, seeing, hearing and thinking. The organs related to these are the nostrils with the vital-force, the eyes, the mouth with its voice, the ears and the mind. Each of these can be made a vehicle of contact with the Whole, which dwells in them, though hidden. Each of them, in itself, is only a part of the Whole but each of them is a vehicle for the Whole and the One. Thus, the verse enjoins the seeking for the Whole in the part, not the error of a fetishistic loss of the Whole in an exclusive attention to the part. Each god exists not for itself, but as a "footprint" or "trace" of the invisible *Puruṣa* which inhabits it. The Self is the Integral Reality in which the fragmentation of the cosmos resulting from Separation is overcome in the reconstitution of the *Puruṣa*:

> He who meditates on one or the other of them does not know for he is incomplete with one or another of these. The *Ātman* is to be meditated on for in it all these become One. This *Ātman* is the foot-trace of this Whole (*sarvam*), for by it one knows this Whole, just as one can find again by its footprints what was lost.

> 8. This Self is dearer than a son, dearer than wealth, dearer than everything else, because It is innermost. If one holding the Self dear were to say to a person who speaks of anything other than the Self as dear, that he, the latter, will lose what

> he holds dear – and the former is certainly competent to do so – it will indeed come true. One should meditate upon the Self alone as dear. He who meditates upon the Self alone as dear – what he holds dear will not perish.

The next paragraph reiterates the absolute immanence of *Ātman* in each being, moving from the objective apprehension of *Ātman* in the fragmented parts of the cosmos to the subjective apprehension of the *Ātman* as the nearest and dearest in and of oneself. One, who holds the *Ātman* to be one's dearest and meditates on one's *Ātman* exclusively as dear, never loses whatever one holds dear, since it is the *Ātman* that is the Self of all this and this is one's own Self. Later in the *Upaniṣad*, this meditation is reiterated by Yājñavalkya in a famous passage in his colloquy with his wife Maitreyī, where he says to her it is not for the sake of the wife that the wife is dear, but for the sake of the self (*BU* II.4.45, IV.5.6), opening thereby a relationship with the wife that addresses the deepest Self of all through relationship. If the previous paragraph was a reference to the *yoga* methods of *Prakṛti*, such as *prāṇāyāma, mantra, darśana* or *jñāna-yoga* as paths to the integral Divine through a change of objective, the present paragraph turns us to a method of *Puruṣa*, the subjective path of Relationship through Love of the most intimate Being.

This is followed by two paragraphs to an even deeper approach to the Subject, what may be called the *yoga* of direct knowledge by identity:

> 9. They say: "Since men think that by the Knowledge of *Brahman* they become all, what, pray, was it that *Brahman* knew by which It became all?"
>
> 10. *Brahman* indeed was this in the beginning. It knew itself only as "I am *Brahman*". Therefore, it became all. Whoever among the gods had this knowing, also became That. It is the same with the seers (*ṛṣis*), the same with men. The seer Vāmadeva, having realized this self as That, came to know:

> "I was Manu and the sun". And to this day, whoever in a like manner knows the self as "I am *Brahman*", becomes all this universe. Even the gods cannot prevent his becoming this, for he has become their Self. Now, if a man worships another deity, thinking: "He is one and I am another", he does not know. He is like an animal to the gods. As many animals serve a man, so does each man serve the gods. Even if one animal is taken away, it causes anguish to the owner; how much more so when many are taken away! Therefore, it is not pleasing to the gods that men should know this.

This may be compared with what Zen Buddhism calls "sudden enlightenment" or Kashmir Śaivism calls the method of no method (*anupāya*) (Lakshmanjoo 2015: 33-40). Paragraph 9 initiates this approach by returning us to the start of the *brāhmaṇa*, how did *Brahman* come to the knowledge of itself as all? As we saw at the very beginning, *Puruṣa* "looked around" and saw itself everywhere. This action of *vijñāna* was spontaneous and unmediated. The verse seeks the answer to this question with an aim to replicate its method in the questioner. There is no method except a call to the most primordial remembrance of this original reflexive self-regard. Paragraph 10 announces this in the form of one of the Great Sayings (*mantras*) of the Upaniṣads, the *mahāvākya, aham brahmāsmi* (I am *Brahman*). Just the Knowledge-Idea is an orientation that can unaccountably reopen the ever-present reflexive self-regard of *vijñāna* that is indeed all this cosmos and all its beings. That is what resides in all as the *Puruṣa, Ātman* and *Brahman*, other than Whom there is nothing.

But this knowledge is kept hidden within the forgetting of the Separation, maintained by the cosmic automatisms ruled by the gods. Worshipping these gods for material boons, as was the custom at the time, only keeps the orbits of automatism in place and the gods in control. The *Upaniṣad* has already affirmed that the gods are the creations of mortals in their reverse Sacrifice towards Wholeness. The gods reside in us, but we must exceed the gods in the self-knowledge that has become the cosmos and that is our true identity.

Paragraphs 11 to 15 address the castes:

> 11. In the beginning this was indeed *Brahman*, one only without a second (*ekam evādvitīyam*). He, being one, did not flourish. He projected, further, an excellent form, the *kṣatra* power, even those who are *kṣatra*s (rulers) among the gods: Indra, Varuṇa, Soma (Moon), Rudra, Parjanya, Yama, Mṛtyu (Death) and Īśāna. Therefore, there is none higher than the kṣatriyas. Thus, at the Rājasūya sacrifice, the brāhmaṇa sits below and worships the kṣatriya. He confers that glory on kṣatriyahood alone. But brāhmaṇahood is nevertheless the source of kṣatriyahood. Therefore, even though the king is exalted in the sacrifice, at the end of it he resorts to brāhmaṇahood as his source. He who slights a brāhmaṇa strikes at his own source. He becomes more evil, as one who slights his superior.
>
> 12. Yet He did not flourish. He projected the Viś (the commonalty) – those classes of gods who are designated in groups: Vasus, Rudras, Ādityas, Viśvedevas and Maruts.
>
> 13. Still He did not flourish. He projected the śūdra order as Pūṣaṇ. This earth is verily Pūṣaṇ (the nourisher); for it nourishes all that exists.
>
> 14. Yet He did not flourish. He projected, further, that excellent form (*dharma*). This *dharma* is the controller of the kṣatriya. Therefore, there is nothing higher than *dharma*. So, even a weak man hopes to defeat a stronger man through *dharma*, as one does with the help of a king. Verily, that which is *dharma* is truth. Thus, if a man speaks the truth, they say he speaks what is just and if he speaks what is just, they say he speaks the truth; for justice alone is both these.
>
> 15. So these, the brāhmaṇa, the kṣatriya, the vaiśya and the śūdra. Among the gods *Brahman* became fire and among men He became the brāhmaṇa. He became a kṣatriya through

> kṣatriya power, a vaiśya through vaiśya power and a śūdra through śūdra power. Therefore, by fire, people desire the world of the gods and (a place) among men (in the power of) a brāhmaṇa. For *Brahman* existed (predominantly) in these two forms. Now, if a man departs from this world without realizing his own world, it, being unknown, does not protect him – as the Vedas, unrecited, or as a deed unaccomplished, do not protect him. Nay, even if one who does not know It should perform here on earth a great many meritorious acts, those acts will in the end surely perish for him. One should meditate only on the Self (*Ātman*) as the world. He who meditates upon the Self (*Ātman*) as the world – his work does not perish; for, from this very Self (*Ātman*), he creates whatever he desires.

These paragraphs bring us both to a reconsideration of the Puruṣa Sūkta of the *Ṛgveda* and to a reconsideration of the caste system as it was practised at the time of the *Upaniṣad*. This *brāhmaṇa* contains several allusions to the Puruṣa Sūkta of the *Ṛgveda* but addresses them in its own way. The creation of creatures and the gods, put forward in the Puruṣa Sūkta as conserving the harmonious order of the *Puruṣa* in its Sacrificial self-becoming of the cosmos, is challenged in the name of individual identity with the *Puruṣa*. It is not the gods or their order that one is to search for first, but one's identity with *Puruṣa*. One would then know that the *Puruṣa* has become all these and since one is no other than the *Puruṣa*, the gods are our own creation. In paragraphs 11 to 15, the fourfold order of works in the kingdom through the castes is reviewed. At the time of the *Upaniṣad*, a collusion between the brāhmaṇas and kṣatriyas had become hegemonic in the political control of the kingdoms. The *Upaniṣad*'s feature a revisionary scheme where *Brahman* knowledge is not restricted to the brāhmaṇas. In several Upaniṣads, the teachers of *Brahman* knowledge are kṣatriyas or the other castes, including śūdras. The *Chāndogya Upaniṣad*, along with the *Bṛhadāraṇyaka*, one of the two earliest Upaniṣads, features several such counter-cultural examples. The

Bṛhadāraṇyaka highlights the teacher Yājñavalkya, who may have been a brāhmaṇa, but a very unconventional one. Paragraph 11 begins by privileging the kṣatriya over all the castes but brings in the brāhmaṇa as subordinate in political status but superior in moral status. As an Āraṇyaka, the *Bṛhadāraṇayaka* was in all likelihood meant for kṣatriyas, since it begins with the image of the Sacrificial Horse, used in the Aśvamedha *yajña*, carried out by aspiring emperors (*cakravartins*). The *Upaniṣad* also features centrally the relation between the unconventional brāhmaṇa, Yājñavalkya and a *Brahman*-knowing philosopher-king, Janaka. It is this ideal relationship that is being referred to in this description of the two higher castes. At the same time, the following two paragraphs, 12 and 13, make clear that these two castes are incomplete by themselves or even together and that the other two castes, the vaiśya and śūdra, are no less necessary or important to the Whole. The vaiśya is related to the power of the collective or the people (*viś*), while the śūdra is related to the power of nourishment. Each of these is also related to a set of gods and, hence, a world. Finally, paragraph 14 points to the fact that all four castes, taken together, are incomplete, and take their completeness from a fifth source or root, *dharma*, which is the Truth. This, of course, was the ancient idea of caste polity, based on the root of *dharma* being the *Puruṣa*, who had become the four castes. The *Upaniṣad*, in reiterating this Idea, calls for the proper understanding of the caste-based system in terms of *dharma* (spiritual Right). By this, it does not mean the Dharmaśāstras, texts of legal injunction codifying *dharma*, which were yet to be written, but the realization of *Puruṣa* by each caste, leading to the proper functioning of the part in terms of the Whole and One.

Paragraph 15 brings the consideration of the castes to an end by complexifying the privilege accorded to the brāhmaṇa. As the other castes have been related to sets of gods, the brāhmaṇa is related here to *Brahman*, by implication *dharma*. In the Veda, the

God Agni (Fire) is the priest of the Sacrifice, hence represents *dharma* among the gods, while among men, the brāhmaṇa is the priest who represents *dharma*. Hence, the aspiration of people who wish to have a place in the world of the gods by the power of Agni or among men by the power of the brāhmaṇa is acknowledged. The question of who is a brāhmaṇa, whether it is a hereditary status or one defined by some special property is not explored except to relate Brahmā also to Agni among the gods. We may remember the story of Satyakāma Jābāla from the *Chāndogya Upaniṣad*, where the brāhmaṇa was pointedly denied hereditary status and equated instead to a speaker of truth. The equation of *dharma* with truth in the previous paragraph makes the same case by implication. Further, the assertion is made in this paragraph that individuals who do not "know their own world" before departing are not protected. This world pertains to their functional soul quality (*dharma*). Even if they perform a great and holy work, the good they incur gets exhausted. The verse ends by affirming that all beings should meditate on the *Ātman* as their true world; work done by such a person yields results that are not exhausted because he/she can create what he/she desires from union with the Self.

These paragraphs on caste are strongly reminiscent of the *Bhagavadgītā*, which may have drawn some of its teachings on caste and *dharma* from these verses. The *Gītā* (and its contextual text, the *Mahābhārata*) is centrally concerned with the question of *dharma* and its relation to the castes. It makes a strong assertion that it is better to do badly works of one's own *svadharma* than doing well works of another's *dharma* (*BG* III.35). This is similar to the injunction of these paragraphs of the *Bṛhadāraṇyaka*. By the 18th chapter of the *Gītā*, it is clear that *svadharma* is neither hereditary nor hierarchical, but what arises from the *svabhāva* (soul quality) (*BG* XVIII.41-48). Finally, the *Gītā*'s last word translates the source of *dharma* to the *Puruṣottama* or Supreme *Puruṣa*, enjoining a complete surrender directly to this *Puruṣa*, since it is the root also of the *svadharma* (*BG* XVIII.66). Similarly, the *Bṛhadāraṇyaka* enjoins a complete surrender to the Supreme *Ātman* who, as the Supreme *Puruṣa*, is the source of all Works, understood as *yajña*, the reverse sacrifice leading back to the reconstitution of *Puruṣa* in the creatures. Both the radical decentralization of the caste system and integral universalism of the individual are worth noting here. There is a world – i.e. a relative universal perspective – for each caste and each class of beings, but the self (*ātman*) of each individual challenges any caste or class hierarchism, as might be supposed to prevail in Vedic society, empowering the individual for equal access to the power that holds the world together. At the same time, it affirms the fact that all diversities that have their relative approaches to universalism (their world) belong ultimately to one world (the world) whose Self (*Ātman*) is individuated as the self (*ātman*) of each individual.

In paragraph 16, the self-regard of *Ātman* as *Puruṣa* recognizing itself everywhere is again invoked, now from the perspective of the creature who seeks to know the truth of Works:

> 16. Now, this self (*ātman*) is the world (*lokāḥ*) of all beings. Insofar as he offers oblations in the fire and performs sacrifices, he becomes the world of the gods. Insofar as he studies the Vedas, he becomes the world of the *ṛṣis*. Insofar as he makes offerings to the forefathers and desires offspring, he becomes the world of the forefathers. Insofar as he gives shelter and food to humans, he becomes the world of humans. Insofar as he gives fodder and water to the animals, he becomes the world of the animals. Insofar as beasts and birds, and even ants find a living in his home, he becomes their world. Just as one wishes no injury to one's body, so do all beings wish no injury to him who has this knowledge. All this, indeed, has been known and well investigated.

The paragraph elaborates the ending of paragraph 15 in that

works done in union with the *Ātman* bring whatever results are desired. This is simply because *Ātman* has become everything. Hence, in union with *Ātman*, one can become any world of self-knowing one chooses by extension of identity.

The concluding paragraph of the *brāhmaṇa* returns us to the wants of the *Ātman*:

> 17. In the beginning this was just the self (*ātman*), one only. He desired: "Let me have a wife, so that I may be born as the child; and let me have wealth, so that I may perform rites." This much, indeed, is the range of desire; even if one wishes, one cannot get more than this. Therefore, to this day, a man who is single desires: "Let me have a wife, so that I may be born as the child; and let me have wealth, so that I may perform rites". So long as he does not obtain each one of these, he thinks he is incomplete. Now, his completeness: The mind is his self, speech his wife, the vital breath his child, the eye his human wealth, for he finds it with the eye; the ear his divine wealth, for he hears it with the ear; the body his instrument of rites, for he performs rites through the body. So, this sacrifice has five factors – the animals have five factors, men have five factors and all this that exists has five factors. He who knows this obtains all this.

We saw this in the cosmogonic sequence, where *Puruṣa* as Subject experienced the Bliss of Relation upon objectifying itself and hence sought to enjoy this Bliss through Separation leading to a cosmos of plurality in which the relation of *Puruṣa* with *Prakṛti* was multiplied in innumerable creatures. The object of the Bliss of Relation was the wife, the self-multiplication of subjective/objective polarity in the creatures was its offspring and the reverse sacrifice of these multiplied creatures in reconstituting the integral *Puruṣa* was conducted through the expenditure of experience and energy. This was the wealth needed for the performance of Sacrifice. The *Upaniṣad* concludes by detailing the subjective equivalents of these wishes in each individual.

Together they reconstitute the *Puruṣa* bringing integrality. This is the assemblage of the gods – the mind as the self, the word as the wife, the breath as the offspring, the eye as human wealth and the ear as divine wealth. We have encountered this fivefold before, in paragraph 7, when we were told that these are each the seat of the integral *Ātman*, knowing which all these are known together as One. These are the gods with which the description of the Sacrificial Horse began and these are the gods with which the fourth *brāhmaṇa* ends. They are each a special name and form of *Ātman*. Surrender to *Ātman* is to be made through each and all of these, making them the channels for the experience of *Ātman*, in the replication by the individual of the *vijñāna* of *Ātman/Puruṣa* which has become the cosmos and each of its creatures as part of the Measure of its unbounded infinity.

Food
Adhyāya I: Brāhmaṇa 5

1. The father produced seven kinds of food through Intelligence and concentration. One is common to all. Two he portioned to the gods. Three he kept for his Self. And one he gave to the animals. On it rests everything – what lives and what does not. Why are they not exhausted, although they are eaten everyday? He who knows this cause of their permanence eats food with *pratīka* (the image). He goes to the gods, he lives on strength. Thus the verses.

2. When the father produced seven kinds of food through Intelligence and Will means that the father indeed produced them through Intelligence and Will. "One is common to all eaters", means this food that is eaten is the common food of all eaters. He who venerates this food is never free from sin, for it is mixed. "Two he portioned to the gods" means the fire offerings and the will behind these offerings. Therefore, both of these are offered to the gods. Some, however, say, those two are the new and full moon sacrifices. Therefore, one should not be engrossed with sacrifices for material ends. "One he gave to the animals" – it is milk. For men and animals first live on milk alone. Therefore, they first make a newborn babe lick clarified butter or suckle it. And they speak of a new-born calf as one not yet eating grass. "On it rests everything – what lives and what does not" means that on milk indeed rests all this that lives and that does not. It is said that by making offerings of milk in the fire for a year one conquers further death. One should not think thus. He who knows this conquers further death the very day he makes that offering, for he offers all his food to the gods. "Why are they not exhausted, although they are always being eaten?" – means that the Person (*Puruṣa*) is indeed the cause of their permanence, for he produces this food again and again. "He who knows this cause of their permanence" means that the *Puruṣa* is indeed the cause of their permanence, for he produces this food through his

continuous work of concentration. Should he not do this, it will be exhausted. "He eats food with *pratīka*." The mouth is the *pratīka*, he eats with the mouth. "He attains the gods, he lives on strength." This is an eulogy.

3. "Three he made for his-Self": Mind, Speech and the Life-force, these he made for himself. (One says), "My mind was elsewhere, I did not see it", "My mind was elsewhere, I did not hear it". It is through the mind that one sees and hears. Desire, purpose, doubt, faith, lack of faith, steadiness, unsteadiness, shame, intelligence and fear – all these are but the mind. Even if one is touched from behind, one knows it through the mind; therefore (the mind exists). And any kind of sound is but Speech, for it serves to determine a thing but it cannot itself be revealed. *Prāṇa, apāna, vyāna, udāna* and *samāna* – all these forms of breathing are but the Life-force. This body is identified with these – with Speech, Mind and the Life-force.

4. These are the three worlds. Speech is this world (the Earth), Mind is the Midworld and the Life-force is that world (Heaven).

5. These are the three Vedas. Speech is the *R̥gveda*, Mind is the *Yajurveda* and the Life-force the *Sāmaveda*.

6. These are the gods, the ancestors and men. Speech is the gods, Mind the ancestors and the Life-force men.

7. These are the father, mother and child. Mind is the father, Speech the mother and the Life-force the child.

8. These are what is known, what it is desirable to know and what is unknown. Whatever is known is a form of Speech, for it is the Knower. Speech protects him by becoming that (which is known).

9. Whatever it is desirable to know is a form of Mind, for the Mind is what it is desirable to know. Mind protects him by becoming that (which it is desirable to know).

10. Whatever is unknown is a form of the Life-force, for the Life-force is what is unknown. The Life-force protects him by becoming that (which is unknown).

11. The earth is the body of Speech and Fire is its form of Illumination. And as far as Speech extends, so far extends the Earth and so far does this Fire.

12. Heaven is the body of this mind and that Sun is its form of Illumination. And as far as the mind extends, so far extends heaven and so far does that Sun. These two had intercourse and from that the Life-force was born. It is Indra, the Lord of gods. It is unrivalled. A second is indeed a rival. He who knows this has no rival.

13. Water is the body of this Life-force and that Moon is its form of Illumination. And as far as the Life-force extends, so far extends Water and so far does that Moon. These are all equal and all Infinite. He who meditates upon these as finite wins a finite world, but he who meditates upon these as Infinite wins an infinite world.

14. This Prajāpati has sixteen digits and is represented by the year. The nights are his fifteen digits and the constant one is his sixteenth digit. He waxes and wanes by the nights. Through this sixteenth digit, he permeates all these living beings on the night of *amāvasyā* and rises the next morning. Therefore, on this night one should not take the life of living beings, not even of a lizard, in sole adoration of this deity.

15. The person here who knows this is indeed himself Prajāpati who has sixteen digits and is represented by the year. Wealth constitutes his fifteen digits and the Self his sixteenth digit. He is filled as well as wasted by wealth. This Self stands for the hub and wealth is the felloe. Therefore, if a man loses everything, but he himself lives, people say that he has only lost his felloe.

16. There are indeed three worlds, the world of men, the world of the ancestors and the world of the gods. This world of men is to be won through the son alone and by no other work; the world of the ancestors through works; and the world of the gods through Knowledge. The world of the gods is the best of the worlds. Therefore, they praise Knowledge.

17. Now, therefore, the transmission: When a man thinks he will die, he says to his son, "You are *Brahman*, you are the sacrifice and you are the world". The son replies, I am *Brahman*, I am the sacrifice and I am the world. Whatever is studied is all unified in *Brahman*. Whatever sacrifices there are, are all unified in *yajña*. And whatever worlds there are, are all unified in this world. Great, indeed, is the All. "He, being the All, will liberate me from this world." Therefore, a son who is this instructed is known as the Master of the world; therefore, is the son instructed. When one who knows this departs from this world, he enters his son with his breaths (*prāṇa*). Whatever wrong may have been done by him, the son liberates him from all that; therefore, he is called a son. The father stands firm in this world through the son. Then the divine immortal breaths enter him.

18. From the earth and from fire Divine Speech enter him. That is the Divine Speech through which whatever he says is fulfilled.

19. From heaven and from the sun the Divine Mind enters him. That is the Divine Mind through which he becomes only blissful and never mourns.

20. From water and from the moon the Divine Life-force enters him. That is the Divine Life-force which, whether it moves or is stationary, feels no pain nor is injured. He who knows this becomes the Self of all beings. As is this deity, so is he. As all beings take care of this deity, so do they take care of him. Howsoever these beings may grieve, that grief of theirs is connected with them. But only merit goes to him. No demerit ever goes to the gods.

21. Now a consideration of the resolution/praxis: Prajāpati projected the organs of action. These, on being created, quarrelled with one another. The organ of Speech took a resolution, "I will go on speaking". The eye: "I will see". The ear: "I will hear". And so did the other organs according to their functions. Death captured them in the form of fatigue – it overtook them and having overtaken them it controlled them.

Therefore, the organ of speech invariably gets tired and so do the eye and the ear. But death did not capture the "central breath" in the body. The organs resolved to know it. "This is the greatest among us that, when it moves or does not move, feels no pain nor is injured. Well, let us all be of its form." They all assumed its form. Therefore, they are called by this name of *prāṇa*. That family in which a man is born who knows this, is indeed named after him. And he who competes with one who knows this shrivels and after shrivelling dies at the end. This is with reference to the Self.

22. Now with reference to the gods: Fire made a resolution, "I will go on burning". The sun: "I will give heat". The moon: "I will shine". And so did the other gods according to their functions. As is the Life-force in the body among these organs, so is Vāyu (Wind) among these gods. Other gods sink, but not Wind. Wind is the deity that never sets.

23. Now there is this verse: "The gods observed the resolution of that from which the sun rises and in which he sets. It is (followed) today and it will be (followed) tomorrow." The sun indeed rises from the Life-force and also sets in it. What these (gods) observed then, they observe to this day. Therefore, a man should observe a single resolution – do the functions of the *prāṇa* and *apāna*, lest the evil of death should take him. And if he observes it, he should seek to finish it. Through it he attains identity with this deity and lives in the same world with it.

Being and Becoming: The Horse Sacrifice

THE enigmatic esotericism of the *Bṛhadāraṇyaka Upaniṣad* develops itself in relation to the symbolic ritualization of the Veda, subjecting its elements and intentions to mystic deformations and deconstructions so as to unfamiliarize their common meanings and turn them into profound contemplations of cosmic and psychological truths, and practices. In this vein, the first *adhyāya* of the *Bṛhadāraṇyaka Upaniṣad* takes up the Horse sacrifice (Aśvamedha *yajña*), meant for the establishment of emperors (*cakravartin*) and turns it into a cosmogenetic symbol. In this the original sense of the Vedic *cakravartin*, the One who makes the circle (*cakra*) rotate (*vartin*) as the solar godhead is established, as is the significance of its sacrifice, creating the basis for the play of multiplicity in/as Space and Time. Multiplicity in Space is the fragmentation of the One, while multiplicity in Time is the discretization of continuity, its subjection to creations, preservations, destructions, returns, mutations and evolution. If the first *brāhmaṇa* establishes the eternal Time-Image of the *cakravartin* (Time is the Self of the Horse sacrificial), with its relational elements forming a virtual Ideal Engine (*yantra*), the second *brāhmaṇa* dramatizes the Fall of Being into the realm of Becoming in terms of the sacrifice of the Horse and its evolution in/as the Time of cosmos and replicating and evolving individuals.

The paradoxical gap between Being and Becoming is an ever-renewed Absence which is the Memory-Image of the origin of cosmic Time, "as in a dark beginning of all things" (Aurobindo 1997, vols 21-22: 1). This Sacrifice, Fall or Absence is at the heart of the polarity which forms the Engine of Becoming, an Immortality that has lost itself in a Death, a Death that hungers for its Origin in Immortality. Hence, the Death with which the second *brāhmaṇa* begins is not an absolute Death nor an original Death, it is the semblance of an origin and it is a shadow of Immortality, perpetually haunted by its memory, as its double. This haunting awakes as a Hunger (*aśanāyā mṛtyu*) (*BU* I.2.1) in the heart of the cosmos, providing it with a Will-to-individuation and cosmogenesis. This disembodied Will-to-embodiment, appearing from the churning between Death and the ghost of its Origin, evolves the cosmic elements. These are given in order as the Substances or States of Being, Mind (*manaḥ*), Speech of Prayer/Aspiration (*arcā*), Water (*āpaḥ*), Earth (*pṛthvī*), Fire (*agni*), the Vital Energy, the solar Idea; horizontal Space made up of the eight Directions and vertical Space made up of the three strata, Earth, Midworld and Heaven (*BU* I.2.1-3). Together they form the evolving foundation and replication of the Horse in the virtuality of cosmic Becoming.

Cosmic Evolution

It is worth taking note here of the sequence of emergent properties. The Death of Becoming is instinct with Intelligence. Its first self-awareness is that of a disembodied Mind with a will-to-embodiment. This Instinct and Will are the foundation of the work or toil that fills the cosmos, a toil to individuate and exceed Death. From the friction of opposites, Death and its hidden origin/telos of Immortality, Fire is born. This fire is initially latent; in the second stanza of the second *brāhmaṇa*, its hidden presence is manifest through a play of the sound-syllables *ṛ* and *ca* (*BU* I.2.1). *Arcā* refers ritually to the stanzas of the hymns of adoration of the *Ṛgveda*. Here, it indicates the Word of Aspiration, invoking the telos as Attractor. "Moving about" (*acara*), uttering the Word of Aspiration (*arca*) are the forms of Work which produce the elements, according to this *Upaniṣad*, at first Water (*āpaḥ*), a symbol of differentiated Consciousness, then through a process of settling and solidification, Earth (*pṛthvī*) and with further settling and concentration (*tapas*), manifest Fire (*agni*). But with the appearance of Water, a subjective element becomes apparent to the disembodied Mind of the cosmic Subject, Death. This is *kaṁ* (joy) (*BU* I.2.1, tr. Aurobindo 2001: 269). The *Upaniṣad*, at this point, links *arca*, the word of prayer to *arka* or radiance. *Arka* is also a name of the Sun, the source of Radiance. The *Upaniṣad* asserts that joy (*kaṁ*) is the essence of the radiant principle behind the word uttered in prayer. We are thus shown that the heart of cosmic toil is the Joy of the Solar principle, the Real-Idea or Being that has sacrificed itself to appear as Death in the Becoming. It is an assertion of the immanence of the Real-Idea (*cakravartin*), the Centre of the Circle that makes all things move in their orbits, within the fragmented Becoming which has lost its centre. It is also an assertion of the principle of Eternity and Immortality in the heart of Death, seeding its Mind with the Joy of cosmogenesis and evolution. This equation of the radiant principle (*arka*) and of bliss (*kaṁ*) as its essence accompanies the manifest emergence of Fire (*agni*), which may be considered the soul of the immanent Solar Principle. It is the heart of the reverse or return Sacrifice from the Sacrifice of the Horse. From here the second *brāhmaṇa* begins referring to the cosmogenesis in terms of the replicated cosmic Horse. Fire is its Self, which divided itself into three, the other two parts being the Sun and the Wind. We are immediately brought into remembrance of the beginning of the first *brāhmaṇa*, which describes the head of the Horse in terms of these three principles:

> Dawn is the head of the horse sacrificial. The Sun is his eye, his breath is the Wind, his wide open mouth is Fire, the master might universal .... – *BU* I.1.1

These are the gods that best represent the Self of the Horse and can lead to its Self-experience. They represent the eternal principles of the Heaven-world, which take their stations in the three vertical strata of the axis mundi which is formed subsequent to their appearance in cosmic Becoming – the Sun in the solar world of Mind-Heaven, the Wind in the midworld of Life and Fire burning within Matter. They integrate the Self of the Horse and give it a cosmic foundation.

Vedic Resonances

Just as with the image of the Horse and its relation to the Vedic ritual of the Horse Sacrifice (Aśvamedha) in the first *brāhmaṇa*, the Vedic resonances of the second *brāhmaṇa* should not be missed. Just as Vedic rituals of state like the Aśvamedha structured the macropolis (*rājya maṇḍala* – imperial circle), the ritual of the Fire Sacrifice (*yajña*) structured the life of the individual or family. Just as the larger goals of the Horse Sacrifice were peace, justice and plenty for the inhabitants of the polis, the goals of the fire sacrifice were food, wealth, happiness and progeny for the individual and the family or communal group. The reduction of these rituals to material meanings and goals is being complicated and revised in cosmological and psychological terms in the Upaniṣads. In the second *brāhmaṇa*, the attention is being shifted from the image of the *cakravartin* as the solar Time-Image of the Horse to its immanence in the Becoming, in other words, to a displacement of authority from centre to periphery.

The elements that constitute the emergence of cosmos in the second *brāhmaṇa* are all key to the Vedic fire sacrifice, though marshalled in a different order appropriate to the emergence of cosmos as an act of reverse sacrifice. In the Vedic fire sacrifice, the directions are marked out and enclosed, the altar built and the wood-fire lit in the altar. Then the objects of sacrifice such as clarified butter (*ghee*), milk, water, grains and rice cakes were offered to the fire accompanied by the recitation of Vedic hymns (*arcā*). In the second *brāhmaṇa*, a hidden Fire is the secret Agent within the Mind of Death, through whose covert working the Word of Aspiration and Adoration is what emerges first and then successively, water, earth and overt fire. The overt emergence of Fire gives virtual cosmic body to the Horse in the Becoming, along with its vital energy (*vāyu*) and the solar Idea (*āditya*), after which the eight directions of horizontal Space and the three strata of vertical Space are established by its objective body parts (*BU* I.2.3). In later Tāntric practice, a similar process is followed by the individual practitioner to undo the "given" relation of elements and "rebuild" a divine body by an inner process of reconstitution (*nyāsa*). The psychological possibilities of the Vedic fire ritual are thus indicated in this manner, along with a cosmogonic description.

Food

The other aspect of the Vedic ritual that is of particular importance to our consideration of the fifth *brāhmaṇa* is the place of food. I have mentioned how the reduction of the goal of Vedic rituals to food is a major concern of the Upaniṣads. The Upaniṣads address this by an oft-repeated attention to food, nuancing, deepening and universalizing its meaning. The equation of Matter with food and rice in the word *annam* is one of the devices by which the phenomenology of food is turned cosmological and psychological. In *brāhmaṇa* 2, the ground is laid for such a cosmological consideration of food when Death is equated with Hunger. Death as Hunger desires "food", but this Hunger is insatiable, infinite, since Death is marked by Absence and only its realization of its origin as the Eternal Time-Image can satiate it. Yet, such a realization, in a logical sense, will mean the end of the cosmos, since it is insatiable Hunger that proliferates as the infinite cosmos. The second *brāhmaṇa* sees Hunger behind the restoration of the cosmic virtual image of the Horse in the Becoming, which is then pushed to replicate variations or simulacra of this image as the operation of its immanent Memory in the form of individuation. This is indicated after the establishment of the virtual image of the cosmic Horse in the desire for "a double". This double of the cosmos is a form of individuation. Every form of individuation is a unique microcosm of the macrocosm. The need for a double is described as a desire for companionship ("would that a second *ātman* were born for me"), but in reality, it is also a desire for food. For this process of actualizing an infinite material cosmos, Death is said to have intercourse with Speech (*Vāc*) by its Mind. This implies the mapping out of the idea-space of Death, that is the infinite variety of beings in primary relation to Death, a cosmos marked by relationality with Death. The language universe formed of such an intercourse encompasses forms of individuation evolving around survival and endurance against the erasure of self by Death. Are they walled in by the Mind of Death or does their other parent, the Word, have a Power that stretches beyond these walls? Death hides Immortality in its bosom, yet it is necessary for a Becoming of multiplicity in Time and Space, hence its creatures must be subject to Death even as they actualize degrees and forms of "overmortality", to adapt a word of the philosopher Bernard Stiegler.[1] This world is the domain of Death (*mṛtyu*). Hence, it is known as *marta*, in its Indo-European roots, a world of mortality, Matter, Inconscience, Death which houses Life as a temporary guest. Hence, this infinite Mind-Space of the intercourse of Death with the Word is all food for Death. Yet, all its creatures are also marked by the Hunger of Death not only for food but also for an end to Death, its origin in Immortality. Hence, the Horse's simulacra in the Mind-Space of Death are each allowed to manifest its own Immortality by proliferating in kind. The second *brāhmaṇa* expresses this laconically as an afterthought of Death, which after producing its "double" or "second Self", is about to eat it as its food but in a moment of profound calculative reason, lets it live so that it may replicate itself and multiply the consumables for Death. Yet, hidden behind this hesitation and reasoning is also an aspiration that the forms of immortality expressed by this double may not be limited to the replicability by quantitative multiplication or by reincarnation, which both remain fodder for Death, but by the realization of the immortal Self (*Ātman*). A form of individuation that realizes the immortal Self is no longer food for Death's insatiable Hunger, but the Self of All, including Death. As Death, it is the Eater of all things. Here, the notion of food becomes different, it is no longer the consumption which puts an end to things, but the Enjoyment of the Self by the Self, both beyond change and within the mutations of Time.

---

1 "... overmortality [*surmortalité*] [is] that which, when it is thought starting from being-towards-death, nevertheless allows to account for the fact that psychic individuation always carries itself forward, as originarily collective in this sense, going beyond itself, into a future that exceeds its own disappearance."
– Stiegler 2009: 48-49

The complex moment of the creation of an individuating double, the microcosm replicating the macrocosm, has other resonances than Death's intent (*BU* I.2.4). Born of the Infinite and Eternal, however, hidden by its Shadow, it must express Infinity and Eternity. If Death is Thanatos, the urge to dissolution and Nothingness, the individuating microcosm is born of the intercourse of Death and the Word, hence is constituted equally of Intelligence and the telos of the Integral Self. Hence, in Death's hesitation can be read also the slippage of the Word, its escape from the jaws of Death with the cry "Bhāṇ" (ibid.). Though Vedic terms such as *ṛk* and *vāk* are used in this *brāhmaṇa* for the Word, one may bring to mind that fact that language is also called *bhāṣā*, in which the syllable *bhā* means to shine. The cry *bhāṇ* is the escape of the Intelligent principle from the determinism of Matter and its journey towards a singular Wholeness and Immortality through individuation. This will to persist against the pursuit of the Ender opens the gate to the expression of its Infinity in a variety of ways. The two most material of these ways are replication through reproduction and through reincarnation. The remainder of *brāhmaṇa* 2 deals in a cryptic way with the persistence beyond Death by means of replication through reincarnation (*BU* I.2.6-7), while *brāhmaṇa* 4 deals with the multiplication of species by means of replication through reproduction. This latter is the population of the horizontal plane of the Horse's virtual existence in the Becoming. Yet, both these forms of replication are marked from the start as Death's belonging and only multiply its food source. But they are both also answers to the question raised in the fifth *brāhmaṇa*, "Why aren't they exhausted when they are eaten every day?" (*BU* I.5.1). Born of Infinity, they express Infinity in their own ways, by unending linear progression and horizontal expansion. However, *brāhmaṇa* 3 opens the way of the gods (*devayāna*), the path to individuation which exceeds Death and wins Immortality (*BU* I.3). In this way, one is not subject to Death, but is an equal of the gods, an Immortal, that knows Death as another god. It knows its truth beyond the mutations of Death and in its persistence through them. It enjoys all things as food, just like Death, where food takes on a non-material significance, as the Enjoyment (*bhoga*) of the infinite qualities of the Self in the play of the Becoming. This status is achieved by the gods joining together under the leadership of "the Breath in the mouth", "the Āṅgirasa Ayāsya" (*BU* I.3.7-8), a mysterious esoteric principle which is behind and secretly hidden in all the gods, such as Fire, Breath and the Word, and is their integral Soul and/or Self.

The Brāhmaṇa of Food

Brāhmaṇa 5 brings these meditations together on the subject of Food. At its beginning, it invokes Prajāpati, the Father of Creatures, the Creator, as producing seven kinds of Food through intelligence (*medhā*) and concentration of force (*tapas*).

> 1. The father produced seven kinds of food (*anna*) through Intelligence (*medhā*) and Concentration (*tapas*). One is common to all (*sādhāraṇa*). Two he portioned to the gods (*deva*). Three he kept for his Self (*Ātman*). And one he gave to the animals (*paśu*). On it rests everything – what lives and what does not. Why are they not exhausted, although they are eaten every day? He who knows this cause of their permanence eats food with *pratīka* (image). He goes to the gods, he lives on strength (*ūrjam*). Thus the verses.[2]

We saw in *brāhmaṇa* 2 how Intelligence and Will are behind the emergence of the elements leading to the cosmos following the Sacrifice of the Horse.[3] Thus, in an inversion, Prajāpati, the god of Creation takes here the same place as Death in *brāhmaṇa* 2. Here the seven kinds of Food are given in terms of the beings

---

2 All translations by the author unless explicitly mentioned.

3 Death-Hunger first creates Mind and then wills "let me have a self" (*BU* I.2.1).

to whom they are portioned – one common to all (*sādhāraṇa*), two to the gods (*devāḥ*), three for the Self (*Ātman*) and one for living creatures (*paśu*). It raises the question we have already touched on, "Why aren't they exhausted when they are eaten every day?" and states the reward for solving this riddle: "The man who knows it as the inexhaustible – he eats food with his face, he reaches the gods, he lives on invigorating food". "The man who knows it as the inexhaustible" points to the integral knowledge of Food that is indicated in this *brāhmaṇa*. Food is substance, food is sustenance, food is support for individuation and evolution, food is enjoyment and food is Immortality. This is the integral scope of food developed by this *brāhmaṇa*.

The Praxis of Food

After introducing the varieties of food in terms of their consumers in its compact beginning, it then proceeds to expand on the meaning of these seven kinds of food.

> 2. When the father produced seven kinds of food through Intelligence and Will means that the father indeed produced them through Intelligence and Will. "One is common to all eaters" means, this food that is eaten is the common food of all eaters. He who venerates this food is never free from sin (*pāpa*), for it is mixed (*miśra*). "Two he portioned to the gods" means the fire offerings (*hutam*) and the will behind these offerings (*prahutam*). Therefore, both of these are offered to the gods. Some, however, say, those two are the new and full moon sacrifices. Therefore, one should not be engrossed with sacrifices for material ends. "One he gave to the animals" – it is milk (*payaḥ*). For men and animals first live on milk alone. Therefore, they first make a new-born babe lick clarified butter (*ghṛtam*) or suckle it. And they speak of a new-born calf as one not yet eating grass. "On it rests everything – what lives and what does not" means that on milk indeed rests all this that lives and that does not. It is said that by making offerings of milk in the fire for a year one conquers further death (*punarmṛtyu*). One should not think thus. He who knows this

> conquers further death the very day he makes that offering, for he offers all his food to the gods. "Why are they not exhausted, although they are always being eaten?" – means that the Person (*Puruṣa*) is indeed the cause of their permanence, for he produces this food again and again. "He who knows this cause of their permanence" means that the *Puruṣa* is indeed the cause of their permanence, for he produces this food through his continuous work (*karma*) of concentration (*dhiyā dhiyā*). Should he not do this, it will be exhausted. "He eats food with *pratīka*." The mouth (*mukha*) is the *pratīka*, he eats with the mouth. "He attains the gods, he lives on strength (*ūrjam*)." This is a eulogy.

It identifies the "common" food for all as *anna*, that "which is eaten here". Those who venerate this food do not escape from sin, for it is mixed. We have considered the word *anna*. In the Upaniṣads, it means food, rice and Matter. It is the staple rice and it is the equation of food with Matter. In terms of the Vedic sacrifice, it refers to the rice cakes (*puroḍāśa*) and in terms of the domestic *yajña*, it refers to the reduction of its goal to material ends. The *Upaniṣad* is making clear here that this goal of the Vedic *yajña* does not bring freedom from sin and evil. We can relate this also to the food of Death. "All is the food of Death", refers to all material things, things based in Matter (*marta*), marked by Death (*mṛtyu*). All material things are in a state of constant transformation, consuming and being consumed. In Sri Aurobindo's annotation of this aspect:

> All Matter according to the *Upaniṣad* is food and this is the formula of the material world that "the eater eating is himself eaten".
> – 2005: 204

To mistake the goal of the Vedic *yajña* with material food brings no escape from this compulsion to Death. Nor does it bring freedom from sin (*pāpa*) and evil. In invoking sin, the *Upaniṣad* brings to mind the vertical scale of the cosmos, the higher meanings and laws of Food, leading to its ultimate meaning as the Self of Death, Immortality.

If, as Matter, food is Substance, subject to the law of perpetual transformation of Substance, as the Life-principle established in Matter, food is Sustenance. It flows across boundaries, supporting and nourishing Life. Here we can think of the food made for all living creatures (*paśu*), which the *Upaniṣad* gives as milk. Milk (and clarified butter, ghee, also invoked in this *brāhmaṇa* as a milk substitute) is another constituent of the Vedic *yajña*. Milk is a product of the Cow, another primary animal in the Vedic system, like the Horse, which is at the centre of this *Upaniṣad*. If the Horse stands for Divine Force, the Power of the kṣatriya, the Cow stands for Divine Knowledge, the Power of the brāhmaṇa. In expressing the law of Sustenance, food ascends to a function that heralds a universal exchange based in Amity and Love. Sri Aurobindo sees this as an evolutionary advance:

> ... it has to progress from the type of a mutually devouring hunger to the type of a mutual giving, of an increasingly joyous sacrifice of interchange; – the individual gives himself to other individuals and receives them back in exchange; the lower gives itself to the higher and the higher to the lower so that they may be fulfilled in each other; the human gives itself to the Divine and the Divine to the human; the All in the individual gives itself to the All in the universe and receives its realized universality as a divine recompense. Thus the law of Hunger must give place progressively to the law of Love, the law of Division to the law of Unity, the law of Death to the law of Immortality. – 2005: 207-08

Brāhmaṇa 5 universalizes this law extending it from living creatures to include all beings, living and non-living, deepening the meaning of the word *paśu*. *Paśu*, commonly meaning "creature" in its etymological sense, means that which is bound, since a *pāśa* is a knot or tie. All living things are bound to the universal Law of Death, but in a deeper sense, this is the universal Law of Sacrifice, since it is by Sacrifice that the Divine has become fragmented and by Sacrifice seeks to reconstitute itself into Wholeness. Thus, the Sustenance represented by milk represents a higher universal meaning to that of Hunger that is Death. Related to this revised meaning the *brāhmaṇa* raises a popular convention related to Vedic milk sacrifice: "This is said that by making offerings with milk for a year one conquers further death". It denies this superstition, replacing it by the Law of universal Sacrifice. In every self-offering, it is the Universe that offers itself and the Universe that accepts the offering. This knowledge of food as universal sustenance in every particular, if experienced through the act of every offering, can bring the contact and eventually the union with the Cosmic Puruṣa and Śakti. This Cosmic Puruṣa is what is described in the second *brāhmaṇa* as the reconstituted virtual-image of the Horse in the Becoming following the Sacrifice. This teaching later becomes the bedrock of the *Gītā*'s *karma-yoga*. Thus, the *brāhmaṇa* says of this deeper discovery of the universal Sacrifice: "He who knows this conquers further Death the very day he makes the offering, for he offers all his food to the gods". The gods here are the cosmic powers, the functionaries of the Cosmic Being, who keep the cosmos in operation, maintaining it within the bounds of an Order that prevents it from dissolution.

Ascent of the Puruṣa in the Praxis of Food

With the cosmic Sacrifice, we are in the horizontal domain of the Directions (*dik*) of the existing cosmos. There is also the vertical domain of the Strata of Ascent and Descent, the Ladder of Consciousness. Above the Life-principle is the realm of Mind, the zone of Ideas and Meaning. If the Life-principle, in the sacrifice of Love and Amity reaches the gods, it is the offerings purified by burning (*huta*) that is meant for the gods in their proper domain, the Mind Heavens. We are coming closer to the esoteric heart of the Vedic Sacrifice here, where the psychic element, Fire, the "breath within the mouth" of the third *brāhmaṇa* is invoked. We become aware here of the inner alchemy involved in the *Upaniṣad*'s transfiguration of the Vedic Sacrifice. The material sense of the ritual is rejected at the very start as the domain of Death's Hunger and that of the compromised struggle of Good and Evil, the gods and the demons. Instead, a transformative psychology of the ritual relates it to a different sense of Food and Sacrifice which resignifies it in terms of the relation with Death, its individuation towards Immortality. It orients the Life-principle towards Nurture and identification with the psychic principle of cosmic Exchange. This begins our journey away from subjection to Death in the discovery of a universal principle of Immortality in Mutuality. But as in the virtual constitution of the Horse in *brāhmaṇa* 2, the principle of individuation reaches self-consciousness with the overt discovery of Fire, Agni, the psychic element in the individual. This is the emergence of Person, *Puruṣa* or psychic being. The Sacrifice ascends to the Mind-realm, the zone of the gods. Here, the *brāhmaṇa* says, to the gods were given two kinds of Food, *hutam* and *prahutam*. If *hutam* is the fire offering, *prahutam*, adding the prefix *pra*, signifying protension, "reaching forward", to *hutam*, is the intent of the offering, the Will to Wholeness and Immortality in it. It is these two that are meant for the gods. Food here exceeds Substance and Sustenance to include the Enjoyment of Meaning in all experience. All experience contains a symbolic aspect of Sacrifice to the vertical dimension of the Origin, the Real-Idea of the Horse in the first *brāhmaṇa*, the Wholeness and Immortality of the Solar One prior to the Sacrifice, which remains the Unborn in the Births of the Becoming. It is this that sustains the gods.

After speaking of *hutam* and *prahutam*, the discussion of the two kinds of food for the gods introduces an alternative. "They also say they are the new moon and full moon sacrifices." This alternative is only followed by a statement in passing: "Therefore, one should not sacrifice for material ends". Like *hutam* and *prahutam*, the full moon and new moon represent manifest and unmanifest forms of expression. If the full moon is the expressed part of the offering (*pravṛtti*), the new moon is the cessation of expression (*nivṛtti*) and gestation for new expression. The sphere of Meaning includes both the visible and the invisible, and the food for the gods is made another occasion for warning against the material reduction of the sacrifice.

Riddle of the Brāhmaṇa as a Problem of Becoming

Ascending to the zone of Meaning, the question posed about Food at the beginning of the *brāhmaṇa* comes to light – "Why aren't they exhausted, when they are eaten everyday?" The Sacrifice of the Horse is the Becoming of the Being of the Real-Idea of Radical Infinity. Hence, it expresses the Infinity of the Being in the Becoming through the concentrated Will of the Real-Idea. The Sacrifice is referred to as an originary Event, the starting point of Time; but this is just a "manner of speaking" unavoidable and necessary to the ontology of temporality, made up of beginnings, middles and ends. In fact, the Becoming in all its becomings is an "eternal recurrence of Being", to adapt Nietzsche's phrase. As we saw at the start, it is the loosing of the multiplicity of Infinite Being in a cosmos of Time and Space. But this is accomplished as an act of Concentration and Will (*tapas*). The Self-Sacrifice of the One to its infinite potential is the Time-Image that lives in each unit of temporality and spatiality, marked by the beginning, middle and end of all discrete measure. It is the One that has become these Many in the Being of the Sacrifice, by its Force of concentrated Will (*tapas*). This translates to a perennial and perpetual Becoming in Space and Time, each becoming upheld inexhaustibly by the *tapas* of the Being in the Sacrifice. This Being, figured as the Horse of the Aśvamedha in *brāhmaṇa* 1, is none other than the *Puruṣa*, radical Infinity as Person. If the tenth *maṇḍala* of the *Ṛgveda* spoke of this Being of Sacrifice in the image of a post-Anthropos, the *Bṛhadāraṇyaka Upaniṣad* replaces the Anthropic by the Equine. This complicates the anthropocentric bias of the Veda, at the same time displacing its Brāhmanic privilege towards the kṣatriya. However, if this was all, we would be justified in thinking of this displacement as a sleight of hand, since the Horse exists in such an image only to empower the Human Emperor, an anthropocentric Power Source. But the State-Idea in the image of the Horse is itself displaced and decentralized in favour of the individuation of the individual, the Each of the Many. The One that has become the Many is not to be found in-itself outside the Many but is immanent in Each of the Many as the alchemic Fire Sacrifice that reveals its identity as the One and the All in the Each. The *tapas* by which the Being becomes through Sacrifice is a Space-Time-Image, it pervades infinite Space and inhabits beginningless and unending Time. By it the Being becomes innumerably, infinitely and unendingly.

The discovery of this identity of each becoming with the Being, of the Sacrifice as the magic act (*māyā*) of the Infinite One, releasing its Infinity and remaining One in all and each of its infinite portions, is the answer to the riddle of the *brāhmaṇa* – "Why aren't they exhausted when they are eaten everyday?" The *brāhmaṇa* asserts: "The *Puruṣa* is indestructible, It gives birth to Food repeatedly." It then invokes the statement of the answer to the riddle given at the start of the *brāhmaṇa*: "Who knows it as the inexhaustible, he eats Food with his image (*pratīka*), he goes to the gods, he lives on strength", unpacking it phrase by phrase. "Who knows it as the inexhaustible – in other words, the *Puruṣa* is indestructible, it gives birth to Food as its work through continuous meditation. If it were not to do this, the food would be exhausted", an invocation of the *tapas* (concentrated will) of the *Puruṣa* in the continuous upholding of the Sacrifice in Space–Time. "He eats food with his image (*pratīka*), in other words, the image (*pratīka*) is the mouth (or chief) (*mukha*), he eats with the mouth, he goes to the gods, he lives by strength, this is praise."

These enigmatic lines are taken in a rather banal sense by

most translators as eating face forward and by the mouth. But to unpack their sense we need to go back to the first and third *brāhmaṇas*, which speak about the gods. The gods enumerated in the first *brāhmaṇa* constitute the head of the Horse – the Sun (*Āditya*) constituting the eyes of the Horse, Fire, Agni, constituting the Mouth of the Horse and Wind (*Vāyu*) constituting the breath of the Horse. Again in the second *brāhmaṇa*, during the reconstitution of the Horse as a virtual image or cosmic image of the Becoming following the Sacrifice, it is Fire which is the first of the gods to emerge and then divide itself into the three gods, Fire, Sun and Wind, making up the head or "face" of the Horse with Fire as its Mouth. These three gods also take their position as the controllers of the three strata in the verticality of the axis mundi or World-Stair. In the later Upaniṣads, Fire (*agni*) is seen as the Divinity of the Earth or Material World (*pṛthvī*), Wind (*vāyu*) as the Divinity of the Midworld or Life-World (*antarikṣa*) and the Sun (*āditya*) as the Divinity of Heaven or the Mindworld (*dyauṣ*). However, as we will see, in this *adhyāya*, the positions of the Sun and Wind are inverted, since it is the Horse, Idea of Power that is being privileged here. Vāyu, Lord of Wind, is exalted as the Divinity of Heaven, the Sun (*āditya*) as the Divinity of the Midworld and Fire (*agni*) of the Material World.

Food as Experience and Expression of Self

> 3. "Three he made for his-Self (*ātman*)": Mind, Speech and the Life-force, these he made for himself. (One says), "My mind was elsewhere, I did not see it", "My mind was elsewhere, I did not hear it". It is through the mind that one sees and hears. Desire, purpose, doubt, faith, lack of faith, steadiness, unsteadiness, shame, intelligence and fear – all these are but the mind. Even if one is touched from behind, one knows it through the mind; therefore (the mind exists). And any kind of sound is but Speech, for it serves to determine a thing but it cannot itself be revealed. *Prāṇa, apāna, vyāna, udāna* and *samāna* – all these are forms of breathing but the Life-force. This body is identified with these – with Speech, Mind and the Life-force.

In the third *brāhmaṇa*, dealing with the contest of the gods and demons (*devas* and *asuras*), the gods are given as Speech (*Vāc*), Life-force (*prāṇa*), Sight (*cakṣu*), Hearing (*śrotra*) and Mind (*mana*) (*BU* I.3.2-6). These are subjective correlates of the objectified gods Sun (*Āditya*), Wind (*Vāyu*) and Fire (*Agni*) respectively. We can see the correlations in terms of the organology of the Horse's head. Since Fire is its Mouth, the Word is the subjective correlate of Fire; since the Sun is its Eye, Sight, its associate, Hearing and their ancestor Mind are the subjective correlates of the Sun; and since Wind is its Breath, the Life-force is the subjective correlate of the Wind. In the third *brāhmaṇa*, these gods each try to vanquish the demons but fail until they are led by a mysterious Stranger, "the breath in the mouth", Ayāsya Āṅgirasa (*BU* I.3.7). This is asserted as the essence of all the body parts (*aṅga-rasa*), the eater of food, the leader of all the gods, who huddling around it partake of its eating. It thus constitutes the image of the Whole assemblage of the gods, the strata and the Being in each becoming. It is Breath and Word and Fire, yet it is invisible and hidden.

With this in mind, we are in a better position to understand the enigmatic lines about eating with the image (*pratīka*) and by the face/mouth (*mukha*), as well as the succeeding lines about the three kinds of food reserved for itself by Prajāpati. The "breath in the mouth", the hidden God who is the essence of the limbs and the leader of the gods, is the true Divine Eater of Food in the cosmos and the individual. By Eater of Food one may conceive of it as the Experiencer, Subject or immanent *Puruṣa*. All experience belongs to it and nourishes by it all the gods in all the strata and all the body parts. It is the image (*pratīka*) because it integrates all these in itself. In the first hymn of the *Ṛgveda* and in many hymns thereafter, this primacy and essentiality of function is given to Fire, Agni. It is the priest and leader of the Sacrifice, it is invoked as a god to "bring all the gods". This is the psychic being, crystallized image of the individualized integral Divine immanent in all becomings. *Mukha* (face) here is the mouth, since this hidden god is known as the "breath in the mouth" and the mouth is the organ associated with psychic Fire and the Word; but *mukha* is also a pun for chief, the leader of the gods, the priest of the reverse Sacrifice leading to Integrality and Immortality.

The *brāhmaṇa* introduces the riddle at its heart and its solution after talking of the food for the gods, and it continues to discuss the three kinds of food reserved for itself by Prajāpati. We are told that these are Mind (*mana*), Speech (*vāk*) and the Life-force (*prāṇa*). We have already encountered these three among the five introduced in *brāhmaṇa* 3. The third paragraph of *brāhmaṇa* 5 refers to this in its reduction of Sight and Hearing to Mind, all Sound to Speech and the Five Breaths to the Life-force. Moving from the gods of the objective cosmos we encounter their subjective counterparts in the Food for the Self. Prajāpati, the Creator, here is none other than Death which is Hunger in the second *brāhmaṇa* and both are names for the Real-Idea of the Sacrifice of the Being of the Becoming, the Self of all selves. Just as the psychic being is the essence and Self of the gods immanent in the individual, the Real-Idea of the Sacrifice is the essence and Self of the gods at the supramental Origin. Knowing the two as one is the apotheosis of Food, the enjoyment of Immortality in all experience in the field of Death.[4] The three gods reserved for itself by Prajāpati are psychic handles for this knowledge, since in the immanence, the psychic being and in the Supermind, the Real-Idea are the essence of all three and can be known in seeking for their essence. Between the multiplicity of individual immanence and the Oneness of Supermind are the universal strata of Earth, Life-world and Mind-world, in each of which one of these gods presides. Thus, seeking for the Self in these strata is accomplished through each of these gods. These gods are thus doors through which to seek the integral knowledge of

---

4 This idea is the specialized message of the *Īśa Upaniṣad*.

Oneness, the Self of the Being, the cosmic Being and Becoming in all its strata and the individual being and its becomings in Space and Time.

The Cosmic Trinities

4. These are the three worlds. Speech is this world (the Earth), Mind is the Midworld (*antarikṣa*) and the Life-force (*prāṇa*) is that world (*heaven*).

5. These are the three Vedas. Speech is the *Ṛgveda*, Mind is the *Yajurveda* and the Life-force is the *Sāmaveda*.

6. These are the gods (*deva*s), the ancestors (*pitṛ*s) and men (*manuṣya*). Speech is the gods, mind the ancestors and the Life-force men.

7. These are the father, mother and child. Mind is the father, Speech the mother and the Life-force the child.

8. These are what is known, what it is desirable to know and what is unknown. Whatever is known is a form of Speech, for it is the Knower. Speech protects him by becoming that (which is known).

9. Whatever it is desirable to know is a form of Mind, for the Mind is what it is desirable to know. Mind protects him by becoming that (which it is desirable to know).

10. Whatever is unknown is a form of the Life-force, for the Life-force is what is unknown. The Life-force protects him by becoming that (which is unknown).

11. The earth is the body of Speech and Fire is its form of Illumination. And as far as Speech extends, so far extends the Earth and so far does this Fire.

12. Heaven is the body of this mind and that Sun is its form of Illumination. And as far as the mind extends, so far extends heaven and so far does that Sun. These two had intercourse and from that the Life-force was born. It is Indra, the Lord of gods. It is unrivalled. A second is indeed a rival. He who knows this has no rival.

> 13. Water is the body of this Life-force and that Moon is its form of Illumination. And as far as the Life-force extends, so far extends Water and so far does that Moon. These are all equal and all Infinite. He who meditates upon these as finite wins a finite world, but he who meditates upon these as Infinite wins an infinite world.

From stanza 4 to 13, the Trinity that is described as the food for the Self is elaborated in terms of other cosmic Trinities and adulated. In *brāhmaṇa* 2 we saw how the intercourse of the Mind (*mana*) of Death with Speech (*vāk*) produced the cosmos of individuation, the doubles or simulacra of Becoming. This is referenced in the Trinity in terms of the Father being the Mind, the Mother being Speech and the child being the Life-force born of their coupling. The Trinity of Speech, Mind and Life-force is also mapped respectively to the Earth, the Midworld and the Heaven; the *Ṛgveda*, the *Yajurveda* and the *Sāmaveda*; gods, ancestors and humans; the known, the to-be-known and the unknown. Next the three are mapped to forms of Illumination, the Speech to Fire, the Mind to the Sun and the Life-force to the Moon, as to the media respectively of earth, sky and water. In stanza 12, there is an explicit reiteration of the intercourse of Mind and Speech or Sun and Fire to produce the Life-force. Here, the Life-force is also equated to Indra Lord of the Mind-Heavens and of Knowledge. All these correspondences are established to provide an orientation to cosmic realities as related and as Divine. Each of these principles is asserted to be equal of extent and Infinite. A veneration of the cosmos in all its related principles seen each as infinite is the key to the solution of the riddle and to the experience of all things in the cosmos as "Food" equated with the experience of Immortality. Failing this, viewing these principles as finite, one experiences a world of limits and is a victim of Death.

Time as the Self of the Horse

We have moved from Food seen as Substance of Matter subject

to Sacrifice seen as the Law of Death to Food seen as Sustenance of Life belonging to Sacrifice seen as the Law of Mutuality and Love, to Food seen as Idea in Mind belonging to Sacrifice seen as the Law of Knowledge and Will, to Food seen as Experience in Self belonging to Sacrifice seen as Law of Self-Manifestation. This progression has followed the creative process of Prajāpati, God or Father of Creatures, or literally Lord of beings subject to Birth. In *brāhmaṇa* 2, the cosmic creation was seen as the generative process of Death. These two gods, Mṛtyu (Death) and Prajāpati, represent two ways of viewing the same thing, the consequence of the Sacrifice of the Real-Idea of Infinite Person, seen here as the Divine Horse. This Sacrifice is the paradoxical gap between Being and Becoming, and between the One and the Many. Death and Birth, Mṛtyu and Prajāpati, both mark the Becoming with its multiplicity of becomings. They are the repeating Time-steps of the galloping Horse, making for the progressions of multiple creatures. In the very first *brāhmaṇa*, we are told Time-unit or Year (*saṁvatsara*) is the Self or Being of the Horse (*BU* I.1.1). In the second *brāhmaṇa*, after the objective establishment of the Being of cosmic Becoming, its subjective Space emerges through the intercourse of Death with Speech. This subjective Space or Space of Subject is measured by Time-units of Gestation, Life, Death and Rebirth. This periodicity is given as the Year or the duration of the earth's revolution around the Sun, or in a relative sense, the Sun's seasonal cycle on the Earth. We are told at this point that the seed of the union of Death with Speech was the annual Time-unit (*saṁvatsara*), Time now came into existence, it did not exist before this (*BU* I.2.3). This is the individuated replication of the Self of the Horse. Thus, Mṛtyu, Prajāpati and the Divine Horse of the Sacrifice are all emblems of the Solar Divinity of the Veda. Having arrived at the Food reserved by Prajāpati for Himself, the Trinity of primary gods that form the Head of the Sacrificial Horse (*BU* I.1.1) or the Organs of Experience, Life and Expression, we have moved to the border between the Object and the Subject, the liminal gods of the borderland. We are in contact with the Self of the Divine Person, who is none other than the Self of All and Each.

Thus, it is this Self of the Becoming that is now described in terms of Time and periodicity:

> 14. This Prajāpati has sixteen digits (*ṣoḍaśa kalā*) and is represented by the year (*saṁvatsara*). The nights are his fifteen digits and the constant one (*dhruva*) is his sixteenth digit. He waxes and wanes by the nights. Through this sixteenth digit he permeates all these living beings on the night of *amāvasyā* and rises the next morning. Therefore, on this night one should not take the life of living beings, not even of a lizard, in sole adoration of this deity.
>
> 15. The person here who knows this is indeed himself Prajāpati who has sixteen digits and is represented by the year. Wealth constitutes his fifteen digits and the Self his sixteenth digit. He is filled as well as wasted by wealth. This Self stands for the hub and wealth is the felloe. Therefore, if a man loses everything, but he himself lives, people say that he has only lost his felloe.

Bound by the sacrificial duration, it is the solar cycle or Year. This is itself divided in cycles constituted by the lunar phases, *kalā* (digits) of the moon in its waxing and waning cycle of fifteen days each. In this description, too, is an implicit triplicity, for the digits of the moon take their form due to its transitions around the earth, which mediates its relation with the Sun. But if this description could exhaust the Self of the Becoming, it would be nothing other than a Machine or in the language of the *Upaniṣad*, the spokes and rim (felloe) of a Wheel. But this periodicity is determined by the Self and cannot determine it. It thus retains an indeterminable and unchanging (*dhruva*) sixteenth part for itself, the hub of the Wheel. We are told that the night of the *amāvasyā* is the Night of Gestation (*nivṛtti*), when the sixteenth part, the Self, occupies all the beings of Life (breathing beings) and is born again the next morning. The cycle of the waxing and waning Moon constitutes the Nights of Expression (*pravṛtti*) when the self-born (*svayambhū*) Idea of the Self manifests progressively in evolutionary phases leading to its full expression with the Full Moon and subsequent progressive reabsorption. We find this idea replicated in the *Śākta Tantra* with the fifteen Nitya Devīs related to the fifteen nights of the waxing (*śukla pakṣa*) and waning (*kṛṣṇa pakṣa*) moon and Tripurasundarī, the Supremely Beautiful Goddess of the Three Worlds as the "sixteenth" fixed point forming the centre of the Circle. For this reason, She is also called *Ṣoḍaśī* (Sixteenth). In the second *brāhmaṇa,* with the description of the self-replication of Death (the Sacrificed Horse) the Year is the Night of Gestation, followed by a Year of Expression leading to a repetition of the Sacrifice. This is the very meaning of the Becoming, multiple recursive cycles of progressive manifestation of the Radical Infinity of the Time-Image of the Sacrificial Horse, eternal as plural Being, perennial as Being-in-Becoming, perpetual as plural Becoming. This is the supramental Real-Idea of Cosmos. The freedom of the Self occupies the lives of all creatures in the Night of Gestation, when the Idea of the next cycle is self-born in all the creatures and manifests itself through the remainder of the Time-cycle. But the free Self is no less present in the creatures through the Nights of Expression, choosing its manifestation and retaining its uniqueness in creative freedom. All repetitions are the perpetual returns of Difference-in-Itself. This is the solution to the riddle on Food – the Being of Radical Infinity, who as Real-Idea becomes innumerably, perpetually, perennially and without end, through its discretizations in Space and Time, in other words, as the repetition of innumerable variations transforming through processes of birth, life, death and rebirth. Realizing this, one becomes the Real-Idea, at once Being and Becoming in all becomings.

Overmortality and the Three Worlds

> 16. There are indeed three worlds, the world of men, the world of the ancestors and the world of the gods. This world of men is to be won through the son (*putra*) alone and by no other work; the world of the ancestors through works (*karma*); and the world of the gods through Knowledge (*vidyā*). The world of the gods is the best of the worlds. Therefore, they praise Knowledge (*vidyā*).

The fifth *brāhmaṇa*, proceeding from its meditation on the kinds of Food, introduced the meaning of Food to Matter, the Life-force, the Mind and the Self. Thus, we have a Trinity ascending to the Self. The Food of the Self (*ātman*) is itself a Trinity, the three principal gods, Mind, Speech and the Life-force. These gods are themselves the subjective properties of the Self, which become the governing Powers of the three zones of Matter, Life and Mind. Before coming to the consolidation of the Whole in the image of the subjective Self of Prajāpati as Being and Becomings, this Trinity of Mind, Speech and Life-force is extended into a variety of cosmic trinities, so as to universalize its perception in the aspirant and lead towards its integral realization. At the end of the extension, Mind, Speech and the Life-force, which we saw as the subjective correlates of the Vedic gods Āditya (Sun), Agni (Fire) and Vāyu (Wind) constituting the Eye, Mouth and Breath of the sacrificial Horse, are equated respectively to sources of illumination Sun, Fire and Moon, and the universal media of Sky, Earth and Water respectively. Fire is the Sun descended into the Earth and pluralized as the inhabitant in all beings/becomings; Moon is the astral Wisdom of the subjective consciousness of the universe, represented by Water; and Sun is the constant source of solar Knowledge illuminating the heights of the Mind Heavens from Beyond. These three realms are equated at this point respectively, to the world of humans (*manuṣya*, mind-creatures), the ancestors (*pitṛ*s) and the gods (*deva*s). The Earth or world of humans is the world of the present, the coexistence of plurality in the spatial contraction of Time expressing through Matter. The world of Ancestors (*pitṛs*) is the world of the accumulated Wisdom of the past, the expansion of Time as collective Memory in the watery medium of subliminal Consciousness. The world of the gods is the spontaneous world of Gnosis, both eternal and encompassing the three times, Past, Present and Future. In a relation with the Earth, the world of the Ancestors is that of the Past, a retention, while the world of the gods is that of the Future, a protention. Each has its own relation to Death or Overmortality. The world of humans is subject to perpetual transformation of Substance. Overmortality here is the transmission of material memory, Speech as the genetic code, carried forward in Time through Matter. One may think of another kind of material Overmortality, that of rebirth. But this involves the eternal soul, Agni lodged in Matter. The world of the ancestors is that of the fluid exchanges of the Life-energies represented in the medium of Water and manifest in the Breath. Behind it is the accumulated wisdom of the ancestors, represented by the Moon. Overmortality here is the realization of mutual Sacrifice as the Law of the cosmos, the Immortality of the cosmic Being and Consciousness as carried in the Life-force. The world of the gods is that of the Immortality of the Person realizing itself as the Being and the Becoming. It is the Gnosis of the Sun in the supramental Space represented by Sky and projecting and illumining the Cosmic Mind. Possession of this Knowledge brings the full individuation of Immortality in the One, the All and the Each. The sixteenth stanza of the fifth *brāhmaṇa* summarizes these forms of Overmortality by asserting that one is victorious over the realm of the humans through the son (*putra*) not through any work (*karma*); one is victorious over the world of the ancestors through Works, implying the works of universal Sacrifice (*yajña*); and one is victorious over the world of the gods through Knowledge (*vidyā*), meaning the realization of the Real-Idea in its double status as Being and Becoming, the

Sun in Space and the Fire on Earth. Possessing the three together is the integral Knowledge.

Transmission, Descent and Transformation

This is followed from stanza 17 by esoteric verses on the transmission (*sampratiḥ*) of this integral Knowledge at the time of Death:

> 17. Now therefore the transmission (*sampratiḥ*): When a man thinks he will die, he says to his son, "You are *Brahman*, you are the sacrifice (*yajña*) and you are the world (*loka*)". The son replies, I am *brahman*, I am the sacrifice and I am the world. Whatever is studied is all unified in the *brahman*. Whatever sacrifices there are, are all unified in *yajña*. And whatever worlds there are, are all unified in this world (*loka*). Great, indeed, is the All (*sarvam*). "He, being the All, will liberate me from this world." Therefore, a son who is this instructed is known as the Master of the world; therefore is the son instructed. When one who knows this departs from this world, he enters his son with his breaths (*prāṇa*). Whatever wrong may have been done by him, the son liberates him from all that; therefore, he is called a son (*putra*). The father stands firm in this world through the son. Then the divine immortal breaths enter him.

When a person thinks he is about to depart, he should address his son with a view to the transmission of his realization. The term *putra*, used for son, is explicated in stanza 17 as the one who frees the father from wrong-doing. This implies a breakdown of *putra* in terms of *puḥ*, related to *pur* or *pra*, going before or forward and *tra*, to liberate, in other words, the son is one who "liberates forward" or liberates in future time his father. "Son" and "birth" are terms often used in the Veda. Like "food", "son" is considered one of the goals of the sacrifice. But again like "food", it can have other semantic values. In the Veda, an esoteric meaning of "son" can be the birth of a new formation of consciousness by the power of *yoga*. One that "liberates in future time" can also mean a "spiritual son" (*śiṣya*) in the *guru–śiṣya* tradition of the *Upaniṣad* or even the soul or psychic being, moving towards new lives through rebirth. Hence, *sampratiḥ* transmission is a form of *śaktipāt*, transference of realization from one person to another, deemed a descendant, with intent to furthering one's line of spiritual progress. All Time is progression of Consciousness from a Zero state of the Sacrifice to a conscious realization of the Origin and its manifestation in/as plurality in Time. Of necessity, this journey through Ignorance (*avidyā*) to Knowledge (*vidyā*) is a progressive setting-right, a liberation in future time. The "son" here, therefore, can mean any individual or even any inner formation of the dying person who/that is chosen by his/her/its capacity to carry forward the spiritual realization.

The term *śaktipāt* is a later invention, more common in traditions of Tantra and Śaivism. But it has been known in various traditions. Behind it is the "descent of Consciousness" as a power of transformation. The realizer of the Integral Real-Idea must in fact practise some kind of *śaktipāt* on his/her own nature to bring the realization into the "realm of the humans", i.e. into the body. In premodern times, the anointing or coronation of a king, in many traditions, was a symbolic act of *śaktipāt*, where the divinity of a god was invoked to enter the king as a representative of the Divine. The Horse Sacrifice itself, which is at the centre of this *Upaniṣad*, was conducted to transfer such Divine Power to the *cakravartin*. But here, in the culture of the *Upaniṣad*, the idea of *śaktipāt* is being democratized and invoked in individuals, whether in a father–son filial situation or in a *guru–śiṣya* hermitage situation. In fact, the latter context is not unknown even today. One hears the use of the term in certain Tāntric or Kashmir Śaiva contexts, such as when Swami Muktānanda announced his descendants and anointed them, as it were, through *śaktipāt*. But the act is even more common than the word. We hear of Sri Ramakrishna passing on his realization to Swami Vivekananda a few days before his passing. Similarly, the Mother has attested to Sri Aurobindo's passing his realization on to her at the time of his passing.

Stanza 17 discusses this process in terms of the preparation of the "son". This preparation or receptive orientation consists in repeating the words "I am *Brahman*, I am *yajña*, I am the world (*loka*)". We have seen how each of these categories is related to one of the three worlds, *Brahman*, the ontology of Knowledge (*vidyā*), with the world of the gods; *yajña*, the ontology of mutuality in Sacrifice with the world of the ancestors and *loka*, world, the ontology of transformations of Substance in plural contexts (worlds) with the world of humans. Each of these repetitions is an act of concentration, drawing the power of transcendental Knowledge, universal Sacrifice and cosmic transformation into oneself. The thought of each is accompanied with a focus on its universality. All that one has learnt comes from the One Knowledge (*vidyā*), all that one has sacrificed comes from the One Sacrifice and all the worlds one has inhabited belong to the One World. Opening oneself to the Source of all three, one is attuned to the Origin, the Subject. This is referred to as the Whole (*sarvam*). The "father" passes the intent of transmission to "the son" with the thought, "Being thus the Whole, he liberates me from this world". A son who is thus instructed becomes one with the world and the father enters him with all his breaths (*prāṇas*). At this point, the *Upaniṣad* develops its creative etymology of "son" (*putra*) as he who "liberates in future time".

> 18. From the earth and from fire Divine Speech enters him. That is the Divine Speech through which whatever he says is fulfilled.
>
> 19. From heaven and from the sun the Divine Mind enters him. That is the Divine Mind through which he becomes only blissful and never mourns.
>
> 20. From water and from the moon the Divine Life-force enters him. That is the Divine Life-force which, whether it moves

> or is stationary, feels no pain nor is injured. He who knows this becomes the Self of all beings. As is this deity, so is he. As all beings take care of this deity, so do they take care of him. Howsoever these beings may grieve, that grief *of* theirs is connected with them. But only merit goes to him. No demerit ever goes to the gods.

All the faculties of divine realization are referred to as breaths (*prāṇa*) here. They enter the "son" from their respective divine realms, Divine Speech (Daivī Vāk) from the Earth (Pṛthvī) and Fire (Agni), the Divine Mind (Daivam Mana) from the Heaven (Divaḥ) and the Sun (Āditya), the Divine Life-force (Daiva Prāṇa) from the Water and the Moon (Candra). With them come their divine Powers or *siddhi*s. Whatever he says comes to pass, whatever he thinks, he becomes, always of bliss and never of suffering; whether his breath is active or still, it remains unperturbed and uninjured. He becomes one with the Divine Self, the Self of all Beings. As it is with this Origin so it is with him, he is free of the dualities, only the unshadowed Good comes to him, no evil is his.

Madhyama Prāṇa and Vāyu as Integrative Divinities

The *brāhmaṇa* ends with three stanzas, which adulate an integrative source among all the faculties and all the gods, and identifies this as the "central breath" (*madhyama prāṇa*) among the faculties and Wind (*Vāyu*) among the gods:

> 21. Now a consideration of the resolution/praxis (*vrata*): Prajāpati projected the organs of action. These, on being created, quarrelled with one another. The organ of Speech took a resolution, "I will go on speaking". The eye: "I will see". The ear: "I will hear". And so did the other organs according to their functions. Death captured them in the form of fatigue – it overtook them and having overtaken them it controlled them. Therefore, the organ of speech invariably gets tired and so do the eye and the ear. But death did not capture the "central breath" (*madhyama prāṇa*) in the body. The organs resolved to

> know it. "This is the greatest among us that, when it moves or does not move, feels no pain nor is injured. Well, let us all be of its form." They all assumed its form. Therefore, they are called by this name of "Prāṇa". That family in which a man is born who knows this is indeed named after him. And he who competes with one who knows this shrivels and after shrivelling dies at the end. This is with reference to the Self.
>
> 22. Now with reference to the gods: Fire took a resolution, "I will go on burning". The sun: "I will give heat". The moon: "I will shine". And so did the other gods according to their functions. As is the Life-force in the body among these organs, so is Vāyu (Wind) among these gods. Other gods sink, but not Wind. Wind is the deity that never sets.
>
> 23. Now there is this verse: "The gods observed the resolution of that from which the sun rises and in which he sets. It is (followed) today and it will be (followed) tomorrow." The sun indeed rises from the Life-force and also sets in it. What these (gods) observed then, they observe to this day. Therefore, a man should observe a single resolution – do the functions of the *prāṇa* and *apāna* (*prāṇāyāma*), lest the evil of death should take him. And if he observes it, he should seek to finish it. Through it he attains identity with this deity and lives in the same world with it.

These stanzas sound similar to and rehearse the idea behind *brāhmaṇa* 2, dealing with the conflict between the gods (*deva*s) and demons (*asura*s). There it was the mysterious "breath within the mouth" that was held to be the impregnable leader of all the gods. Here, all the faculties such as Speech, Sight, Hearing are referred to as breaths (*prāṇa*s) and it is the "central breath" (*madhyama prāṇa*) that is their leader. The emphasis on the Breath is a specific handle of this *adhyāya* of the *Upaniṣad*. Different Upaniṣads and different *adhyāya*s focus on different such handles of praxis through which to mediate their realization. We have seen how this *adhyāya* begins with the Divine Horse, a symbol of Royalty and Power. It is thus the Life-force that is chosen by this *adhyāya* as the central Deity to approach the integral Divine. In *brāhmaṇa* 2 the psychic integral is referred to as the "breath within the Mouth". But this breath within the mouth is described as the essence (*rasa*) of all the body parts (*aṅga*s), Aṅgirasa. It is the essence of all the faculties and one with them. It can equally be called Speech or other gods since it is equally the Power in all. Yet, by calling it the "breath in the mouth", the Life-force (*prāṇa*) becomes the central handle for praxis to get to this psychic element. The praxis of the Life-force is *yajña*, sacrifice of the life activities. The sacrifice of the life activities (*prāṇa*s) to the Integral One can be thought of as the central praxis leading to the integral Divine. One could think of this as portending the *karma-yoga* of the *Bhagavadgītā*, written perhaps a millennium later. The sacrifice of Works, the sacrifice of Knowledge and the sacrifice of Relations, such as that between the sexes, between parents and children, and between preceptor and student, in all cases to the Integral Divine, lead to the finding of this central Divinity within the individual and in the cosmos. In verses 21 and 22 there is no duality as between the gods and the demons; the problem is the uncoordinated individualism of the faculties and the gods. The problem of the integral begins with the recognition of plurality without unity. The assemblage of the faculties as of the gods must develop or discover a will to integrality. The integral is already the Truth of the universal solar Gnosis as of the individual psychic Fire. Here, this is asserted in terms of the universal Wind God (Vāyu) and the individual psychic Life-force (*prāṇa*) showing a pointer to a resolved praxis (*vrata*). This concludes the fifth *brāhmaṇa* of the first *adhyāya* of the *Bṛhadāraṇyaka Upaniṣad*.

Triplicity
Adhyāya I: Brāhmaṇa 6

1. Indeed, here (all) is a triplicity of name, form and work. Of these, for names, speech is the source, for from it all names arise. It is the one (*sāman*) in them, for it is the same for all names. It is their *Brahman*, for it supports all names.

2. Next, of forms, the eye is the source (*uktha*), for from it all forms arise. It is the one (*sāman*) in them, for it is the same for all forms. It is their *Brahman* (self), for it supports all forms.

3. Next, of work, the self (*ātman*) is the source (*uktha*), for from it all works arise. It is the one (*sāman*) in them, for it is the same for all works. It is their *Brahman*, for it supports all works. These three together are one – this self (*ātman*); and the self (*ātman*), though one, is these three. This is the immortal covered by the real: the vital breath (*prāṇa*) is the immortal and name and form are the real and by them the immortal is covered.

THE short sixth and last *brāhmaṇa* (section) of the first *adhyāya* (chapter) serves as the conclusion of the *adhyāya*. It continues the trend of thought with which the fifth *brāhmaṇa* ends and pulls together a central thread that runs through the *adhyāya* at the same time. The fifth *brāhmaṇa* ends with the process of replication. This process itself ends with the entry of the three divine faculties, Speech (*vāc*), Mind (*mana*) and Breath (*prāṇa*), into the replicating individual (*BU* I.5.18-20). These psychological faculties are related to the three cosmic gods and sources of Light, Fire (Agni), Sun (Āditya) and Moon (Candramā) and to three cosmic media, earth (*pr̥thivī*), heaven (*dyauṣ*) and water (*āpas*) respectively. These correspondences are related to the Vedic schemes of mapping macrocosm and microcosm, folding cosmology into psychology. Hence, we find the combinations Speech–Fire–Earth, Mind–Sun–Heaven and Breath–Moon–Water (*BU* I.5.18-20). The set Speech–Fire–Earth corresponds to the world of Matter (*bhū*) or Earth (*pr̥thivī*), the set Breath–Moon–Water to the Midworld (*antarikṣa*) or world of Life (*bhuvar*) and the set Mind–Sun–Heaven to the world of Heaven (*dyauṣ*) or Mind (*svar*). The three sets correspond to the opening description of the *adhyāya*, that of the sacrificial cosmic Horse, with its Head figured as the Dawn with the Sun (Āditya) as its Eye (*cakṣu*), the Wind (*vāta*) as its Breath (*prāṇa*) and the Fire (Agni) as its Mouth (*vyattam*) (*BU* I.1.1). The verticality of Earth (*pṛthivī*), Midworld (*antarikṣa*) and Heaven (*dyauṣ*), or Matter, Life and Mind is even physiognomically followed in this description, the "highest" being the Eye, the "middle" the Nostrils and the "lowest" the Mouth.

Though this verticality is clearly hierarchic, its sequence is not necessarily that privileged by the *Upaniṣad*. To start with, we need to acknowledge the choice of the Horse as the initiating image of the *adhyāya* and a displacement of the anthropocentric *Puruṣa* of the Vedic Puruṣa Sūkta (*ṚV* X.90). The Sacrificial Horse indicates the kṣatriya, representing the soul force (*vīrya*) of the *vīra* (hero), or what Sri Aurobindo refers to as the Higher Vital, the victorious aspirant Life-force. Indeed, as a body of wisdom the *Upaniṣads* themselves have been thought by several scholars, including Sri Aurobindo, to be an expression of kṣatriyas. They are marked by a bold restatement of Vedic truths, displacing the superiority of brāhmaṇas and of the symbolic structure of Vedic society around rituals mediated by brāhmaṇa priests, sometimes in favour of the kṣatriyas and sometimes towards other castes or classes of society and in all cases, towards a decentralization and pluralization of spiritual access in terms of the equation of conscious Being (*Brahman*) and individual soul (*ātman*). The *Bṛhadāraṇyaka Upaniṣad* highlights the relations between a truth-seeking king Janaka and an unconventional brāhmaṇa, Yājñavalkya, who challenges the wise men and women of the court or responds to them with enigmatic wisdom, always pointing towards the experience of the identity of *Brahman* and *ātman*.

A Praxis for Kṣatriyas

The first *adhyāya* of the *Upaniṣad* provides an esoteric framework for this dramatized representation of the *Upaniṣad*, by extending a number of narrations on the origins of creation based on the supramental Time-Image of the Sacrificial Horse and its reconstitution in cosmic Being and Becoming arising from Sacrifice. The Horse Sacrifice (Aśvamedha), as mentioned earlier, is specific to the coronation of kṣatriya emperors or *cakravartins*, literally "turners of the wheel", a reference to the solar centre of our cosmic system. Later, in the fourth *brāhmaṇa* of the *Upaniṣad*, the creation of the four *varṇa*s is described as *Brahman* expressing itself integrally in/as creation in stages (*BU* I.4.11-16). In the presentation, the kṣatriya is the first expression given pre-eminence as the ruling power (*rājanya*) of all beings, hence the greatest, greater than the *brāhmaṇa*, who "prostrates himself" to the kṣatriya during the royal anointment rituals (*BU* I.4.11). But the *brāhmaṇa* is considered the "womb" (*yoni*) of the kṣatriya, hence to be adored and respected by the kṣatriya (ibid.). The enigma of this mutual relation is developed later, when it is declared that *Brahman* manifested directly as fire (*agni*) among the gods and brāhmaṇa (integral knowledge) among humans (*BU* I.4.15). Brāhmaṇa here is the integral knowledge born in human beings. By expression of its *kṣatra* power, it produced the kṣatriya, by its vaiśya power it produced the vaiśya and by its śūdra power it produced the śūdra (ibid.). Hence, power (*kṣatra tejas* of the kṣatriya), collective unity (*viśva-saṁgraha* of the vaiśya) and nurture (*poṣaṇa śakti* of the śūdra) are shown to be progressive emanations of *Brahman*. This is an early example of the idea of *caturvyūha* (emanational) manifestation, which we later find in the theory of the *avatāra-vibhava* in Pāñcarātra cosmogony (Srinivasan 1979: 39-54). In the fourth *brāhmaṇa* of the *Bṛhadāraṇyaka*, *Brahman* in its self-expression was not fulfilled by the manifestation of these four emanations and manifested further as *dharma* surpassing the "ruling power" of the kṣatriya

(*BU* I.4.14). *Dharma* is that which holds together the cosmos and all its beings and their expressions. If there is hierarchy among the *varṇas*, *dharma* exceeds the highest and can be invoked equally by the lowest (ibid.). The *Upaniṣad* declares that though humans wish to reach the world of the gods (fulfilment of spiritual goals) through fire and the world of the humans (fulfilment of social goals) through the brāhmaṇa, if they die without knowing their own world, it is of no use to them (*BU* I.4.15). At this point, the *Upaniṣad* declares that all individuals should only venerate their own Self (*ātman*) as their world (*BU* I.4.16).

This is a very interesting sequence in which the absolute and the macrocosm are equated with the essence of the individual as microcosm, passing emanationally through the cosmic and social structures laid down by the Vedic society. We find, first a displacement of the brāhmaṇa-centric system towards a kṣatriya-centric one; next, a reinstatement of the brāhmaṇa but a further decentralization through the acknowledgement of the other *varṇa*s as necessary to the integral expression of *Brahman*; next, the establishment of the principle of *dharma* as superior to all *varṇa*s and the true authority of the kṣatriya; and finally a complete decentralization of *dharma* to all individuals as their own selves (*ātman*) known as the foundation of all worlds (*loka*s). We can think of this as a precursor to the *Gītā*'s (XVIII.40-48) idea of *dharma* inhering in each individual as soul-quality, *svadharma* based in the unique individualization of *Brahman* in the form of *svabhāva* (see Aurobindo 1997: 507-25). But most germane to our purpose here, this restructuring is initiated through the centring of the "ruling power" (*rājanya*) of the kṣatriya.

Returning to the system of three psychological powers, gods and their respective "worlds" with which we began, the triplicities Eye (*cakṣu*) – Sun (Āditya) – Heaven (*dyauṣ*), Breath (*prāṇa*) – Wind (Vāyu) – Midworld (*antarikṣa*) and Speech (*vāc*) – Fire (Agni) – Earth (*pṛthivī*), though there seems to be a natural hierarchy in this sequence, the *Upaniṣad* jumbles this hierarchy, privileging the second, particularly its individual manifestation *prāṇa* (Life-force) and its god, Vāyu (Wind) over the others. This is the power and the presiding deity of the kṣatriya. At the same time, just as in the discussion of the *varṇa*s, it avoids a rigid systematization, deliberately complexifying this hierarchy through alternative systems throughout its narration. Indeed, such a flexible understanding of system is what the *Bṛhadāraṇyaka Upaniṣad* seems to be encouraging in its reader, a departure from rigid prescriptional sequences and algorithms that, it may be supposed had become a trend in the ritualization of practice in the symbolic society of the Veda. Indeed, if the Upaniṣads represent an attempt at countering this trend, it must be seen as short-lived, since soon after we have the eponymous apophatic enumeration of Sāṁkhya, the algorithmic enumeration of the Buddhist four "noble" truths (*catur ārya satyāni*) and eightfold path, the elaborate enumerations of Jainism, the prescriptions of the Dharmaśāstras and the *kriyā*-based ritual praxis of Tantra and *pūjā*.

Praxeological Systems

Characteristic of the playful subversion of this trend in the *Bṛhadāraṇyaka* is the ninth *brāhmaṇa* of its third *adhyāya*, where Yājñavalkya is queried by Vidagdha Śākalya in the court of King Janaka about the number of gods (*BU* III.9.1-9). Yājñavalkya replies successively, 3003, 303, 33, 6, 3, 2, 1½ and 1. These include the pantheons of Vedic gods, the subject–object systems of the three vertical worlds (earth–midworld–heaven), food, breath and wind (ibid.). The final One is *Brahman*, known both as the Unknowable That (*tyad*) and as Breath (*prāṇa*) (*BU* III.9.9). It is interesting to note the privileging of Wind (Vāyu) and breath (*prāṇa*) and the identity of *prāṇa* and *Brahman* as the One in this narration, repeating the privileging of faculties and gods in the last *brāhmaṇa* of the first *adhyāya*. However, as with the discussion of *varṇa*, this privilege is not asserted in an absolute manner throughout the first *adhyāya*, the basis in *ātman* (Self) of all faculties and in *Brahman* of all gods reiterated throughout and variant hierarchies presented in various *brāhmaṇas*. As a text aimed at kṣatriyas and in a broader sense, at a dynamic understanding of Truth and action, this privilege accorded to the identity of *prāṇa* and *ātman* must be seen not as absolute but praxeological, that is, relative to the practice of kṣatriyas and a *yoga* of works in the world.

Vāyu and *prāṇa* as primary forms of *Brahman* and *ātman* respectively are asserted in the fifth and sixth *brāhmaṇas*, within a system privileging of the three gods, Sun (Āditya), Wind (Vāyu) and Fire (Agni), and psychological properties, sight (or mental perception), breath (Life-force) and speech. In the sixth *brāhmaṇa*, name (*nāma*), form (*rūpa*) and work (*karma*) are asserted as the phenomenological elements of cosmic experience (*BU* I.6.1). These are related to psychological properties of speech (*vāc*), sight (*cakṣu*) and self (*ātman*) (*BU* I.6.1-3). It is interesting that work takes its origin in the self (*ātman*) here. It reminds us of the second *brāhmaṇa*, which begins with the re-emergence of the cosmic Horse from the nothingness of Death. Here, it is the concealed presence of the sacrificed Horse, image of the solar Truth, which becomes the Hunger of Death and desiring a self, becomes a "Mind of Death" which gives birth to the elements, as from a nascent Memory (*BU* I.2.1). Among the first acts of this emergence is the "moving about" (*acarat*) "worshipping" (*arcan*) of this Mind of Death-Hunger (ibid.). Death-Hunger (*aśanāyā mṛtyu*) is another name for the *avidyā* (Ignorance), whose self is soul of Knowledge-seeking. Its primordial activity, in finding a cosmic form for itself is "moving about worshipping", calling on the hidden Transcendent to manifest. This is the essence of "work" in the cosmos. It is seen here as a direct action of *ātman*. The nature of this action as a distributed circulation of aspiring energy is seen in the Veda to be that of the Wind

God (*Vāyu*).[1] However, as with the Veda, gods are seldom distinct in the early *Upaniṣads*. This energy is often attributed to Kratu, the creative Will, equated with Agni, the Fire God[2] as with Vāyu. As pointed to earlier, the sound syllables used to describe this action, *arcan acarat*, are a combination of *ṛ* and *ca*, conducive to imagining the kindling and burning of Fire. Fire itself is a property of the solar deity Āditya, sometimes known as Arka, who is also invoked in this emergence (see *ṚV* IV.16, VI.73). These gods are immanent in the initiating activity of the Self of Ignorance (*avidyā*) and emerge with its worshipping movement. In succession, the cosmic elements with their subjective properties produced by this action are Water (*āpas*), Joy or Bliss (*kaṁ*, identified as the essence of Arka, Fire/Sun – *arkasya arkatvam*), Earth (*pṛthivī*) and Fire (*agni*) (*BU* I.2.1). Fire now made itsself (*ātman*) threefold, remaining one-third Fire and becoming a third Wind (*vāyu*) and a third Sun (Āditya), (re-)forming the triple-souled Self of the emergent cosmic Horse in the Becoming (*BU* I.2.3). We see here, the gods Wind (*vāyu*) and Sun (Āditya) to be the self-transformations of the Fire God, Agni. This is in keeping with the Veda, where Agni is often referred to as a god who carries all the gods and brings them with itself to the seeker (*ṚV* I.1.2, 5). It would seem

---

1 Hymns to Vāyu often refer to its chariot with many horses, signifying a widespread and powerful working. – See *ṚV* IV.48.5 in Aurobindo 1998: 307, 313-14. Vāyu hymns are also most often related to the work of expressing sacrificial energies and the enjoyment of drinking *soma*, the principle of Bliss that is generated in the working, as one may see in the first *ṛk* of *Ṛgveda* IV.48: "Do thou manifest the sacrificial energies that are unmanifested, even as a revealer of felicity and doer of the work; Oh Vāyu, come in thy car of happy light to the drinking of the *soma* wine." – Aurobindo 1998: 306, 310-11

2 In the first hymn of the *Ṛgveda*, Agni is invoked as *kavi-kratu*, the seer-will. Its work of aspiration is intentional and intuitional. – See *Ṛgveda* I.1.5 in Aurobindo 2013: 117-18

here, that unlike the fifth and sixth *brāhmaṇa*, it is Fire which is the primordial Divine. Yet, as if in the same breath (no pun intended), it is referred to, with its transformations as the breath of Life (*prāṇa*) (*BU* I.2.3).

In the sixth *brāhmaṇa* too, Work is seen as an expression of the Self (*ātman*), which is spoken of as one among the triplicity of Speech (*vāc*), Sight (*cakṣu*) and Self (*ātman*), and itself the One Self of the triplicity (*BU* I.6.3). We are reminded that Speech (*vāc*) is related to Fire (*agni*), Sight (*cakṣu*) is related to Sun (Āditya) and Breath (*prāṇa*) is related to Wind (Vāyu) in *brāhmaṇa*s 2 and 3, all three forming the triple souled Self (*ātman*) which is also Breath (*prāṇa*) in *brāhmaṇa* 2. In *brāhmaṇa* 6, the triplicity, while being asserted as one, is also divided into two – the appearance and the reality, the phenomenal and the noumenal (ibid.). The phenomenal is the world of name and form (*nāma–rūpa*), correlated to the gods Speech (*vāc*) and Sight (*cakṣu*) respectively, the noumenal is the Self (*ātman*). Though it has a phenomenal expression in Work (*karma*), it is invisible itself and purely noumenal. However, Speech and Sight, which hide it, are also its parts in essence, being part of its triplicity. Here the *Upaniṣad* can be compared with the Platonic division of the phenomenal and noumenal, and body and soul. We see that the *Upaniṣad*'s division of the two is not a distinct separation, as with Plato (1996). The phenomenal hides the noumenal but inheres in it, just as the noumenal inheres essentially in the phenomenal. This simultaneous independence and inherence of the Self in all the faculties and vice versa is repeated in several of the *brāhmaṇa*s. In *brāhmaṇa* 3, the "breath in the mouth" (*āsye 'ntar prāṇaḥ*) takes the place of the self (*ātman*) of the gods, seen as the faculties of speech (*vāc*), Life-force (*prāṇa*), sight (*cakṣu*), hearing (*śrotra*) and mind (*mana*) (*BU* I.3.7). It is equated to the forefather Aṅgirasa of the Veda, the name disjoined creatively as *aṅga* + *rasa* (essence of the limbs), referring to the inherence or immanence of the *ātman* or One Self in all faculties seen as the limbs or parts of phenomenal experience (*BU* I.3.8). Similarly, these five faculty-gods and the self (*ātman*) are re-invoked in *brāhmaṇa* 4, where the self, though invisible, is spoken of as being signified by the faculties, which function as its "foot-traces"; it is also asserted that to know each and all of the faculties one must meditate on the self (*ātman*) (*BU* I.4.7-8). We see here the epistemological role played by the *ātman* in uniting macrocosm and microcosm due to its transcendence and immanence in the whole and its parts. This is brought home with even greater force later in *brāhmaṇa* 4, when the divided manifestations of *Brahman* as the *varṇa*s and its universal manifestation as *dharma* are both declared to be knowable as one through the *ātman*, which is spoken of as the true world of each being (microcosm) and the world of all beings (macrocosm) (*BU* I.4.15-16). In the words of a later *Upaniṣad*, the *Kaṭha Upaniṣad*, the *ātman* is thus invoked as

> *nityo 'nityānām cetanaścetanānām eko bahunām* ।
>
> The one permanent among transient things, the single consciousness in conscious beings, the one in the many.
> – *KU* II.2.13

Numerologies

As with the narrations of variant structures in the virtual constitution of the cosmic (and individual) Self and as in the case of Yājñavalkya's response to the number of gods, the first *adhyāya* seems to revel in alternative numerologies. We have one Self-presentation of *Brahman* as Real-Idea or Time-Image of Being in the form of the Sacrificial Horse in *brāhmaṇa* 1 (*BU* I.1.1), one Mind of Death-Hunger (*aśanāyā mṛtyu*) which reconstitutes the Horse in cosmic virtuality and replicates it in individual becomings in *brāhmaṇa* 2 (*BU* I.2.1), one "breath in the mouth" which is free of the power of Death and integrates all the cosmic faculties in *brāhmaṇa* 3 (*BU* I.3.7), one post-anthropic world-soul (*ātman* as *Puruṣa*) which, as radical infinity, intuited its Other and split itself into the foundation of relationality, becoming the infinite creatures of the world (*BU* I.4.1-3); and one *Brahman* which expressed its integrality, emanating the four *varṇa*s along with the cosmic principle of *dharma* and became immanent in all beings as *ātman* in *brāhmaṇa* 4 (*BU* I.4.11-13), one middle breath (*madhyama prāṇa*) and one predominant god, Vāyu who never fell under the influence of Death and remains unwearied in their continuance in *brāhmaṇa* 5 (*BU* I.5.21-23) and one self (*ātman*) which is identified as breath (*prāṇa*) hidden by the world of appearances in *brāhmaṇa* 6 (*BU* I.6.3).

We have 2, the Mind of Death and Speech, which, through intercourse, produce all creatures in *brāhmaṇa* 2 (*BU* I.2.4); later in the same *brāhmaṇa*, we have two, the Sun (Āditya) and the Horse Sacrifice (Aśvamedha) or Being and Becoming, which can be known as one in the Self of all things, even Death, bringing immortality (*BU* I.1.7). In *brāhmaṇa* 3, we have the two kinds of cosmic beings produced by Prajāpati, gods and demons (*deva*s and *asura*s), who contend against each other for supremacy (*BU* I.3.1). In *brāhmaṇa* 4, we have the division of *Brahman* to two, which coupled to generate the graded multiplicity of creatures in the cosmos (*BU* I.4.3-4) and in the same *brāhmaṇa*, we also have two, the world of name and form or of Speech and Sight, within which the *ātman* enters as essence, also manifest as *prāṇa* (breath) (*BU* I.4.7).

We have already encountered a number of threes and are faced with the privileging of the number 3 in *brāhmaṇa* 6. These three, Sun (Āditya), Wind (Vāyu) and Fire (Agni), with their corresponding faculties Sight (*cakṣu*), Breath (*prāṇa*) and Speech (*vāc*) are featured in *brāhmaṇa* 1 in the description of the head of the Horse (*BU* I.1.1); again, they repeat in *brāhmaṇa* 2 in the threefold Self of the reconstituted Horse (*BU* I.2.3); in *brāhmaṇa* 5, Prajāpati keeps a variation of these three, here Mind (*mana*), Breath (*prāṇa*) and Speech (*vāc*) for himself, meaning for his *ātman*, in other words, they form the self of the cosmic becoming (*BU* I.5.4). In stanzas 4 to 13 and 16, this threesome is correlated with varieties of threesomes in the universe (*BU* I.5.4-13). In stanza 13, it is asserted that each of these 3 is infinite and each is equal to the others (*BU* I.5.13). Thus, though the privileging of Breath indicates a praxeological preference for this dynamic component in the *Bṛhadāraṇyaka Upaniṣad*, one may conceive of the other two gods, the Sun (Āditya) or the Fire (Agni) or its correlate, Speech (Vāc) as equally primary handles of praxis. Indeed, this is often the case in other and later Upaniṣads. For example, the *Kaṭha* and the *Īśa Upaniṣad*, both privilege the Sun. The *Īśa* ends with the vision of the integral godhead *Brahman* seen as the Sun (*IU* 15-16) and the *Kaṭha* elaborates on the image of the chariot with its goal in the highest seat of Viṣṇu, the solar godhead (*KU* I.3.9). Similarly, the *Māṇḍūkya Upaniṣad*, which is centred on the *praṇava* or the sound-syllable *oṁ*, privileges Speech (Vāc) (Aurobindo 2001: 193-96). In some other *Upaniṣad*s these three are varied; for example, in the allegory of *Brahman* and the blade of grass in the *Kena Upaniṣad* we find the gods Agni (Fire), Vāyu (Wind) and Indra, of whom it is Indra who is privileged. Indra here takes the place of Āditya, being a Mind god (*KeU* III-IV).

There are several other numbers described, for example, the eight planar directions (*dik, diśā*) and three vertical worlds (*pṛthivī, antarikṣa* and *dyauṣ*) in *brāhmaṇa*s 1 and 2, the four *varṇa*s in *brāhmaṇa* 4 and the seven kinds of food produced by Prajāpati in *brāhmaṇa* 5. But the other most common number repeated is five. These are mostly the faculties Speech (*vāc*), Life-force (*prāṇa*), Sight (*cakṣu*), Hearing (*śrotra*) and Mind (*mana*). These are related to the gods Fire (Agni), Wind (Vāyu), Sun (Āditya), Directions (Diśaḥ) and Moon (Candramā). We find them first in *brāhmaṇa* 3 as the gods on earth who dwell with their antagonists, the demons and who are victorious through the help of the "breath in the mouth", who is revealed as the self and essence of all the gods united in it as in a transindividual. In *brāhmaṇa* 5, as we saw, we have the three gods, Mind, Speech and

Breath, that Prajāpati keeps for himself. In stanza 3 of *brāhmaṇa* 5, Mind (*mana*) is made to subsume Sight (*cakṣu*) and Hearing (*śrotra*). If we accept this reduction, then the five faculties are reduced to three, related once more to the three major gods, seen as praxeological handles of *ātman* realization. Privileging the Breath, the fifth *brāhmaṇa* ends with the praxical core of the first *adhyāya*:

> *... ekam eva vratam caretprāṇyāc caiva apānyāc ca nen mā pāpmā mṛtyur apnuvad iti yady u caret samāpipayiṣet teno etasyai devatāyai sāyujyaṁ salokatāṁ jayati* ||
>
> Let a person perform one observance only, he should breathe in and breathe out, wishing, "May not the evil of Death capture me". And when he performs it, let him try to complete it. Thereby he wins union with that divinity and residence in the same world with him.

The "union with that divinity" is a reference to *brāhmaṇa* 2, stanza 7:

> *eṣa ha vā aśvamedho ya eṣa tapati tasya saṁvatsara ātmā ayam agnir arka stasyeme lokā ātmāna stāv etāv arkāśvamedhau so punar ekaiva devatā bhavati mṛtyureva āpa punarmṛtyuṁ jayati nainaṁ mṛtyurāpnoti mṛtyurasyātmā bhavati etāsāṁ devatānām eko bhavati* ||
>
> Verily, that (Sun) which gives heat is the Horse sacrifice. His body is the year. This fire is the *arka*, whose selves are these worlds. So these two are the *arka* and the Aśvamedha (Horse sacrifice). These two, again, become one god, indeed, Death. He who knows this conquers repeated death; death cannot overcome him; death becomes his self; and he becomes one with these deities.

Here, the original status of the Sacrificial Horse as the Real-Idea or Being as presented in the first *adhyāya* is invoked as the solar godhead, while its sacrificed earthly Becoming is identified with the sacrificial Fire (*arka*) aspiring to establish its latent identity with the Real-Idea of Being. This Self of Being and Becoming seen as One is the *yoga* that knows its timeless immortality and its temporal eternity. It is the self of all the gods, even Death, hence superior to its/their instrumentality. The breathing practice prescribed in *brāhmaṇa* 6, therefore, needs to be understood in its fullness in terms of this double identity with the Self of Being and Becoming. This fulfils the goal of the *Upaniṣad* set up in stanza 28 of the third *brāhmaṇa*:

> *asato mā sadgamaya tamaso mā jyotirgamaya mr̥tyormā 'mr̥taṁ gamaya*

॥ *oṁ śāntīḥ śāntīḥ śāntiḥ* ॥

The Book of Honey
Adhyāya II: Madhu Kāṇḍa

Brāhmaṇa 1: Experiencers and the Experiencer

1. *Oṁ*. Once there lived a man of the Gārgya clan named Dṛpta-Bālāki, who was a teacher of Vedic knowledge. He said to Ajātaśatru, king of Kāśī: "I will tell you about *Brahman*". Ajātaśatru said: "For this proposal I will give you a thousand (cows). People will indeed come running, saying: 'Janaka, Janaka'."

2. Gārgya said: "That person (*puruṣa*) who is in the sun, I worship him as *Brahman*." Ajātaśatru said: "Please do not talk to me about him. I adulate him as all-surpassing, as the head and king of all beings." Whosoever thus adulates him becomes all-surpassing, the head and king of all beings.

3. Gārgya said: "That person (*puruṣa*) who is in the moon, I worship him as *Brahman*." Ajātaśatru said: "Please do not talk to me about him. I adulate him as the great, white-robed King Soma." Whosoever thus adulates him has abundant *soma* pressed for him everyday and his food never runs short.

4. Gārgya said: "That person (*puruṣa*) who is in the lightning, I worship him as *Brahman*." Ajātaśatru said: "Please do not talk to me about him. I adulate him as the radiant one." Whosoever thus adulates him becomes radiant and his progeny too becomes radiant.

5. Gārgya said: "This person (*puruṣa*) who is in Space (*ākāśa*), I worship him as *Brahman*." Ajātaśatru said: "Please do not talk about him. I adulate him as full and unexhausted." Whosoever thus adulates him is filled with progeny and cattle, and his progeny will never be extinct.

6. Gārgya said: "This person (*puruṣa*) who is in the Wind (Vāyu), I worship him as *Brahman*." Ajātaśatru said: "Please

do not talk about him. I adulate him as the Lord (Indra), as irresistible and as the unvanquished army." Whosoever thus adulates him becomes ever victorious, invincible and a conqueror of enemies.

7. Gārgya said: "This person (*puruṣa*) who is in fire (*agni*), I worship him as *Brahman*." Ajātaśatru said: "Please do not talk about him. I adulate him as irresistible." Whosoever thus adulates him becomes irresistible and his progeny becomes irresistible.

8. Gārgya said: "This person (*puruṣa*) who is in water, I worship him as *Brahman*." Ajātaśatru said: "Please do not talk about him. I adulate him as an image." Whosoever thus adulates him, to him comes what is like him, not what is unlike him and to him are born children who are like him.

9. Gārgya said: "This person (*puruṣa*) who is in the mirror/ideal, I worship him as *Brahman*." Ajātaśatru said: "Please do not talk about him. I adulate him as the shining one." Whosoever thus adulates him becomes shining and his progeny too becomes shining and he outshines all those with whom he comes in contact.

10. Gārgya said: "The sound that arises behind a man while he walks, I worship as *Brahman*." Ajātaśatru said: "Please do not talk about him. I adulate him as life." Whosoever thus adulates him reaches his full life-span on this earth and life does not depart from him before the completion of that time.

11. Gārgya said: "This person (*puruṣa*) who is in the directions, I worship him as *Brahman*." Ajātaśatru said: "Please do not talk about him. I adulate him as the double who never leaves us." Whosoever thus adulates him receives a double who does not part with him.

12. Gārgya said: "This person (*puruṣa*) who consists of shadow, I worship him as *Brahman*." Ajātaśatru said: "Please do not talk about him. I adulate him as death." Whosoever thus adulates him reaches his full life-span on this earth and death does not overtake him before the completion of that time.

13. Gārgya said: "This person (*puruṣa*) who is in the self (*ātman*), I worship him as *Brahman*." Ajātaśatru said: "Please do not talk about him. I adulate him as self-possessed." Whosoever thus adulates him becomes self-possessed and his progeny too becomes self-possessed. Gārgya remained silent.

14. Ajātaśatru said: "Is this all?" "That is all." "By knowing that much one cannot know *Brahman*." "Let me approach you as a student," said Gārgya.

15. Ajātaśatru said: "It is contrary to normal practice that a brāhmaṇa should approach a kṣatriya, thinking: 'He will teach me about *Brahman*.' Nevertheless, I will instruct you." So saying, he took Gārgya by the hand and rose. They came to a sleeping man. Ajātaśatru addressed him by these names: "Oh Soma, great king dressed in white." The man did not get up. The king touched him with his hand. Then he awoke.

16. Ajātaśatru said: "When this man was thus asleep, where was the person consisting of knowledge (*vijñānamaya puruṣa*) and whence did it return?" Gārgya did not know the answer.

17. Ajātaśatru said: "When this man was asleep, the person of knowledge (*vijñānamaya puruṣa*) having gathered the cognitive functions of the life-energies (*prāṇa*) and rests in the Space (*ākāśa*) within the heart. When this person absorbs these (cognitive functions) thus, it is said to be in dream-state. Then breath, speech, sight, hearing and mind are in the grasp of this person (of knowledge)."

18. Wherever he may travel in his dreams, these become his worlds. He then may become a great king or a high brāhmaṇa or may attain high or low states. Even as a great king, taking with him his retinue of citizens, moves about, according to his pleasure, within his own domain, so does the self (*ātman*), taking with it the life-functions (*prāṇa*), move about according to its pleasure, in the body.

19. Next, when he enters the state of dreamless sleep (*suṣupti*) – when it does not know anything – returning through the 72,000 nerves called *hitā*, which extend from the heart to the

> pericardium it comes to rest in the pericardium. As a young man or an emperor or a great brāhmaṇa lives, having reached the summit of bliss, so does he rest.
>
> 20. The spider moves along the thread it spins, or as small sparks fly in all directions from a fire, even so from this Self (*ātman*) emerge all the life-functions (*prāṇas*), all worlds (*lokas*), all gods (*devas*), all beings (*bhūtāni*). Its secret name (*upaniṣad*) is "the Truth of truth". The vital breaths are the truth and this is their truth.

THE first *adhyāya* of the *Bṛhadāraṇyaka Upaniṣad* established its ontology and ontogenesis in terms of contemplative philosophy. The first two *brāhmaṇas* confronted us with the Real-Idea of cosmic Being and Becoming through the Time-Image of the regnal Horse and its sacrifice, reconstitution and reproductions. The third *brāhmaṇa* introduced an axiology in terms of the struggle between the gods and demons furthering an evolution of consciousness individualized by the secret "breath in the mouth" or psychic spirit-entity. The fourth *brāhmaṇa* established the identity of *Brahman* (Being) and *ātman* (Self) as foundation and as cosmic distribution. The fifth *brāhmaṇa* dealt with the varieties of experience in terms of food and its inexhaustible function in sustaining and evolving the cosmos; and the short sixth and final *brāhmaṇa* returned us to a reduction to three divinities or cosmic handles of contemplation and identity from the numerologies introduced in the previous *brāhmaṇas*; and further reduced these finally to two exoteric realities, name and form (*nāma–rūpa*), and one esoteric one hidden by these two, the hidden breath (*prāṇa*), which it identified with Self.

This *adhyāya* may thus be considered a cosmic ontology. *Adhyāya* 2 shifts the theatre of contemplation to the human psyche, a move from a cosmology to a psychology. The first *brāhmaṇa* of the second *adhyāya* already introduces us to this through a dialogue between two humans who represent two castes, a brāhmaṇa and a kṣatriya. To highlight the countercultural aspect of this dialogue, the teaching roles are reversed – the brāhmaṇa begins by extending a teaching to the kṣatriya, but the latter betters him in each case and turns the table on him when the brāhmaṇa asks to become his disciple and is given a psychological lesson on *Brahman*. This *brāhmaṇa* is a foretaste of the second *kāṇḍa* of the *Upaniṣad*, the Muni Kāṇḍa, constituting the third and fourth *adhyāyas*, which is staged as conversations between the unconventional brāhmaṇa sage Yājñavalkya and the philosopher-king Janaka or between Yājñavalkya and the other scholars (*paṇḍits*) of Janaka's court. In fact, a number of references from the start of this *brāhmaṇa* relate us to the next *kāṇḍa*, shadowing the future. In this respect, it is not just a dialogue between a brāhmaṇa and a kṣatriya, but between two styles of knowledge, book knowledge and knowledge of experience. It is thus reminiscent of Platonic dialogues, conducted between Socrates and the Sophists. The Sophists are professional philosophers and orators, who are less concerned about the subject they are talking about than in the cleverness of the argument. Socrates, on the other hand, stands for existential thinking, philosophy as transformative inquiry into living and its possibilities and imperatives. Dṛpta-Bālāki is introduced as an *anūcāna*, an scholar and explainer of the Vedas. Though not exactly a Sophist, he is like them in not being primarily interested in experience but rather in book knowledge. Like the more conventional brāhmaṇa scholars in Janaka's court, he understands *Brahman* in terms of the gods or cosmic functionaries instead of the infinite Absolute. Dṛpta-Bālāki is introduced to us as a Gārgya, prefiguring one of the more erudite and wise opponents of Yājñavalkya from the court of Janaka, the female scholar Gārgī. Similarly, the King Ajātaśatru starts his conversation with Dṛpta-Bālāki with a snide comment referring to King Janaka, accepting the brāhmaṇa's offer to teach him about *Brahman* with the counter of mock payment of a thousand (cows) as a consequence of fame gained as a king through comparison with Janaka (the people will run hither saying "Janaka, Janaka").

We have noted, towards the end of *brāhmaṇa* 3 of the first *adhyāya*, the double entendre around the word *sama* in relation to *Brahman*. On one level, the stanzas refer to the *Sāmaveda* (Veda of song) whose hymns were used in Vedic rituals. *Svara* (voice or vocal tone) and accuracy of intonation is held to be its perfection. This also refers to the Vedic use of the word *Brahman*, which means the Vedic Word, in literal ritual interpretation, the perfect enunciation of the scriptural texts which was meant to make the gods manifest. At another level, that of the revised semantics of the *Upaniṣad*, *Brahman* was the "smooth space" of the undifferentiated absolute consciousness, equal everywhere, which had differentiated itself in becoming cosmos. *Sama* at this register meant equal, the ontological basis of absolute *Brahman*; and *svara* was the "fourth world" or Supermind beyond earth (*pṛthvī*), midworld (*antarikṣa*) and heaven (*dyauṣ*), the forgotten mystical goal of the Vedic *ṛṣis*. *Brāhmaṇa* 1 of *adhyāya* II intends a similar distinction – the Vedic understanding of *Brahman* as different gods attained through ritual invocation and the Upaniṣadic revision to refer to the experience of a non-dual consciousness attainted through contemplation and psychological identity.

Dṛpta-Bālāki successively indicates a number of cosmic functionaries, the gods, referring to each of them as *Brahman*. In each case, Ajātaśatru dismisses the identification with the words "Do not talk to me about him" and proceeds to explain the specific function served by the deity and the result of worshipping him. In this manner, the narrative cycles through twelve deities or "persons" (*puruṣa*), each of whom is identified as *Brahman*. We have encountered several of these as cosmic functionaries related to the sacrificial horse of *adhyāya* I, *brāhmaṇas* 1 and 2, also identified as gods in *brāhmaṇa* 3. *Brāhmaṇa* 3 was an allegory designed to show how the gods are subject to the dualities and cannot overcome their contraries without the aid of "the breath in the mouth", an identifier for the dynamic form of the self (*ātman*). Here, attention is drawn to the bounded infinity that each of them represents, a relative infinity belonging to a world of relations subject to the relation of the Subject and the Object.

In early Greek classical philosophy, the question of Being is posed by Aristotle in two ways – Being is the indescribable ground of all beings; but it makes itself available in experience as the totality of our experience of all beings. The latter access to Being is that of it which is subject to a cosmic phenomenology. It is the "greatest of all beings", a comparative superlative, rather than the "Being of all beings".[1] It is this limitation that characterizes the gods, each one the greatest of its domain, but not free from the bounds of this domain. The gods start from the greatest of them all, the sun God, equated in the Veda to the Supreme Being. A solar myth underlies the Veda and its metaphoricity pervades Vedic society. We have seen this in the case of the *cakravartin* and ritual of the sacrificial horse. Thus, Dṛpta-Bālāki's identification of *Brahman* begins with the sun, but Ajātaśatru dismisses it summarily, putting it in its functional place: "I worship him as all-surpassing, the head and king of all beings. He who worships him becomes all-surpassing, the head and king of all beings." The king of all kings, the emperor (*cakravartin*) is by definition bound in its relationality to the realm of beings – i.e. existence. Its ontology is not independent or absolute. In saying this, Ajātaśatru immediately claims a difference-in-kind between *Brahman* and the realm of existence. *Brahman* is Being in Aristotle's sense of the "Being of all beings" not "the greatest or totality of all beings". It is also the Being beyond all beings, that which grants being to each being yet remains unexhausted by all beings.

---

[1] As discussed by Heidegger in *Introduction to Metaphysics*, pp. 199-200, 1959, New Haven, CT: Yale University Press.

Dṛpta-Bālāki continues his identification through alternative supremes, each a god of its domain – the persons (*puruṣas*) of the moon, the lightning, space, wind, fire, water, mirror-reflection or ideal, the sound which follows one, the directions, the shadow and the sense of self. The first three are sources of illumination, the next four are the subtle or fluid media of manifestation, the last four are related to the phenomenal constitution of the individual. As the sun illuminates the objective world, the moon illuminates the subjective world and lightning illuminates the fragmented world of mental intuition. Ether, wind, fire and water constitute four of the five elements of the Upaniṣadic conception, the subtle elements which precede materiality. Each of these extends a world of its own. These are followed by four persons related to an inferential sense of phenomenal individual existence. First comes the person in the mirror or the ideal (*ādarśa*), who reflects an ideal image; Ajātaśatru identifies him as "the shining one", both because it is an image of light and an ideal image. Next is the person of the sound which follows one; this is an enigmatic idea referring either to an occult experience or to the "buzz" created by one's activities.

Our present creates our past in its wake through the plural images it leaves in the minds and words of others, the sound that follows one. Ajātaśatru identifies this as the being of life. This is followed by the being of the directions. We saw in *brāhmaṇa* 3 of *adhyāya* I how the directions were related to hearing; they present us with a located sense of self in the world. Ajātaśatru identifies this being with one's "double", a spatial image through which one is located. Next is the person of the shadow; Ajātaśatru identifies this with death, the inverse image that is tied to us and reminds us of non-being that doubles our existence and waits to erase it into the unknowable. The final inferential being is our sense of self. It is interesting to see that the word *ātman* is used for this, demonstrating the current existence of two senses to the word *ātman*. Somewhat later, in the fifth century, BCE, the Buddha, in his second sermon, proceeds through a demonstration of the absence of a permanent self to the phenomenal constituents of individual experience (*skanda*). The term *anātman* used here for the Buddha's demonstration assumes the meaning of *ātman* as "permanent self", by definition lacking in the impermanent constituents of phenomenal experience. It also means that in common usage *ātman* was confused with these phenomenal constituents, as it is here. Ajātaśatru assumes that Dṛpta-Bālāki means this loose sense of the ego (*aham*) when he says *ātman* and Dṛpta-Bālāki does not contest this repudiation. Ajātaśatru identifies this person as "self-possessed" (*ātmanvī*), characterized by a distinct finite sense of self, not the independent self (*ātman*).

Dṛpta-Bālāki has exhausted his understanding of *Brahman* at this point. Ajātaśatru asks him is he has anything more to say and Dṛpta-Bālāki says that is all. "With just this much it is not known" asserts Ajātaśatru and Dṛpta-Bālāki experiences a moment of reversal, asking Ajātaśatru to become his teacher. As if to rub in the countercultural significance of this act, the text makes Ajātaśatru state explicitly that this violates the convention relating to brāhmaṇas and kṣatriyas but he will make an exception and teach Dṛpta-Bālāki. In the Introduction, I have discussed the possible kṣatriya origin of the Upaniṣads, particularly the early ones. While this is probable, the reversal of caste roles could equally be a countercultural strategy of the imagination characterizing this form of minor literature. It is interesting to note the irony of history in the canonization of the Upaniṣads as Vedic texts, "the end of the Veda" and indeed, post-Śaṅkara, as "the essence of the Veda". While this last may be true from a certain point of view, without noting its countercultural intent, it is merely an appropriation that serves one or more orthodoxies.

Ajātaśatru then displaces the consideration of *Brahman* from the cosmological to the psychological by dramatizing the experience of the cosmos in terms of the human experiencer and its states or conditions (*avasthā*) of experience. Ajātaśatru takes

Dṛpta-Bālāki to a sleeping man and upon waking him, raises the question of the experiencer in its states of waking and sleep. It is interesting to note that his question is asked with respect to the *Vijñānamaya Puruṣa*. Radhakrishnan translates this as "person consisting of intelligence" and Olivelle translates it as "person consisting of perception". If we are to go by other early Upaniṣads, such as the *Taittirīya Upaniṣad, vijñāna* is neither intelligence nor perception but gnosis, what Sri Aurobindo refers to as Supermind. The *Taittirīya Upaniṣad* locates it beyond the Mind (*mana*). It is the Mind that is responsible for the trenchant experience of dualities, at the foundation of which is the duality of the Subject and Object. The experiencer in us is immersed in the world of the Object and knows its Subjecthood in its terms. In the waking experience it is the waking subject, bound by the laws of waking experience; in the dreaming experience, it is the dreaming subject, the laws of whose world are quite different and more fluid than those of the waking experience. However, the experiencer is the same in each case and is possessed of the same apparatus of senses, mind and other life-functions (*prāṇa*). In the first *adhyāya* of the *Bṛhadāraṇyaka Upaniṣad*, these life-functions are identified in terms of the subjective functions of the gods, seeing, hearing, thinking, breathing and speaking. In the third *brāhmaṇa*, the god related to seeing is the Sun, to hearing are the Directions, to thinking is the Moon, to breathing is the Wind and to speaking is Fire. By the time of the *Kaṭha Upaniṣad*, this experiencing apparatus is identified in terms of the body (*śarīra*), the senses (*indriya*), the mind (*mana*) and the intelligence (*buddhi*). Perhaps following this, in Sāṁkhya, the apparatus becomes the senses (*indriya*), the sense-mind (*manas*), the ego (*ahaṁkāra*) and the intelligence (*buddhi*). The experiencer in all these cases is *Puruṣa* (or *ātman* in the case of the *Kaṭha Upaniṣad*), but in this second *adhyāya* of the *Bṛhadāraṇyaka Upaniṣad* it is identified as *Vijñānamaya Puruṣa* (Person of Gnosis). The apparatus and faculties of knowledge are the properties of the

Being of Knowledge, who takes the knowledge of these faculties with it to locate itself hermetically in the space within the heart (*antar-hṛdaya ākāśa*) during dreaming sleep. It is no longer the subject of the waking world nor is the waking world with its laws of coherence of time, space and individuality its object. It may change its subjecthood to become a king or brāhmaṇa or other being or creature and roam about in other worlds with other laws of time and space which are then its object. This contemplation is meant to complicate our notion of the Being of Knowledge we all are. The Being of Knowledge experiences itself differently through different modes of knowledge under different conditions of experience, yet the Being of Knowledge supersedes its conditions of knowledge and remains the same. Finally, passing through a special channel (*nāḍī*) named *hitā* in a system of 72,000 channels, it enters a covering of the heart. The term used for this is *purītatam*, which is the pericardium, a membraneous envelope of the heart, in later Sanskrit. Evidently, the text is referring to an esoteric anatomy in this verse, perhaps the equivalent of "the cave of the heart" which is considered the seat of the reincarnating self in the *Kaṭha Upaniṣad*. Here, the Being of Knowledge enters the state of deep dreamless sleep, the term used being *suṣupti*, literally sleep in sleep. This term is repeated in the *Māṇḍūkya Upaniṣad* for the third condition of (non-)experience, beyond the waking and the dreaming. In the *Māṇḍūkya Upaniṣad*, there is a fourth condition, merely known as "the fourth" (*turīya*) to refer to an absolute unmanifest condition. The state of *suṣupti* takes the experiencer out of the subject–object system into the origin beyond subject and object and hence beyond experience. The question of whether the Being of Knowledge is able to determine other conditions of knowledge for itself is not discussed. In entering the dreamless sleep it realizes utter non-duality as a sublime state of stasis in bliss, described in comparison with the "highest bliss (*ānanda*) that a youth, a king or a great brāhmaṇa (*mahā*-brāhmaṇa) might rest in (as a state of non-experience). One sees here an affirmation of the *Taittirīya Upaniṣad*'s identification of Bliss (*ānanda*) as the non-dual foundation of all existence and experience. This is also dealt with in *brāhmaṇa* 5 of this *adhyāya* of the *Bṛhadāraṇyaka Upaniṣad*, the Madhu *brāhmaṇa* or *brāhmaṇa* of Honey, which gives its name to the first two *adhyāya*s as Madhu Kāṇḍa. But, is this a state of Knowledge also, since the Being of Knowledge is experiencing itself in this state? This question is left unanswered here.

However, the *brāhmaṇa* ends with a stanza affirming this Self (once more the term *ātman* is used here, undoubtedly in a different sense than that used by Dṛpta-Bālāki and in implication as equivalent to the *Vijñānamaya Puruṣa*) as the creative source of Subject, Object and World. Its manifestations are likened to the lines of thread spun by a spider or the sparks emerging from a fire: "As a spider spins forth its thread, as sparks fly from a fire, so indeed do all vital functions (*prāṇa*), all worlds, all gods and all beings spring from this Self (*ātman*). Its secret name (*upaniṣad*) is the truth of truths. For the *prāṇa*s are the truth and this is the truth of the *prāṇa*s." In this way, the *brāhmaṇa*, after challenging the misidentification of *Brahman* with the gods, integrates them along with the worlds, the creatures and the experiencing apparatus and forces of each individual (*prāṇa*s) in the non-dual origin of the Being of Knowledge (*Vijñānamaya Puruṣa*) in its independent condition, equated with the Self (*ātman*) and with *Brahman*. Even though located in the esoteric anatomy of each individual, this is the transcendent *Brahman*, One without a second (*ekamevādvitīyam brahma*) present in and as each vital function (*prāṇa*), each creature, each god and each world. Implicit in the *brāhmaṇa* is the creative function of this self-becoming, one and infinite at the same time, which mobilizes the laws by which it holds together the subjective experiences, creatures and gods in each world of experience. It does so by the power of Knowledge or Gnosis (*vijñāna*) which is its Truth of Truths and its secret name (*Upaniṣad*). It is instructive to compare this self and person to the *Puruṣa* of Sāṁkhya. Sāṁkhya is a dualistic system, it separates *Puruṣa* from the appearances of *Prakṛti*. Like the *Vijñānamaya Puruṣa*, *Puruṣa* of Sāṁkhya can be known outside the play of the senses and the world. However, *Puruṣa* of Sāṁkhya is without quality, no quality can be asserted of it, since all quality belongs to *Prakṛti*, which is ontologically separate from *Puruṣa*. In the case of the *Vijñānamaya Puruṣa*, it is the non-dual Source of Subject and Object, its intrinsic self-experience (*svānubhava*) is bliss (*ānanda*) and its self-nature (*svabhāva*) is knowledge. This differentiates Vedānta from Sāṁkhya, the first is primordially and integrally non-dual, while the latter remains dual.

Brāhmaṇa 2: The Fractal Cosmic Individual

1. He who knows the new-born (calf) together with its dwelling space, its activity space, its post and its rope, keeps away his seven hostile kinsmen. The central breath is indeed the calf; this (body) is its dwelling space, this (head) its activity space, the life-breath (*prāṇa*) its post and food its rope.

2. The seven undecaying ones stand in attendance (on the calf): through these red lines in the eye, Rudra is united with him; through the water in the eye, Parjanya; through the pupil of the eye, Āditya; through the black (of the eye), Agni; through the white, Indra; through the lower eyelid, the earth (*pṛthvī*) and through the upper eyelid, heaven (*dyauṣ*). He who knows this, his food does not diminish.

3. Regarding this, there is the following verse: "There is a bowl which has its mouth below and bottom up. Within it, a glory of universal forms is placed. Seven sages sit on its rim and speech is the eighth, which communicates with *Brahman*." What is called the "bowl which has its mouth below and bottom up" is this head of ours, for it is a bowl which has its mouth below and which bulges at the top. When it is said: "Manifold knowledge has been put into it", this refers to the

life-breaths; these indeed represent manifold knowledge. When it is said: "Seven sages sit on its rim", this refers to the organs of life-functions; they indeed are the sages. "Speech which communicates with *Brahman*, is the eighth" because the organ of speech is the eighth and communicates with *Brahman*.

4. These two (ears) are Gautama and Bharadvāja: this one (the right) is Gautama and this one (the left), Bharadvāja. These two eyes are Viśvāmitra and Jamadagni: this one (the right) is Viśvāmitra and this one (the left), Jamadagni. These two nostrils are Vasiṣṭha and Kaśyapa: this one (the right) is Vasiṣṭha and this one (the left), Kaśyapa. The tongue is Atri, for through the tongue food is eaten. Atri is the same as *atti* (eating). He who knows this becomes the eater of everything and everything becomes his food.

Having established its monistic foundation in terms of knowledge or gnosis in the first *brāhmaṇa*, the second *brāhmaṇa* breaks into three contemplative images relating microcosm, macrocosm and the non-dual inhabitant. It begins with an image of a new-born calf (*śiśu*) tied to a post by a rope in its stable. The terms of the image are explicated – the calf is the central breath, the post is breath or vitality, the rope is food, the living space of the stable is the body and the activity space of the stable is the head. This, then is a contemplation of the human body with the inhabitant shown to be the "central breath". We have come across this central breath before in *adhyāya* I, in *brāhmaṇa* 3 it was called "the breath in the mouth". We identified it there as the vital aspect of the soul, pneuma or "holy ghost". The image of a psychic breath tied to the body by material means is a surreal image and speaks to the nexus between the non-material and materiality in human experience. Matter, according to Indian psychology, is generally described as part physical or gross (*sthūla*) and part non-physical or subtle (*sūkṣma*). This is also the general premodern animistic description of physicality, revived in philosophical terms in our time by Henri Bergson (1988).[2]

2 See the Introduction to *Matter and Memory*, pp. 9-16.

Thus, the distance between the rope and the post measures the gradations of the flesh moving from physical materiality to non-physical vitality. It also redefines "food" to be both what we eat and what we experience in terms of the energetic component of our interactions. The vital aspect of the soul (the central breath) is tied to this spectrum of physicality and contained within it. Its foundation is the frame of the body and its covering is the head, representing the mental component. Contemplating this allows us to centre the immaterial and unformed aspect of the psychic entity as the inhabitant in the body. It also shows us the function of food, vitality and the body. We do not eat or experience/ exercise our vitality for their own sake but for the sake of that which they feed and enrich with experience, the subtle soul, keeping it tied to the physical existence. Contemplating this image allows us to align our functions, establishing the union (*yoga*) for which they exist according to the *Upaniṣad*.

The image also refers to the seven hostile kinsmen, who are kept at bay if one knows this and experiences it. This returns us to *brāhmaṇa* 3 of the first *adhyāya*, the contest of the gods and demons. The gods there are individualized and made functional in the human vital functions – seeing, hearing, smelling/ breathing, thinking and speaking/eating. They are related to the organs the eyes, the ears, the nostrils, the mind and the mouth. The divine potential of each of these is contested by the demons, who know how to infect each of them with evil. Thus, in a way, we can say that each of these gods comes with its demonic counterpart – the evil potential in each of the vital functions. The seven hostile kinsmen are these evil opposites of the gods in the vital functions physically specialized in the orifices of the sense organs. They operate in and as the two eyes, the two ears, the two nostrils and the mouth. As with the third *brāhmaṇa*, where it took the intervention of the breath in the mouth to tip the balance in favour of the gods for overcoming the demons and establishing a divine transformation, here too, we are told that it is this psychic constitution of the human physical/vital/ mental system that keeps away the influence of the demons. Interestingly, they are called "the hostile kinsmen" because they are intimately tied to their opposites, the divine potential of the senses and vital functions.

This image of the physical/vital/psychic individual is followed by an abrupt microscopic zoom into the eye seen in reflexological terms. If the gods inhabit different parts of the horse's body in the first *brāhmaṇa* of *adhyāya* I and if they inhabit the different senses/vital functions in *brāhmaṇa* 3 (tacitly referred to in the previous stanza), this close-up of the eye establishes the fractal constitution of the cosmos. Not only are the cosmic functionaries present in each individual in their varied parts and functions, they are all equally present in each part of each individual. This brings to mind the *pūrṇam* chant which is expressed in *adhyāya* V of the *Bṛhadāraṇyaka Upaniṣad* V.1.1. The whole in emanating a part of itself does not cease to be the whole in and as the part; nor does the remainder after emanation lose any of its wholeness. In this consideration of the eye, seven imperishable/immortal gods reside in its various parts – Rudra in the red streaks of the eye, Parjanya in the water of the eye, Āditya in the pupil of the eye, Agni in the black of the eye, Indra in the white of the eye, Pṛthvī (Earth) in the lower eyelid and Dyauṣ (heaven) in the upper eyelid. Once we establish the central constitution of the psychic individuality, we proceed in this stanza to sacralize each part of the body by contemplating its divine constitution. This contemplation is an early instance of the visualization praxis of *nyāsa* in Tantra, by which the goddesses are established in each part of the body leading to a divine transformation.

This image is followed by a zooming out to see the head as an inverted bowl with the Vedic *ṛṣi*s (seers) seated on its rim and Speech (*vāk*) as that which communicates with *Brahman*. Inside the bowl is placed a glory of universal forms (*viśva-rūpa*).

This time, the vital functions/senses are imaged not as gods but as seers. The glory of universal forms are said to be placed in the "breaths" or vital energies in the mind which is physically located in the head. The outer gates of these vital breaths are the senses that are identified with the *ṛṣis*. These are given in three sets of pairs which are indicated orally without explicit naming. This refers to the oral and secret nature of transmission, where the senses would be physically indicated by the teacher. These three sets are clearly the two eyes, the two ears and the nostrils. The seventh seer sits on the tongue. The seers (in pairs) are: Gautama and Bharadvāja, Viśvāmitra and Jamadagni, Vasiṣṭha and Kaśyapa. The seventh seer on the tongue is Atri. Seers, instead of gods, refer to the receptive function of the sense-intuitions. We are reminded of Blake's famous lines:

> If the doors of perception were cleansed, everything would appear to man as it is: infinite.[3]

Each sense, operating in its purity is a seer that perceives the universal and infinite (glory of universal forms) in the particular and finite. This *yoga* of the senses serves a function of communication with *Brahman* through the word of the poet (*kavi*). The other function of the mouth, i.e. eating, is served by the *ṛṣi* Atri. As with Aditi in *brāhmaṇa* 2, Atri is turned into a pun for eating (*atti*). This is an aspect of the *Upaniṣad*'s humour, at the same time relating eating to a sacred function of nourishing the soul (the central breath) in its woṛk of individuating the cosmos and connecting heaven and earth.

Brāhmaṇa 3: This, That and the One

> 1. Truly, there are two forms of *Brahman*: having appearance and lacking appearance, mortal and immortal, immobile and mobile, actual and transcendental.

---

[3] William Blake, 1868, *The Marriage of Heaven and Hell*, p. 14, London: John Camden Hotten.

> 2. The form having appearance is that which is other than Wind (Vāyu) and the intermediate space (*antarikṣa*). It is mortal, immobile and actual (*sat*). The essence (*rasa*) of that which has appearance, which is mortal, which is immobile and which is actual is that which gives heat (*tapati*), for that is the essence of the actual (*sat*).
>
> 3. Now the form without appearance: It is Wind (Vāyu) and the intermediate space. It is immortal, it is mobile and it is transcendental (*tyat*). The essence of that which is without appearance, which is immortal, which is mobile and which is transcendental (*tyat*) is the Person (*Puruṣa*) in this circle (*maṇḍala*), for that Person is the essence of the transcendental (*tyat*). This is with reference to the gods (*ādhidaiva*).
>
> 4. Now with reference to the self (*adhyātma*): The form having appearance is that which is other than the life-breath (*prāṇa*) and the space (*ākāśa*) of the inner self (*antarātmā*). It is mortal, it is immobile and it is actual (*sat*). The essence of that which has appearance, which is mortal, which is immobile and which is actual is the eye; for it (the eye) is the essence of the actual (*sat*).
>
> 5. Now the form without appearance: It is the life-breath (*prāṇa*) and the space (*ākāśa*) of the inner self (*antarātmā*). It is immortal, it is mobile and it is transcendental (*tyat*). The essence of that which has no appearance, which is immortal, which is mobile and which is transcendental is the person (*puruṣa*) that is in the right eye, for that person is the essence of the transcendental (*tyat*).
>
> 6. The form of that person is like a cloth dyed with turmeric, or like pale sheep's wool, or like the scarlet insect called *indragopa*, or like a tongue of fire, or like a white lotus, or like a flash of lightning. He who knows this attains divinity (*śrī*) like a flash of lightning. Now, therefore, the injunction (*ādeśa*): "Not this, not this" (*neti, neti*); for there is nothing else beyond this "Not this". Now its name: "The Truth of truth". The life-breath (*prāṇa*) is truth (*satyam*) and this is the Truth of that.

Having related the microcosmic and the macrocosmic, the

individual and the cosmos, the realm of the self (*ātman*) and the realm of the gods (*devas*) in *brāhmaṇa* 2, the *adhyāya* moves to a cosmological topography in *brāhmaṇa* 3. This topography acknowledges our experience of the paradoxical conjoining of materiality and immateriality in individual and cosmos. Reality or Truth (*Satyam*) is broken into the actual (*sat*) and the virtual or transcendental (*tyam*). What the senses experience is the empirical appearance of the actual (*sat*) while what remains transcendental is the immaterial foundation of the material. Together they compose *Satyam* (Truth). This is *Brahman* but each of these components is also pronounced from the outset as a form (*rūpa*) of *Brahman*. "There are two forms of *Brahman*, with fixed shape and shapeless, mortal and immortal, stable and changing, *sat* and *tyat*." The word play is significant here, since it indicates the integral nature of these two conjoined realms, refusing dismissal of either. This is relevant to note when comparing the Upaniṣads to their later interpretations by the Vedāntic scholars of the post-eighth century CE. Moreover, it is also significant because the privileging of idealism in the later Upaniṣads and more so in later interpretations of the Upaniṣads prioritizes the non-material as eternal and static, while in this topography, the empirical is acknowledged first as the unchanging.

Brahman having sensible form, which is mortal and unchanging is that which is other than the Wind (Vāyu) and the intermediate world (*antarikṣa*); in other words, it is the world of Matter (*Pṛthvī*). This is the actual form of *Brahman*. Its essence is declared to be that which gives heat. Matter is considered a form of dense concentration of consciousness (*tapas*); concentration of consciousness results in heat. This is also a reference to Agni, the God of Fire, which is the solar presence immanent in Matter. Alternately, the form without sensible appearance is the Wind (Vāyu) and the intermediate world (*antarikṣa*). This is immortal, dynamic and transcendental (*tyat*). Its essence is the Person (*Puruṣa*) in the (solar) cosmic circle. This distinction is then asserted as pertaining to the gods or cosmic functionaries (*ādhidaiva*), in other words, to the macrocosm.

The *brāhmaṇa* then asserts the same distinction for the individual microcosm, calling it that which pertains to the self (*ādhyātmika*). Here, that which has sensible appearance (*mūrta*), is stable or fixed, mortal and actual is other than the life-breath (*prāṇa*) and the space (*ākāśa*) of the inner self (*antarātman*); in other words, this is the physical body; its essence (*rasa*) is asserted to be the eye. We are reminded of the microscopic eye reflexological description of the previous *brāhmaṇa* following the description of the physical–psychical complex. The eyes are the windows of the soul, its primary material receptors for experience or soul-food.

That which is without sensible appearance is asserted to be the life-breath and the space of the inner self; it is immortal, dynamic and transcendental (*tyat*). Its essence is the Person (*Puruṣa*) in the right eye for that is the essence of the transcendental.

This is how the macrocosm and microcosm are both described in terms of materiality as actual and vitality as transcendental. The essence of both is the solar realm – of the material the concentrated force of the solar *tapas* for the cosmos and the eye for the individual – the equation of the eye of the sacrificial horse with the sun in *brāhmaṇa* 1 is invoked here; and of the virtual, the *Puruṣa* (Person, Subject) of the sun for the cosmos and of the eye for the individual. The solar Person (*Puruṣa*) is the seer through his eye and the world he sees comes to light through the sun. The eye and the sun are thus receiver and transmitter of its non-dual self-imaginings in/as cosmos and individual.

In a final stanza, two sets of approaches to this non-dual *Puruṣa* who is the source of the two realms in both cosmos and individual are offered – a cataphatic approach for the empirical and material, and an apophatic approach for the transcendental. The cataphatic is a set of sensible images that serve as symbols or signals for anamnesis – i.e. the psychic memory that connects the two realms. These are given as a golden cloth, white wool, a small scarlet insect (*indragopa*), a flame, a white lotus and a flash of lightning. It is unknown if the saffron robe was a sign of renunciation (*saṁnyāsa*) at the time of composition of this text, but even if it was and if the image referenced this as a starting point, each of these images is offered as a contemplation beyond expected conventions or ideological propaganda, a phenomenology of signs. The colours white or red or gold predominate, as integrating or penetrating focus awakening a state of pre-literate gnosis. A golden cloth may open an undivided smooth space of solar origin, the Vedic realm of Aditi, which has modulated itself into the invisible and dynamic intermediate region (*antarikṣa*) of the Wind (Vāyu) and the visible stable world of Matter (Pṛthvī). White wool, in its softness and sublimity, like snow or cloud, evokes a fathomless depth of maternal wisdom supporting existence. The small scarlet insect (*indragopa*), like an intense ruby crystal, evokes a primordial consciousness-particle that can locate itself instantly at any point as an act of concentration (*tapas*), as the power of manifesting the unmanifest. A flame can awake the sleeping will to knowledge involved as the solar origin in matter, a sign of the psychic memory, the knower of births (*jātaveda*). The white lotus is an image of the evolution of consciousness from the inconscient and its passage through the gradations of consciousness till its disclosure as a great divine bloom of harmonious complex oneness, the Mother of solar origin, Aditi. A flash of lightning is the operation of hidden knowledge as an inexplicable intuition, sometimes thought of as the action of Divine Grace, a hurled shaft of Indra bridging the transcendental and empirical worlds, bringing "sudden enlightenment". It is this image of sudden or inexplicable enlightenment that is made the capstone of the cataphatic series with the favourite stock phrase of this *kāṇḍa* denoting the method of no method (*anupāya*) – *ya evam veda* – he who knows this: "He who knows this attains divinity (*asya śrīr bhavati*) like a sudden flash of lightning". Thus, these images are signs with diverse divine potential, any or some or all of them may provide a key at the sensible or imaginary level for a divine opening for different people. Each is a door and an indication to integral fulfilment.

However, the stanza follows this cataphatic set with an apophatic praxis – "Now therefore the injunction (*ādeśa*) not this, not this (*neti neti*) for there is nothing beyond this, this that it is not this". Following the cataphatic images, it weans us from every foothold of a referent; if any of the images opens a door for us, we cannot attach ourselves to any known sensory, energetic or intellectual experience of the image as defining or limiting that to which it leads. The image itself then reveals itself to be nothing we have known or could know about it but the unknowable self-revealed in becoming to the aspirant as the non-dual Person (Puruṣa) that s/he is. The stanza ends by reconstituting the two "forms of *Brahman*", the material and the transcendental, the *sat* and the *tyam* whose separate existences it had explicated: "Now it is name – the truth of the truth (*satasya satyam*)". We realize a telescoped system of truths – *tyam* (that, the transcendental) was the truth of *sat* (the actual, the material) and the integral solar *Puruṣa* who reconstitutes the division of these two (*satyam*) is the truth of the transcendental: "Indeed, the life-breath (*prāṇa*) is truth (*satyam*) and He is the truth (*satyam*) of that".

Brāhmaṇa 4: Separative Knowledge and Gnosis

1. "Maitreyī", said Yājñavalkya, "Look, I am about to leave this place. So let me make a settlement between you and Kātyāyanī."

2. Thereupon Maitreyī said: "Sir, if indeed the whole earth, full of wealth was mine, would I be immortal through that?" "No", said Yājñavalkya, "as the life of the rich, so would your life be.

Of Immortality, however, there is no hope through wealth."

3. Then Maitreyī said: "What should I do with that which would not make me immortal? That which you know (as the means of attaining immortality), sir, tell me that."

4. Yājñavalkya replied: "Beloved, indeed you have been dear to me and now you speak dear words. Come, sit down; I will explain to you. As I am explaining, concentrate (*nididhyāsana*) on what I say."

5. Then Yājñavalkya said: "Truly, not for the desire of the husband is the husband beloved, he is beloved for the desire of the self. Not for the desire of the wife is the wife beloved, she is beloved for the desire of the self. Not for the desire of the sons are the sons beloved, they are beloved for the desire of the self. Not for the desire of wealth is wealth beloved, it is beloved for the desire of the self. Not for the desire of the brāhmaṇa is the brāhmaṇa beloved, he is beloved for the desire of the self. Not for the desire of the kṣatriya is the kṣatriya beloved, he is beloved for the desire of the self. Not for the desire of the worlds are the worlds beloved, they are beloved for the desire of the self. Not for the desire of the gods are the gods beloved, they are beloved for the desire of the self. Not for the desire of beings are beings beloved, they are beloved for the desire of the self. Not for the desire of the Whole is the Whole beloved, it is beloved for the desire of the self. Truly, Maitreyī, it is the Self that is meant to be seen, heard, reflected on and entered into oneness with. By seeing, hearing, reflection and knowledge of the Self, all this is known."

6. "The *brāhma* (priestly) power abandons one who thinks of it as residing in anything other than the self. The *kṣatra* (ruling) power abandons one who thinks of it as residing in anything other than the self. The worlds abandon one who thinks of them as residing in anything other than the self. The gods abandon one who thinks of them as residing in anything other than the self. The beings abandon one who thinks of them as residing in anything other than the self. The Whole abandons one who thinks of it as residing in anything other than the self.

This *brāhma* power, this *kṣatra* power, these worlds, these gods, these beings and this Whole are that Self (*ātman*)."

7. "As when a drum is beaten, its external sounds cannot be grasped, but by grasping the drum or the drummer the sounds are grasped."

8. "As when a conch is blown, its external sounds cannot be grasped, but by grasping the conch or the blower of the conch the sounds are grasped."

9. "As when a *vīṇā* (string instrument) is struck, its external sounds cannot be grasped, but by grasping the *vīṇā* or the player of the *vīṇā* the sounds are grasped."

10. "As from a fire kindled with wet fuel various kinds of smoke issue forth, even so, my dear, the *Ṛgveda*, the *Yajurveda*, the *Sāmaveda*, the *Atharvāṅgirasa*, history (*itihāsa*), mythology (*purāṇa*), arts (*vidyā*), the Upaniṣads, verses (*śloka*s), aphorisms (*sūtra*s), elucidations (*anuvyākhyāna*s) and explanations (*vyākhyāna*s) are the inhalations and exhalations (*niḥśvasitāni*) of this immense Being. All these are indeed its breathing."

11. "As the ocean is the destination of all waters, as the skin is the destination of all touch, as the nostrils are the destination of all smells, as the tongue is the destination of all tastes, as the ear is the destination of all sounds, as the mind is the destination of all intentions, as the heart is the destination of all forms of knowledge, as the hands are the destination of all actions, as the sexual organ is the destination of all pleasures, as the anus is the destination of all excretions, as the feet are the destination of all movements, as the organ of speech is the destination of all the Vedas."

12. "As a lump of salt dropped in water dissolves and cannot be grasped separately anymore, but wherever we taste the water it tastes salt, even so, my dear, this great Being, infinite, shoreless is dense with Knowledge (*vijñānaghana*). Arising with these beings it disappears with their destruction. Having departed there is no sense-knowledge (*saṁjñā*). This I say, my dear." So said Yājñavalkya.

13. Then Maitreyī said: "Just here you have bewildered me, Sir, by saying that after departure there is no more sense-knowledge (*saṁjñā*)." Yājñavalkya replied: "Certainly I am not saying anything confusing. This is sufficient for the knowledge of *vijñāna*."

14. "For when there is any duality, then one smells another, one sees another, one hears another, one speaks to another, one thinks of another, one knows another. But when all has become the Self, then what should one smell and by what means, what should one see and by what means, what should one hear and by what means, what should one speak and by what means, what should one think and by what means, what should one know and by what means? That by which all is known, by what means can that be known; by what, my dear, should one know the Knower?"

The second *adhyāya* started with a conversation between a kṣatriya king who was a knower of *Brahman* and a brāhmaṇa priest who worshipped the gods. The conversation, apart from its countercultural social message, opened a contemplative consideration of the relationship between the cosmological and the psychological in terms of *Brahman* and *ātman*. This consideration continued in a more theoretical vein through *brāhmaṇa*s 2 and 3, where the double constitution of cosmological and psychological was further doubled in terms of the empirical and the transcendental. Following on the introduction of correspondences in the image of the sacrificial horse in *adhyāya* I *brāhmaṇa* 1, these *brāhmaṇa*s related the material–vital complex between individual and cosmos in terms of the relationship of the Sun and eye, deriving them both back to the *Puruṣa*. *Puruṣa* has become cosmos and individual by manifesting as the cosmic functions in both. In the cosmos, these functions manifest through the cosmic functionaries, the gods and in the individual they manifest through the vital functions, named here the *prāṇa*s. A prime such correspondence, which was chosen for explication in these *brāhmaṇa*s was the function of visibility manifest cosmically through the sun and individually through the eye. The implication of these contemplations was to seek the non-dual source of the correspondence as the Person (*Puruṣa*) through the function of sight.

Brāhmaṇa 4 returns us to a conversation so as to bring these ideas into our expected existence and in this case, for the first time, brings the conversation into the intimate domestic domain. Thus, this is the demonstration of another, perhaps most fitting, context for the intimate speech of "sitting near" (*upaniṣad*). We are also introduced for the first time to Yājñavalkya, the protagonist of the third and fourth *adhyāyas*, who is traditionally held to be the author of this *Upaniṣad*. The *brāhmaṇa* starts abruptly with Yājñavalkya announcing to one of his (two) wives Maitreyī that he is leaving this place and wishes to make a settlement with both his wives. Yājñavalkya's entries into the text are often with a shock and a flourish, in keeping with his unconventional nature, which forces thought. In this first appearance, we realize that he is taking a decision to leave his household, though we are not told why or where. We also realize that he has two wives, among whom he will divide his belongings. Those familiar with Indian legends would not be surprised with kings having two wives, but for a *brāhmaṇa* to have two wives was less expected. Later, we will see that Yājñavalkya thinks nothing of amassing wealth from contests, indeed does so in a tongue in cheek manner as if to expose the hypocrisy of others. This abrupt gesture of renunciation is equally a shock, demonstrating that wealth or wives are equally nothing when he decides to seek other aims of life. Radhakrishnan gives an explicit social content to this gesture, as referring to the transition from the life of the householder (*gṛhasthya*) to that of a forest-dwelling renunciant (*vānaprastha*), but this conclusion is unwarranted, since it is very unlikely that these formal institutionalized stages of life existed at this time. Yājñavalkya is not following a convention, it is more likely that he is taking a spontaneous existential action, that might have later become a model for an institutional convention.

Why he is departing and what he thinks of material possessions comes to light through the response of Maitreyī, who smells a rat – what is Yājñavalkya in search for that he is renouncing his possessions with impunity? She asks – If all the wealth of the world was mine would I be immortal through that? She tests out the stakes for immortality and Yājñavalkya's sardonic humour is awakened in his answer: "No, with riches you will only be a rich person. Through wealth one cannot expect immortality." Immortality eludes the market, it is not a commodity to be bought or sold. Maitreyī then rejects the offer of material settlement by Yājñavalkya, since it will not bring the knowledge of immortality and asks Yājñavalkya to impart what he knows of this knowledge. Yājñavalkya is pleased with Maitreyī's aspiration and proceeds to instruct her. The set-up for this instruction is a literal demonstration of *Upaniṣad*, the intimate wisdom of "sitting near". The qualities of physical and affective intimacy and the concentration leading to non-duality that are involved in this transmission are dramatized in Yājñavalkya's reply to Maitreyī prior to instruction: "Beloved, indeed you have been dear to me and now you speak dear words. Come, sit down; I will explain to you. As I am explaining, concentrate on what I say." The term used for the attitude Yājñavalkya expects from Maitreyī as he explains is given as *nididhyāsana*. This word will recur as the culminating essence of Yājñavalkya's formula for praxis – *darśana, śravaṇa, manana, nididhyāsana* (seeing, hearing, reflecting and entering into non-dual relation). *Nididhyāsana* is an empathic depth of concentration leading to deep relationality and union.

The gist of Yājñavalkya's instruction is carried in stanza 5 of the *brāhmaṇa*, a section of text which is among the most famous in the Upaniṣads and, certainly, of all passages in the *Bṛhadāraṇyaka Upaniṣad*. Referring one by one to husband, wife, son, wealth, brāhmaṇa, kṣatriya, worlds, gods, beings and the cosmic Whole or All (*sarva*), he says that each of these is not desirable for its own sake but desirable for the sake of the self (*ātman*). Hence, it is the self (*ātman*) that should be seen, heard, contemplated and entered into intimate relation and union with. By seeing, hearing, mentally contemplating (*matya*) and entering into knowledge through union (*vijñānena*) with the Self (*ātman*) everything (*sarva*) can be known (*vidita*).

This passage is reminiscent of *brāhmaṇa* 4 of *adhyāya* I, where after introducing the castes and their inherence in Divine Law (*dharma*) and after a mention of the need for each to know its world, the Self (*ātman*) is asserted as the world of each and all of them. Here the worlds of both private and public, domestic and political relations are invoked and shown to take their non-dual origin in the Self (*ātman*). However, this is demonstrated here through a concise linguistic strategy which forces the affect to a dialectical consideration of the self (*ātman*). Each of the relations mentioned above has an affective power over us. Each of these is desirable, but Yājñavalkya forces a reversal of gaze from object to subject. Whatever is desirable is because I find it desirable. At an empirical level, this desirability may hide itself in nobility, piety or compassion, but could not exist if it did not serve a selfish affect. The more this affect is wrapped up in an empirical sense of separate self, the more possessive I am about its objects. This is self as ego (*ahaṁkāra*), which is a distorted or limited self (*ātman*). It reminds us of the erroneous use of *ātman* made by Dṛpta-Bālāki in *brāhmaṇa* 1 of this *adhyāya*, which Ajātaśatru rejects. Understanding each of these relations in this manner is a psychologically unsentimental disillusionment to one's self-deceptions. This is a starting point to a deeper contemplation of the basis of one's relations. However, it is not untrue that what I find desirable in others is because I am receptive to its qualities that exist universally in the objective world. And as the previous *brāhmaṇa* has held, behind the empirical or actual self is the transcendental immanent self (*ātman*) and person (*Puruṣa*), who is the source of experience. This has become the empirical experiencer as the empirical self and its objects of experience in the objective world. The subjective–objective experience of all things is in truth for the experience of this experiencer, the Self of selves and worlds (*ātman*). After recognizing the subjective root of desirability, we can open to the intuition of the non-dual subject and self of subjective and objective reality through depth and intensity of contemplation. This contemplation is indicated as a form of praxis in the famous lines which have reverberated through the history of Indian spirituality in a variety of contexts ranging from *pūjā* ritual to seed-syllable (*bīja mantra*) initiation and professional training in fields such as music (*saṅgīta*), art (*śilpa*) and architecture (*sthāpatya*): "Oh Maitreyī, it is the Self (*ātman*) that must be/is meant to be seen (*draṣṭavya*), heard (*śrotravya*), contemplated (*mantavya*) and known through union (*nididhyāsanavya*)." The empirical experience of seeing or hearing things which move us with joy should be subject to continuous contemplative introspection leading to an intuition of the non-dual self of both the object of relation and oneself. It is as if the object of one's relation is experienced within oneself at a transcendental level of immanence, felt as both personal and universal.

The next stanza turns its revisionary attention more explicitly to the caste system, as with *brāhmaṇa* 3 of *adhyāya* I. But as with the previous stanza on relations, this consideration is couched in terms of power. The brāhmaṇa power (power for knowledge) will abandon those who do not recognize it as residing in the *ātman*, the kṣatriya power (power to rule and administer) will abandon those who do not recognize it as residing in the *ātman*; the same is asserted for the gods, all beings and the cosmic Whole. The power of each of these will abandon the person who mistakes them to reside in anything other than the Self. All these are asserted to be nothing but the Self.

The *brāhmaṇa* then extends three sonic metaphors – that of a drum, a conch and a string instrument (*vīṇā*). In each case we are told that we cannot "catch the sound" in itself but only by catching the subject or the instrument of sound production. This returns us to the twofold constitution of all things as empirical and immanent transcendental described in the previous *brāhmaṇa*. That which cannot be materially grasped because it transcends the senses, can be grasped by its empirical traces. As a corollary, empirical events may be signs that indicate transcendental realities. The metaphor is then carried into the domains of the life-breaths and the elements. In *brāhmaṇa* 6 of *adhyāya* I we were told that the transcendental truth of beings is the life-breath (*prāṇa*), which is hidden by the empirical manifestations of name and form (*nāma–rūpa*). Here, this is expressed through the metaphor of fire burning damp fuel which produces variegated smoke depending on the objects burned. In the same manner, the Vedas, histories, sciences, poetry, aphorisms, commentaries and the secret knowledge of the Upaniṣads itself are all produced as the in-breathing and out-breathing of this immense Being, the Self of all selves. Just as the destination of all water is the ocean and the destinations of all the life-activities (*prāṇa*) – touch, smell, taste, sight, hearing, intention, knowledge, works, enjoyment, expulsion, movement and truth-speech (*veda*) are their respective organs – skin, nostrils, tongue, eyes, ears, mind, heart, hands, sex organ, anus, feet and the word (*vāg*) – so is the destination of all sensible expression of the non-sensible self (*ātman*). These metaphors are meant to expand the contemplation on the formula for imperative praxis – all things experienced through the senses (*darśana, śravaṇa*) should be taken as signs of the self (*ātman*) through contemplation (*manana*), leading to knowledge by identity of the self (*nididhyāsana*).

This set of metaphors is concluded by Yājñavalkya with a figure that is repeated in a variety of contexts in the Upaniṣads, a favourite illustration of *Brahman* – just as a chunk of salt dropped in water loses its separate existence in being dissolved, but becomes part of the water and can be found anywhere in it as the essence of its taste, so too is this vast, infinite, limitless Being dense with knowledge (*vijñānaghana*). It arises out of and together with these existences and disappears with their disappearance. In its departure, there is no more separate empirical knowledge (*saṁjñā*). It should be noted that this image of *Brahman/ātman* is one that pertains to knowledge in its distinction between separative knowledge and knowledge by identity or gnosis. The terms used for these two forms of knowledge are *saṁjñāna* (or in short *saṁjñā*) and *vijñāna*. These two terms are oft-repeated in the Upaniṣads and later Indian philosophical thought. We find their use also in Buddhism, for example in the second sermon of the Buddha, where the organs of phenomenal knowledge (*skanda*) are described. Over time, the terms mutate in meaning but in this early period, *saṁjñā* is sense-knowledge, contingent on the separation into subjects and objects, and *vijñāna* is comprehensive knowledge, unified knowledge of principles or truths-of-being by which all differentiation into existences occurs and into which they are absorbed into latency on destruction. *Saṁjñā* is empirical knowledge as we have it, received through the senses and interpreted and known by the mental subject, but *vijñāna* cannot be known by the mind, which is bound by the separation of subject and object for its operation; *vijñāna* can only be had through a non-dual faculty at the origin of this separation and of its maintenance by the mind. Sri Aurobindo has referred to this faculty as Supermind.

The essence of knowledge is not a pure conscious transcendental existence in which the very possibility of the experience of separative knowledge disappears, it is another dimension of knowledge, its origin, that from which the separative knowledge of the world is made possible. This essence of knowledge is alien to us, hence Maitreyī is confused and expresses her bewilderment to Yājñavalkya about his statement regarding the disappearance of empirical knowledge (*saṁjñā*) in departing from earthly existence. In responding, Yājñavalkya invokes the criterion of philosophical precision: "I have said nothing confusing," he responds, "this is the sufficient statement for *vijñāna*." That which bewilders the mind is the condition for opening to a knowledge that is hidden to mind. To indicate it is the condition for opening to its hidden truth, to try to explain it in the language of the mind is to provide the illusion of understanding without experience. Yājñavalkya refuses the path of this illusion. In conclusion, he reiterates the distinction between separative knowledge being based on the experience of duality, of subjects and objects, and the sensing of "others" in varied sense experience. In becoming the non-dual self, the possibility of separative knowledge returns to its source, the knower of the mental knower and its objects. Thus, Yājñavalkya ends with the contemplative enigma – "By what should one know that by which all this is known? By what, my dear, should one know the knower?"

Brāhmaṇa 5: The Section of Honey

1. This Earth is the honey of all beings and all beings are the honey of this earth. Likewise, the radiant, immortal person (*puruṣa*) who is in this earth and with respect to the self (*adhyātma*) the radiant, immortal person (*puruṣa*) who is in the body, he indeed is but this Self. This is Immortal, this is *Brahman*, this is the Whole.

2. This water is the honey of all beings and all beings are the honey of this water. Likewise, the radiant, immortal person (*puruṣa*) who is in this water and with respect to the self (*adhyātma*) the radiant, immortal person (*puruṣa*) who is in the sexual energy (*retas*), he indeed is but this Self. This is Immortal, this is *Brahman*, this is the Whole.

3. This fire is the honey of all beings and all beings are the

honey of this fire. Likewise, the radiant, immortal person (*puruṣa*) who is in this fire and with respect to the self (*adhyātma*) the radiant, immortal person (*puruṣa*) who is made of Speech (*vāṅmaya*), he indeed is but this Self. This is Immortal, this is *Brahman*, this is the Whole.

4. This Wind is the honey of all beings and all beings are the honey of this Wind. Likewise, the radiant, immortal person (*puruṣa*) who is in this Wind and with respect to the self (*adhyātma*) the radiant, immortal person (*puruṣa*) who is in the life-breath (*prāṇas*), he indeed is but this Self. This is Immortal, this is *Brahman*, this is the Whole.

5. This Sun is the honey of all beings and all beings are the honey of this Sun. Likewise, the radiant, immortal person (*puruṣa*) who is in this Sun and with respect to the self (*adhyātma*) the radiant, immortal person (*puruṣa*) who is in the Sight (*cakṣus*), he indeed is but this Self. This is Immortal, this is *Brahman*, this is the Whole.

6. These directions are the honey of all beings and all beings are the honey of these directions. Likewise, the radiant, immortal person (*puruṣa*) who is in the directions and with respect to the self (*adhyātma*) the radiant, immortal person (*puruṣa*) who is in the hearing (*śrotra*), he indeed is but this Self. This is Immortal, this is *Brahman*, this is the Whole.

7. This moon is the honey of all beings and all beings are the honey of this moon. Likewise, the radiant, immortal person (*puruṣa*) who is in this moon and with respect to the self (*adhyātma*) the radiant, immortal person (*puruṣa*) who is in the mind (*manas*), he indeed is but this Self. This is Immortal, this is *Brahman*, this is the Whole.

8. This lightning is the honey of all beings and all beings are the honey of this lightning. Likewise, the radiant, immortal person (*puruṣa*) who is in this lightning and with respect to the self (*adhyātma*) the radiant, immortal person (*puruṣa*) who is in

radiance (*taijasa*), he indeed is but this Self. This is Immortal, this is *Brahman*, this is the Whole.

9. This thunder-cloud is the honey of all beings and all beings are the honey of this thunder-cloud. Likewise, the radiant, immortal person who is in this space and with respect to the self (*adhyātma*) the radiant, immortal person in sound and in tone, he indeed is but this Self. This is Immortal, this is *Brahman*, this is the Whole.

10. This Space (*ākāśa*) is the honey of all beings and all beings are the honey of this Space (*ākāśa*). Likewise, the radiant, immortal person who is in this space and with respect to the self (*adhyātma*) the radiant, immortal person in the space of the heart, is but this Self. This is Immortal, this is *Brahman*, this is the Whole.

11. This *dharma* (Law, principle which holds together) is the honey of all beings and all beings are the honey of this *dharma*. Likewise, the radiant, immortal person who is in this *dharma* and with respect to the self, the radiant, immortal person devoted to *dharma* in the body, is indeed but this Self. This is Immortal, this is *Brahman*, this is the Whole.

12. This truth is the honey of all beings and all beings are the honey of this truth. Likewise, the radiant, immortal person who is in this truth and the radiant, immortal person devoted to truth is indeed but this Self. This is Immortal, this is *Brahman*, this is the Whole.

13. This Mental Being is the honey of all beings and all beings are the honey of this Mental Being. Likewise, the radiant, immortal person who is in the Mental Being and with respect to the Self, the radiant, immortal person in the human being is indeed but this Self. This is Immortal, this is *Brahman*, this is the Whole.

14. This self (*ātman*) is the honey of all beings and all beings are the honey of this self. Likewise, the radiant, immortal

person in the self and with respect to the (individual) self, the radiant, immortal person in the self, is indeed but this Self. This is Immortal, this is *Brahman*, this is the Whole.

15. Truly this Self is the ruler of all beings, the king of all beings. Just as all the spokes are fixed in the nave and the felloe of a chariot wheel, so are all beings, all gods, all worlds, all life-functions and all these individual selves held together in the Self.

16. This, verily, is the honey (*madhu*-doctrine) which Dadhyañc Ātharvaṇ taught the Aśvins. The *ṛṣi* perceived this and said: "Oh heroes, that awesome profitable mastery of yours I will disclose, as the thunder-cloud (discloses) the rain – that *madhu*-doctrine which Dadhyañc Ātharvaṇ taught you through the head of a horse."

17. This, verily, is the honey (*madhu*-doctrine) which Dadhyañc Ātharvaṇ taught the Aśvins. The *ṛṣi* perceived this and said: "Oh Aśvins, on Dadhyañc Ātharvaṇ you fixed a horse's head. As promised, he revealed to you Tvaṣṭṛ's honey, Oh mighty ones, that remains a secret with you."

18. This, verily, is the honey (*madhu*-doctrine) which Dadhyañc Ātharvaṇ taught the Aśvins. The *ṛṣi* perceived this and said: "He made forts with two feet; He made forts with four feet. Becoming a bird, at the beginning the Person (*puruṣa*) entered the fort." This very Person (*puruṣa*) is the fort-dweller (*purīśayaḥ*) in all forts (*pura*). There is nothing that is not protected by Him, nothing that is not pervaded by Him.

19. This, verily, is the honey (*madhu*-doctrine) which Dadhyañc Ātharvaṇ taught the Aśvins. The *ṛṣi* perceived this and said: "He became the likeness of every form. All forms exist to reveal him. The Lord (Indra), through His magical power (*māyā*), travels abroad in many forms; for to Him are yoked 110 horses." He is himself the horses; He is himself tens and thousands, many and infinite. This *Brahman* is without an earlier or a later, without an inside or an outside. This

> self is *Brahman* (*ayam ātma brahma*), all-experiencing. This is the teaching.

This section known traditionally as *madhu brāhmaṇa* brings to a close the content of the volume (*kāṇḍa*) to which it gives its name, Madhu Kāṇḍa, the volume of honey. The volume is made up of the first two chapters (*adhyāyas*) of the *Bṛhadāraṇyaka Upaniṣad*, which we have been considering. Throughout the *brāhmaṇas* of these two *adhyāyas*, the constitution of the cosmos is referred to in terms of the cosmic gods and their psychological counterparts. *Brāhmaṇa* 1 of the second *adhyāya* invoked these gods only to supersede them by the true subject that experiences through them. In *brāhmaṇa* 4 of this *adhyāya* cosmic experience was seen to take its origin in the subject, eventually in the Self (*ātman*) realized in terms of the essence of knowledge or the being of knowledge (*vijñānamaya puruṣa*). Now in this final *brāhmaṇa*, the root of all experience, including knowledge is shown as bliss (*ānanda*), imaged here as honey (*madhu*). All the gods and all the corresponding psychological functions are forms of bliss as is their experiencer, the subject. This metaphor hearkens back to hymn I.90 of the *Ṛgveda*, where four lines invoke the Divine Bliss as pervading and flowing in the cosmos in the image of honey:

> *6. May a honeyed wind blow for him who grows in Truth, may the rivers sprinkle honey,*
> *So may medicinal plants be honeyed for us.*
>
> *7. Honeyed be the night and honeyed the dawns, honeyed the terrestrial kingdom;*
> *Honeyed be our Father Heaven to us.*
>
> *8. May the trees be full of honey for us and full of honey Sūrya, the Sun-God:*
> *May his herds become honeyed for us.*

Brāhmaṇa five asserts a similar expression of cosmic bliss. The Time-Image of the Horse with which we started in *brāhmaṇa* one of the *Upaniṣad* has been taken apart through the *brāhmaṇas* of these first two *adhyāya*s, studied in its inner and outer relations, shown to be present in macrocosm and microcosm, established in the priorities of its gods, discovered in its origin as the self of all selves, shown in its essence of knowledge (*vijñānamaya*) and finally the whole is realized as the creative expression of Bliss pervading all the gods and their psychological workings as their sap and deepest essence (*rasa*).

The significance of the movement of literary forms through the second *adhyāya* should also not be lost on us. The *adhyāya* starts with a dialogue in which the gods are invoked but successively put aside as in the apophatic praxis of *neti neti*, culminating in an inward reversal and the discovery of *Brahman* in the self. This is followed by two *brāhmaṇa*s presenting images relating the empirical and transcendental aspects of reality for contemplation. After this, we return to the conversation form in the dialogue of Yājñavalkya and Maitreyī, dramatizing the ideas presented so far, so as to make them intimate and relational (*upaniṣad*), ending with the goal of realizing the non-dual source of gnosis (*vijñāna*) at the heart of all reality. This has also been a movement from the materiality of the first *brāhmaṇa* to the vitality and mentality of the second and third *brāhmaṇa*s and finally the supramentality of the fourth one, in the Upaniṣadic sequence, a movement from *anna* to *prāṇa*, *manaḥ* and finally *vijñāna*, the knowledge-essence or the non-dual Logos of the cosmos. The next step is the Subject of Bliss (*Ānandamaya Puruṣa*) who has become all this and exists as its essence, sweetness or honey. This is asserted in a choral form. It is like an impersonal hymn sung in unison by all the cosmic powers announcing the unity of the cosmos in causeless Bliss. It begins with the Earth (*pṛthvī*), then follows the sequence of elements which we saw emerging in the reconstitution of the cosmic horse in *brāhmaṇa* 2 of the first *adhyāya* – Water, Fire, Wind, Sun, Directions, Moon, Lightning, Thunder, Space – and continues to more abstract principles – *dharma* (the law-holding things, gnosis), *satyam* (truth), *mānusam* (mental beings, humanity) – ending with the Self (*ātman*). These cosmic powers are each asserted as being the honey for all beings along with its reciprocal reality of all beings being honey for it, thus establishing the relational oneness of existence in blissful mutuality of sacrifice. The use of the term honey also grounds the entire multilayered reality of Bliss in Matter as a form of food (*anna*), the very essence of taste. Each cosmic power is also asserted to be a form of the radiant immortal Divine Person (*tejomayaḥ amṛtamayaḥ puruṣaḥ*) who is simultaneously declared to be present in the individual (at the level of the self (*ātman*) as the person (*puruṣa*) of its corresponding psychological organ). These correspondences have been established in the previous *brāhmaṇa*s, starting with the first *brāhmaṇa* of the first *adhyāya* but continuing throughout, for example, more extensively in the third *brāhmaṇa* – the body for Earth, the sexual energy (*retas*) for Water, speech for Fire, the life-breath (*prāṇa*) for Wind, the eye for the Sun, the ear for the Directions, the mind for the Moon, radiance for Lightning, sound and tone for Thunder, the soul-space in the heart for Space (*ākāśa*), soul-law for cosmic Law (*dharma*), truthfulness for Truth, the human being for the Mental Being, the individual self (*ātman*) for the cosmic Self (*Ātman*). In each case, this *Puruṣa*, who is the self is declared to be immortal (*amṛta*), *Brahman* and the Whole (*sarva*). Each choral line is a repeated pattern of words in which only the terms for the cosmic god and its individual organ or functional quality are varied. With the last of these, pertaining to the Self (*ātman*), we arrive at the self-evident root of the pattern, the completion of the hermeneutic circle, which signifies only itself:

> 14. This self (*ātman*) is the honey of all beings and all beings are the honey of this self. The radiant and immortal person in this self and the radiant and immortal person in this self, this is indeed the self. It is the immortal, it is *Brahman*, it is the Whole.

The Self is then imaged as the emperor (*cakravartin*). We will recollect that the *Bṛhadāraṇyaka Upaniṣad* begins with the sacrificial Horse of the ritual leading to the establishment of the *cakravartin* (emperor). Just as the image of the Horse has been decoded as the cosmos with the Self (*ātman*) as its essence, the *cakravartin* who absorbs the power of the horse sacrifice is shown to be nothing other than the Self (*ātman*). *Cakravartin* means "turner of the wheel" and is a translation to political terms of the solar godhead at the centre of the solar system (*sūrya maṇḍala*). In its image the "imperial circle" of the emperor was known as the *rājya maṇḍala*. As with the ritual, the *Upaniṣad* is here displacing the feudal symbolism of Vedic society to centre it in the self (*ātman*) of each person. Each self is really a self-perception of the Self of all selves; hence each self is equally the centre of the cosmic circle.

> 15. This very self (*ātman*) is the lord and king of all beings. As all the spokes are fastened to the hub and the rim of a wheel, so to one's self (*ātman*) are fastened all beings, all the gods, all the worlds, all the breaths and all these selves (*ātman*).[4]

From stanzas 16 to 19, the *brāhmaṇa* breaks into verses (*ṛk*) referring to an enigmatic myth mentioned in several verses of the *Ṛgveda* as well as the *Śatapatha Brāhmaṇa* which forms the larger textual body in which the *Bṛhadāraṇyaka Upaniṣad* is contained. The *ṛk* contained in stanza 16 is taken from *Ṛgveda* I.116.12 in which the seer Kakṣivān, son of Dīrghatamas, addresses the Aśvins. Stanza 17 includes another *ṛk* attributed to the same *ṛṣi* Kakṣivān (*ṚV* I.117.22). The myth is related to the imparting of the secret of honey to the Aśvins by the Sage Dadhyañc. As told in the *Śatapatha Brāhmaṇa*, Indra bestowed the secret knowledge of Madhu to the Sage Dadhyañc with the condition that were he to disclose it to anyone, Indra would cut off his head. The Aśvin twins, who came to know of this, devised a way

---

4 This is an image reminiscent of the first line of the *Īśa Upaniṣad*.

to coax Dadhyañc to divulge the secret to them. Being divine surgeons, they replaced Dadhyañc's head with that of a horse. Dadhyañc divulged the secret to the Aśvins with this horse's head. When Indra struck off this head, the Aśvins replaced it with Dadhyañc's original head.

Stanzas 16 and 17 refer to this myth. There are three secret hints and precursors to this enigma in the prior *brāhmaṇa*s of the Madhu Kāṇḍa: the eternal event of the Horse with which the *kāṇḍa* begins, the divine horsemen, the Aśvins and the image of the head as an upturned vessel with seers (*ṛṣi*s) seated on its rim and the Divine Word communicating with heaven from its mouth from *brāhmaṇa* 2 of this *adhyāya*. We have noted how the sacrificial Horse is a solar image, symbol of solar kingship, divine Force. The Aśvins, similarly, are solar Horsemen, heralds and scouts of the Dawn who bring the joy and enthusiasm of approaching daybreak to the denizens of the Night, preparing their receptivity and their aspiration. As twins, they represent the dual qualities of being and becoming, represented in the senses by seeing and hearing or revelation and inspiration, respectively. Divine surgeons, they effect an exchange, bringing the power of solar force to the Night and receiving in return from it, the bliss of physical aspiration. This exchange is represented by the bestowal of the horse's head to Dadhyañc. The name Dadhyañc, derived from *dadhi* (curd), represents solar intelligence in the physical mind. Son of the Ṛṣi Atharvan, Dadhyañc's full name is Dadhyañc Ātharvaṇ. Atharva refers to immobility and brings to mind the two zones of *brāhmaṇa* 3 – the immobile and the mobile, the empirical or material and the transcendental or spiritual. Thus Dadhyañc Ātharvaṇ represents the physical earth mind transforming into divinized mentality and the myth expresses the secret process of evolutionary transition. Each "new Day" manifests a new potency of consciousness, a quantum leap which is prepared and effected by the being of the higher consciousness through a secret exchange, awakening the potential of the new consciousness which lies latent in the old. In these stanzas, such a transition is intended, one materialized Mind to the solar consciousness of Supermind. The Aśvins are the heralds and representatives of this solar consciousness. They temporarily uplift this mental consciousness of the earth with solar force and the earth responds with an appropriate solar aspiration, the secret word which brings the knowledge of the physical embodiment of Bliss to the solar world represented by the Aśvins. The net result is the divinization of Matter and the materialization of the solar consciousness. The Aśvins learn the secret of earthly bliss (*madhu*) which enables them to materialize, while the human is lifted to the solar consciousness temporarily for the exchange. Once the exchange is effected, the human regains its natural mental qualities, but now transformed into its overmental or supramental operations. The image of the upturned vessel in *brāhmaṇa* 2 prepares us for this transformation. As an upturned vessel, it empties downwards the divine forces of the solar world. The upturned vessel was later used on temple pillar capitals as symbols of the continuous descent of Divine Consciousness to Earth. On the other hand, as a head with seers seated on its rim in the form of the senses representing the vital functions, it is the transformed and divinized mental consciousness with its vital functions turned to channels of divine receptivity. Its mouth communicates through Speech with *Brahman*, implying the transmission of the secret knowledge of Bliss (*madhu*), in the physical to the transcendental, bringing in return the supramental divinization of Matter and the integral realization of Divine Bliss (*ānanda*).[5]

Stanza 18 starts by repeating the terms of the Dadhyañc myth and then breaks into verse related to the building of forts with 2 ft and 4 ft into which he becomes a bird and enters. The Aśvins

[5] This discussion of the Dadhyañc myth is based on the commentary of Kapali Shastry (1947) in *Lights on the Upanishads*, pp. 126-64.

jointly represent the *Puruṣa* of the solar consciousness. The *ṛk* reiterates the general process of evolutionary transition. The *Puruṣa* of a higher consciousness prepares the materials of nature to be an adequate instrument for its expression and then inhabits it. Forts with 2 and 4 ft refer to animal and human life forms. Though self (*ātman*) is everywhere, in all things and *puruṣa* (person) is potentially present in all individuals, the degrees of its potentia are awakened by successive corresponding *puruṣa*s from higher planes of consciousness. In this *ṛk*, the *Puruṣa* of the transcendental hemisphere known as *vidyā*, prepares living beings and enters them as their individuating centre, helping them to evolve to their divine types. We see here a new creative etymology of *Puruṣa* as the dweller of the *pura* (fort), fort-dweller. Person is a qualitative degree of self, equipped to express itself through an ensemble for individuation. Protected by its outer walls, it is a fort, a contained microcosm internalizing or folding the macrocosm. The bird is a descending power of light, the solar Person that miniaturizes itself to enter the new construction as its inhabitant. However, it is potentially already present in the form and its materials and in its descent, awakens its potential within the individuating being which it has prepared. Hence, the stanza following the *ṛk* asserts that the *Puruṣa* lives in all forts; there is nothing that is not protected or secured by him. We may recollect *brāhmaṇa* 2 of the first *adhyāya*, dealing with the sacrifice of the Horse. In its sacrificed state the Horse is dismembered and formless, yet the entire Horse is potentially present in its self-oblivion. In its evolutionary reconstitution, cosmically as a whole and innumerably as individuals, it is this spirit or soul of the Horse that is present in every particle and becomes progressively activated in its degrees of completeness through the evolution. In these passages on the Dadhyañc and Aśvins myth, the secret process of this evolution is held out as a panentheistic exchange in which the dispersed particles of the sacrificed *Puruṣa* are evolving towards individuations in which each individual will embody the wholeness of the Divine *Puruṣa*. This process is effected as a transpersonal exchange between the Divine *Puruṣa* and its sacrificed and individuating parts.

Stanza 19 repeats for a fourth and last time the exchange of Dadhyañc and the Aśvins and further elaborates the process of the individuation and embodiment of the *Puruṣa* that it has introduced in the previous stanzas. The *ṛk* in this stanza is taken from a Ṛgvedic hymn by Bharadvāja (*ṚV* VI.47.18). The first line of the *ṛk* is famous and has been oft-repeated in the history of Indian thought:

> *rūpam rūpam pratirūpo babhūva* ।
> *tadasya rūpam praticakṣaṇāya* ॥

> *Form and form, all forms he has become.*
> *Each of these forms exists to reveal him.*

As with all translations, there may be variant meanings. Kapali Shastry translates these lines:

> *To every form he has remained the counter-form;*
> *That is his form for us to face and see.*[6]

In either case, if we are to read it in the light of the non-dual conclusion of the stanza, it is a non-dual understanding that should prevail. In the first case, the *Puruṣa* has become all the forms it inhabits. In the language of Sāṁkhya (which is yet to appear at this time) *Puruṣa* has become all the forms of *prakṛti*. In the second case, *Puruṣa* exists as an inseparable transcendental part of every empirical form. This second reading would be in tune with *brāhmaṇa* 3 of the second *adhyāya*. The second line equally demonstrates the ambiguity of the Sanskrit language due to its syntax-free structure and phonemic flexibility. This ambiguity is deliberate from the viewpoint of consciousness, allowing for a ploygonal contemplation. "Each of these forms exists to reveal him" provides a monistic basis for expressionism

---

[6] Kapali Sastry, T.V., 1947, *Lights on the Upanishads*, p. 148.

and evolution, while "That is his form for us to face and see" puts the onus on relationality and reciprocity. These lines are followed by a vision of Indra who, by the power of his *māyā* (magic), travels abroad in all these forms, identified here as 10,000 horses to which Indra is yoked. Indra here must be understood in the literal sense as king or emperor, thus returning us through this image to the idea of the *cakravartin* and the horse sacrifice. The *cakravartin* is the "central ruling power" *kṣatras*, that should be equated with the law that holds the cosmos together. Earlier, we have been told that this is the *ātman*, in its potency as the *Puruṣa* or person of gnosis (*Vijñānamaya Puruṣa*) as well as of bliss (*madhu, Ānandamaya Puruṣa*). The stanza concludes by equating this *Puruṣa* with all his horses, indeed with innumerable and every instrumental form, multiple and infinite, connecting with the beginning lines of the *ṛk* if we take it to mean that it is the *Puruṣa* that has become all the forms it inhabits, while remaining at the centre of each of them as well as independent and unchanged in all its becomings. It is thus "inside", "as" and "outside" all things. The stanza (and the *brāhmaṇa, adhyāya* and *kāṇḍa*) ends with a description of *Brahman* in terms of absolute non-duality which yet assumes the terms of all differentiations in the cosmos. This same is asserted to be the self of each and all selves: "This *Brahman* is without a before and an after, without an inner and an outer. This *Brahman* is the all-experiencing self (*ātman*)." The grand excursus of cosmic, anthropological and transcendental reality establishes a many-sided relational differentiation, leading to a radical identification of each and all with the One (*Brahman*) which is equally the self (*ātman*) of each. "That is the teaching", it says in conclusion.

Appendix
Bṛhadāraṇyaka Upaniṣad: Text, Transliteration and Translation

Adhyāya I: Brāhmaṇa 1

ॐ उषा वा अश्वस्य मेध्यस्य शिरः । सूर्यश्चक्षुर्वातः प्राणो व्यात्तमग्निर्वैश्वानरः संवत्सर आत्माश्वस्य मेध्यस्य । द्यौः पृष्ठमन्तरिक्षमुदरं पृथिवी पाजस्यम् । दिशः पार्श्वे अवान्तरदिशः पर्शव ऋतवोऽङ्गानि मासाश्चार्धमासाश्च पर्वाण्यहोरात्राणि प्रतिष्ठा नक्षत्राण्यस्थीनि नभो माँसानि । ऊवध्यँ सिकताः सिन्धवो गुदा यकृच्च क्लोमानश्च पर्वता ओषधयश्च वनस्पतयश्च लोमानिउद्यन् पूर्वार्धो निम्लोचञ्जघनार्धो तद्विजृम्भते तद्विद्योतते यद्विधूनुते तत्स्तनयति यन्मेहति तद्वर्षति वागेवास्य वाक् ॥ १॥

oṁ uṣā vā aśvasya medhyasya śiraḥ । sūryaścakṣurvātaḥ prāṇo vyāttamagnirvaiśvānaraḥ saṁvatsara ātmāśvasya medhyasya । dyauḥ pṛṣṭhamantarikṣamudaraṁ pṛthivī pājasyam । diśaḥ pārśve avāntaradiśaḥ parśava ṛtavo 'ṅgāni māsāścārdhamāsāśca parvāṇyahorātrāṇi pratiṣṭhā nakṣatrāṇyasthīni nabho māṁsāni । ūvadhyaṁ sikatāḥ sindhavo gudā yakṛcca klomānaśca parvatā oṣadhayaśca vanaspatayaśca lomāni udyan pūrvārdho nimlocañjaghanārdho tadvijṛmbhate tadvidyotate yadvidhūnute tatstanayati yanmehati tadvarṣati vāgevāsya vāk ॥1॥

Oṁ, Dawn is the head of the sacrificial horse, the sun its eye, the wind its life-breath (*prāṇa*), its open mouth the Vaiśvānara fire, cyclical Time (*saṁvatsara*, the year) is the Self (*ātmā*) of the sacrificial horse. Heaven its back, the intermediate region its belly, the earth its hoof, the four directions its sides, the intermediate directions its ribs, the seasons its limbs, the months and half-months its joints, days and nights its feet, the stars its bones, the clouds its flesh. Its half-digested food is the sand, the rivers its blood-vessels, its liver and lungs the mountains, medicinal plants and vegetation its hair. Its forepart is the rising sun and its hind part the setting sun. When it stretches lightning flashes, when it shakes its body then it thunders, when it urinates then it rains and its neighing is indeed the Word (*vāk*).

अहर्वा अश्वं पुरस्तान्महिमाऽन्वजायत तस्य पूर्वे समुद्रे योनी रात्रिरेनं पश्चान्महिमान्वजायत तस्यापरे समुद्रे योनिरेतौ वा अश्वं महिमानावभितः संबभूवतुः। हयो भूत्वा देवानवहद्वाजी गन्धर्वानर्वाऽसुरानश्वो मनुष्यान् समुद्र एवास्य बन्धुः समुद्रो योनिः ॥२॥

aharvā aśvaṁ purastānmahimā 'nvajāyata tasya pūrve samudre yonī rātrirenaṁ paścānmahimānvajāyata tasyāpare samudre yoniretau vā aśvaṁ mahimānāvabhitaḥ saṁbabhūvatuḥ । *hayo bhūtvā devānavahadvājī gandharvānarvā 'surānaśvo manuṣyān samudra evāsya bandhuḥ samudro yoniḥ* ॥2॥

Day was the glory that was born in front of the horse (as it ran). Its womb is the eastern ocean. Night was the glory that was born behind it. Its womb is the other ocean. These are the glories that came into being on either end of the horse. As Haya it carried the gods, as Vājī the *gandharvas*, as *arvan*, the *asuras*, as Aśva, humans. The sea is its brother and the sea its womb.

Adhyāya I: Brāhmaṇa 2

नैवेह किंचनाग्र आसीन्मृत्युनैवेदमावृतमासीत्। अशनाययाशनाया हि मृत्युस्तन्मनोऽकुरुतात्मन्वी स्यामिति। सोऽर्चन्नचरत्तस्यार्चत आपोऽजायन्तार्चते वै मेकमभूदिति। तदवार्कस्यार्कत्वम् कँ ह वा अस्मै भवति य एवमेतदर्कस्यार्कत्वं वेद ॥१॥

naiveha kiñcanāgra āsīnmṛtyunaivedamāvṛtamāsīt । *aśanāyayāśanāyā hi mṛtyustanmano 'kurutātmanvī syāmiti* । *so 'rcannacarattasyārcata āpo 'jāyantārcate vai mekamabhūditi* । *tadevārkasyārkatvaṁ kaṁ ha vā asmai bhavati ya evametadarkasyārkatvaṁ veda* ॥2॥

Nothing whatever existed here in the beginning. By Death all this was covered-by hunger (*aśanāyayā*); hunger, verily, is Death. That created Mind, (thus thinking) "let me have a Self (*ātman*)". He moved about (*acarat*) worshipping (*arcan*). From his worshipping (*arcata*), water (*āpo*) was produced. "Indeed, while worshipping, bliss (*kaṁ*) came into being" (Death thought); that indeed is the fiery solar essence (*arkasya arkatvam*). Thus, bliss, indeed, is born to him who knows (*ya evam veda*) the fiery solar essence (*arkasya arkatvam*).

आपो वा अर्कस्तद्यदपाँ शर आसीतत्समहन्यत सा पृथिव्यभवत्तस्यामश्राम्यत्तस्य श्रान्तस्य तप्तस्य तेजोरसो निरवर्तताग्निः ॥२॥

āpo vā arkastadyadapām̐ śara āsītsamahanyata sā pṛthivyabhavat-tasyāmaśrāmyattasya śrāntasya taptasya tejoraso niravartatāgniḥ ॥2॥

Water, indeed, is solar fire (*arka*). That which was foam of water compacted; that became the earth. On that he toiled. From the concentrated energy of his exhausting labour, the essence of heat emerged. That was fire (*agni*).

स त्रेधात्मानं व्यकुरुतादित्यं तृतीयं वायुं तृतीयँ स एष प्राणस्त्रेधा विहितः। तस्य प्राची दिक्शिरोऽसौ चासौ चेर्मौ। अथास्य प्रतीची दिक् पुच्छमसौ चासौ च सक्थ्यौ दक्षिणा चोदीची च पार्श्वे द्यौः पृष्ठमन्तरिक्षमुदरमियमुरः स एषोप्सु प्रतिष्ठितो यत्र क्वचैति तदेव प्रतितिष्ठत्येवं विद्वान्॥३॥

sa tredhātmānaṁ vyakurutādityaṁ tṛtīyaṁ vāyuṁ tṛtīyam̐ sa eṣa prāṇastredhā vihitaḥ । tasya prācī dikṣiro 'sau cāsau cermau । athāsya pratīcī dik pucchamasau cāsau ca sakthyau dakṣiṇā codīcī ca pārśve dyauḥ pṛṣṭhamantarikṣamudaramiyamuraḥ sa eṣopsu pratiṣṭhito yatra kvacaiti tadeva pratitiṣṭhatyevaṁ vidvān ॥3॥

He divided Himself into three: the Sun (Āditya) one-third and the Wind (Vāyu) one-third. This is that Life-force (*prāṇa*) divided threefold. His head is the east and His arms are that (the north-east) and that (the south-east). His rear is the west and His hip-bones are that (the north-west) and that (the south-west). His sides are the south and the north. The heaven (*dyauṣ*) is his back, the intermediate region (*antarikṣa*) his belly and this (earth) is his chest. Thus, He stands firm on water. He who knows this stands firm wherever he goes.

सोऽकामयतः द्वितीयो म आत्मा जायेतेति स मनसा वाचं मिथुनँ समभवदशनाया मृत्युस्तद्यद्रेत आसीत्स संवत्सरोऽभवत्। न ह पुरा ततः संवत्सर आस तमेतावन्तं कालमबिभः। यावान्त्संवत्सरातमेतावतः कालस्य परस्तादसृजत तं जातमभिव्याददात्स भाणकरोत्सैव वागभवत्॥४॥

so 'kāmayataḥ dvitīyo ma ātmā jāyeteti sa manasā vācaṁ mithunaṁ̐ samabhavadaśanāyā mṛtyustadyadreta āsītsa saṁvatsaro 'bhavat । na ha purā tataḥ saṁvatsara āsa tametāvantaṁ kālamabibhaḥ । yāvāntsaṁvatsarātametāvataḥ kālasya parastādasṛjata taṁ jātamabhivyādadātsa bhāṇakarotsaiva vāgabhavat ॥4॥

He desired: "Let a second self (*ātman*) be born of Me" and He, Death that is Hunger (*aśanāyā mṛtyu*), brought about the intercourse (*mithuna*) of mind (*mana*) with speech (*vāc*). What was the seed there became the year (cyclical Time). Prior to that there had been no year. He (Death) bore him in himself for as long as a year and after that time projected him. Then, when he was born, Death opened His mouth to devour him. He cried "Bhāṇ!" and that, indeed, became speech.

स ऐक्षत यदि वा इममभिमँस्ये कनीयोऽन्नं करिष्य इति स तया वाचा तेनात्मनेदँ सर्वमसृजत यदिदं किंचर्चो यजूँषि सामानि छन्दाँसि यज्ञान् प्रजाः पशून्। स यद्यदेवासृजत तत्तदत्तुमध्रियत। सर्वं वा अत्तीति तददितेरदितित्वँ सर्वस्यैतस्यात्ता भवति सर्वमस्यान्नं भवति य एवमेतददितेरदितित्वं वेद ॥५॥

sa aikṣata yadi vā imamabhimaṁ̐sye kanīyo 'nnaṁ kariṣya iti sa tayā vācā tenātmanedaṁ̐ sarvamasṛjata yadidaṁ kiñcarco yajūṁ̐ṣi sāmāni chandāṁ̐si yajñān prajāḥ paśūn । sa yadyadevāsṛjata tattadat-tumadhriyata । sarvaṁ vā attīti tadaditeradititvaṁ̐ sarvasyaitasyāttā bhavati sarvamasyānnaṁ bhavati ya evametadaditeradititvaṁ veda ॥5॥

He thought: "If I kill him, I shall have but little food"; therefore, through that speech (*vāc*) and that self (*ātmā*) He brought forth all this, whatever there is: the *Ṛk*s, the *Yajus*, the *Sāma*s, the metres, the sacrifices, men and animals. Whatever He created that He resolved to eat. Verily, because He eats (*atti*) everything, therefore, (He is) the essence (Adititva) of Aditi. He who knows this essence (Adititvam) of Aditi becomes the eater of everything and everything becomes his food.

सोऽकामयत भूयसा यज्ञेन भूयो यजेयेति सोऽश्राम्यत्स तपोऽतप्यत तस्य श्रान्तस्य तप्तस्य यशो वीर्यमुदक्रामत् प्राणा वै यशो वीर्यं तत्प्राणेषूत्क्रान्तेषु शरीरँ श्वयितुमध्रियत तस्य शरीर एव मन आसीत् ॥ ६॥

so 'kāmayataḥ bhūyasā yajñena bhūyo yajeyeti so 'śrāmyatsa tapo 'tapyata tasya śrāntasya taptasya yaśo vīryamudakrāmat prāṇā vai yaśo vīryaṁ tatprāṇeṣūtkrānteṣu śarīraṁ̐ śvayitumadhriyata tasya śarīra eva mana āsīt ॥ 6 ॥

He desired: "Let me sacrifice again with a greater sacrifice." He laboured and gathered heat through austerity. From him thus full of exertion and heated, his glory and virtue came forth. The life-forces (*prāṇa*s) indeed are glory and virtue. When the *prāṇa*s go forth, the body begins to swell, but even so the mind is set in the body.

सोऽकामयतः मेध्यं म इदँ स्यादात्मन्व्यनेन स्यामिति। ततोऽश्वः समभवद्यदश्वत्तन्मेध्यमभूदिति। तदेवाश्वमेधस्याश्वमेधत्वं। एष ह वा अश्वमेधं वेद य एनमेवं वेद तमनवरुद्ध्यैवामन्यत तँ संवत्सरस्य परस्तादात्मन आलभत पशून्देवताभ्यः प्रत्यौहत्। तस्मात्सर्वदेवत्यं प्रोक्षितं प्राजापत्यमालभन्ते एष ह वा अश्वमेधो य एष तपति तस्य संवत्सर आत्मायमग्निरर्कस्तस्येमे लोका आत्मानस्तावेतावर्काश्वमेधौ सोपुनरेकैव देवता भवति मृत्युरेवाप पुनर्मृत्युं जयति नैनं मृत्युराप्नोति मृत्युरस्यात्मा भवत्येतासां देवतानामेको भवति ॥७॥

so 'kāmayataḥ medhyaṁ ma idaṁ̐ syādātmanvyanena syāmiti । *tato 'śvaḥ samabhavadyadaśvattanmedhyamabhūditi tadevāśvamedhasyāśvamedhatvaṁ* । *eṣa ha vā aśvamedhaṁ veda ya enamevaṁ veda tamanavaruddhyaiṁ̐vāmanyata taṁ̐ saṁvatsarasya parastādātmana ālabhata* । *paśūndevatābhyaḥ pratyauhat* । *tasmātsarvadevatyaṁ prokṣitaṁ prājāpatyamālabhante eṣa ha vā aśvamedho ya eṣa tapati tasya saṁvatsara ātmāyamagnirarkastasyeme lokā ātmānastāvetāvarkāśvamedhau sopunarekaiva devatā bhavati mṛtyurevāpa punarmṛtyuṁ jayati nainaṁ mṛtyurāpnoti mṛtyurasyātmā bhavatyetāsāṁ devatānāmeko bhavati* ॥ 7 ॥

He desired: "Let this (body) of Mine be fit for a sacrifice and let Me have a self (*ātman*) through this." Because the body swelled (*aśvat*), therefore it came to be called horse (*aśva*). And because it became fit for sacrifice (*medhya*), therefore the Horse sacrifice came to be known as Aśvamedha. He who knows this verily knows the Horse sacrifice. Letting it remain free, he reflected. At the end of a year he sacrificed it to himself and dispatched the other animals to the gods. Therefore, priests even now sacrifice to Prajāpati the sanctified (horse) dedicated to all the gods. Verily, that (sun) which radiates heat (*tapati*) is the Horse sacrifice. His self is the year (cyclical time). This fire (*agni*) is the *arka* (solar essence), whose selves are these worlds. So these two, fire and the sun, are the *arka* and the Aśvamedha (Horse sacrifice). These two, again, become the same god, Death. He who knows this conquers further death; death cannot overcome him; death becomes his self; and he becomes one with these deities.

Adhyāya I: Brāhmaṇa 3

द्वया ह प्राजापत्या देवाश्चासुराश्च ततः कानीयसा एव देवा ज्यायसा असुरास्त एषु लोकेष्वस्पर्धन्त ते ह देवा ऊचुर्हन्तासुरान्यज्ञ उद्गीथेनात्ययामेति ॥ १॥

dvayā ha prājāpatyā devāścāsurāśca tataḥ kānīyasā eva devā jyāyasā asurāsta eṣu lokeṣvaspardhanta te ha devā ūcurhantāsurānyajña udgīthenātyayāmeti ॥1 ॥

Two were the classes descending from the Lord of Creatures (Prajāpati): the gods (*devas*) and the demons (*asuras*). Of these, the gods were the younger and the demons the elder. They struggled with one another for mastery of these worlds. The gods said, let us overcome the demons at the sacrifice by means of the Udgītha (the ascending song, the *oṁ*).

ते ह वाचमूचुस्त्वं न उद्गायेति तथेति तेभ्यो वागुदगायत् यो वाचि भोगस्तं देवेभ्य आगायद्यत् कल्याणं वदति तदात्मने ते विदुरनेन वै न उद्गात्रात्येष्यन्तीति तमभिद्रुत्य पाप्मनाविध्यन्त्स यः स पाप्मा यदेवेदमप्रतिरूपं वदति स एव स पाप्मा ॥ २॥

te ha vācamūcustvaṁ na udgāyeti tatheti tebhyo vāgudagāyat yo vāci bhogastaṁ devebhya āgāyadyat kalyāṇaṁ vadati tadātmane te viduranena vai na udgātrātyeṣyantīti tamabhidrutya pāpmanāvidhyantsa yaḥ sa pāpmā yadevedamapratirūpaṁ vadati sa eva sa pāpmā ॥2 ॥

They said to the organ of speech: "Chant the Udgītha (ascending song) for us". "So be it", said speech and ascended singing for them. Whatever enjoyment belongs to speech, it brought to the gods, whatever blessing is in speech, it brought for itself (*ātman*). They (the *asuras*) knew that through this singer they (the *devas*) will overcome us. They rushed at it and pierced it with evil. That evil which consists in improper speech, that is that evil.

अथ ह प्राणमूचुस्त्वं न उद्गायेति तथेति तेभ्यः प्राण उदगायद्यः प्राणे भोगस्तंदेवेभ्य आगायद्यत् कल्याणं जिघ्रति तदात्मने ते विदुरनेन वै न उद्गात्राऽत्येष्यन्तीति तमभिद्रुत्य पाप्मनाऽविध्यन्त्स यः स पाप्मा यदेवेदमप्रतिरूपं जिघ्रति स एव स पाप्मा ॥ ३॥

atha ha prāṇamūcustvaṁ na udgāyeti tatheti tebhyaḥ prāṇa udagāyadyaḥ prāṇe bhogastaṁ devebhya āgāyadyat kalyāṇaṁ jighrati tadātmane te viduranena vai na udgātrā 'tyeṣyantīti tamabhidrutya pāpmanā 'vidhyantsa yaḥ sa pāpmā yadevedamapratirūpaṁ jighrati sa eva sa pāpmā ॥3 ॥

Then they said to the life-breath (*prāṇa*): "Chant the Udgītha (ascending song) for us". "So be it", said the life-breath and ascended singing for them. Whatever enjoyment belongs to the life-breath, it brought to the gods, whatever blessing is in smell, it brought for itself (*ātman*). They (the *asuras*) knew that through this singer they (the *devas*) will overcome us. They rushed at it and pierced it with evil. That evil which consists in improper smell, that is that evil.

अथ ह चक्षुरूचुस्त्वं न उद्गायेति तथेति तेभ्यश्चक्षुरुदगायद् यश्चक्षुषि भोगस्तं देवेभ्य आगायद्यत्कल्याणं पश्यति तदात्मने ते विदुरनेन वै न उद्गात्रात्येष्यन्तीति तमभिद्रुत्य पाप्मनाविध्यन्त्स यः स पाप्मा यदेवेदमप्रतिरूपं पश्यति स एव स पाप्मा ॥४॥

atha ha cakṣurūcustvaṁ na udgāyeti tatheti tebhyaścakṣurudagāyad yaścakṣuṣi bhogastaṁ devebhya āgāyadyatkalyāṇaṁ paśyati tadātmane te viduranena vai na udgātrātyeṣyantīti tamabhidrutya pāpmanāvidhyantsa yaḥ sa pāpmā yadevedamapratirūpaṁ paśyati sa eva sa pāpmā ॥4॥

Then they said to the eye: "Chant the Udgītha (ascending song) for us". "So be it", said the eye and ascended singing for them. Whatever enjoyment belongs to the eye, it brought to the gods, whatever blessing is in sight, it brought for itself (*ātman*). They (the *asuras*) knew that through this singer they (the *devas*) will overcome us. They rushed at it and pierced it with evil. That evil which consists in improper seeing, that is that evil.

अथ ह श्रोत्रमूचुस्त्वं न उद्गायेति तथेति तेभ्यः श्रोत्रमुदगायद्यः श्रोत्रे भोगस्तं देवेभ्य आगायद्यत्कल्याणँ शृणोति तदात्मने ते विदुरनेन वै न उद्गात्रात्येष्यन्तीति तमभिद्रुत्य पाप्मनाऽविध्यन्त्स यः स पाप्मा यदेवेदमप्रतिरूपँ शृणोति स एव स पाप्मा ॥५॥

atha ha śrotramūcustvaṁ na udgāyeti tatheti tebhyaḥ śrotramud-agāyadyaḥ śrotre bhogastaṁ devebhya āgāyadyatkalyāṇam̐ śṛṇoti tadātmane te viduranena vai na udgātrātyeṣyantīti tamabhidrutya pāpmanā 'vidhyantsa yaḥ sa pāpmā yadevedamapratirūpam̐ śṛṇoti sa eva sa pāpmā ॥5॥

Then they said to the ear: "Chant the Udgītha (ascending song) for us". "So be it", said the ear and ascended singing for them. Whatever enjoyment belongs to the ear, it brought to the gods, whatever blessing is in hearing, it brought for itself (*ātman*). They (the *asuras*) knew that through this singer they (the *devas*) will overcome us. They rushed at it and pierced it with evil. That evil which consists in improper hearing, that is that evil.

अथ ह मन ऊचुस्त्वं न उद्गायेति तथेति तेभ्यो मन उद्गायद्यो मनसि भोगस्तं देवेभ्य आगायद्यत् कल्याणँ संकल्पयति तदात्मने ते विदुरनेन वै न उद्गात्रात्येष्यन्तीति तमभिद्रुत्य पाप्मनाविध्यन्त्स यः स पाप्मा यदेवेदमप्रतिरूपँ संकल्पयति स एव स पाप्मैवमु खल्वेता देवताः पाप्मभिरुपासृजन्नेवमेनाः पाप्मेनाविध्यन् ॥६॥

atha ha mana ūcustvaṁ na udgāyeti tatheti tebhyo mana udagāyadyo manasi bhogastaṁ devebhya āgāyadyat kalyāṇam̐ saṅkalpayati tadātmane te viduranena vai na udgātrātyeṣyantīti tamabhidrutya pāpmanāvidhyantsa yaḥ sa pāpmā yadevedamapratirūpaṁ saṅkalpayati sa eva sa pāpmaivamu khalvetā devatāḥ pāpmabhirupāsṛjannevamenāḥ pāpmenā 'vidhyan ||6 ||

Then they said to the mind: "Chant the Udgītha (ascending song) for us". "So be it", said the mind and ascended singing for them. Whatever enjoyment belongs to the mind, it brought to the gods, whatever blessing is in thought, it brought for itself (*ātman*). They (the *asura*s) knew that through this singer they (the *deva*s) will overcome us. They rushed at it and pierced it with evil. That evil which consists in improper thinking, that is that evil.

अथ हेममासन्यं प्राणमूचुस्त्वं न उद्गायेति तथेति तेभ्य एष प्राण उदगायत्ते विदुरनेन वै न उद्गात्रात्येष्यन्तीति तदभिद्रुत्य पाप्मनाविव्यस्यन्स यथाश्मानमृत्वा लोष्टो विध्वँसे तैवँ हैव विध्वँसमाना विष्वञ्चो विनेशुस्ततो देवा अभवन् परासुरा भवत्यात्मना परास्य द्विषन्भ्रातृव्यो भवति य एवं वेद ॥७॥

atha hemamāsanyaṁ prāṇamūcustvaṁ na udgāyeti tatheti tebhya eṣa prāṇa udagāyatte viduranena vai na udgātrātyeṣyantīti tadabhidrutya pāpmanāvivyatsyansa yathāśmānamṛtvā loṣṭo vidhvaṁ̐se taiva haiva vidhvaṁ̐samānā viṣvañco vineśustato devā abhavan parāsurā bhavatyātmanā parāsya dviṣanbhrātṛvyo bhavati ya evaṁ veda ||7 ||

Then they said to the vital breath in the mouth: "Chant the Udgītha (ascending song) for us". "So be it", said the vital breath and ascended singing for them. They (the *asura*s) knew that through this singer they (the *deva*s) will overcome us. They rushed at it, intending to pierce it with evil. But as a clod of earth striking against a rock is scattered, even so they were scattered in all directions and destroyed. Thereupon, the gods became established in their true selves and the demons perished. He who knows this becomes his true self and his spiteful kinsman perishes.

ते होचु क्व नु सोऽभूद्यो न इत्थमसक्तेत्ययमास्येऽन्तरितिसोऽयास्य आङ्गिरसोऽङ्गानाँ हि रसः ॥८॥

te hocu kva nu so 'bhūdyo na itthamasaktetyayamāsye 'ntariti so 'yāsya āṅgiraso 'ṅgānām̐ hi rasaḥ ॥8 ॥

Then the organs said: "Where is that which joined us to our true selves?" After deliberation they discovered that it was here, within the mouth (*asye*). Hence, the vital breath (*prāṇa*) is called *ayāsya* and also, because it is the essence (*rasa*) of the limbs (*aṅga*) of the body, *aṅgirasa*.

सा वा एषा देवता दूर्नाम दूरँ ह्यस्या मृत्युर्दूरँ ह वा अस्मान्मृत्युर्भवति य एवं वेद ॥९॥

sā vā eṣā devatā dūrnāma dūram̐ hyasyā mṛtyurdūram̐ ha vā asmānmṛtyurbhavati ya evaṁ veda ॥9 ॥

That deity is called *dūra*, because death is far (*dūra*) from it. From him who knows this, death is far away.

सा वा एषा देवतैतासां देवतानां पाप्मानं मृत्युमपहृत्य यत्रासां दिशामन्तस्तद्गमयांचकार तदासां पाप्मनो विन्यदधात्तस्मान्न जनमियान्नान्तमियान्नेत्पाप्मानं मृत्युमन्ववायानीति ॥१०॥

sā vā eṣā devataitāsāṁ devatānāṁ pāpmānaṁ mṛtyumapahatya yatrāsāṁ diśāmantastadgamayāṁcakāra tadāsāṁ pāpmano vinyadadhāttasmānna janamiyānnāntamiyānnetpāpmānaṁ mṛtyumanvavāyānīti ॥10 ॥

Verily that divinity took away the evil of these gods, even death and carried it to where the end of the quarters is. There it deposited their evils. Therefore, let no one visit persons (of that region), or travel to the country beyond the border, lest he should meet there with evil, with death.

सा वा एषा देवतैतासां देवतानां पाप्मानं मृत्युमपहृत्याथैनां मृत्युमत्यवहत् ॥११॥

sā vā eṣā devataitāsāṁ devatānāṁ pāpmānaṁ mṛtyumapahatyāthaināṁ mṛtyumatyavahat ॥11 ॥

That divinity, after removed the evil, the death of the gods, carried them beyond death.

स वै वाचमेव प्रथमामत्यवहत्सा यदा मृत्युमत्यमुच्यत सोऽग्निरभवत्सोऽयमग्निः परेण मृत्युमतिक्रान्तो दीप्यते ॥ १२॥

sa vai vācameva prathamāmatyavahatsā yadā mṛtyumatyamucyata so 'gnirabhavatso 'yamagniḥ pareṇa mṛtyumatikrānto dīpyate ॥12॥

Indeed it transported Speech first. When (Speech) was freed from death, it became fire. That fire, having transcended Death, shines beyond its reach.

अथ प्राणमत्यवहत्स यदा मृत्युमत्यमुच्यत स वायुरभवत्सोऽयं वायुः परेण मृत्युमतिक्रान्तः पवते ॥ १३॥

atha prāṇamatyavahatsa yadā mṛtyumatyamucyata sa vāyura bhavatso 'yaṁ vāyuḥ pareṇa mṛtyumatikrāntaḥ pavate ॥13॥

Then it carried the life-breaths. When that was freed from death, it became Wind (Vāyu). That Wind, having transcended death, blows beyond its reach.

अथ चक्षुरत्यवहत्तद्यदा मृत्युमत्यमुच्यत स आदित्योऽभवत् सोऽसावादित्यः परेण मृत्युमतिक्रान्तस्तपति ॥ १४॥

atha cakṣuratyavahattadyadā mṛtyumatyamucyata sa ādityo 'bhavatso 'sāvādityaḥ pareṇa mṛtyumatikrāntastapati ॥14॥

Then it carried the Eye. When that was freed from death, it became the sun (*sūrya*). That sun, having transcended death, shines beyond its reach.

अथ श्रोत्रमत्यवहत्तद्यदा मृत्युमत्यमुच्यत ता दिशोऽभवँस्ता इमा दिशः परेण मृत्युमतिक्रान्ताः ॥ १५॥

atha śrotramatyavahattadyadā mṛtyumatyamucyata tā diśo 'bhavam̐stā imā diśaḥ pareṇa mṛtyumatikrāntāḥ ॥15॥

Then it carried the Ear. When it was freed from death, it became the quarters (*diśaḥ*). Those quarters, having transcended death, remain beyond its reach.

अथ मनोऽत्यवहत्तद्यदा मृत्युमत्यमुच्यत स चन्द्रमा अभवत्सोऽसौ परेण मृत्युमतिक्रान्तो भात्येवँ ह वा एनमेषा देवता मृत्युमतिवहति य एवं वेद ॥१६॥

atha mano 'tyavahattadyadā mṛtyumatyamucyata sa candramā abhavatso 'sau pareṇa mṛtyumatikrānto bhātyevaṁ ha vā enameṣā devatā mṛtyumativahati ya evaṁ veda ॥16॥

Then it carried the mind. When the mind was freed from death it became the moon (*candra*). That moon, having transcended death, shines beyond its reach. Thus, verily, that divinity carries beyond death him who knows this.

अथात्मनेऽन्नाद्यमागायद्यद्धि किञ्चान्नमद्यतेऽनेनैव तदद्यत इह प्रतितिष्ठति ॥१७॥

athātmane 'nnādyamāgāyadyaddhi kiñcānnamadyate 'nenaiva tadadyata iha pratitiṣṭhati ॥17॥

Next it (the breath in the mouth) obtained food for itself by singing. For whatever food is eaten, is eaten by that (the vital breath) alone. In it (the vital breath) is established.

ते देवा अब्रुवन्नेतावद्वा इदँ सर्वं यदन्नं तदात्मन आगासीरनु नोऽस्मिन्नन्न आभजस्वेति ते वै माभिसंविशतेति तथेति तँ समन्तं परिण्यविशन्त तस्माद्यदनेनान्नमत्ति तेनैतास्तृप्यन्त्येवँ ह वा एनँ स्वा अभिसंविशन्ति भर्ता स्वानाँ श्रेष्ठः पुर एता भवत्यन्नादोऽधिपतिर्य एवं वेद य उ हैवंविदँ स्वेषु प्रति प्रतिर्बुभूषति न हैवालं भार्येभ्यो भवत्यथ य एवैतमनुभवति यो वै तमनु भार्यान् बुभूर्षति स हैवालं भार्येभ्यो भवति ॥१८॥

te devā abruvannetāvadvā idaṁ sarvaṁ yadannaṁ tadātmana āgāsīranu no 'sminnanna ābhajasveti te vai mābhisaṁviśateti tatheti taṁ samantaṁ pariṇyaviśanta। *tasmādyadanenānnamatti tenaitāstṛpyantyevaṁ ha vā enaṁ svā abhisaṁviśanti bhartā svānāṁ śreṣṭhaḥ pura etā bhavatyannādo 'dhipatirya evaṁ veda ya u haivaṁvidaṁ sveṣu prati pratirbubhūṣati na haivālaṁ bhāryebhyo bhavatyatha ya evaitamanubhavati yo vai tamanu bhāryānbubhūrṣati sa haivālaṁ bhāryebhyo bhavati* ॥18॥

These gods said: "Indeed, just this much is all the food there is and you have obtained for yourself by singing. Now let us have a share of this food." "Then sit around facing me." "So be it." They sat down around it on all sides. That is why whatever food one eats through it satisfies also these others. So do his relatives gather around him who knows this; he becomes their supporter, the foremost among them and their leader; an eater of food and their lord. Whoever, among his kinsmen, desires to be a rival of the man who has this knowledge will be unable to support his own dependents. On the other hand, he who follows him (the knower of the vital breath) and who, following him, desires to support his dependents, indeed, is able to do so.

सोऽयास्य आङ्गिरसोऽङ्गानाँ हि रसः प्राणो वा अङ्गानाँ रसः प्राणो हि वा अङ्गानाँ रसस्तस्माद्य-
स्मात्कस्माच्चाङ्गात्प्राण उत्क्रामति तदेव तच्छुष्यत्येष हि वा अङ्गानाँ रसः ॥१९॥

so 'yāsya āṅgiraso 'ṅgānāṁ hi rasaḥ prāṇo vā aṅgānāṁ rasaḥ prāṇo hi vā aṅgānāṁ rasastasmādyasmātkasmāccāṅgātprāṇa utkrāmati tadeva tacchuṣyatyeṣa hi vā aṅgānāṁ rasaḥ ॥19॥

It is Aṅgirasa Ayāsya , for it is the essence (*rasa*) of the limbs (*aṅga*). Indeed, this life-breath (*prāṇa*) is the essence of the limbs, yes indeed this life-breath (*prāṇa*) is the essence of the limbs. From whichever limb this life-breath departs, that limb is sure to wither; for it is the very essence of the limbs.

एष उ एव बृहस्पतिर्वाग् वै बृहती तस्या एष पतिस्तस्मादु बृहस्पतिः ॥२०॥

eṣa u eva bṛhaspatirvāg vai bṛhatī tasyā eṣa patistasmādu bṛhaspatiḥ ॥20।

And it is also Bṛhaspati. Speech is Bṛhatī and this is its lord (*pati*). Therefore, it is called Bṛhaspati.

एष उ एव ब्रह्मणस्पतिर्वाग् वै ब्रह्म तस्या एष पतिस्तस्मादु ब्रह्मणस्पतिः ॥२१॥

eṣa u eva brahmaṇaspatirvāg vai brahma tasyā eṣa patistasmādu brahmaṇaspatiḥ ॥21॥

And it is also Brahmaṇaspati. Speech is *Brahman* and this is its lord (*pati*). Therefore, it is called Brahmaṇaspati.

एष उ एव साम वाग् वै सामैष सा चामश्चेति तत्साम्नः सामत्वं। यद्वेव समः प्लुषिणा समो मशकेन समो नागेन सम एभिस्त्रिभिर्लोकैः समोऽनेन सर्वेण तस्माद्वेव सामाश्नुते साम्नः सायुज्यँ सलोकतां जयति य एवमेतत्साम वेद ॥२२॥

eṣa u eva sāma vāg vai sāmaiṣa sā cāmaśceti tatsāmnaḥ sāmatvaṁ । *yadveva samaḥ pluṣiṇā samo maśakena samo nāgena sama ebhistribhirlokaiḥ samo 'nena sarveṇa tasmādveva sāmāśnute sāmnaḥ sāyujyam̐ salokatāṁ jayati ya evametatsāma veda* ॥22॥

And this also is *Sāman*, the Equal. Speech is verily *Sāman*. It is she (*sā*) and he (*ama*). That is the equality (*sāmatvam*) of the Equal (*sāman*). Or, because it is equal (*sama*) to a white ant, equal to a mosquito, equal to an elephant, equal to these three worlds, or even equal to all others, therefore, it is indeed the Equal (*sama*). He who knows this *Sāma* enjoys union with it and lives in the same world with the *Sāman*.

एष उ वा उद्गीथः प्राणो वा उत्प्राणेन हीदँ सर्वमुत्तब्धं वागेव गीथोच्चगीथा चेति स उद्गीथः ॥२३॥

eṣa u vā udgīthaḥ prāṇo vā utprāṇena hīdam̐ sarvamuttabdhaṁ vāgeva gīthoccagīthā ceti sa udgīthaḥ ॥23॥

And it is also the ascending song, Udgītha. The life-breath is verily ascension (*ut*), for by the life-breath all this is upheld (*uttabdham*). Speech is *gīthā* (song). And ascending (*ut*) song (*gīthā*) is therefore *Udgītha*.

तद्धापि ब्रह्मदत्तश्चैकितानेयो राजानं भक्षयन्नुवाचायं त्यस्य राजा मूर्धानं विपातयताद्यदितोऽयास्य आङ्गिरसोऽन्येनोदगायदिति वाचा च ह्येव स प्राणेन चोदगायदिति ॥२४॥

taddhāpi brahmadattaścaikitāneyo rājānaṁ bhakṣayannuvācāyaṁ tyasya rājā mūrdhānaṁ vipātayatādyadito 'yāsya āṅgiraso 'nyenodagāyaditi vācā ca hyeva sa prāṇena codagāyaditi ॥24॥

As to this there also Brahmadatta Caikitāneya, while drinking the King elixir [Soma], said: "May this King strike off my head if I say that the Aṅgirasa Ayāsya sang the Udgītha by any other means, for by Speech and the Life-breath alone did he sing it.

तस्य हैतस्य साम्नो यः स्वं वेद भवति हास्य स्वं तस्य वै स्वर एव स्वं तस्मादार्त्विज्यं करिष्यन्वाचि स्वरमिच्छेत तया वाचा स्वरसम्पन्नयार्त्विज्यं कुर्यात्तस्माद्यज्ञे स्वरवन्तं दिदृक्षन्त एवाथो यस्य स्वं भवति भवति हास्य स्वं य एवमेतत्साम्नः स्वं वेद ॥२५॥

tasya haitasya sāmno yaḥ svaṁ veda bhavati hāsya svaṁ tasya vai svara eva svaṁ tasmādārtvijyaṁ kariṣyanvāci svaramiccheta tayā vācā svarasampannayārtvijyaṁ kuryāttasmādyajñe svaravantaṁ didṛkṣanta evātho yasya svaṁ bhavati bhavati hāsya svaṁ ya evametatsāmnaḥ svaṁ veda ॥25॥

He who knows the wealth of this Sāman obtains wealth. Tone (*svara*), indeed, is its wealth (*sva*). Therefore, let one who is going to perform the sacrificial work as a priest desire that his voice may be rich in tone and let him perform the sacrifice with that voice rich in tone. Therefore, people desire a priest with a rich tone at a sacrifice, like one who has wealth. He who thus knows thus the wealth of the Sāman obtains wealth.

तस्य हैतस्य साम्नो यः सुवर्णं वेद भवति हास्य सुवर्णं तस्य वै स्वर एव सुवर्णं भवति हास्य सुवर्णं य एवमेतत्साम्नः सुवर्णं वेद ॥२६॥

tasya haitasya sāmno yaḥ suvarṇaṁ veda bhavati hāsya suvarṇaṁ tasya vai svara eva suvarṇaṁ bhavati hāsya suvarṇaṁ ya evametatsāmnaḥ suvarṇaṁ veda ॥26॥

He who knows the gold (*suvarṇa*) of the Sāman obtains gold. Tone (*svara*) is verily its gold (*suvarṇa*). He who thus knows what is the gold of the Sāman obtains gold.

तस्य हैतस्य साम्नो यः प्रतिष्ठां वेद प्रति ह तिष्ठति तस्य वै वागेव प्रतिष्ठा वाचि हि खल्वेष एतत्प्राणः प्रतिष्ठितो गीयतेऽन्न इत्यु हैक आहुः ॥२७॥

tasya haitasya sāmno yaḥ pratiṣṭhāṁ veda prati ha tiṣṭhati tasya vai vāgeva pratiṣṭhā vāci hi khalveṣa etatprāṇaḥ pratiṣṭhito gīyate 'nna ityu haika āhuḥ ॥27॥

He who knows the support of the Sāman obtains a foundation. Speech verily is its support. For, supported in speech, the life-breath is transformed into a song. Some, however, say food (*anna*) is the support.

अथातः पवमानानामेवाभ्यारोहः स वै खलु प्रस्तोता साम प्रस्तौति स यत्र प्रस्तुयात्तदेतानि जपेदसतो मा सद्गमय तमसो मा ज्योतिर्गमय मृत्योर्माऽमृतं गमयेति स यदाहासतो मा सद्गमयेति मृत्युर्वा असत्सदमृतं मृत्योर्माऽमृतं गमयामृतं मा कुर्वित्येवैतदाह तमसो मा ज्योतिर्गमयेति मृत्युर्वै तमो ज्योतिरमृतं मृत्योर्माऽमृतं गमयामृतं मां कुर्वित्येवैतदाह मृत्योर्माऽमृतं गमयेति नात्र तिरोहितमिवास्ति। अथ यानीतराणि स्तोत्राणि तेष्वात्मनेऽन्नाद्यमागायेत्तस्मादु तेषु वरं वृणीत यं कामं कामयेत तँ स एष एवंविदुद्गातात्मने वा यजमानाय वा यं कामं कामयते तमागायति तद्धैतल्लोकजिदेव न हैवालोक्यताया आशास्ति य एवमेतत्साम वेद ॥२८॥

athātaḥ pavamānānāmevābhyārohaḥ sa vai khalu prastotā sāma prastauti sa yatra prastuyāttadetāni japedasato mā sadgamaya tamaso mā jyotirgamaya mṛtyormā 'mṛtaṁ gamayeti sa yadāhāsato mā sadgamayeti mṛtyurvā asatsadamṛtaṁ mṛtyormā 'mṛtaṁ gamayāmṛtaṁ mā kurvityevaitadāha tamaso mā jyotirgamayeti mṛtyurvai tamo jyotiramṛtaṁ mṛtyormā 'mṛtaṁ gamayāmṛtaṁ māṁ kurvityevaitadāha mṛtyormā 'mṛtaṁ gamayeti nātra tirohitamivāsti ।
atha yānītarāṇi stotrāṇi teṣvātmane 'nnādyamāgāyettasmādu teṣu varaṁ vṛṇīta yaṁ kāmaṁ kāmayeta taṁ̐ sa eṣa evaṁvidudgātātmane vā yajamānāya vā yaṁ kāmaṁ kāmayate tamāgāyati taddhaitallokajideva na haivālokyatāyā āśāsti ya evametatsāma veda ॥28॥

Next follows the repetition (*abhyāroha*) only of the purificatory hymns (*pavamāna*). The priest called *prastotṛ* indeed chants the *sāman*; while he chants it, let the sacrificer recite these [*Yajur* verses]: "Lead me from the unreal to the real. From darkness lead me to light. From death lead me to immortality." When he says: "Lead me from the unreal to the real", "the unreal" means death and the "real", immortality; so it says, "From death lead me to immortality", that is to say, "Make me immortal". When it says: "From darkness lead me to light", "darkness" means death and "light", immortality; so it says: "From death lead me to immortality", that is to say, "Make me immortal". "From death lead me to immortality", there is nothing that is hidden here. Whatever the other hymns by them one should obtain food for one's self. Therefore, in them he should ask a boon (*vara*) – anything he desires. Whatever objects this singer of the ascending word (*udgātṛ*), endowed with such knowledge, desires for himself or for the sacrifice (*yajamāna*), that he obtains. This, indeed, is world conquering. He who thus knows the *sāman*, for him, there is no fear of being without a world.

Adhyāya I: Brāhmaṇa 4

आत्मैवेदमग्र आसीत् पुरुषविधः सोऽनुवीक्ष्य नान्यदात्मनोऽपश्यत् सोऽहमस्मीत्यग्रे व्याहरत्ततो-ऽहंनामाभवत्तस्मादप्येतर्ह्यामन्त्रितोऽहमयमित्येवाग्र उक्त्वाथान्यन्नाम प्रब्रूते यदस्य भवति स यत्पूर्वोऽस्मात्सर्वस्मात्सर्वान्पाप्मन औषत्तस्मात्पुरुष ओषति ह वै स तं योऽस्मात्पूर्वो बुभूषति य एवं वेद ॥ १॥

ātmaivedamagra āsīt puruṣavidhaḥ so 'nuvīkṣya nānyadātmano 'paśyat so 'hamasmītyagre vyāharattato 'haṁnāmābhavattasmādapyetarhyāmantrito 'hamayamityevāgra uktvāthānyannāma prabrūte yadasya bhavati sa yatpūrvo 'smātsarvasmātsarvānpāpmana auṣattasmātpuruṣa oṣati ha vai sa taṁ yo 'smātpūrvo bubhūṣati ya evaṁ veda ॥1 ॥

In the beginning, this universe was *Ātman* alone, in the shape of Person (*Puruṣa*). It looked around and saw nothing other than Itself. He first said *so 'ham asmi* (I am He). Therefore arose the name I (*aham*). Hence, even now, when a person is addressed, he first says: "It is I" and then says whatever other name he may have. And because It burnt (*auṣat*) all evils, before it, therefore, It is called *Puruṣa* (Person). He who knows this verily burns up him who/what wishes to be ahead of him.

सोऽबिभेत्तस्मादेकाकी बिभेति स हायमीक्षांचक्रेः यन्मदन्यन्नास्ति कस्मान्नु बिभेमीति तत एवास्य भयं वीयाय कस्माद्ध्यभेष्यद्द्वितीयाद्वै भयं भवति ॥ २॥

so 'bibhettasmādekākī bibheti sa hāyamīkṣāṁcakreḥ yanmadanyannāsti kasmānnu bibhemīti tata evāsya bhayaṁ vīyāya kasmāddhyabheṣyaddvitīyādvai bhayaṁ bhavati ॥2 ॥

He was afraid. Therefore, one who is alone is afraid. He thought: "There is none other than I, of what am I afraid?" Thereupon His fears were gone; for what was there to fear? Assuredly, it is from a second that fear arises.

स वै नैव रेमे तस्मादेकाकी न रमते स द्वितीयमैच्छत् स हैतावानास यथा स्त्रीपुमाँसौ संपरिष्वक्तौ स इममेवात्मानं द्वेधाऽपातयत्ततः पतिश्च पत्नी चाभवतां तस्मादिदमर्धबृगलमिव स्व इति ह स्माह याज्ञवल्क्यस्तस्मादयमाकाशः स्त्रिया पूर्यत एव ताँ समभवत्ततो मनुष्या अजायन्त ॥३॥

sa vai naiva reme tasmādekākī na ramate sa dvitīyamaicchat sa haitāvānāsa yathā strīpumām̐sau sam̐pariṣvaktau sa imame vātmānam̐ dvedhā 'pātayattataḥ patiśca patnī cābhavatām̐ tasmād idamardhabṛgalamiva sva iti ha smāha yājñavalkyastasmādayamākāśaḥ striyā pūryata eva tām̐ samabhavattato manuṣyā ajāyanta ॥3 ॥

He indeed had no delight. Therefore, when alone, a person has no delight. He desired a second. He became the size of a man and woman in close embrace. He divided this self into two. From that division arose husband (*pati*) and wife (*patnī*). Therefore, as Yājñavalkya said, this (body) is one half of a split pea. Therefore, this space is indeed filled by the wife. He united with her. From that human beings were born.

सा हेयमीक्षांचक्रे कथं नु मात्मान एव जनयित्वा संभवति हन्त तिरोऽसानीति सा गौरभवदृषभ इतरस्ताँ समेवाभवत्ततो गावोऽजायन्त वडवेतराभवदश्ववृष इतरो गर्दभीतरा गर्दभ इतरस्ताँ समेवाभवत्तत एकशफमजायताजेतराभवद्वस्त इतरोऽविरितरा मेष इतरस्ताँ समेवाभवत्ततोऽजावयोऽजायन्तैवमेव यदिदं किं च मिथुनमापिपीलिकाभ्यस्तत्सर्वमसृजत ॥४॥

sā heyamīkṣām̐cakre katham̐ nu mātmāna eva janayitvā sam̐bhavati hanta tiro 'sānīti sā gaurabhavadṛṣabha itarastām̐ samevābhavattato gāvo 'jāyanta vaḍavetarābhavadaśvavṛṣa itaro gardabhītarā gardabha itarastām̐ samevābhavattata ekaśaphamajāyatājetarābhavadvasta itaro 'viritarā meṣa itarastām̐ samevābhavattato 'jāvayo 'jāyantaivameva yadidam̐ kim̐ ca mithunamāpipīlikābhyastatsarvamasṛjata ॥4 ॥

She thought: "How can he unite with me after having produced me from himself? Well, let me hide myself." She became a cow, the other became a bull and was united with her; from that cows were born. The one became a mare, the other a stallion; the one became a she-ass, the other a he-ass and was united with her; from that one-hoofed animals were born. The one became a she-goat, the other a he-goat; the one became an ewe, the other became a ram and was united with her; from that goats and sheeps were born. Thus, indeed, he produced everything that exists in pairs, down to the ants.

सोऽवेदहं वाव सृष्टिरस्म्यहँ हीदँ सर्वमसृक्षीति ततः सृष्टिरभवत्सृष्ट्याँ हास्यैतस्यां भवति य एवं वेद ॥५॥

so 'vedahaṁ vāva sṛṣṭirasmyahaṁ̐ hīdaṁ̐ sarvamasṛkṣīti tataḥ sṛṣṭirabhavatsṛṣṭyāṁ̐ hāsyaitasyāṁ bhavati ya evaṁ veda ॥5॥

He knew: "Indeed, I am the creation, for I produced all this." Therefore, He became the creation. He who knows this becomes this creation.

अथेत्यभ्यमन्थत्स मुखाच्च योनेर्हस्ताभ्यां चाग्निमसृजत तस्मादेतदुभयमलोमकमन्तरतोऽलोमका हि योनिरन्तरतस्तद्यदिदमाहुरमुं यजामुं यजेत्येकैकं देवमेतस्यैव सा विसृष्टिरेष उ ह्येव सर्वे देवा अथ यत्किंचेदमार्द्रं तद्रेतसोऽसृजत तदु सोम एतावद्वा इदँ सर्वमन्नं चैवान्नादश्च सोम एवान्नमग्निरन्नादः सैषा ब्रह्मणोऽतिसृष्टिर्यच्छ्रेयसो देवानसृजताथ यन्मर्त्यः सन्नमृतानसृजत तस्मादतिसृष्टिरतिसृष्ट्याँ हास्यैतस्यां भवति य एवं वेद ॥६॥

athetyabhyamanthatsa mukhācca yonerhastābhyāṁ cāgnimasṛjata tasmādetadubhayamalomakamantarato 'lomakā hi yonirantarata-stadyadidamāhuramuṁ yajāmuṁ yajetyekaikaṁ devametasyaiva sā visṛṣṭireṣa u hyeva sarve devā atha yatkiñcedamārdraṁ tadretaso 'sṛjata tadu soma etāvadvā idaṁ̐ sarvamannaṁ caivānnādaśca soma evānnamagnirannādaḥ saiṣā brahmaṇo 'tisṛṣṭiryacchreyaso devānasṛjatātha yanmartyaḥ sannamṛtānasṛjata tasmādatisṛṣṭiratisṛṣṭyāṁ̐ hāsyaitasyāṁ bhavati ya evaṁ veda ॥6॥

Then he rubbed back and forth thus and produced fire from the vagina, the mouth and the hands. Therefore, both the hands and mouth are hairless inside as the vagina is hairless inside. When they say "Sacrifice to him", "Sacrifice to that one", these are all his manifestations: he himself is all the gods. Now, whatever is liquid, He produced from semen; and that is Soma. This whole (world) is just food and the eater of food. Soma is food; and fire, the eater of food. This is the highest creation of Brahmā, that He created the gods, who are superior to Him. This is the highest creation because He, although mortal Himself, manifested the immortal. He who knows this truly becomes a creator in this highest creation.

तद्धेदं तर्ह्यव्याकृतमासीत्तन्नामरूपाभ्यामेव व्याक्रियतेऽसौनामायमिदँरूप इति तदिदमप्येतर्हि नामरूपाभ्यामेव व्याक्रियतेऽसौनामायमिदँरूप इति स एष इह प्रविष्टः। आ नखाग्रेभ्यो यथा क्षुरः क्षुरधानेऽवहितः स्याद्विश्वम्भरो वा विश्वम्भरकुलाये तं न पश्यन्ति। अकृत्स्नो हि स प्राणन्नेव प्राणो नाम भवति। वदन् वाक्पश्यँश्चक्षुः शृण्वन् श्रोत्रं मन्वानो मनस्तान्यस्यैतानि कर्मनामान्येव स योऽत एकैकमुपास्ते न स वेदाकृत्स्नो ह्येषोऽत एकैकेन भवतात्मेत्येवोपासीतात्र ह्येते सर्व एकं भवन्ति तदेतत्पदनीयमस्य सर्वस्य यदयमात्माऽनेन ह्येतत्सर्वं वेद। यथा ह वै पदेनानुविन्देदेवं कीर्तिँ श्लोकं विन्दते य एवं वेद ॥७॥

taddhedaṁ tarhyavyākṛtamāsīttannāmarūpābhyāmeva vyākriyate 'saunāmāyamidaṁ̐rūpa iti tadidamapyetarhi nāmarūpābhyāmeva vyākriyate 'saunāmāyamidaṁ̐rūpa iti sa eṣa iha praviṣṭaḥ। ā nakhāgrebhyo yathā kṣuraḥ kṣuradhāne 'vahitaḥ syādviśvambharo vā viśvambharakulāye taṁ na paśyanti। akṛtsno hi sa prāṇanneva prāṇo nāma bhavati। vadan vākpaśyaṁ̐ścakṣuḥ śṛṇvan śrotraṁ manvāno manastānyasyaitāni karmanāmānyeva sa yo 'ta ekaikamupāste na sa vedākṛtsno hyeṣo 'ta ekaikena bhavatātmetyevopāsītātra hyete sarva ekaṁ bhavanti tadetatpadanīyamasya sarvasya yadayamātmā 'nena hyetatsarvaṁ veda। yathā ha vai padenānuvindedevaṁ kīrtiṁ̐ ślokaṁ vindate ya evaṁ veda ॥7॥

Now, all this universe was then undifferentiated. It became differentiated by name and form: it was known by such and such a name and such and such a form. Thus, to this day this universe is differentiated by name and form; so it is said: "He has such a name and such a form." This Self has entered into these bodies up to the very tips of the nails, as a razor lies hidden in its case, or as fire, which sustains the world, lies hidden in its source. People do not see the Self, for when viewed in parts It is incomplete: when breathing, It is called the vital breath (*prāṇa*); when speaking, the organ of speech; when seeing, the eye; when hearing, the ear; when thinking, the mind. These are merely Its names according to Its functions. He who meditates on one or another of Its aspects does not know, for It is then incomplete: the Self is separated from Its totality by being associated with a single characteristic. The Self alone is to be meditated upon, for in It all these become unified. Of all these, this Self alone should be known, for in it all these become one. This Self is the foot-trace of all this, for by it one knows all this, just as by its footprints one can find again (a lost cow). He who knows this obtains fame and association with dear ones.

तदेतत्प्रेयः पुत्रात्प्रेयो वित्तात्प्रेयोऽन्यस्मात्सर्वस्मादन्तरतरं यदयमात्मा स योऽन्यमात्मनः प्रियं ब्रुवाणं ब्रूयात् प्रियँ रोत्स्यतीतीश्वरो ह तथैव स्यादात्मानमेव प्रियमुपासीत स य आत्मानमेव प्रियमुपास्ते न हास्य प्रियं प्रमायुकं भवति ॥८॥

tadetatpreyaḥ putrātpreyo vittātpreyo 'nyasmātsarvasmādantarataraṁ yadayamātmā sa yo 'nyamātmanaḥ priyaṁ bruvāṇaṁ brūyāt priyam̐ rotsyatītīśvaro ha tathaiva syādātmānameva priyamupāsīta sa ya ātmānameva priyamupāste na hāsya priyaṁ pramāyukaṁ bhavati ॥8॥

This Self is dearer than a son, dearer than wealth, dearer than everything else, because It is innermost. If one holding the Self dear were to say to a person who speaks of anything other than the Self as dear, that he, the latter, will lose what he holds dear – and the former is certainly competent to do so – it will indeed come true. One should meditate upon the Self alone as dear. He who meditates upon the Self alone as dear – what he holds dear will not perish.

तदाहुर्यद्ब्रह्मविद्यया सर्वं भविष्यन्तो मनुष्या मन्यन्ते किमु तद्ब्रह्माऽवेद्यस्मात्तत्सर्वमभवदिति ॥९॥

tadāhuryadbrahmavidyayā sarvaṁ bhaviṣyanto manuṣyā manyante kimu tadbrahmā 'vedyasmāttatsarvamabhavaditi ॥9॥

They say: "Since men think that by the Knowledge of *Brahman* they become all, what, pray, was it that *Brahman* knew by which It became all?"

ब्रह्म वा इदमग्र आसीत् तदात्मानमेवावेदहं ब्रह्मास्मीति तस्मात्तत् सर्वमभवत् तद्यो यो देवानां प्रत्यबुध्यत स एव तदभवत्तथर्षीनां तथा मनुष्याणां तद्धैतत्पश्यन्नृषिर्वामदेवः प्रतिपेदेऽहं मनुरभवँ सूर्यश्चेति तदिदमप्येतर्हि य एवं वेदाऽहं ब्रह्मास्मीति स इदँ सर्वं भवति तस्य ह न देवाश्चनाभूत्या ईशत आत्मा ह्येषाँ स भवत्यथ योऽन्यां देवतामुपास्तेऽन्योऽसावन्योऽहमस्मीति न स वेद यथा पशुरेवँ स देवानां यथा ह वै बहवः पशवो मनुष्यं भुञ्ज्युरेवमेकैकः पुरुषो देवान् भुनक्त्येकस्मिन्नेव पशावादीयमानेऽप्रियं भवति किमु बहुषु तस्मादेषां तन्न प्रियं यदेतन्मनुष्या विद्युः ॥१०॥

brahma vā idamagra āsīt tadātmānamevāvedahaṁ brahmāsmīti tasmāt tatsarvamabhavat tadyo yo devānāṁ pratyabudhyata sa eva tadabhavattatharṣīnāṁ tathā manuṣyāṇāṁ taddhaitat-paśyannṛṣirvāmadevaḥ pratipede 'haṁ manurabhavaṁ̐ sūryaśceti tadidamapyetarhi ya evaṁ vedā 'haṁ brahmāsmīti sa idaṁ̐ sarvaṁ bhavati tasya ha na devāścanābhūtyā īśata ātmā hyeṣāṁ̐ sa bhavatyatha yo 'nyāṁ devatāmupāste 'nyo 'sāvanyo 'hamasmīti na sa veda yathā paśurevaṁ̐ sa devānāṁ yathā ha vai bahavaḥ paśavo manuṣyaṁ bhuñjyurevamekaikaḥ puruṣo devān bhunaktyekasminneva paśāvādīyamāne 'priyaṁ bhavati kimu bahuṣu tasmādeṣāṁ tanna priyaṁ yadetanmanuṣyā vidyuḥ ॥10॥

Brahman indeed was this in the beginning. It knew itself only as "I am *Brahman*". Therefore, it became all. Whoever among the gods had this knowing, also became That. It is the same with the seers (*ṛṣi*s), the same with men. The seer Vāmadeva, having realized this self as That, came to know: "I was Manu and the sun". And to this day, whoever in a like manner knows the self as "I am *Brahman*", becomes all this universe. Even the gods cannot prevent his becoming this, for he has become their Self. Now, if a man worships another deity, thinking: "He is one and I am another", he does not know. He is like an animal to the gods. As many animals serve a man, so does each man serves the gods. Even if one animal is taken away, it causes anguish to the owner; how much more so when many are taken away! Therefore, it is not pleasing to the gods that men should know this.

ब्रह्म वा इदमग्र आसीदेकमेव तदेकँ सन्न व्यभवत्तच्छ्रेयोरूपमत्यसृजत क्षत्रं यान्येतानि देवत्रा क्षत्राणीन्द्रो वरुणः सोमो रुद्रः पर्जन्यो यमो मृत्युरीशान इति तस्मात् क्षत्रात्परं नास्ति तस्माद्ब्राह्मणः क्षत्रियमधस्तादुपास्ते राजसूये क्षत्र एव तद्यशो दधाति सैषा क्षत्रस्य योनिर्यद्ब्रह्म। तस्माद्यद्यपि राजा परमतां गच्छति ब्रह्मैवान्तत उपनिश्रयति स्वां योनिं य उ एनँ हिनस्ति स्वाँ स योनिमृच्छति स पापीयान् भवति यथा श्रेयाँ सँ हिँ सित्वा ॥ ११॥

brahma vā idamagra āsīdekamevaṁ tadeka sanna vyabhavattacchreyorūpamatyasṛjata kṣatraṁ yānyetāni devatrā kṣatrāṇīndro varuṇaḥ somo rudraḥ parjanyo yamo mṛtyurīśāna iti tasmāt kṣatrātparaṁ nāsti tasmādbrāhmaṇaḥ kṣatriyamadhastādupāste rājasūye kṣatra eva tadyaśo dadhāti saiṣā kṣatrasya yoniryadbrahma ।
tasmādyadyapi rājā paramatāṁ gacchati brahmaivāntata upaniśrayati svāṁ yoniṁ ya u enaṁ hinasti svāṁ sa yonimṛcchati sa pāpīyān bhavati yathā śreyāṁsāṁ hiṁsitvā ॥11॥

In the beginning this was indeed *Brahman*, one only without a second. He, being one, did not flourish. He projected, further, an excellent form, the *kṣatra* power, even those who are *kṣatra*s (rulers) among the gods: Indra, Varuṇa, Soma (Moon), Rudra, Parjanya, Yama, Mṛtyu (Death) and Īśāna. Therefore, there is none higher than the kṣatriyas. Thus, at the Rājasūya sacrifice, the brāhmaṇa sits below and worships the kṣatriya. He confers that glory on kṣatriyahood alone. But brāhmaṇahood is nevertheless the source of kṣatriyahood. Thus, even though the king is exalted in the sacrifice, at the end of it he resorts to brāhmaṇahood as his source. He who slights a brāhmaṇa strikes at his own source. He becomes more evil, as one who slights his superior.

स नैव व्यभवत् स विशमसृजत यान्येतानि देवजातानि गणश आख्यायन्ते वसवो रुद्रा आदित्या विश्वेदेवा मरुत इति ॥ १२॥

sa naiva vyabhavat sa viśamasṛjata yānyetāni devajātāni gaṇaśa ākhyāyante vasavo rudrā ādityā viśvedevā maruta iti ॥12॥

Yet He did not flourish. He projected the *viś* (the commonalty) – those classes of gods who are designated in groups: the Vasus, Rudras, Ādityas, Viśvedevas and Maruts.

स नैव व्यभवत् स शौद्रं वर्णमसृजत पूषणमियं वै पूषेयँ हीदँ सर्वं पुष्यति यदिदं किंच ॥ १३॥

sa naiva vyabhavat sa śaudraṁ varṇamasṛjata pūṣaṇamiyaṁ vai pūṣeyaṁ̐ hīdaṁ̐ sarvaṁ puṣyati yadidaṁ kiṁca ॥3॥

Still He did not flourish. He projected the śūdra order as Pūṣaṇ. This earth is verily Pūṣaṇ (the nourisher); for it nourishes all that exists.

स नैव व्यभवत्तच्छ्रेयोरूपमत्यसृजत धर्मं तदेतत् क्षत्रस्य क्षत्रं यद्धर्मस्तस्माद्धर्मात्परं नास्त्यथो अबलीयान् बलीयाँ समाशँसते धर्मेण यथा राज्ञैवं यो वै स धर्मः सत्यं वै तत्तस्मात् सत्यं वदन्तमाहुर्धर्मं वदतीति धर्मं वा वदन्तँ सत्यं वदतीत्येतद्ध्येवैतदुभयं भवति ॥ १४॥

sa naiva vyabhavattacchreyorūpamatyasṛjata dharmaṁ tadetat-kṣatrasya kṣatraṁ yaddharmastasmāddharmātparaṁ nāstyatho abalīyān balīyāṁ̐ samaṁ̐śasate dharmeṇa yathā rājñaivaṁ yo vai sa dharmaḥ satyaṁ vai tattasmātsatyaṁ vadantamāhurdharmaṁ vadatīti dharmaṁ vā vadantaṁ̐ satyaṁ vadatītyetaddhyevaitadubhayaṁ bhavati ॥4॥

Yet He did not flourish. He projected, further, that excellent form, *dharma*. This *dharma* is the controller of the kṣatriya. Therefore, there is nothing higher than *dharma*. So, even a weak man hopes to defeat a stronger man through *dharma*, as one does with the help of a king. Verily, that which is *dharma* is truth. Hence, if a man speaks the truth, they say he speaks what is just and if he speaks what is just, they say he speaks the truth; for justice alone is both these.

तदेतद्ब्रह्म क्षत्रं विट् शूद्रस्तदग्निनैव देवेषु ब्रह्माभवद्ब्राह्मणो मनुष्येषु क्षत्रियेण क्षत्रियो वैश्येन वैश्यः शूद्रेण शूद्रस्तस्मादग्नावेव देवेषु लोकमिच्छन्ते ब्राह्मणे मनुष्येष्वेताभ्याँ हि रूपाभ्यां

ब्रह्माभवत्। अथ यो ह वा अस्माल्लोकात्स्वं लोकमदृष्ट्वा प्रैति स एनमविदितो न भुनक्ति यथा वेदो वाननूक्तोऽन्यद्वा कर्माकृतं यदिह वा अप्यनेवंविद् महत्पुण्यं कर्म करोति तद्धास्यान्ततः क्षीयत एवात्मानमेव लोकमुपासीत स य आत्मानमेव लोकमुपास्ते न हास्य कर्म क्षीयते अस्माद्ध्येवात्मनो यद्यत्कामयते तत्तत्सृजते ॥ १५॥

tadetadbrahma kṣatraṁ viṭ śūdrastadagninaiva deveṣu brahmābhavadbrāhmaṇo manuṣyeṣu kṣatriyeṇa kṣatriyo vaiśyena vaiśyaḥ śūdreṇa śūdrastasmādagnāveva deveṣu lokamicchante brāhmaṇe manuṣyeṣvetābhyām̐ hi rūpābhyāṁ brahmābhavat । atha yo ha vā asmāllokātsvaṁ lokamadṛṣṭvā praiti sa enamavidito na bhunakti yathā vedo vānanūkto 'nyadvā karmākṛtaṁ yadiha vā apyanevaṁvid mahatpuṇyaṁ karma karoti taddhāsyāntataḥ kṣīyata evātmānameva lokamupāsīta sa ya ātmānameva lokamupāste na hāsya karma kṣīyate asmāddhyevātmano yadyatkāmayate tattatsṛjate ॥15॥

So these, the brāhmaṇa, the kṣatriya, the vaiśya and the śūdra. Among the gods *Brahman* became fire and among men He became the brāhmaṇa. He became a kṣatriya through kṣatriya power, a vaiśya through vaiśya power and a śūdra through śūdra power. Therefore, by fire people desire the world of the gods and (a place) among men (in the power of) a brāhmaṇa. For *Brahman* existed (predominantly) in these two forms. Now, if a man departs from this world without realizing his own World, It, being unknown, does not protect him – as the Vedas, unrecited, or as a deed unaccomplished, do not protect him. Nay, even if one who does not know It should perform here on earth a great many meritorious acts, those acts will in the end surely perish for him. One should meditate only upon the World of the Self (*ātman*). He who meditates upon the World of the Self (*ātman*), his work does not perish; for from this very *ātman* he creates whatever he desires.

अथो अयं वा आत्मा सर्वेषां भूतानां लोकः स यज्जुहोति यद्यजते तेन देवानां लोकोऽथ यदनुब्रूते तेन ऋषीणामथ यत्पितृभ्यो निपृणाति यत्प्रजामिच्छते तेन पितॄणामथ यन्मनुष्यान्वासयते यदेभ्योऽशनं ददाति तेन मनुष्याणामथ यत्पशुभ्यस्तृणोदकं विन्दति तेन पशूनां यदस्य गृहेषु

श्वापदा वयाँस्यापिपीलिकाभ्य उपजीवन्ति तेन तेषां लोको यथा ह वै स्वाय लोकायारिष्टिमिच्छेदेवँ हैवंविदे सर्वाणि भूतान्यरिष्टिमिच्छन्ति तद्वा एतद्विदितं मीमाँसितम् ॥ १६॥

atho ayaṁ vā ātmā sarveṣāṁ bhūtānāṁ lokaḥ sa yajjuhoti yadyajate tena devānāṁ loko 'tha yadanubrūte tena ṛṣīṇāmatha yatpitṛbhyo nipṛṇāti yatprajāmicchate tena pitṝṇāmatha yanmanuṣyānvāsayate yadebhyo 'śanaṁ dadāti tena manuṣyāṇāmatha yatpaśubhyastṛṇodakaṁ vindati tena paśūnāṁ yadasya gṛheṣu śvāpadā vayām̐syāpipīlikābhya upajīvanti tena teṣāṁ loko yathā ha vai svāya lokāyāriṣṭimicchedevam̐ haivaṁvide sarvāṇi bhūtānyariṣṭimicchanti tadvā etadviditaṁ mīmām̐sitam ॥

Now, this self is the world of all beings. Insofar as he offers oblations in the fire and performs sacrifices, he becomes the world of the gods. Insofar as he studies the Vedas, he becomes the world of the *ṛṣis*. Insofar as he makes offerings to the forefathers and desires offspring, he becomes the world of the forefathers. Insofar as he gives shelter and food to humans, he becomes the world of humans. Insofar as he gives fodder and water to the animals, he becomes the world of the animals. Insofar as beasts and birds and even ants find a living in his home, he becomes their world. Just as one wishes no injury to one's body, so do all beings wish no injury to him who has this knowledge. All this, indeed, has been known and well investigated.

आत्मैवेदमग्र आसीदेक एव सोऽकामयत जाया मे स्यादथ प्रजायेयाथ वित्तं मे स्यादथ कर्म कुर्वीयेत्येतावान् वै कामो नेच्छँश्चनातो भूयो विन्देत्तस्मादप्येतर्ह्येकाकी कामयते जाया मे स्यादथ प्रजायेयाथ वित्तं मे स्यादथ कर्म कुर्वीयेति स यावदप्येतेषामेकैकं न प्राप्नोत्यकृत्स्न एव तावन्मन्यते तस्यो कृत्स्नता मन एवास्यात्मा वाग्जाया प्राणः प्रजा चक्षुर्मानुषं वित्तं चक्षुषा हि तद्विन्दते श्रोत्रं देवँ श्रोत्रेण हि तच्छृणोत्यात्मैवास्य कर्मात्मना हि कर्म करोति स एष पाङ्क्तो यज्ञः पाङ्क्तः पशुः पाङ्क्तः पुरुषःपाङ्क्तमिदँ सर्वं यदिदं किंच तदिदँ सर्वमाप्नोति य एवं वेद ॥१७॥

ātmaivedamagra āsīdeka eva so 'kāmayata jāyā me syādatha prajāyeyātha vittaṁ me syādatha karma kurvīyetyetāvān vai kāmo necchām̐ścanāto bhūyo vindettasmadapyetarhyekākī kāmayate jāyā me syādatha prajāyeyātha vittaṁ me syādatha karma kurvīyeti sa yāvadapyeteṣāmekaikaṁ na prāpnotyakṛtsna eva tāvanmanyate tasyo kṛtsnatā mana evāsyātmā vāgjāyā prāṇaḥ prajā cakṣurmānuṣaṁ vittaṁ caksuṣā hi tadvindate śrotraṁ devaṁ śrotreṇa hi tacchṛṇotyātmaivāsya karmātmanā hi karma karoti sa eṣa pāṅkto yajñaḥ pāṅktaḥ paśuḥ pāṅktaḥ puruṣaḥpāṅktamidaṁ sarvaṁ yadidaṁ kicaṁ tadidaṁ sarvamāpnoti ya evaṁ veda ॥17 ॥

In the beginning this was just the self, one only. He desired: "Let me have a wife, so that I may be born as the child; and let me have wealth, so that I may perform rites." This much, indeed, is the range of desire; even if one wishes, one cannot get more than this. Therefore, to this day, a man who is single desires: "Let me have a wife, so that I may be born as the child; and let me have wealth, so that I may perform rites." So long as he does not obtain each one of these, he thinks he is incomplete. Now, his completeness: The mind is his self, speech his wife, the vital breath his child, the eye his human wealth, for he finds it with the eye; the ear his divine wealth, for he hears it with the ear; the body his instrument of rites, for he performs rites through the body. So, this sacrifice has five factors – the animals have five factors, men have five factors and all this that exists has five factors. He who knows this obtains all this.

Adhyāya I: Brāhmaṇa 5

यत्सप्तान्नानि मेधया तपसाजनयत्पिता। एकमस्य साधारणं द्वे देवानभाजयत्। त्रीण्यात्मनेऽकुरुत पशुभ्य एकं प्रायच्छत्तस्मिन्त्सर्वं प्रतिष्ठितं यच्च प्राणिति यच्च न कस्मात्तानि न क्षीयन्तेऽद्यमानानि सर्वदा। यो वैतामक्षितिं वेद सोऽन्नमत्ति प्रतीकेन स देवानपि यच्छति स ऊर्जमुपजीवतीति श्लोकाः ॥१॥

yatsaptānnāni medhayā tapasājanayatpitā। ekamasya sādhāraṇaṁ dve devānabhājayat। trīṇyātmane 'kuruta paśubhya ekaṁ prāyacchattasmintsarvaṁ pratiṣṭhitaṁ yacca prāṇiti yacca na। kasmāttāni na kṣīyante 'dyamānāni sarvadā। yo vaitāmakṣitiṁ veda so 'nnamatti pratīkena sa devānapiyacchati sa ūrjamupajīvatīti ślokāḥ ॥1 ॥

The father produced seven kinds of food (*anna*) through Intelligence (*medhā*) and Concentration (*tapas*). One is common to all (*sādhāraṇa*). Two he portioned to the gods (*deva*s). Three he kept for his Self (*ātman*). And one he gave to the animals (*paśu*). On it rests everything – what lives and what does not. Why are they not exhausted, although they are eaten everyday? He who knows this cause of their permanence eats food with *pratīka* (the image). He goes to the gods, he lives on strength. Thus the verses.

यत्सप्तान्नानि मेधया तपसाजनयत्पितेति मेधया हि तपसाऽजनयत्पितैकमस्य साधारणमितीदमेवास्य तत्साधारणमन्नं यदिदमद्यते स य एतदुपास्ते न स पाप्मनो व्यावर्तते मिश्रँ ह्येत द्वै देवानभाजयदिति हुतं च प्रहुतं च तस्माद्देवेभ्यो जुह्वति च प्र च जुह्वत्यथो आहुर्दर्शपूर्णमासाविति। तस्मान्नेष्टियाजुकः स्यात्पशुभ्य एकं प्रायच्छदिति तत्पयः पयो ह्येवाग्रे मनुष्याश्च पशवश्चोपजीवन्ति तस्मात् कुमारं जातं घृतं वै वाग्रे प्रतिलेहयन्ति स्तनं वानुधापयन्त्यथ वत्सं जातमाहुरतृणाद इति। तस्मिन् सर्वं प्रतिष्ठितं यच्च प्राणिति यच्च नेति पयसि हीदँ सर्वं प्रतिष्ठितं यच्च प्राणिति यच्च न। तद्यदिदमाहुः संवत्सरं पयसा जुह्वदप पुनर्मृत्युं जयतीति न तथा विद्याद्यदहरेव जुहोति तदहः पुनर्मृत्युमपजयत्येवंविद्वान्सर्वँ हि देवेभ्योऽन्नाद्यं प्रयच्छति। कस्मात्तानि न क्षीयन्तेऽद्यमानानि सर्वदेति पुरुषो वा अक्षितिः स हीदमन्नं पुनः पुनर्जनयते। यो वैतामक्षितिं वेदेति पुरुषो वा अक्षितिः स हीदमन्नं धिया धिया जनयते। कर्मभिर्यद्धैतन्न कुर्यात्क्षीयेत ह सोऽन्नमत्ति प्रतीकेनेति मुखं प्रतीकं मुखेनेत्येतत्स देवानपि गच्छति स ऊर्जमुपजीवतीति प्रशँसा ॥२॥

yatsaptānnāni medhayā tapasājanayatpiteti medhayā hi tapasā 'janayatpitaikamasya sādhāraṇamitīdamevāsya tatsādhāraṇamannaṁ yadidamadyate sa ya etadupāste na sa pāpmano vyāvartate miśraṁ̐ hyetadvai devānabhājayaditi hutaṁ ca prahutaṁ ca tasmāddevebhyo juhvati ca pra ca juhvatyatho āhurdarśapūrṇamāsāviti । *tasmānneṣṭiyājukaḥ syātpaśubhya ekaṁ prāyacchaditi tatpayaḥ payo hyevāgre manuṣyāśca paśavaścopajīvanti tasmāt kumāraṁ jātaṁ ghṛtaṁ vai vāgre pratilehayanti stanaṁ vānudhāpayantyatha vatsaṁ jātamāhuratṛṇāda iti* । *tasmin sarvaṁ pratiṣṭhitaṁ yacca prāṇiti yacca neti payasi hīdaṁ̐ sarvaṁ pratiṣṭhitaṁ yacca prāṇiti yacca na* । *tadyadidamāhuḥ saṁvatsaraṁ payasā juhvadapa punarmṛtyuṁ jayatīti na tathā vidyādyadahareva juhoti tadahaḥ punarmṛtyumapajayatyevaṁvidvānsarvaṁ̐ hi devebhyo 'nnādyaṁ prayacchati । kasmāttāni na kṣīyante 'dyamānāni sarvadeti puruṣo vā akṣitiḥ sa hīdamannaṁ punaḥ punarjanayate । yo vaitāmakṣitiṁ vedeti puruṣo vā akṣitiḥ sa hīdamannaṁ dhiyā dhiyā janayate । karmabhiryaddhaitanna kuryātkṣīyeta ha so 'nnamatti pratīkeneti mukhaṁ pratīkaṁ mukhenetyetatsa devānapi gacchati sa ūrjamupajīvatīti praśaṁsā* ॥2॥

When the father produced seven kinds of food through Intelligence and Will, it means that the father indeed produced them through Intelligence and Will. "One is common to all eaters" means, this food that is eaten is the common food of all eaters. He who venerates this food is never free from sin (*pāpa*), for it is mixed (*miśram*). "Two he portioned to the gods", means the fire offerings (*hutam*) and the will behind these offerings (*prahutam*). Therefore, both of these are offered to the gods. Some, however, say, those two are the new and full moon sacrifices. Therefore, one should not be engrossed with sacrifices for material ends. "One he gave to the animals" – it is milk (*payaḥ*). For men and animals first live on milk alone. Therefore, they first make a new-born babe lick clarified butter (*ghṛta*) or suckle it. And they speak of a new-born calf as one not yet eating grass. "On it rests everything – what lives and what does not" means that on milk indeed rests all this that lives and that does not. It is said that by making offerings of milk in the fire for a year one conquers further death (*punarmṛtyu*). One should not think thus. He who knows this conquers further death the very day he makes that offering, for he offers all his food to the gods. "Why are they not exhausted, although they are always being eaten?" – means that the Person (*Puruṣa*) is indeed the cause of their permanence, for he produces this food again and again. "He who knows this cause of their permanence" means that the *Puruṣa* is indeed the cause of their permanence, for he produces this food through his continuous work (*karma*) of concentration (*dhiyā dhiyā*). Should he not do this, it will be exhausted. "He eats food with *Pratīka*." The mouth (*mukha*) is the *Pratīka*, he eats with the mouth. "He attains the gods, he lives on strength (*ūrjā*)." This is a eulogy.

त्रीण्यात्मनेऽकुरुतेति मनो वाचं प्राणं तान्यात्मनेऽकुरुतान्यत्रमना अभूवं नादर्शमन्यत्रमना अभूवं नाश्रौषमिति मनसा ह्येव पश्यति मनसा शृणोति। कामः सङ्कल्पो विचिकित्सा श्रद्धाऽश्रद्धा धृतिरधृतिर्ह्रीर्धीर्भीरित्येतत्सर्वं मन एव तस्मादपि पृष्ठत उपस्पृष्टो मनसा विजानाति यः कश्च शब्दो वागेव सैषा ह्यन्तमायत्तैषा हि न प्राणोऽपानो व्यान उदानः समानोऽन इत्येतत्सर्वं प्राण एवैतन्मयो वा अयमात्मा वाङ्मयो मनोमयः प्राणमयः ॥३॥

trīṇyātmane 'kuruteti mano vācaṁ prāṇaṁ tānyātmane 'kurutānyatramanā abhūvaṁ nādarśamanyatramanā abhūvaṁ nāśrauṣamiti manasā hyeva paśyati manasā śṛṇoti । *kāmaḥ saṅkalpo vicikitsā śraddhā 'śraddhā dhṛtiradhṛtirhrīrdhīrbhīrityetatsarvaṁ mana eva tasmādapi pṛṣṭhata upaspṛṣṭo manasā vijānāti yaḥ kaśca śabdo vāgeva saiṣā hyantamāyattaiṣā hi na prāṇo 'pāno vyāna udānaḥ samāno 'na ityetatsarvaṁ prāṇa evaitanmayo vā ayamātmā vāṅmayo manomayaḥ prāṇamayaḥ* ॥

"Three he made for his-Self (*ātman*)": Mind, Speech and the Life-force, these he made for himself. (One says), "My mind was elsewhere, I did not see it", "My mind was elsewhere, I did not hear it". It is through the mind that one sees and hears. Desire, purpose, doubt, faith, lack of faith, steadiness, unsteadiness, shame, intelligence and fear – all these are but the mind. Even if one is touched from behind, one knows it through the mind; therefore (the mind exists). And any kind of sound is but Speech, for it serves to determine a thing but it cannot itself be revealed. *Prāṇa, apāna, vyāna, udāna* and *samāna* – all these are but the Life-force. This body is identified with these – with Speech, Mind and the Life-force.

त्रयो लोका एत एव वागेवायं लोको मनोऽन्तरिक्षलोकः प्राणोऽसौ लोकः ॥४॥

trayo lokā eta eva vāgevāyaṁ loko mano 'ntarikṣalokaḥ prāṇo 'sau lokaḥ ॥4॥

These are the three worlds. Speech is this world (the Earth),

Mind is the Midworld (*antarikṣa*) and the Life-force (*prāṇa*) is that world (Heaven).

त्रयो वेदा एत एव वागेवर्ग्वेदो मनो यजुर्वेदः प्राणः सामवेदः ॥५॥

trayo vedā eta eva vāgevargvedo mano yajurvedaḥ prāṇaḥ sāmavedaḥ ॥5 ॥

These are the three Vedas. Speech is the *Ṛgveda,* Mind is the *Yajurveda* and the Life-force the *Sāmaveda*.

देवाः पितरो मनुष्या एत एव वागेव देवा मनः पितरः प्राणो मनुष्याः ॥६॥

devāḥ pitaro manuṣyā eta eva vāgeva devā manaḥ pitaraḥ prāṇo manuṣyāḥ ॥6 ॥

These are the gods (*deva*s), the ancestors (*pitṛ*s) and men (*manuṣya*s). Speech is the gods, Mind the ancestors and the Life-force men.

पिता माता प्रजैत एव मन एव पिता वाङ्माता प्राणः प्रजा ॥७॥

pitā mātā prajaita eva mana eva pitā vāṅmātā prāṇaḥ prajā ॥7 ॥

These are the father, mother and child. Mind is the father, Speech the mother and the Life-force the child.

विज्ञातं विजिज्ञास्यमविज्ञातमेत एव यत् किंच विज्ञातं वाचस्तद्रूपम् वाग्घि विज्ञाता वागेनं तद्भूत्वाऽवति ॥८॥

vijñātaṁ vijijñāsyamavijñātameta eva yat kiṁca vijñātaṁ vācastadrūpam vāgghi vijñātā vāgenaṁ tadbhūtvā 'vati ॥8 ॥

These are what is known, what it is desirable to know and what is/unknown. Whatever is known is a form of Speech, for it is the Knower. Speech protects him by becoming that (which is known).

यत्किञ्च विजिज्ञास्यं मनसस्तद्रूपम् मनो हि विजिज्ञास्यं मन एनं तद्भूत्वावति ॥९॥

yatkiñca vijijñāsyaṁ manasastadrūpam mano hi vijijñāsyaṁ mana enaṁ tadbhūtvāvati ॥9 ॥

Whatever it is desirable to know is a form of Mind, for the Mind is what it is desirable to know. Mind protects him by becoming that (which it is desirable to know).

यत्किञ्चाविज्ञातं प्राणस्य तद्रूपं प्राणो ह्यविज्ञातः प्राण एनं तद्भूत्वावति ॥१०॥

yatkiñcāvijñātaṁ prāṇasya tadrūpaṁ prāṇo hyavijñātaḥ prāṇa enaṁ tadbhūtvāvati ॥10॥

Whatever is unknown is a form of the Life-force, for the Life-force is what is unknown. The Life-force protects him by becoming that (which is unknown).

तस्यै वाचः पृथिवी शरीरं ज्योतीरूपमयमग्निस्तद्यावत्येव वाक्तावती पृथिवी तावानयमग्निः ॥११॥

tasyai vācaḥ pṛthivī śarīraṁ jyotīrūpamayamagnistadyāvatyeva vāktāvatī pṛthivī tāvānayamagniḥ ॥11॥

The earth is the body of Speech and Fire is its form of Illumination. And as far as Speech extends, so far extends the Earth and so far does this Fire.

अथैतस्य मनसो द्यौः शरीरं ज्योतीरूपमसावादित्यस्तद्यावदेव मनस्तावती द्यौस्तावानसावादित्यस्तौ मिथुनँ समैतां ततः प्राणोऽजायत स इन्द्रः स एषोऽसपत्नो द्वितीयो वै सपत्नो नास्य सपत्नो भवति य एवं वेद ॥१२॥

athaitasya manaso dyauḥ śarīraṁ jyotīrūpamasāvādityastadyāvadeva manastāvatī dyaustāvānasāvādityastau mithunam̐ samaitāṁ tataḥ prāṇo 'jāyata sa indraḥ sa eṣo 'sapatno dvitīyo vai sapatno nāsya sapatno bhavati ya evaṁ veda ॥12॥

Heaven is the body of this mind and that Sun is its form of Illumination. And as far as the mind extends, so far extends heaven and so far does that Sun. These two had intercourse, and from that the Life-force was born. It is Indra, the Lord of gods. It is unrivalled. A second is indeed a rival. He who knows this has no rival.

अथैतस्य प्राणस्यापः शरीरं ज्योतीरूपमसौ चन्द्रस्तद्यावानेव प्राणस्तावत्य आपस्तावानसौ चन्द्रस्त एते सर्व एव समाः सर्वेऽनन्ताः स यो हैतानन्तवत उपास्तेऽन्तवन्तँ स लोकं जयत्यथ यो

हैताननन्तानुपास्तेऽनन्तँ स लोकं जयति ॥ १३॥

athaitasya prāṇasyāpaḥ śarīraṁ jyotīrūpamasau candrastadyāvāneva prāṇastāvatya āpastāvānasau candrasta ete sarva eva samāḥ sarve 'nantāḥ sa yo haitānantavata upāste 'ntavantam̐ sa lokaṁ jayatyatha yo haitānanantānupāste 'nantam̐ sa lokaṁ jayati ॥13॥

Water is the body of this Life-force, and that Moon is its form of Illumination. And as far as the Life-force extends, so far extends Water and so far does that Moon. These are all equal and all Infinite. He who meditates upon these as finite wins a finite world, but he who meditates upon these as Infinite wins an infinite world.

स एष संवत्सरः प्रजापतिः षोडशकलस्तस्य रात्रय एव पञ्चदशकला ध्रुवैवास्य षोडशी कला स रात्रिभिरेवा च पूर्यतेऽप च क्षीयते सोऽमावास्या रात्रिमेतयाँ षोडश्या कलया सर्वमिदं प्राणभृदनुप्रविश्य ततः प्रातर्जायते तस्मादेताँ रात्रिं प्राणभृतः प्राणं न विच्छिन्द्यादपि कृकलासस्यैतस्या एव देवताया अपचित्यै ॥ १४॥

sa eṣa saṁvatsaraḥ prajāpatiḥ ṣoḍaśakalastasya rātraya eva pañcadaśakalā dhruvaivāsya ṣoḍaśī kalā sa rātribhirevā ca pūryate 'pa ca kṣīyate so 'māvāsyām̐ rātrimetayā ṣoḍaśyā kalayā sarvamidaṁ prāṇabhṛdanupraviśya tataḥ prātarjāyate tasmādetām̐ rātriṁ prāṇabhṛtaḥ prāṇaṁ na vicchindyādapi kṛkalāsasyaitasyā eva devatāyā apacityai ॥14॥

This Prajāpati has sixteen digits (*ṣoḍaśa kalā*) and is represented by the year (*saṁvatsara*). The nights are his fifteen digits and the constant one (*dhruva*) is his sixteenth digit. He waxes and wanes by the nights. Through this sixteenth digit he permeates all these living beings on the night of *amāvasyā* and rises the next morning. Therefore, on this night, one should not take the life of living beings, not even of a lizard, in sole adoration of this deity.

यो वै स संवत्सरः प्रजापतिः षोडशकलोऽयमेव स योऽयमेवंवित्पुरुषस्तस्य वित्तमेव पञ्चदशकला आत्मैवास्य षोडशी कला स वित्तेनैवा च पूर्यतेऽप च क्षीयते तदेतन्नभ्यं यदयमात्मा प्रधिर्वित्तं तस्माद्यद्यपि सर्वज्यानिं जीर्यत आत्मना चेज्जीवति प्रधिनाऽगादित्येवाहुः ॥ १५॥

yo vai sa saṁvatsaraḥ prajāpatiḥ ṣoḍaśakalo'yameva sa yo 'yame-vaṁvitpuruṣastasya vittameva pañcadaśakalā ātmaivāsya ṣoḍaśī kalā sa vittenaivā ca pūryate 'pa ca kṣīyate tadetannabhyaṁ yadayamātmā pradhirvittaṁ tasmādyadyapi sarvajyāniṁ jīryata ātmanā cejjīvati pradhinā 'gādityevāhuḥ ॥15॥

The person here who knows this is indeed himself Prajāpati who has sixteen digits and is represented by the year. Wealth constitutes his fifteen digits and the Self his sixteenth digit. He is filled as well as wasted by wealth. This Self stands for the hub and wealth is the felloe. Therefore, if a man loses everything, but he himself lives, people say that he has only lost his felloe.

अथ त्रयो वाव लोका मनुष्यलोकः पितृलोको देवलोक इति सोऽयं मनुष्यलोकः पुत्रेणैव जय्यो नान्येन कर्मणा कर्मणा पितृलोको विद्यया देवलोको देवलोको वै लोकानाँ श्रेष्ठस्तस्माद्विद्यां प्रशँसन्ति ॥ १६॥

atha trayo vāva lokā manuṣyalokaḥ pitṛloko devaloka iti so 'yaṁ manuṣyalokaḥ putreṇaiva jayyo nānyena karmaṇā karmaṇā pitṛloko vidyayā devaloko devaloko vai lokānāṁ śreṣṭhastasmādvidyāṁ praśaṁsanti ॥16॥

There are indeed three worlds, the world of men, the world of the ancestors and the world of the gods. This world of men is to be won through the son (*putra*) alone and by no other work; the world of the ancestors through works (*karma*); and the world of the gods through knowledge (*vidyā*). The world of the gods is the best of the worlds. Therefore, they praise knowledge (*vidyā*).

अथातः सम्प्रत्तिर्यदा प्रैष्यन्मन्यतेऽथ पुत्रमाह त्वं ब्रह्म त्वं यज्ञस्त्वं लोक इति स पुत्रः प्रत्याहाहं ब्रह्माहं यज्ञोऽहं लोक इति यद्वै किंचानूक्तं तस्य सर्वस्य ब्रह्मेत्येकता। ये वै के च यज्ञास्तेषाँ सर्वेषां यज्ञ इत्येकता ये वै के च लोकास्तेषाँ सर्वेषां लोक इत्येकतैतावद्वा इदँ सर्वमेतन्मा सर्वँ सन्नयमितोऽभुनजदिति तस्मात् पुत्रमनुशिष्टं लोक्यमाहुस्तस्मादेनमनुशासति स यदैवंविद-स्माल्लोकात्प्रैत्यथैभिरेव प्राणैः सह पुत्रमाविशति स यद्यनेन किंचिदक्ष्णयाऽकृतं भवति तस्मादेनँ सर्वस्मात्पुत्रो मुञ्चति तस्मात्पुत्रो नाम स पुत्रेणैवास्मिँल्लोके प्रतितिष्ठत्यथैनमेते देवाः प्राणा अमृता आविशन्ति ॥ १७॥

athātaḥ samprattiryadā praiṣyanmanyate 'tha putramāha tvaṁ brahma tvaṁ yajñastvaṁ loka iti sa putraḥ pratyāhāhaṁ brahmāhaṁ yajño 'haṁ loka iti yadvai kiṁcānūktaṁ tasya sarvasya brahmetyekatā । ye vai ke ca yajñāsteṣām̐ sarveṣāṁ yajña ityekatā ye vai ke ca lokāsteṣām̐ sarveṣāṁ loka ityekataitāvadvā idam̐ sarvametanmā sarvam̐ sannayamito 'bhunajaditi tasmāt putramanuśiṣṭaṁ lokyamāhustasmādenamanuśāsati sa yadaivaṁvidasmāllokātpraityathaibhireva prāṇaiḥ saha putramāviśati sa yadyanena kiṁcidakṣṇayā 'kṛtaṁ bhavati tasmādenam̐ sarvasmātputro muñcati tasmātputro nāma sa putreṇaivāsmim̐lloke pratitiṣṭhatyathainamete devāḥ prāṇā amṛtā āviśanti ॥17॥

Now, therefore, the transmission (*samprattiḥ*): When a man thinks he will die, he says to his son, "You are *Brahman*, you are the sacrifice (*yajña*) and you are the world (*loka*)". The son replies, "I am *Brahman*, I am the sacrifice and I am the world". Whatever is studied is all unified in *Brahman*. Whatever sacrifices there are, are all unified in *yajña*. And whatever worlds there are, are all unified in this world (*loka*). Great, indeed, is the All (*sarva*). "He, being the All, will liberate me from this world." Therefore, a son, who is this instructed, is known as the Master of the world; therefore, is the son instructed. When one who knows this departs from this world, he enters his son with his breaths (*prāṇa*). Whatever wrong may have been done by him, the son liberates him from all that; therefore, he is called a son (*putra*). The father stands firm in this world through the son. Then the divine immortal breaths enter him.

पृथिव्यै चैनमग्नेश्च दैवी वागाविशति सा वै दैवी वाग्यया यद्यदेव वदति तत्तद्भवति ॥ १८॥

pṛthivyai cainamagneśca daivī vāgāviśati sā vai daivī vāgyayā yadyadeva vadati tattadbhavati ॥18॥

From the earth and from fire, Divine Speech enter him. That is the Divine Speech through which whatever he says is fulfilled.

दिवश्चैनमादित्याच्च दैवं मन आविशति तद्वै दैवं मनो येनानन्द्येव भवत्यथो न शोचति ॥ १९॥

divaścainamādityācca daivaṁ mana āviśati tadvai daivaṁ mano yenānandyeva bhavatyatho na śocati ॥19॥

From heaven and from the sun the Divine Mind enters him. That is the Divine Mind through which he becomes only blissful and never mourns.

अद्भ्यश्चैनं चन्द्रमसश्च दैवः प्राण आविशति स वै दैवः प्राणो यः संचरँश्चासंचरँश्च न व्यथतेऽथो न रिष्यति स एवंवित्सर्वेषां भूतानामात्मा भवति यथैषा देवतैवँ स यथैतां देवताँ सर्वाणि भूतान्यवन्त्येवँ हैवंविदँ सर्वाणि भूतान्यवन्ति यदु किंचेमाः प्रजाः शोचन्त्यमैवासां तद्भवति पुण्यमेवामुं गच्छति न ह वै देवान् पापं गच्छति ॥२०॥

adbhyaścainaṁ candramasaśca daivaḥ prāṇa āviśati sa vai daivaḥ prāṇo yaḥ saṁcaraṁ̐ścāsaṁcaraṁ̐śca na vyathate 'tho na riṣyati sa evaṁvitsarveṣāṁ bhūtānāmātmā bhavati yathaiṣā devataivaṁ̐ sa yathaitāṁ devatāṁ̐ sarvāṇi bhūtānyavantyevaṁ̐ haivaṁvidaṁ̐ sarvāṇi bhūtānyavanti yadu kiṁcemāḥ prajāḥ śocantyamaivāsāṁ tadbhavati puṇyamevāmuṁ gacchati na ha vai devān pāpaṁ gacchati ॥20॥

From water and from the moon the Divine Life-force enters him. That is the Divine Life-force which, whether it moves or is stationary, feels no pain nor is injured. He who knows this becomes the Self of all beings. As is this deity, so is he. As all beings take care of this deity, so do they take care of him. Howsoever these beings may grieve, that grief of theirs is connected with them. But only merit goes to him. No demerit ever goes to the gods.

अथातो व्रतमीमाँसा प्रजापतिर्ह कर्माणि ससृजे तानि सृष्टान्यन्योन्येनास्पर्धन्त वदिष्याम्येवाहमिति वाग्दध्रे द्रक्ष्याम्यहमिति चक्षुः श्रोष्याम्यहमिति श्रोत्रमेवमन्यानि कर्माणि यथाकर्म तानि मृत्युः श्रमो भूत्वोपयेमे तान्याप्नोत्तान्याप्त्वा मृत्युरवारुन्ध तस्माच्छ्राम्यत्येव वाक् श्राम्यति चक्षुः श्राम्यति श्रोत्रमथेममेव नाप्नोद्योऽयं मध्यमः प्राणस्तानि ज्ञातुं दध्रिर अयं वै नः श्रेष्ठो यः संचरँश्चासंचरँश्च न व्यथतेऽथो न रिष्यति हन्तास्यैव सर्वे रूपमसामेति त एतस्यैव सर्वे रूपमभवँस्तस्मादेत एतेनाख्यायन्ते प्राणा इति तेन ह वाव तत्कुलमाचक्षते यस्मिन्कुले भवति य एवं वेद य उ हैवंविदा स्पर्धतेऽनुशुष्यत्यनुशुष्य हैवान्ततो म्रियत इत्यध्यात्मम् ॥२१॥

athāto vratamīmāṁsā prajāpatirha karmāṇi sasṛje tāni sṛṣṭānyanyonyenāspardhanta vadiṣyāmyevāhamiti vāgdadhre drakṣyāmyahamiti cakṣuḥ śroṣyāmyahamiti śrotramevamanyāni karmāṇi yathākarma tāni mṛtyuḥ śramo bhūtvopayeme tānyāpnottānyāptvā mṛtyuravārundha tasmācchrāmyatyeva vāk śrāmyati cakṣuḥ śrāmyati śrotramathemameva nāpnodyo 'yaṁ madhyamaḥ prāṇastāni jñātuṁ dadhrira ayaṁ vai naḥ śreṣṭho yaḥ saṁcaraṁścāsaṁcaraṁśca na vyathate 'tho na riṣyati hantāsyaiva sarve rūpamasāmeti ta etasyaiva sarve rūpamabhavaṁstasmādeta etenākhyāyante prāṇā iti tena ha vāva tatkulamācakṣate yasminkule bhavati ya evaṁ veda ya u haivaṁvidā spardhate 'nuśuṣyatyanuśuṣya haivāntato mriyata ityadhyātmam ॥21 ॥

Now a consideration of the resolution/praxis (*vrata*): Prajāpati projected the organs of action. These, on being created, quarrelled with one another. The organ of Speech took a resolution, "I will go on speaking". The eye: "I will see". The ear: "I will hear". And so did the other organs according to their functions. Death captured them in the form of fatigue – it overtook them and having overtaken them it controlled them. Therefore, the organ of speech invariably gets tired and so do the eye and the ear. But death did not capture the "central breath" (*madhyama prāṇa*) in the body. The organs resolved to know it. "This is the greatest among us that, when it moves or does not move, feels no pain nor is injured. Well, let us all be of its form." They all assumed its form. Therefore, they are called by this name of *prāṇa*. That family in which a man is born, who knows this, is indeed named after him. And he who competes with one who knows this shrivels and after shrivelling dies at the end. This is with reference to the Self.

अथाधिदैवतम् ज्वलिष्याम्येवाहमित्यग्निर्दध्रे तप्स्याम्यहमित्यादित्यो भास्याम्यहमिति चन्द्रमा एवमन्या देवता यथादैवतँ स यथैषां प्राणानां मध्यमः प्राण एवमेतासां देवतानां वायुर्म्लोचन्ति ह्यन्या देवता न वायुः सैषानस्तमिता देवता यद्वायुः ॥२२॥

athādhidaivatam jvaliṣyāmyevāhamityagnirdadhre tapsyāmyahamityādityo bhāsyāmyahamiti candramā evamanyā devatā yathādaivataṁ sa yathaiṣāṁ prāṇānāṁ madhyamaḥ prāṇa evametāsāṁ devatānāṁ vāyurmlocanti hyanyā devatā na vāyuḥ saiṣānastamitā devatā yadvāyuḥ ॥22॥

Now with reference to the gods: Fire made a resolution, "I will go on burning". The sun: "I will give heat". The moon: "I will shine". And so did the other gods according to their functions. As is the Life-force in the body among these organs, so is Vāyu (Wind) among these gods. Other gods sink, but not Wind. Wind is the deity that never sets.

अथैष श्लोको भवति यतश्चोदेति सूर्योऽस्तं यत्र च गच्छतीति प्राणाद्वा एष उदेति प्राणेऽस्तमेति तं देवाश्चक्रिरे धर्मँ स एवाद्य स उ श्व इति यद्वा एतेऽमुर्ह्यध्रियन्त तदेवाप्यद्य कुर्वन्ति। तस्मादेकमेव व्रतं चरेत्प्राण्याच्चैवापान्याच्च नेन्मा पाप्मा मृत्युराप्नुवदिति यद्यु चरेत्समापिपयिषेत्तेनो एतस्यै देवतायै सायुज्यँ सलोकतां जयति ॥२३॥

athaiṣa śloko bhavati yataścodeti sūryo 'staṁ yatra ca gacchatīti prāṇādvā eṣa udeti prāṇe 'stameti taṁ devāścakrire dharmaṁ sa evādya sa u śva iti yadvā ete 'murhyadhriyanta tadevāpyadya kurvanti । *tasmādekameva vrataṁ caretprāṇyāccaivāpānyācca nenmā pāpmā mṛtyurāpnuvaditi yadyu caretsamāpipayiṣetteno etasyai devatāyai sāyujyaṁ salokatāṁ jayati* ॥23॥

Now there is this verse: "The gods observed the resolution of that from which the sun rises and in which he sets. It is (followed) today and it will be (followed) tomorrow." The sun indeed rises from the Life-force and also sets in it. What these (gods) observed then, they observe to this day. Therefore, a man should observe a single resolution – do the functions of the *prāṇa* and *apāna* (*prāṇāyāma*), lest the evil of death should take him. And if he observes it, he should seek to finish it. Through it, he attains identity with this deity and lives in the same world with it.

Adhyāya I: Brāhmaṇa 6

त्रयं वा इदं नाम रूपं कर्म तेषां नाम्नां वागित्येतदेषामुक्थमतो हि सर्वाणि नामान्युत्तिष्ठन्त्येतदेषाँ सामैतद्धि सर्वैर्नामभिः सममेतदेषां ब्रह्मैतद्धि सर्वाणि नामानि बिभर्ति ॥ १॥

trayaṁ vā idaṁ nāma rūpaṁ karma teṣāṁ nāmnāṁ vāgityetade-ṣāmukthamato hi sarvāṇi nāmānyuttiṣṭhantyetadeṣām̐ sāmaitaddhi sarvairnāmabhiḥ samametadeṣāṁ brahmaitaddhi sarvāṇi nāmāni bibharti ॥1 ॥

Indeed, here (all) is a triplicity of name, form and work. Of these, for names, speech is the source, for from it all names arise. It is the one (*sāman*) in them, for it is the same for all names. It is their *Brahman*, for it supports all names.

अथ रूपाणां चक्षुरित्येतदेषामुक्थमतो हि सर्वाणि रूपाण्युत्तिष्ठन्त्यतदेषाँ सामैतद्धि सर्वै रूपैः सममेतदेषां ब्रह्मैतद्धि सर्वाणि रूपाणि बिभर्ति ॥ २॥

atha rūpāṇāṁ cakṣurityetadeṣāmukthamato hi sarvāṇi rūpāṇyut-tiṣṭhantyatadeṣām̐ sāmaitaddhi sarvai rūpaiḥ samametadeṣāṁ brahmaitaddhi sarvāṇi rūpāṇi bibharti ॥2 ॥

Next, of forms, the eye is the source (*uktha*), for from it all forms arise. It is the one (*sāman*) in them, for it is the same for all forms. It is their *Brahman* (self), for it supports all forms.

अथ कर्मणामात्मेत्येतदेषामुक्थमतो हि सर्वाणि कर्माण्युत्तिष्ठन्त्येतदेषाँ सामैतद्धि सर्वैः कर्मभिः सममेतदेषां ब्रह्मैतद्धि सर्वाणि कर्माणि बिभर्ति तदेतत्त्रयँ सदेकमयमात्मात्मो एकः सन्नेतत्त्रयं तदेतदमृतँ सत्येन छन्नं प्राणो वा अमृतं नामरूपे सत्यं ताभ्यामयं प्राणश्छन्नः ॥ ३॥

atha karmaṇāmātmetyetadeṣāmukthamato hi sarvāṇi karmāṇyuttiṣṭhantyetadeṣām̐ sāmaitaddhi sarvaiḥ karmabhiḥ samametadeṣāṁ brahmaitaddhi sarvāṇi karmāṇi bibharti tadetattrayam̐ sadekamayamātmātmo ekaḥ sannetattrayaṁ tadetadamṛtam̐ satyena channaṁ prāṇo vā amṛtaṁ nāmarūpe satyaṁ tābhyāmayaṁ prāṇaśchannaḥ ॥3 ॥

Next, of work, the self (*ātman*) is the source (*uktha*), for from it all works arise. It is the one (*sāman*) in them, for it is the same for all works. It is their *Brahman*, for it supports all works. These three together are one – this self (*ātmā*); and the self (*ātma*), though one, is these three. This is the immortal covered by the real: the vital breath (*prāṇa*) is the immortal and name and form are the real and by them this life is covered.

Adhyāya II: Brāhmaṇa 1

दृप्तबालाकिर्हानूचानो गार्ग्य आस स होवाचाजातशत्रुं काश्यं ब्रह्म ते ब्रवाणीति स होवाचाजातशत्रुः सहस्रमेतस्यां वाचि दद्मो जनको जनक इति वै जना धावन्तीति ॥१॥

dṛptabālākirhānūcāno gārgya āsa sa hovācājātaśatruṁ kāśyaṁ brahma te bravāṇīti sa hovācājātaśatruḥ sahasrametasyāṁ vāci dadmo janako janaka iti vai janā dhāvantīti ॥1॥

Once there lived a man of the Gārgya clan named Dṛpta-Bālāki, who was a teacher of Vedic knowledge. He said to Ajātaśatru, king of Kāśī: "I will tell you about *Brahman*". Ajātaśatru said: "For this proposal I will give you 1,000 (cows). People will indeed come running, saying: 'Janaka, Janaka'."

स होवाच गार्ग्यो य एवासावादित्ये पुरुष एतमेवाहं ब्रह्मोपास इति स होवाचाजातशत्रुर्मा मैतस्मिन्संवदिष्ठा अतिष्ठाः सर्वेषां भूतानां मूर्धा राजेति वा अहमेतमुपास इति स य एतमेवमुपास्तेऽतिष्ठाः सर्वेषां भूतानां मूर्धा राजा भवति ॥२॥

sa hovāca gārgyo ya evāsāvāditye puruṣa etamevāhaṁ brahmopāsa iti sa hovācājātaśatrurmā maitasminsaṁvadiṣṭhā atiṣṭhāḥ sarveṣāṁ bhūtānāṁ mūrdhā rājeti vā ahametamupāsa iti sa ya etamevamupāste 'tiṣṭhāḥ sarveṣāṁ bhūtānāṁ mūrdhā rājā bhavati ॥2॥

Gārgya said: "That person (*puruṣa*) who is in the sun, I worship him as *Brahman.*" Ajātaśatru said: "Please do not talk to me about him. I adulate him as all-surpassing, as the head and king of all beings." Whosoever thus adulates him becomes all-surpassing, the head and king of all beings.

स होवाच गार्ग्यो य एवासौ चन्द्रे पुरुष एतमेवाहं ब्रह्मोपास इति स होवाचाजातशत्रुर्मा मैतस्मिन्संवदिष्ठा बृहन्पाण्डरवासाः सोमो राजेति वा अहमेतमुपास इति स य एतमेवमुपास्तेऽहरहर्ह

सुतः प्रसुतो भवति नास्यान्नं क्षीयते ॥३॥

sa hovāca gārgyo ya evāsau candre puruṣa etamevāhaṁ brahmopāsa iti sa hovācājātaśatrurmā maitasminsaṁvadiṣṭhā bṛhanpāṇḍaravāsāḥ somo rājeti vā ahametamupāsa iti sa ya etamevamupāste 'haraharha sutaḥ prasuto bhavati nāsyānnaṁ kṣīyate ॥3 ॥

Gārgya said: "That person (*puruṣa*) who is in the Moon, I worship him as *Brahman.*" Ajātaśatru said: "Please do not talk to me about him. I adulate him as the great, white-robed king Soma." Whosoever thus adulates him has abundant *soma* pressed for him everyday and his food never runs short.

स होवाच गार्ग्यो य एवासौ विद्युति पुरुष एतमेवाहं ब्रह्मोपास इति स होवाचाजातशत्रुर्मा मैतस्मिन्संवदिष्ठातेजस्वीति वा अहमेतमुपास इति स य एतमेवमुपास्ते तेजस्वी ह भवति तेजस्विनी हास्य प्रजा भवति ॥४॥

sa hovāca gārgyo ya evāsau vidyuti puruṣa etamevāhaṁ brahmopāsa iti sa hovācājātaśatrurmā maitasminsaṁvadiṣṭhāstejasvīti vā ahametamupāsa iti sa ya etamevamupāste tejasvī ha bhavati tejasvinī hāsya prajā bhavati ॥4 ॥

Gārgya said: "That person (*puruṣa*) who is in the Lightning, I worship him as *Brahman.*" Ajātaśatru said: "Please do not talk to me about him. I adulate him as the radiant one." Whosoever thus adulates him becomes radiant and his progeny too becomes radiant.

स होवाच गार्ग्यो य एवायमाकाशे पुरुष एतमेवाहं ब्रह्मोपास इति स होवाचाजातशत्रुर्मा मैतस्मिन्संवदिष्ठाः पूर्णमप्रवर्तीति वा अहमेतमुपास इति स य एतमेवमुपास्ते पूर्यते प्रजया पशुभिर्नास्यास्माल्लोकात्प्रजोद्वर्तते ॥५॥

sa hovāca gārgyo ya evāyamākāśe puruṣa etamevāhaṁ brahmopāsa iti sa hovācājātaśatrurmā maitasminsaṁvadiṣṭhāḥ pūrṇamapravartīti vā ahametamupāsa iti sa ya etamevamupāste pūryate prajayā paśubhi-rnāsyāsmāllokātprajodvartate ॥5 ॥

Gārgya said: "This person (*puruṣa*) who is in Space (*ākāśa*), I worship him as *Brahman.*" Ajātaśatru said: "Please do not talk about him. I adulate him as full and unexhausted." Whosoever thus adulates him is filled with progeny and cattle, and his progeny will never be extinct.

स होवाच गार्ग्यो य एवायं वायौ पुरुष एतमेवाहं ब्रह्मोपास इति स होवाचाजातशत्रुर्मा मैतस्मिन्संवदिष्ठा इन्द्रो वैकुण्ठोऽपराजिता सेनेति वा अहमेतमुपास इति स य एतमेवमुपास्ते जिष्णुर्हापराजिष्णुर्भवत्यन्यतस्त्यजायी ॥६॥

sa hovāca gārgyo ya evāyaṁ vāyau puruṣa etamevāhaṁ brahmopāsa iti sa hovācājātaśatrurmā maitasminsaṁvadiṣṭhā indro vaikuṇṭho 'parājitā seneti vā ahametamupāsa iti sa ya etamevamupāste jiṣṇurhāparājiṣṇurbhavatyanyatastyajāyī ॥6 ॥

Gārgya said: "This person (*puruṣa*) who is in the Wind (Vāyu), I worship him as *Brahman.*" Ajātaśatru said: "Please do not talk about him. I adulate him as the Lord (Indra), as irresistible and as the unvanquished army." Whosoever thus adulates him becomes ever victorious, invincible and a conqueror of enemies.

स होवाच गार्ग्यो य एवायमग्नौ पुरुष एतमेवाहं ब्रह्मोपास इति स होवाचाजातशत्रुर्मा मैतस्मिन्संवदिष्ठा विषासहिरिति वा अहमेतमुपास इति स य एतमेवमुपास्ते विषासहिर्ह भवति विषासहिर्हास्य प्रजा भवति ॥७॥

sa hovāca gārgyo ya evāyamagnau puruṣa etamevāhaṁ brahmopāsa iti sa hovācājātaśatrurmā maitasminsaṁvadiṣṭhā viṣāsahiriti vā ahametamupāsa iti sa ya etamevamupāste viṣāsahirha bhavati viṣāsahirhāsya prajā bhavati ॥7 ॥

Gārgya said: "This person (*puruṣa*) who is in Fire (Agni), I worship him as *Brahman.*" Ajātaśatru said: "Please do not talk about him. I adulate him as irresistible." Whosoever thus adulates him becomes irresistible and his progeny becomes irresistible.

स होवाच गार्ग्यो य एवायमप्सु पुरुष एतमेवाहं ब्रह्मोपास इति स होवाचाजातशत्रुर्मा मैतस्मिन्संवदिष्ठाः प्रतिरूप इति वा अहमेतमुपास इति स य एतमेवमुपास्ते प्रतिरूपँ

हैवैनमुपगच्छति नाप्रतिरूपमथो प्रतिरुपोऽस्माज्जायते ॥ ८ ॥

sa hovāca gārgyo ya evāyamapsu puruṣa etamevāhaṁ brahmopāsa iti sa hovācājātaśatrurmā maitasminsaṁvadiṣṭhāḥ pratirūpa iti vā ahametamupāsa iti sa ya etamevamupāste pratirūpaṁ haivainam-upagacchati nāpratirūpamatho pratirupo 'smājjāyate ॥8 ॥

Gārgya said: "This person (*puruṣa*) who is in Water, I worship him as *Brahman.*" Ajātaśatru said: "Please do not talk about him. I adulate him as an image." Whosoever thus adulates him, to him comes what is like him, not what is unlike him and to him are born children who are like him.

स होवाच गार्ग्यो य एवायमादर्शे पुरुष एतमेवाहं ब्रह्मोपास इति स होवाचाजातशत्रुर्मा मैतस्मिन्संवदिष्ठा रोचिष्णुरिति वा अहमेतमुपास इति स य एतमेवमुपास्ते रोचिष्णुर्ह भवति रोचिष्णुर्हास्य प्रजा भवत्यथो यैः सन्निगच्छति सर्वाँस्तानतिरोचते ॥ ९॥

sa hovāca gārgyo ya evāyamādarśe puruṣa etamevāhaṁ brahmopāsa iti sa hovācājātaśatrurmā maitasminsaṁvadiṣṭhā rociṣṇuriti vā ahametamupāsa iti sa ya etamevamupāste rociṣṇurha bhavati rociṣṇurhāsya prajā bhavatyatho yaiḥ sannigacchati sarvāṁstānatirocate ॥9 ॥

Gārgya said: "This person (*puruṣa*) who is in the mirror/ideal, I worship him as *Brahman.*" Ajātaśatru said: "Please do not talk about him. I adulate him as the shining one." Whosoever thus adulates him becomes shining and his progeny too becomes shining and he outshines all those with whom he comes in contact.

स होवाच गार्ग्यो य एवायं यन्तं पश्चाच्छब्दोऽनूदेत्येतमेवाहं ब्रह्मोपास इति स होवाचाजातशत्रुर्मा मैतस्मिन्संवदिष्ठा असुरिति वा अहमेतमुपास इति स य एतमेवमुपास्ते सर्वँ हैवास्मिँल्लोक आयुरेति नैनं पुरा कालात्प्राणो जहाति ॥ १० ॥

sa hovāca gārgyo ya evāyaṁ yantaṁ paścācchabdo 'nūdetyetamevāhaṁ brahmopāsa iti sa hovācājātaśatrurmā maitasminsaṁvadiṣṭhā asuriti vā ahametamupāsa iti sa ya etamevamupāste sarvaṁ haivāsmiṁlloka āyureti nainaṁ purā kālātprāṇo jahāti ॥10 ॥

Gārgya said: "The sound that arises behind a man while he walks, I worship as *Brahman.*" Ajātaśatru said: "Please do not talk about him. I adulate him as life." Whosoever thus adulates him reaches his full lifespan on this earth and life does not depart from him before the completion of that time.

स होवाच गार्ग्यो य एवायं दिक्षु पुरुष एतमेवाहं ब्रह्मोपास इति स होवाचाजातशत्रुर्मा मैतस्मिन्संवदिष्ठा द्वितीयोऽनपग इति वा अहमेतमुपास इति स य एतमेवमुपास्ते द्वितीयवान् ह भवति नास्माद्गणश्छिद्यते ॥११॥

sa hovāca gārgyo ya evāyaṁ dikṣu puruṣa etamevāhaṁ brahmopāsa iti sa hovācājātaśatrurmā maitasminsaṁvadiṣṭhā dvitīyo 'napaga iti vā ahametamupāsa iti sa ya etamevamupāste dvitīyavān ha bhavati nāsmādgaṇaśchidyate ॥11 ॥

Gārgya said: "This person (*puruṣa*) who is in the directions, I worship him as *Brahman.*" Ajātaśatru said: "Please do not talk about him. I adulate him as the double who never leaves us." Whosoever thus adulates him receives a double who does not part with him.

स होवाच गार्ग्यो य एवायं छायामयः पुरुष एतमेवाहं ब्रह्मोपास इति स होवाचाजातशत्रुर्मा मैतस्मिन्संवदिष्ठा मृत्युरिति वा अहमेतमुपास इति स य एतमेवमुपास्ते सर्वँ हैवास्मिँल्लोक आयुरेति नैनं पुरा कालान्मृत्युरागच्छति ॥१२॥

sa hovāca gārgyo ya evāyaṁ chāyāmayaḥ puruṣa etamevāhaṁ brahmopāsa iti sa hovācājātaśatrurmā maitasminsaṁvadiṣṭhā mṛtyuriti vā ahametamupāsa iti sa ya etamevamupāste sarvam̐ haivāsmim̐lloka āyureti nainaṁ purā kālānmṛtyurāgacchati ॥12 ॥

Gārgya said: "This person (*puruṣa*) who consists of shadow, I worship him as *Brahman.*" Ajātaśatru said: "Please do not talk about him. I adulate him as death." Whosoever thus adulates him reaches his full lifespan on this earth and death does not overtake him before the completion of that time.

स होवाच गार्ग्यो य एवायमात्मनि पुरुषो एतमेवाहं ब्रह्मोपास इति स ह उवाचाजातशत्रुर्मा मैतस्मिन्संवदिष्ठा आत्मन्वीति वा अहमेतमुपास इति स य एतमेवमुपास्त आत्मन्वीह

भवत्यात्मन्विनी हास्य प्रजा भवति स ह तूष्णीमास गार्ग्यः ॥१३॥

sa hovāca gārgyo ya evāyamātmani puruṣo etamevāhaṁ brahmopāsa iti sa ha uvācājātaśatrurmā maitasminsaṁvadiṣṭhā ātmanvīti vā ahametamupāsa iti sa ya etamevamupāsta ātmanvīha bhavatyātmanvinī hāsya prajā bhavati sa ha tūṣṇīmāsa gārgyaḥ ॥13॥

Gārgya said: "This person (*puruṣa*) who is in the self (*ātman*), I worship him as *Brahman*." Ajātaśatru said: "Please do not talk about him. I adulate him as self-possessed." Whosoever thus adulates him becomes self-possessed and his progeny too becomes self-possessed. Gārgya remained silent.

स होवाचाजातशत्रुरेतावन्नू३ इत्येतावद्धीति नैतावता विदितं भवतीति स होवाच गार्ग्य उपत्वायानीति ॥१४॥

sa hovācājātaśatruretāvannū3 ityetāvaddhīti naitāvatā viditaṁ bhavatīti sa hovāca gārgya upatvāyānīti ॥14॥

Ajātaśatru said: "Is this all?" "That is all." "By knowing that much one cannot know *Brahman*." "Let me approach you as a student," said Gārgya.

स होवाचाजातशत्रुः प्रतिलोमं चैतद्यद्ब्राह्मणः क्षत्रियमुपेयाद्ब्रह्म मे वक्ष्यतीति व्येव त्वा ज्ञपयिष्यामीति तं पाणावादायोत्तस्थौ तौ ह पुरुषँ सुप्तमाजग्मतुस्तमेतैर्नामभिरामन्त्रयांचक्रे बृहन् पाण्डरवासः सोमराजन्निति स नोत्तस्थौ तं पाणिन पेषं बोधयांचकार स होत्तस्थौ ॥१५॥

sa hovācājātaśatruḥ pratilomaṁ caitadyadbrāhmaṇaḥ kṣatriyamupeyādbrahma me vakṣyatīti vyeva tvā jñapayiṣyāmīti taṁ pāṇāvādāyottasthau tau ha puruṣaṁ suptamājagmatustametairnāmab hirāmantrayāṁcakre bṛhan pāṇḍaravāsaḥ somarājanniti sa nottasthau taṁ pāṇinā peṣaṁ bodhayāṁcakāra sa hottasthau ॥१५॥

Ajātaśatru said: "It is contrary to normal practice that a brāhmaṇa should approach a kṣatriya, thinking: 'He will teach me about *Brahman*'. Nevertheless, I will instruct you." So saying, he took Gārgya by the hand and rose. They came to a sleeping man. Ajātaśatru addressed him by these names: "Oh Soma!

great king dressed in white". The man did not get up. The king touched him with his hand. Then he awoke.

स होवाचाजातशत्रुर्यत्रैष एतत्सुप्तोऽभूद्य एष विज्ञानमयः पुरुषः क्वैष तदाभूत्कुत एतदागादिति ।
तदु ह न मेने गार्ग्यः ॥१६॥

sa hovācājātaśatruryatraiṣa etatsupto 'bhūdya eṣa vijñānamayaḥ puruṣaḥ kvaiṣa tadābhūtkuta etadāgāditi । *tadu ha na mene gārgyaḥ* ॥16॥

Ajātaśatru said: "When this man was thus asleep, where was the person consisting of knowledge (*vijñānamaya puruṣa*) and whence did it return?" Gārgya did not know the answer.

स होवाचाजातशत्रुर्यत्रैष एतत्सुप्तोऽभूद्य एष विज्ञानमयः पुरुषस्तदेषां प्राणानां विज्ञानेन विज्ञानमादाय य एषोऽन्तर्हृदय आकाशस्तस्मिञ्छेते तानि यदा गृह्णात्यथ हैतत्पुरुषः स्वपिति नाम तद्गृहीत एव प्राणो भवति गृहीता वाग् गृहीतं चक्षुःर्गृहीतँ श्रोत्रं गृहीतं मनः ॥१७॥

sa hovācājātaśatruryatraiṣa etatsupto 'bhūdya eṣa vijñānamayaḥ puruṣastadeṣāṁ prāṇānāṁ vijñānena vijñānamādāya ya eṣo 'ntarhṛdaya ākāśastasmiñchete tāni yadā gṛhṇātyatha haitatpuruṣaḥ svapiti nāma tadgṛhīta eva prāṇo bhavati gṛhītā vāg gṛhītaṁ cakṣur gṛhītaṁ śrotraṁ gṛhītaṁ manaḥ ॥17॥

Ajātaśatru said: "When this man was asleep, the person of knowledge (*vijñānamaya puruṣa*) having gathered the cognitive functions of the life-energies (*prāṇa*) and rests in the Space (*ākāśa*) within the heart. When this person absorbs these (cognitive functions) thus, it is said to be in dream-state. Then breath, speech, sight, hearing and mind are in the grasp of this person (of knowledge)."

स यत्रैतत्स्वप्न्ययाचरति ते हास्य लोकास्तदुतेव महाराजो भवत्युतेव महाब्राह्मण उतेवोच्चावचं निगच्छति स यथा महाराजो जानपदान् गृहीत्वा स्वे जनपदे यथाकामं परिवर्तेतैवमेवैष एतत्प्राणान् गृहीत्वा स्वे शरीरे यथाकामं परिवर्तते ॥१८॥

sa yatraitatsvapnyayācarati te hāsya lokāstaduteva mahārājo bhavatyuteva mahābrāhmaṇa utevoccāvacaṁ nigacchati sa yathā mahārājo jānapadān gṛhītvā sve janapade yathākāmaṁ parivartetaivamevaiṣa etatprāṇān gṛhītvā sve śarīre yathākāmaṁ parivartate ॥18॥

Wherever he may travel in his dreams, these become his worlds. He then may become a great king or a high brāhmaṇa or may attain high or low states. Even as a great king, taking with him his retinue of citizens, moves about, according to his pleasure, within his own domain, so does the self (*ātman*), taking with it the life-functions (*prāṇa*), move about according to its pleasure, in the body.

अथ यदा सुषुप्तो भवति यदा न कस्यचन वेद हिता नाम नाड्यो द्वासप्ततिसहस्राणि हृदयात्पुरीततमभिप्रतिष्ठन्ते ताभिः प्रत्यवसृप्य पुरीतति शेते स यथा कुमारो वा महाराजो वा महाब्राह्मणो वातिघ्नीमानन्दस्य गत्वा शयीतैवमेवैष एतच्छेते ॥१९॥

atha yadā suṣupto bhavati yadā na kasyacana veda hitā nāma nāḍyo dvāsaptatisahasrāṇi hṛdayātpurītatamabhipratiṣṭhante tābhiḥ pratyavasṛpya purītati śete sa yathā kumāro vā mahārājo vā mahābrāhmaṇo vātighnīmānandasya gatvā śayītaivamevaiṣa etacchete ॥19॥

Next, when he enters the state of dreamless sleep (*suṣupti*) – when it does not know anything – returning through the 72,000 nerves called *hitā*, which extend from the heart to the pericardium it comes to rest in the pericardium. As a young man or an emperor or a great brāhmaṇa lives, having reached the summit of bliss, so does he rest.

स यथोर्णवाभिस्तन्तुनोच्चरेद्यथाग्नेः क्षुद्रा विस्फुलिङ्गा व्युच्चरन्त्येवमेवास्मादात्मनः सर्वे प्राणाः सर्वे लोकाः सर्वे देवाः सर्वाणि भूतानि व्युच्चरन्ति तस्योपनिषत्सत्यस्य सत्यमिति प्राणा वै सत्यं तेषामेष सत्यम् ॥२०॥

sa yathorṇavābhistantunoccaredyathāgneḥ kṣudrā visphuliṅgā vyuccarantyevamevāsmādātmanaḥ sarve prāṇāḥ sarve lokāḥ sarve devāḥ sarvāṇi bhūtāni vyuccaranti tasyopaniṣatsatyasya satyamiti prāṇā vai satyaṁ teṣāmeṣa satyam ॥20॥

As the spider moves along the thread it spins, or as small sparks fly in all directions from a fire, even so from this Self (*ātman*) emerge all the life-functions (*prāṇa*s), all worlds (*loka*s), all gods (*deva*s), all beings (*bhūtāni*). Its secret name (*upaniṣad*) is "the Truth of truth". The vital breaths are the truth and this is their truth.

Adhyāya II: Brāhmaṇa 2

यो ह वै शिशुँ साधानँ सप्रत्याधानँ सस्थूणँ सदामं वेद सप्त ह द्विषतो भ्रातृव्यानवरुणद्धयं वाव शिशुर्योऽयं मध्यमः प्राणस्तस्येदमेवाधानमिदं प्रत्याधानं प्राणः स्थूणान्नं दाम ॥१॥

yo ha vai śiśum̐ sādhānam̐ sapratyādhānam̐ sasthūṇam̐ sadāmaṁ veda sapta ha dviṣato bhrātṛvyānavaruṇaddhyayaṁ vāva śiśuryo 'yaṁ madhyamaḥ prāṇastasyedamevādhānamidaṁ pratyādhānaṁ prāṇaḥ sthūṇānnaṁ dāma ॥1 ॥

He who knows the new-born (calf) together with its dwelling space, its activity space, its post and its rope, keeps away his seven hostile kinsmen. The central breath is indeed the calf; this (body) is its dwelling space, this (head) its activity space, the life-breath (*prāṇa*) its post and food its rope.

तमेताः सप्ताक्षितय उपतिष्ठन्ते तद्या इमा अक्षन् लोहिन्यो राजयस्ताभिरेनँ रुद्रोऽन्वायत्तोऽथ या अक्षन्नापस्ताभिः पर्जन्यो या कनीनिका तयादित्यो यत्कृष्णं तेनाग्निर्यच्छुक्लं तेनेन्द्रोऽधरयैनं वर्तन्या पृथिव्यन्वायत्ता द्यौरुत्तरया नास्यान्नं क्षीयते य एवं वेद ॥२॥

tametāḥ saptākṣitaya upatiṣṭhante tadyā imā akṣan lohinyo rājayastābhirenam̐ rudro 'nvāyatto 'tha yā akṣannāpastābhiḥ parjanyo yā kanīnikā tayādityo yatkṛṣṇaṁ tenāgniryacchuklaṁ tenendro 'dharayainaṁ vartanyā pṛthivyanvāyattā dyauruttarayā nāsyānnaṁ kṣīyate ya evaṁ veda ॥2 ॥

The seven undecaying ones stand in attendance (on the calf): through these red lines in the eye, Rudra is united with him; through the water in the eye, Parjanya; through the pupil of the eye, Āditya; through the black (of the eye), Agni; through the white, Indra; through the lower eyelid, the earth (*pṛthvī*); and through the upper eyelid, heaven (*dyauṣ*). He who knows this, his food does not diminish.

तदेष श्लोको भवति। अर्वाग्बिलश्चमस ऊर्ध्वबुध्नस्तस्मिन्यशो निहितं विश्वरूपम्। तस्यासत ऋषयः सप्त तीरे वागष्टमी ब्रह्मणा संविदानेत्यर्वाग्बिलश्चमस ऊर्ध्वबुध्न इतीदं तच्छिर एष ह्यर्वाग्बिलश्चमस ऊर्ध्वबुध्नस्तस्मिन्यशो निहितं विश्वरूपमिति प्राणा वै यशो विश्वरूपं प्राणानेतदाह तस्यासत ऋषयः सप्त तीर इति प्राणा वा ऋषयः प्राणानेतदाह वागष्टमी ब्रह्मणा संविदानेति वाग्ध्यष्टमी ब्रह्मणा संवित्ते ॥३॥

tadeṣa śloko bhavati। arvāgbilaścamasa ūrdhvabudhnastasminyaśo nihitaṁ viśvarūpam। tasyāsata ṛṣayaḥ sapta tīre vāgaṣṭamī brahmaṇā saṁvidānetyarvāgbilaścamasa ūrdhvabudhna itīdaṁ tacchira eṣa hyarvāgbilaścamasa ūrdhvabudhnastasminyaśo nihitaṁ viśvarūpamiti prāṇā vai yaśo viśvarūpaṁ prāṇānetadāha tasyāsata ṛṣayaḥ sapta tīra iti prāṇā vā ṛṣayaḥ prāṇānetadāha vāgaṣṭamī brahmaṇā saṁvidāneti vāgdhyaṣṭamī brahmaṇā saṁvitte ॥३॥

Regarding this there is the following verse: "There is a bowl which has its mouth below and bottom up. Within it, a glory of universal forms is placed. Seven sages sit on its rim and speech is the eighth, which communicates with *Brahman*." What is called the "bowl which has its mouth below and bottom up" is this head of ours, for it is a bowl which has its mouth below and which bulges at the top. When it is said: "Manifold knowledge has been put into it", this refers to the life-breaths; these indeed represent manifold knowledge. When it is said: "Seven sages sit on its rim", this refers to the organs of life-functions; they indeed are the sages. "Speech which communicates with *Brahman*, is the eighth" because the organ of speech is the eighth and communicates with *Brahman*.

इमावेव गोतमभरद्वाजावयमेव गोतमोऽयं भरद्वाज इमावेव विश्वामित्रजमदग्नी अयमेव विश्वामित्रोऽयं जमदग्निरिमावेव वसिष्ठकश्यपावयमेव वसिष्ठोऽयं कश्यपो वागेवात्रिर्वाचा ह्यन्नमद्यतेऽत्तिर्ह वै नामैतद्यदत्रिरिति सर्वस्यात्ता भवति सर्वमस्यान्नं भवति य एवं वेद ॥४॥

imāveva gotamabharadvājāvayameva gotamo 'yaṁ bharadvāja imāveva viśvāmitrajamadagnī ayameva viśvāmitro 'yaṁ jamadagnirimāveva vasiṣṭhakaśyapāvayameva vasiṣṭho 'yaṁ kaśyapo vāgevātrirvācā hyannamadyate 'ttirha vai nāmaitadyadattririti sarvasyāttā bhavati sarvamasyānnaṁ bhavati ya evaṁ veda ॥4॥

These two (ears) are Gautama and Bharadvāja: this one (the right) is Gautama and this one (the left), Bharadvāja. These two eyes are Viśvāmitra and Jamadagni: this one (the right) is Viśvāmitra and this one (the left), Jamadagni. These two nostrils are Vasiṣṭha and Kaśyapa: this one (the right) is Vasiṣṭha and this one (the left), Kaśyapa. The tongue is Atri, for through the tongue food is eaten. Atri is the same as *atti* (eating). He who knows this becomes the eater of everything and everything becomes his food.

Adhyāya II: Brāhmaṇa 3

द्वे वाव ब्रह्मणो रूपे मूर्तं चैवामूर्तं च मर्त्यं चामृतं च स्थितं च यच्च सच्च त्यच्च ॥

dve vāva brahmaṇo rūpe mūrtaṁ caivāmūrtaṁ ca martyaṁ cāmṛtaṁ ca sthitaṁ ca yacca sacca tyacca ॥

Truly, there are two forms of *Brahman*: having appearance and lacking appearance, mortal and immortal, mobile and immobile, actual and transcendental.

तदेतन्मूर्तं यदन्यद्वायोश्चान्तरिक्षाच्च तन्मर्त्यमेतत्स्थितमेतत्सत्तस्यैतस्य मूर्तस्यैतस्य मर्त्यस्यैतस्य स्थितस्यैतस्य सत एष रसो य एष तपति सतो ह्येष रसः ॥२॥

tadetanmūrtaṁ yadanyadvāyoścāntarikṣācca tanmartyametatsthitametatsattasyaitasya mūrtasyaitasya martyasyaitasya sthitasyaitasya sata eṣa raso ya eṣa tapati sato hyeṣa rasaḥ ॥2॥

The form having appearance is that which is other than Wind (*vāyu*) and the intermediate space (*antarikṣa*). It is mortal, immobile and actual (*sat*). The essence (*rasa*) of that which has appearance, which is mortal, which is immobile and which is actual is that which gives heat (*tapati*), for that is the essence of the actual (*sat*).

अथामूर्तं वायुश्चान्तरिक्षं चैतदमृतमेतद्यदेतत्त्यत्तस्यैतस्यामूर्तस्यैतस्यामृतस्यैतस्य यत एतस्यै त्यस्यैष रसो य एष एतस्मिन्मण्डले पुरुषत्यस्य ह्येष रस इत्यधिदेवतम् ॥३॥

athāmūrtaṁ vāyuścāntarikṣaṁ caitadamṛtametadyadetattyat-tasyaitasyāmūrtasyaitasyāmṛtasyaitasya yata etasya tyasyaiṣa raso ya eṣa etasminmaṇḍale puruṣatyasya hyeṣa rasa ityadhidevatam ॥3 ॥

Now the form without appearance: It is Wind (*vāyu*) and the intermediate space. It is immortal, it is mobile and it is transcendental (*tyat*). The essence of that which is without appearance, which is immortal, which is mobile and which is transcendental (*tyat*) is the Person (*puruṣa*) in this circle (*maṇḍala*), for that Person is the essence of the transcendental (*tyat*). This is with reference to the gods (*ādhidaiva*).

अथाध्यात्ममिदमेव मूर्तं यदन्यत्प्राणाच्च यश्चायमन्तरात्मन्नाकाश एतन्मर्त्यमेतत्स्थितमेतत्सत्तस्यै-तस्य मूर्तस्यैतस्य मर्त्यस्यैतस्य स्थितस्यैतस्य सत एष रसो यच्चक्षुः सतो ह्येष रसः ॥४॥

athādhyātmamidameva mūrtaṁ yadanyatprāṇācca yaścāyamanta-rātmannākāśa etanmartyametatsthitametatsattasyaitasya mūrtasyaitasya martyasyaitasya sthitasyaitasya sata eṣa raso yaccakṣuḥ sato hyeṣa rasaḥ ॥4 ॥

Now with reference to the self (*adhyātma*): The form having appearance is that which is other than the life-breath (*prāṇa*) and the space (*ākāśa*) of the inner self (*antarātmā*). It is mortal, it is immobile and it is actual (*sat*). The essence of that which has appearance, which is mortal, which is immobile and which is actual is the eye; for it (the eye) is the essence of the actual (*sat*).

अथामूर्तं प्राणश्च यश्चायमन्तरात्मन्नाकाश एतदमृतमेतद्यदेतत्त्यं तस्यैतस्यामूर्तस्यैतस्यामृतस्यै तस्य यत एतस्य त्यत्यैष रसो योऽयं दक्षिणेक्षन्पुरुषस्तस्य ह्यैष रसः ॥५॥

athāmūrtaṁ prāṇaśca yaścāyamantarātmannākāśa etadamṛtame-tadyadetattyaṁ tasyaitasyāmūrtasyaitasyāmṛtasyaitasya yata etasya tyatyaiṣa raso yo 'yaṁ dakṣiṇekṣanpuruṣastasya hyaiṣa rasaḥ ॥5 ॥

Now the form without appearance: It is the life-breath (*prāṇa*) and the space (*ākāśa*) of the inner self (*antarātmā*). It is immortal, it is mobile and it is transcendental (*tyat*). The essence of that which has no appearance, which is immortal, which is mobile and which is transcendental is the person (*puruṣa*) that is in the right eye, for that person is the essence of the transcendental (*tyat*).

तस्य हैतस्य पुरुषस्य रूपं यथा माहारजनं वासो यथा पाण्ड्वाविकं यथेन्द्रगोपो यथाऽग्न्यर्चिर्यथा पुण्डरीकं यथा सकृद्विद्युत्तँ सकृद्विद्युत्तेव ह वा अस्य श्रीर्भवति य एवं वेदाथात आदेशः नेति नेति न ह्येतस्मादिति नेत्यन्यत्परमस्त्य नामधेयँ सत्यस्य सत्यमिति प्राणा वै सत्यं तेषामेष सत्यम् ॥६॥

tasya haitasya puruṣasya rūpaṁ yathā māhārajanaṁ vāso yathā pāṇḍvāvikaṁ yathendragopo yathā 'gnyarciryathā puṇḍarīkaṁ yathā sakṛdvidyuttaṁ̐ sakṛdvidyutteva ha vā asya śrīrbhavati ya evaṁ vedāthāta ādeśaḥ neti neti na hyetasmāditi netyanyatparamastyatha nāmadheyaṁ̐ satyasya satyamiti prāṇā vai satyaṁ teṣāmeṣa satyam ॥6॥

The form of that person is like a cloth dyed with turmeric, or like pale sheep's wool, or like the scarlet insect called *indragopa*, or like a tongue of fire, or like a white lotus, or like a flash of lightning. He who knows this attains divinity (*śrī*) like a flash of lightning. Now, therefore, the injunction (*ādeśa*): "Not this, not this" (*neti, neti*); for there is nothing else beyond this "Not this". Now its name: "The Truth of truth". The life-breath (*prāṇa*) is truth (*satyam*) and this is the Truth of that.

Adhyāya II: Brāhmaṇa 4

मैत्रेयीति होवाच याज्ञवल्क्य उद्यास्यन्वा अरेऽहमस्मात्स्थानादस्मि हन्त तेऽनया कात्यायन्यान्तं करवाणीति ॥१॥

maitreyīti hovāca yājñavalkya udyāsyanvā are 'hamasmātsthānādasmi hanta te 'nayā kātyāyanyāntaṁ karavāṇīti ॥1॥

"Maitreyī" said Yājñavalkya, "Look, I am about to leave this place. So let me make a settlement between you and Kātyāyanī."

सा होवाच मैत्रेयी यन्नु म इयं भगोः सर्वा पृथिवी वित्तेन पूर्णा स्यात्कथं तेनामृता स्यामिति नेति

होवाच याज्ञवल्क्यो यथैवोपकरणवतां जीवितँ तथैव ते जीवितँ स्यादमृतत्वस्य तु नाशास्ति वित्तेनेति ॥२॥

sā hovāca maitreyī yannuma iyaṁ bhagoḥ sarvā pṛthivī vittena pūrṇā syātkathaṁ tenāmṛtā syāmiti neti hovāca yājñavalkyo yathaivopakaraṇavatāṁ jīvitaṁ tathaiva te jīvitaṁ̐ syādamṛtatvasya tu nāśāsti vitteneti ॥2 ॥

Thereupon Maitreyī said: "Sir, if indeed the whole earth, full of wealth was mine, would I be immortal through that?" "No," said Yājñavalkya, "as the life of the rich, so would your life be. Of Immortality, however, there is no hope through wealth."

सा होवाच मैत्रेयी येनाहं नामृता स्यां किमहं तेन कुर्यां? यदेव भगवान्वेद तदेव मे ब्रूहीति ॥३॥

sā hovāca maitreyī yenāhaṁ nāmṛtā syāṁ kimahaṁ tena kuryāṁ? yadeva bhagavānveda tadeva me brūhīti ॥3 ॥

Then Maitreyī said: "What should I do with that which would not make me immortal? That which you know (as the means of attaining immortality), sir, tell me that."

स होवाच याज्ञवल्क्यः प्रिया बतारे नः सती प्रियं भाषस एह्यास्स्व व्याख्यास्यामि ते व्याचक्षाणस्य तु मे निदिध्यासस्वेति ॥४॥

sa hovāca yājñavalkyaḥ priyā batāre naḥ satī priyaṁ bhāṣasa ehyāssva vyākhyāsyāmi te vyācakṣāṇasya tu me nididhyāsasveti ॥4 ॥

Yājñavalkya replied: "Beloved, indeed you have been dear to me and now you speak dear words. Come, sit down; I will explain to you. As I am explaining, concentrate (*nididhyāsasva*) on what I say."

स होवाच न वा अरे पत्युः कामाय पतिः प्रियो भवत्यात्मनस्तु कामाय पतिः प्रियो भवति न वा अरे जायायै कामाय जाया प्रिया भवत्यात्मनस्तु कामाय जाया प्रिया भवति न वा अरे पुत्राणां कामाय पुत्राः प्रिया भवन्त्यात्मनस्तु कामाय पुत्राः प्रिया भवन्ति न वा अरे वित्तस्य कामाय वित्तं प्रियं भवत्यात्मनस्तु कामाय वित्तं प्रियं भवति न वा अरे ब्रह्मणः कामाय ब्रह्म प्रियं भवत्यात्मनस्तु कामाय ब्रह्म प्रियं भवति न वा अरे क्षत्रस्य कामाय क्षत्रं प्रियं भवत्यात्मनस्तु कामाय क्षत्रं प्रियं

भवति न वा अरे लोकानां कामाय लोकाः प्रिया भवन्त्यात्मनस्तु कामाय लोकाः प्रिया भवन्ति न वा अरे देवानां कामाय देवाः प्रिया भवन्त्यात्मनस्तु कामाय देवाः प्रिया भवन्ति न वा अरे भूतानां कामाय भूतानि प्रियाणि भवन्त्यात्मनस्तु कामाय भूतानि प्रियाणि भवन्ति न वा अरे सर्वस्य कामाय सर्वं प्रियं भवत्यात्मनस्तु कामाय सर्वं प्रियं भवत्यात्मा वा अरे द्रष्टव्यः श्रोतव्यो मन्तव्यो निदिध्यासितव्यो मैत्रेय्यात्मनो वा अरे दर्शनेन श्रवणेन मत्या विज्ञानेनेदँ सर्वं विदितम् ॥५॥

sa hovāca na vā are patyuḥ kāmāya patiḥ priyo bhavatyātmanastu kāmāya patiḥ priyo bhavati na vā are jāyāyai kāmāya jāyā priyā bhavatyātmanastu kāmāya jāyā priyā bhavati na vā are putrāṇāṁ kāmāya putrāḥ priyā bhavantyātmanastu kāmāya putrāḥ priyā bhavanti na vā are vittasya kāmāya vittaṁ priyaṁ bhavatyātmanastu kāmāya vittaṁ priyaṁ bhavati na vā are brahmaṇaḥ kāmāya brahma priyaṁ bhavatyātmanastu kāmāya brahma priyaṁ bhavati na vā are kṣatrasya kāmāya kṣatraṁ priyaṁ bhavatyātmanastu kāmāya kṣatraṁ priyaṁ bhavati na vā are lokānāṁ kāmāya lokāḥ priyā bhavantyātmanastu kāmāya lokāḥ priyā bhavanti na vā are devānāṁ kāmāya devāḥ priyā bhavantyātmanastu kāmāya devāḥ priyā bhavanti na vā are bhūtānāṁ kāmāya bhūtāni priyāṇi bhavantyātmanastu kāmāya bhūtāni priyāṇi bhavanti na vā are sarvasya kāmāya sarvaṁ priyaṁ bhavatyātmanastu kāmāya sarvaṁ priyaṁ bhavatyātmā vā are draṣṭavyaḥ śrotavyo mantavyo nididhyāsitavyo maitreyyātmano vā are darśanena śravaṇena matyā vijñānenedaṁ̐ sarvaṁ viditam ॥5॥

Then Yājñavalkya said: "Truly, not for the desire of the husband is the husband beloved, he is beloved for the desire of the Self. Not for the desire of the wife is the wife beloved, she is beloved for the desire of the self. Not for the desire of the sons are the sons beloved, they are beloved for the desire of the self. Not for the desire of wealth is wealth beloved, it is beloved for the desire of the self. Not for the desire of the brāhmaṇa is the brāhmaṇa beloved, he is beloved for the desire of the self. Not for the desire of the kṣatriya is the kṣatriya beloved, he is beloved for the desire of the self. Not for the desire of the worlds are the worlds beloved, they are beloved for the desire of the self. Not for the desire of the gods are the gods beloved, they are beloved for the desire of the self. Not for the desire of beings are beings beloved, they are beloved for the desire of the self. Not for the desire of the Whole is the Whole beloved, it is beloved for the desire of the self. Truly, Maitreyī, it is the Self that is meant to be seen, heard, reflected on and entered into oneness with. By seeing, hearing, reflection and knowledge of the Self, all this is known."

ब्रह्म तं परादाद्योऽन्यात्रात्मनो ब्रह्म वेद क्षत्रं तं परादाद्योऽन्यत्रात्मनः क्षत्रं वेद लोकास्तं परादुर्योऽन्यत्रात्मनो लोकान्वेद देवास्तं परादुर्योऽन्यत्रात्मनो देवान्वेद भूतानि तं परादुर्योऽन्यत्रात्मनो भूतानि वेद सर्वं तं परादाद्योऽन्यत्रात्मनः सर्वं वेदेदं ब्रह्मेदं क्षत्रमिमे लोका इमे देवा इमानि भूतानीदँ सर्वं यदयमात्मा ॥६॥

brahma taṁ parādādyo 'nyatrātmano brahma veda kṣatraṁ taṁ parādādyo 'nyatrātmanaḥ kṣatraṁ veda lokāstaṁ parāduryo 'nyatrātmano lokānveda devāstaṁ parāduryo 'nyatrātmano devānveda bhūtāni taṁ parāduryo 'nyatrātmano bhūtāni veda sarvaṁ taṁ parādādyo 'nyatrātmanaḥ sarvaṁ vededaṁ brahmedaṁ kṣatramime lokā ime devā imāni bhūtānīdaṁ sarvaṁ yadayamātmā ॥6॥

"The *brāhma* (priestly) power abandons one who thinks of it as residing in anything other than the self. The *kṣatra* (ruling) power abandons one who thinks of it as residing in anything other than the self. The worlds abandon one who thinks of them as residing in anything other than the self. The gods abandon one who thinks of them as residing in anything other than the self. The beings abandon one who thinks of them as residing in anything other than the self. The Whole abandons one who thinks of it as residing in anything other than the self. This *brāhma* power, this *kṣatra* power, these worlds, these gods, these beings and this Whole are that Self (*ātman*)."

स यथा दुन्दुभेर्हन्यमानस्य न बाह्याञ्छब्दाञ्छक्नुयाद्ग्रहणाय दुन्दुभेस्तु ग्रहणेन दुन्दुभ्याघातस्य वा शब्दो गृहीतः ॥७॥

sa yathā dundubherhanyamānasya na bāhyāñchabdāñchaknu-

yādgrahaṇāya dundubhestu grahaṇena dundubhyāghātasya vā śabdo gṛhītaḥ ॥7॥

"As when a drum is beaten, its external sounds cannot be grasped, but by grasping the drum or the drummer the sounds are grasped ...."

स यथा शङ्खस्य ध्मायमानस्य न बाह्याञ्छब्दाञ्छक्नुयाद्ग्रहणाय शङ्खस्य तु ग्रहणेन शङ्खध्मस्य वा शब्दो गृहीतः ॥८॥

sa yathā śaṅkhasya dhmāyamānasya na bāhyāñchabdāñchaknuyādgrahaṇāya śaṅkhasya tu grahaṇena śaṅkhadhmasya vā śabdo gṛhītaḥ ॥8॥

"As when a conch is blown, its external sounds cannot be grasped, but by grasping the conch or the blower of the conch the sounds are grasped ...."

स यथा वीणायै वाद्यमानायै न बाह्याञ्छब्दाञ्छक्नुयाद्ग्रहणाय वीणायै तु ग्रहणेन वीणावादस्य वा शब्दो गृहीतः ॥९॥

sa yathā vīṇāyai vādyamānāyai na bāhyāñchabdāñchaknuyādgrahaṇāya vīṇāyai tu grahaṇena vīṇāvādasya vā śabdo gṛhītaḥ ॥9॥

"As when a *vīṇā* (string instrument) is struck, its external sounds cannot be grasped, but by grasping the *vīṇā* or the player of the *vīṇā* the sounds are grasped ...."

स यथार्द्रैधाग्नेरभ्याहितात्पृथग्धूमा विनिश्चरन्त्येवं वा अरेऽस्य महतो भूतस्य निःश्वसितमेतद्यदृग्वेदो यजुर्वेदः सामवेदोऽथर्वाङ्गिरस इतिहासः पुराणं विद्या उपनिषदः श्लोकाः सूत्राण्यनुव्याख्यानानि व्याख्यानन्यस्यैवैतानि सर्वाणि निःश्वसितानि ॥१०॥

sa yathārdraidhāgnerabhyāhitātpṛthagdhūmā viniścarantyevaṁ vā are 'sya mahato bhūtasya niḥśvasitametadyadṛgvedo yajurvedaḥ sāmavedo 'tharvāṅgirasa itihāsaḥ purāṇaṁ vidyā upaniṣadaḥ ślokāḥ sūtrāṇyanuvyākhyānāni vyākhyānanyasyaivaitāni sarvāṇi niḥśvasitāni ॥10॥

"As from a fire kindled with wet fuel various kinds of smoke issue forth, even so, my dear, the *Ṛgveda*, the *Yajurveda*, the *Sāmaveda*, the *Atharvāṅgirasa*, history (*itihāsa*), mythology (*purāṇa*), arts (*vidyā*), the Upaniṣads, verses (*śloka*s), aphorisms (*sūtra*s), elucidations (*anuvyākhyāna*s) and explanations (*vyākhyāna*s) are the inhalations and exhalations (*niḥśvasitāni*) of this immense Being. All these are indeed its breathing."

स यथा सर्वासामपाँ समुद्र एकायनमेवँ सर्वेषाँ स्पर्शानां त्वगेकायनमेवँ सर्वेषां गन्धानां नासिके एकायनमेवँ सर्वेषाँ रसानां जिह्वैकायनमेवँ सर्वेषाँ रूपाणां चक्षुरेकायनमेवँ सर्वेषाँ शब्दानाँ श्रोत्रमेकायनमेवँ सर्वेषाँ सङ्कल्पानां मन एकायनमेवँ सर्वासां विद्यानाँ हृदयमेकायनमेवँ सर्वेषां कर्मणाँ हस्तावेकायनमेवँ सर्वेषामानन्दानामुपस्थ एकायनमेवँ सर्वेषां विसर्गाणां पायुरेकायनमेवँ सर्वेषामध्वनां पादावेकायनमेवँ सर्वेषां वेदानां वागेकायनम् ॥११॥

sa yathā sarvāsāmapām̐ samudra ekāyanamevam̐ sarveṣām̐ sparśānāṁ tvagekāyanamevam̐ sarveṣāṁ gandhānāṁ nāsike ekāyanamevam̐ sarveṣām̐ rasānāṁ jihvaikāyanamevam̐ sarveṣām̐ rūpāṇāṁ cakṣurekāyanamevam̐ sarveṣām̐ śabdānām̐ śrotramekāyanamevam̐ sarveṣām̐ saṅkalpānāṁ mana ekāyanamevam̐ sarvāsāṁ vidyānām̐ hṛdayamekāyanamevam̐ sarveṣāṁ karmaṇām̐ hastāvekāyanamevam̐ sarveṣāmānandānāmupastha ekāyanamevam̐ sarveṣāṁ visargāṇāṁ pāyurekāyanamevam̐ sarveṣāmadhvanāṁ pādāvekāyanamevam̐ sarveṣāṁ vedānāṁ vāgekāyanam ॥11॥

"As the ocean is the destination of all waters, as the skin is the destination of all touch, as the nostrils are the destination of all smells, as the tongue is the destination of all tastes, as the ear is the destination of all sounds, as the mind is the destination of all intentions, as the heart is the destination of all forms of knowledge, as the hands are the destination of all actions, as the sexual organ is the destination of all pleasures, as the anus is the destination of all excretions, as the feet are the destination of all movements, as the organ of speech is the destination of all the Vedas …."

स यथा सैन्धवखिल्य उदके प्रास्त उदकमेवानुविलीयेत न हास्योद्ग्रहणायेव स्याद्यतो यतस्त्वाददीत लवणमेवैवं वा अर इदं महद्भूतमनन्तमपारं विज्ञानघन एवैतेभ्यो भूतेभ्यः समुत्थाय

तान्येवानुविनश्यति न प्रेत्य संज्ञास्तीत्यरे ब्रवीमीति होवाच याज्ञवल्क्यः ॥१२॥

sa yathā saindhavakhilya udake prāsta udakamevānuvilīyeta na hāsyodgrahaṇāyeva syādyato yatastvādadīta lavaṇamevaivaṁ vā ara idaṁ mahadbhūtamanantamapāraṁ vijñānaghana evaitebhyo bhūtebhyaḥ samutthāya tānyevānuvinaśyati na pretya saṁjñāstītyare bravīmīti hovāca yājñavalkyaḥ ॥12 ॥

"As a lump of salt dropped in water dissolves and cannot be grasped separately anymore, but wherever we taste the water it tastes salt, even so, my dear, this great Being, infinite, shoreless is dense with Knowledge (*vijñānaghana*). Arising with these beings it disappears with their destruction. Having departed there is no sense-knowledge (*saṁjñā*). This I say, my dear." So said Yājñavalkya.

सा होवाच मैत्रेय्यत्रैव मा भगवानमूमुहन्न प्रेत्य संज्ञास्तीति स होवाच याज्ञवल्क्यो न वा अरेऽहं मोहं ब्रवीम्यलं वा अर इदं विज्ञानाय ॥१३॥

sā hovāca maitreyyatraiva mā bhagavānamūmuhanna pretya saṁjñāstīti sa hovāca yājñavalkyo na vā are 'haṁ mohaṁ bravīmyalaṁ vā ara idaṁ vijñānāya ॥13 ॥

Then Maitreyī said: "Just here you have bewildered me, Sir, by saying that after departure there is no more sense-knowledge (*saṁjñā*)." Yājñavalkya replied: "Certainly I am not saying anything confusing. This is sufficient for the knowledge of *vijñāna*."

यत्र हि द्वैतमिव भवति तदितर इतरं जिघ्रति तदितर इतरं पश्यति तदितर इतरँ शृणोति तदितर इतरमभिवदति तदितर इतरं मनुते तदितर इतरं विजानाति यत्र वा अस्य सर्वमात्मैवाभूत्तत्केन कं जिघ्रेत्तत्केन कं पश्येत्तत्केन कँ शृणुयात्तत्केन कमभिवदेत्तत् केन कं मन्वीत तत्केन कं विजानीयाद्येनेदँ सर्वं विजानाति तं केन विजानीयाद्विज्ञातारमरे केन विजानीयादिति ॥१४॥

yatra hi dvaitamiva bhavati taditara itaraṁ jighrati taditara itaraṁ paśyati taditara itaraṁ̐ śṛṇoti taditara itaramabhivadati taditara itaraṁ manute taditara itaraṁ vijānāti yatra vā asya sarvamātmaivābhūttatkena kaṁ jighrettatkena kaṁ paśyettatkena kam̐ śṛṇuyāttatkena kamabhivadettat kena kaṁ manvīta tatkena kaṁ vijānīyādyenedam̐ sarvaṁ vijānāti taṁ kena vijānīyādvijñātāramare kena vijānīyāditi ॥14॥

"For when there is any duality, then one smells another, one sees another, one hears another, one speaks to another, one thinks of another, one knows another. But when all has become the Self, then what should one smell and by what means, what should one see and by what means, what should one hear and by what means, what should one speak and by what means, what should one think and by what means, what should one know and by what means? That by which all is known, by what means can that be known; by what, my dear, should one know the Knower?"

Adhyāya II: Brāhmaṇa 5

इयं पृथिवी सर्वेषां भूतानां मध्वस्यै पृथिव्यै सर्वाणि भूतानि मधु यश्चायमस्यां पृथिव्यां तेजोमयोऽमृतमयः पुरुषो यश्चायमध्यात्मँ शारीरस्तेजोमयोऽमृतमयः पुरुषोऽयमेव स योऽयमात्मेदममृतमिदँ ब्रह्मेदँ सर्वम् ॥१॥

iyaṁ pṛthivī sarveṣāṁ bhūtānāṁ madhvasyai pṛthivyai sarvāṇi bhūtāni madhu yaścāyamasyāṁ pṛthivyāṁ tejomayo 'mṛtamayaḥ puruṣo yaścāyamadhyātmam̐ śārīrastejomayo 'mṛtamayaḥ puruṣo 'yameva sa yo 'yamātmedamamṛtamidaṁ brahmedam̐ sarvam ॥1॥

This Earth is the honey of all beings and all beings are the honey of this earth. Likewise, the radiant, immortal person (*puruṣa*) who is in this earth and with respect to the self (*adhyātma*) the radiant, immortal person (*puruṣa*) who is in the body, he indeed is but this Self. This is Immortal, this is *Brahman*, this is the Whole.

इमा आपः सर्वेषां भूतानां मध्वासामपाँ सर्वाणि भूतानि मधु यश्चायमास्वप्सु तेजोमयोऽमृतमयः पुरुषो यश्चायमध्यात्मँ रैतसस्तेजोमयोऽमृतमयः पुरुषोऽयमेव स योऽयमात्मेदममृतमिदं ब्रह्मेदँ सर्वम् ॥२॥

imā āpaḥ sarveṣāṁ bhūtānāṁ madhvāsāmapām̐ sarvāṇi bhūtāni madhu yaścāyamāsvapsu tejomayo 'mṛtamayaḥ puruṣo yaścāyam-

adhyātmaṁ̐ raitasastejomayo 'mṛtamayaḥ puruṣo 'yameva sa yo 'yamātmedamamṛtamidaṁ brahmedaṁ̐ sarvam ॥2 ॥

This water is the honey of all beings and all beings are the honey of this water. Likewise, the radiant, immortal person (*puruṣa*) who is in this water and with respect to the self (*adhyātma*) the radiant, immortal person (*puruṣa*) who is in the sexual energy (*retas*), he indeed is but this Self. This is Immortal, this is *Brahman*, this is the Whole.

अयमग्निः सर्वेषां भूतानां मध्वस्याग्नेः सर्वाणि भूतानि मधु यश्चायमस्मिन्नग्नौ तेजोमयोऽमृतमयः पुरुषो यश्चायमध्यात्मं वाङ्मयस्तेजोमयोऽमृतमयः पुरुषोऽयमेव स योऽयमात्मेदममृतमिदं ब्रह्मेद सर्वम् ॥३॥

ayamagniḥ sarveṣāṁ bhūtānāṁ madhvasyāgneḥ sarvāṇi bhūtāni madhu yaścāyamasminnagnau tejomayo 'mṛtamayaḥ puruṣo yaścāyamadhyātmaṁ vāṅmayastejomayo 'mṛtamayaḥ puruṣo 'yameva sa yo 'yamātmedamamṛtamidaṁ brahmedaṁ̐ sarvam ॥3 ॥

This fire is the honey of all beings and all beings are the honey of this fire. Likewise, the radiant, immortal person (*puruṣa*) who is in this fire and with respect to the self (*adhyātma*) the radiant, immortal person (*puruṣa*) who is made of Speech (*vāṅmaya*), he indeed is but this Self. This is Immortal, this is *Brahman*, this is the Whole.

अयं वायुः सर्वेषां भूतानां मध्वस्य वायोः सर्वाणि भूतानि मधु यश्चायमस्मिन्वायौ तेजोमयोऽमृतमयः पुरुषो यश्चायमध्यात्मं प्राणस्तेजोमयोऽमृतमयः पुरुषोऽयमेव स योऽयमात्मेदममृतमिदं ब्रह्मेदँ सर्वम् ॥४॥

ayaṁ vāyuḥ sarveṣāṁ bhūtānāṁ madhvasya vāyoḥ sarvāṇi bhūtāni madhu yaścāyamasminvāyau tejomayo 'mṛtamayaḥ puruṣo yaścāyamadhyātmaṁ prāṇastejomayo 'mṛtamayaḥ puruṣo 'yameva sa yo 'yamātmedamamṛtamidaṁ brahmedaṁ̐ sarvam ॥4 ॥

This Wind is the honey of all beings and all beings are the honey of this Wind. Likewise, the radiant, immortal person (*puruṣa*) who is in this Wind and with respect to the self (*adhyātma*) the radiant, immortal person (*puruṣa*) who is in the life-breath (*prāṇas*), he indeed is but this Self. This is Immortal, this is *Brahman*, this is the Whole.

अयमादित्यः सर्वेषां भूतानां मध्वस्यादित्यस्य सर्वाणि भूतानि मधु यश्चायमस्मिन्नादित्ये तेजोमयोऽमृतमयः पुरुषो यश्चायमध्यात्मं चाक्षुषस्तेजोमयोऽमृतमयः पुरुषोऽयमेव स योऽयमात्मेदममृतमिदं ब्रह्मेदँ सर्वम् ॥५॥

ayamādityaḥ sarveṣāṁ bhūtānāṁ madhvasyādityasya sarvāṇi bhūtāni madhu yaścāyamasminnāditye tejomayo 'mṛtamayaḥ puruṣo yaścāyamadhyātmaṁ cākṣuṣastejomayo 'mṛtamayaḥ puruṣo 'yameva sa yo 'yamātmedamamṛtamidaṁ brahmedaṁ̐ sarvam ॥5॥

This sun is the honey of all beings and all beings are the honey of this sun. Likewise, the radiant, immortal person (*puruṣa*) who is in this Sun and with respect to the self (*adhyātma*) the radiant, immortal person (*puruṣa*) who is in the Sight (*cakṣus*), he indeed is but this Self. This is Immortal, this is *Brahman*, this is the Whole.

इमा दिशः सर्वेषां भूतानां मध्वासां दिशाँ सर्वाणि भूतानि मधु यश्चायमासु दिक्षु तेजोमयोऽमृतमयः पुरुषो यश्चायमध्यात्मँ श्रौत्रः प्रातिश्रुत्कस्तेजोमयोऽमृतमयः पुरुषोऽयमेव स योऽयमात्मेदममृतमिदं ब्रह्मेदँ सर्वम् ॥६॥

imā diśaḥ sarveṣāṁ bhūtānāṁ madhvāsāṁ diśāṁ̐ sarvāṇi bhūtāni madhu yaścāyamāsu dikṣu tejomayo 'mṛtamayaḥ puruṣo yaścāyamadhyātmaṁ̐ śrautraḥ prātiśrutkastejomayo 'mṛtamayaḥ puruṣo 'yameva sa yo 'yamātmedamamṛtamidaṁ brahmedaṁ̐ sarvam ॥6॥

These directions are the honey of all beings and all beings are the honey of these directions. Likewise, the radiant, immortal person (*puruṣa*) who is in the directions and with respect to the self (*adhyātma*) the radiant, immortal person (*puruṣa*) who is in the hearing (*śrotra*), he indeed is but this Self. This is Immortal, this is *Brahman*, this is the Whole.

अयं चन्द्रः सर्वेषां भूतानां मध्वस्य चन्द्रस्य सर्वाणि भूतानि मधु यश्चायमस्मिँश्चन्द्रे तेजोमयोऽमृतमयः

पुरुषो यश्चायमध्यात्मं मानसस्तेजोमयोऽमृतमयः पुरुषोऽयमेव स योऽयमात्मेदममृतमिदं ब्रह्मेदँ सर्वम् ॥७॥

ayaṁ candraḥ sarveṣāṁ bhūtānāṁ madhvasya candrasya sarvāṇi bhūtāni madhu yaścāyamasmiṁ̐ścandre tejomayo 'mr̥tamayaḥ puruṣo yaścāyamadhyātmaṁ mānasastejomayo 'mr̥tamayaḥ puruṣo 'yameva sa yo 'yamātmedamamr̥tamidaṁ brahmedaṁ sarvam ॥7॥

This moon is the honey of all beings and all beings are the honey of this moon. Likewise, the radiant, immortal person (*puruṣa*) who is in this moon and with respect to the self (*adhyātma*) the radiant, immortal person (*puruṣa*) who is in the mind (*manas*), he indeed is but this Self. This is Immortal, this is *Brahman*, this is the Whole.

इयं विद्युत्सर्वेषां भूतानां मध्वस्यै विद्युतः सर्वाणि भूतानि मधु यश्चायमस्यां विद्युति तेजोमयोऽमृतमयः पुरुषो यश्चायमध्यात्मं तैजसस्तेजोमयोऽमृतमयः पुरुषोऽयमेव स योऽयमात्मेदममृतमिदं ब्रह्मेदँ सर्वम् ॥८॥

iyaṁ vidyutsarveṣāṁ bhūtānāṁ madhvasyai vidyutaḥ sarvāṇi bhūtāni madhu yaścāyamasyāṁ vidyuti tejomayo 'mr̥tamayaḥ puruṣo yaścāyamadhyātmaṁ taijasastejomayo 'mr̥tamayaḥ puruṣo 'yameva sa yo 'yamātmedamamr̥tamidaṁ brahmedaṁ̐ sarvam ॥8॥

This lightning is the honey of all beings and all beings are the honey of this lightning. Likewise, the radiant, immortal person (*puruṣa*) who is in this lightning and with respect to the self (*adhyātma*) the radiant, immortal person (*puruṣa*) who is in radiance (*taijasa*), he indeed is but this Self. This is Immortal, this is *Brahman*, this is the Whole.

अयँ स्तनयित्नुः सर्वेषां भूतानां मध्वस्य स्तनयित्नोः सर्वाणि भूतानि मधु यश्चायमस्मिन्स्तनयित्नौ तेजोमयोऽमृतमयः पुरुषो यश्चायमध्यात्मँ शाब्दः सौवरस्तेजोमयोऽमृतमयः पुरुषोऽयमेव स योऽयमात्मेदममृतमिदं ब्रह्मेदँ सर्वम् ॥९॥

ayaṁ̐ stanayitnuḥ sarveṣāṁ bhūtānāṁ madhvasya stanayitnoḥ sarvāṇi bhūtāni madhu yaścāyamasminstanayitnau tejomayo 'mr̥tamayaḥ puruṣo yaścāyamadhyātmaṁ̐ śābdaḥ sauvarastejomayo 'mr̥tamayaḥ puruṣo 'yameva sa yo 'yamātmedamamṛtamidaṁ brahmedaṁ sarvam ॥9 ॥

This thunder-cloud is the honey of all beings and all beings are the honey of this thunder-cloud. Likewise, the radiant, immortal person who is in this thunder-cloud and with respect to the self (*adhyātma*) the radiant, immortal person in sound and in tone, he indeed is but this Self. This is Immortal, this is *Brahman*, this is the Whole.

अयमाकाशः सर्वेषां भूतानां मध्वस्याकाशस्य सर्वाणि भूतानि मधु यश्चायमस्मिन्नाकाशे तेजोमयोऽमृतमयः पुरुषो यश्चायमध्यात्मँ हृद्याकाशस्तेजोमयोऽमृतमयः पुरुषोऽयमेव स योऽयमात्मेदममृतमिदं ब्रह्मेदँ सर्वम् ॥१०॥

ayamākāśaḥ sarveṣāṁ bhūtānāṁ madhvasyākāśasya sarvāṇi bhūtāni madhu yaścāyamasminnākāśe tejomayo 'mṛtamayaḥ puruṣo yaścāyamadhyātmaṁ hṛdyākāśastejomayo 'mṛtamayaḥ puruṣo 'yameva sa yo 'yamātmedamamṛtamidaṁ brahmedaṁ sarvam ॥10 ॥

This Space (*ākāśa*) is the honey of all beings and all beings are the honey of this Space (*ākāśa*). Likewise, the radiant, immortal person who is in this space and with respect to the self (*adhyātma*) the radiant, immortal person in the space of the heart, is but this Self. This is Immortal, this is *Brahman*, this is the Whole.

अयं धर्मः सर्वेषां भूतानां मध्वस्य धर्मस्य सर्वाणि भूतानि मधु यश्चायमस्मिन्धर्मे तेजोमयोऽमृतमयः पुरुषो यश्चायमध्यात्मं धार्मस्तेजोमयोऽमृतमयः पुरुषोऽयमेव स योऽयमात्मेदममृतमिदं ब्रह्मेदँ सर्वम् ॥११॥

ayaṁ dharmaḥ sarveṣāṁ bhūtānāṁ madhvasya dharmasya sarvāṇi bhūtāni madhu yaścāyamasmindharme tejomayo 'mṛtamayaḥ puruṣo yaścāyamadhyātmaṁ dhārmastejomayo 'mṛtamayaḥ puruṣo 'yameva sa yo 'yamātmedamamṛtamidaṁ brahmedaṁ sarvam ॥

This *dharma* (law, principle which holds together) is the honey of all beings and all beings are the honey of this *dharma*. Likewise, the radiant, immortal person who is in this *dharma* and with respect to the self, the radiant, immortal person devoted to *dharma* in the body, is indeed but this Self. This is Immortal, this is *Brahman*, this is the Whole.

इदँ सत्यँ सर्वेषां भूतानां मध्वस्य सत्यस्य सर्वाणि भूतानि मधु यश्चायमस्मिन्सत्ये तेजोमयोऽमृतमयः पुरुषो यश्चायमध्यात्मँ सात्यस्तेजोमयोऽमृतमयः पुरुषोऽयमेव स योऽयमात्मेदममृतमिदं ब्रह्मेदँ सर्वम् ॥१२॥

idaṁ satyaṁ sarveṣāṁ bhūtānāṁ madhvasya satyasya sarvāṇi bhūtāni madhu yaścāyamasminsatye tejomayo 'mṛtamayaḥ puruṣo yaścāyamadhyātmaṁ sātyastejomayo 'mṛtamayaḥ puruṣo 'yameva sa yo 'yamātmedamamṛtamidaṁ brahmedaṁ sarvam ॥12॥

This truth is the honey of all beings and all beings are the honey of this truth. Likewise, the radiant, immortal person who is in this truth and the radiant, immortal person devoted to truth is indeed but this Self. This is Immortal, this is *Brahman*, this is the Whole.

इदं मानुषँ सर्वेषां भूतानां मध्वस्य मानुषस्य सर्वाणि भूतानि मधु यश्चायमस्मिन्मानुषे तेजोमयोऽमृतमयः पुरुषः यश्चायमध्यात्मं मानुषः तेजोमयोऽमृतमयः पुरुषो अयमेव स योऽयमात्मेदममृतमिदं ब्रह्मेदँ सर्वम् ॥१३॥

idaṁ mānuṣaṁ sarveṣāṁ bhūtānāṁ madhvasya mānuṣasya sarvāṇi bhūtāni madhu yaścāyamasminmānuṣe tejomayo 'mṛtamayaḥ puruṣaḥ yaścāyamadhyātmaṁ mānuṣastejomayo 'mṛtamayaḥ puruṣo ayameva sa yo 'yamātmedamamṛtamidaṁ brahmedaṁ sarvam ॥13॥

This Mental Being is the honey of all beings and all beings are the honey of this Mental Being. Likewise, the radiant, immortal person who is in the mental being and with respect to the self, the radiant, immortal person in the human being is indeed but this Self. This is Immortal, this is *Brahman*, this is the Whole.

अयमात्मा सर्वेषां भूतानां मध्वस्यात्मनः सर्वाणि भूतानि मधु यश्चायमस्मिन्नात्मनि तेजोमयोऽमृतमयः पुरुषो यश्चायमात्मा तेजोमयोऽमृतमयः पुरुषोऽयमेव स योऽयमात्मेदममृतमिदं ब्रह्मेदँ सर्वम् ॥१४॥

ayamātmā sarveṣāṁ bhūtānāṁ madhvasyātmanaḥ sarvāṇi bhūtāni madhu yaścāyamasminnātmani tejomayo 'mṛtamayaḥ puruṣo yaścāyamātmā tejomayo 'mṛtamayaḥ puruṣo 'yameva sa yo 'yamātmedamamṛtamidaṁ brahmedam̐ sarvam ॥14॥

This self (*ātman*) is the honey of all beings and all beings are the honey of this self. Likewise, the radiant, immortal person in the self and with respect to the (individual) self, the radiant, immortal person in the self, is indeed but this Self. This is Immortal, this is *Brahman*, this is the Whole.

स वा अयमात्मा सर्वेषां भूतानामधिपतिः सर्वेषां भूतानाँ राजा तद्यथा रथनाभौ च रथनेमौ चाराः सर्वे समर्पिता एवमेवास्मिन्नात्मनि सर्वाणि भूतानि सर्वे देवाः सर्वे लोकाः सर्वे प्राणाः सर्व एत आत्मानः समर्पिताः ॥१५॥

sa vā ayamātmā sarveṣāṁ bhūtānāmadhipatiḥ sarveṣāṁ bhūtānām̐ rājā tadyathā rathanābhau ca rathanemau cārāḥ sarve samarpitā evamevāsminnātmani sarvāṇi bhūtāni sarve devāḥ sarve lokāḥ sarve prāṇāḥ sarva eta ātmānaḥ samarpitāḥ ॥15॥

Truly this Self is the ruler of all beings, the king of all beings. Just as all the spokes are fixed in the nave and the felloe of a chariot wheel, so are all beings, all gods, all worlds, all life-functions and all these individual selves held together in the Self.

इदं वै तन्मधु दध्यङ्ङाथर्वणोऽश्विभ्यामुवाच तदेतदृषिः पश्यन्नवोचत्। तद्वां नरा सनये दँस उग्रमाविष्कृणोमि तन्यतुर्न वृष्टिम्। दध्यङ् ह यन्मध्वाथर्वणो वामश्वस्य शीर्ष्णा प्र यदीमुवाचेति ॥१६॥

idaṁ vai tanmadhu dadhyaṅṅātharvaṇo 'śvibhyāmuvāca tadetadṛṣiḥ paśyannavocat । *tadvāṁ narā sanaye dam̐sa ugramāviṣkṛṇomi tanyaturna vṛṣṭim* । *dadhyaṅ ha yanmadhvātharvaṇo vāmaśvasya śīrṣṇā pra yadīmuvāceti* ॥16॥

This, verily, is the honey (*madhu*-doctrine) which Dadhyañc Ātharvaṇ taught the Aśvins. The *ṛṣi* perceived this and said: "Oh heroes! that awesome profitable mastery of yours I will disclose, as the thunder-cloud (discloses) the rain – that *madhu-*

doctrine which Dadhyañc Ātharvaṇ taught you through the head of a horse."

इदं वै तन्मधु दध्यङ्ङाथर्वणोऽश्विभ्यामुवाच तदेतदृषिः पश्यन्नवोचदाथर्वणायाश्विना दधीचेऽश्व्यँ शिरः प्रत्यैरयतम्। स वां मधु प्र वोचदृतायन्त्वाष्ट्रं यद्दस्रावपि कक्ष्यं वामिति॥१७॥

idaṁ vai tanmadhu dadhyaṅṅātharvaṇo 'śvibhyāmuvāca tadetadṛṣiḥ paśyannavocadātharvaṇāyāśvinā dadhīce 'śvyam̐ śiraḥ pratyairayatam । *sa vāṁ madhu pra vocadṛtāyantvāṣṭraṁ yaddasrāvapi kakṣyaṁ vāmiti* ॥17॥

This, verily, is the honey (*madhu*-doctrine) which Dadhyañc Ātharvaṇ taught the Aśvins. The *ṛṣi* perceived this and said: "Oh Aśvins! on Dadhyañc Ātharvaṇ you fixed a horse's head. As promised, he revealed to you Tvaṣṭṛ's honey, Oh mighty ones! that remains a secret with you."

इदं वै तन्मधु दध्यङ्ङाथर्वणोऽश्विभ्यामुवाच तदेतदृषिः पश्यन्नवोचत्। पुरश्चक्रे द्विपदः पुरश्चक्रे चतुष्पदः पुरः स पक्षी भूत्वा पुरः पुरुष आविशदिति। स वा अयं पुरुषः सर्वासु पूर्षु पुरिशयो नैनेन किंचनानावृतम्॥१८॥

idaṁ vai tanmadhu dadhyaṅṅātharvaṇo 'śvibhyāmuvāca tadetadṛṣiḥ paśyannavocat । *puraścakre dvipadaḥ puraścakre catuṣpadaḥ puraḥ sa pakṣī bhūtvā puraḥ puruṣa āviśaditi* । *sa vā ayaṁ puruṣaḥ sarvāsu pūrṣu puriśayo nainena kiṁcanānāvṛtaṁ* ॥18॥

This, verily, is the honey (*madhu*-doctrine) which Dadhyañc Ātharvaṇ taught the Aśvins. The *ṛṣi* perceived this and said: "He made forts with two feet; He made forts with four feet. Becoming a bird, at the beginning the Person (*puruṣa*) entered the fort." This very Person (*puruṣa*) is the fort-dweller (*puriśaya*) in all forts (*pura*). There is nothing that is not protected by Him, nothing that is not pervaded by Him."

इदं वै तन्मधु दध्यङ्ङाथर्वणोऽश्विभ्यामुवाच तदेतदृषिः पश्यन्नवोचद्रूपरूपँ प्रतिरूपो बभूव तदस्य रूपं प्रतिचक्षणाय। इन्द्रो मायाभिः पुरुरूप ईयते युक्ता ह्यस्य हरयः शता दशेत्ययं वै हरयोऽयं वै दश च सहस्राणि बहूनि चानन्तानि च तदेतद्ब्रह्मापूर्वमनपरमनन्तरमबाह्यमयमात्मा ब्रह्म सर्वानुभूरित्यनुशासनम्॥१९॥

idaṁ vai tanmadhu dadhyaṅṅātharvaṇo 'śvibhyāmuvāca tadetadṛṣiḥ paśyannavocadrūparūpaṁ pratirūpo babhūva tadasya rūpaṁ praticakṣaṇāya । *indro māyābhiḥ pururūpa īyate yuktā hyasya harayaḥ śatā daśetyayaṁ vai harayo 'yaṁ vai daśa ca sahasrāṇi bahūni cānantāni ca tadetadbrahmāpūrvamanaparamanantaramabāhyamayamātmā brahma sarvānubhūrityanuśāsanam* ॥19॥

This, verily, is the honey (*madhu*-doctrine) which Dadhyañc Ātharvaṇ taught the Aśvins. The *ṛṣi* perceived this and said: "He became the likeness of every form. All forms exist to reveal him. The Lord (Indra), through His magical power (*māyā*), travels abroad in many forms; for to Him are yoked 110 horses." He is himself the horses; He is himself tens and thousands, many and infinite. This *Brahman* is without an earlier or a later, without an inside or an outside. This self is *Brahman* (*ayam ātma brahma*), all-experiencing. This is the teaching."

Bibliography

Aurobindo, Sri, 1997, *Essays on the Gita*, in *Complete Works of Sri Aurobindo (CWSA)*, vol. 19, Pondicherry: Sri Aurobindo Ashram.

———, 1997, *Savitri*, in *CWSA*, vols 21 and 22, Pondicherry: Sri Aurobindo Ashram.

———, 1998, *Secret of the Veda*, in *CWSA*, vol. 15, Pondicherry: Sri Aurobindo Ashram.

———, 1999, *Synthesis of Yoga*, in *CWSA*, vols 23-24, Pondicherry: Sri Aurobindo Ashram.

———, 2001, *Kena and Other Upanishads*, in *CWSA*, vol. 18, Pondicherry: Sri Aurobindo Ashram.

———, 2003, *Isha Upanishad*, in *CWSA*, vol. 17, Pondicherry: Sri Aurobindo Ashram.

———, 2003, *Early Cultural Writings*, in *CWSA*, vol. 1, Sri Aurobindo Ashram.

———, 2005, *The Life Divine*, in *CWSA*, vols 33 and 34, Pondicherry: Sri Aurobindo Ashram.

———, 2013, *Hymns to the Mystic Fire*, in *CWSA*, vol. 16, Pondicherry: Sri Aurobindo Ashram.

Banerji, Debashish, 2020, *Meditations on the Isha Upanishad: Tracing the Philosophical Vision of Sri Aurobindo*, Kolkata: Sri Aurobindo Samiti and Maha Bodhi Book Agency.

Bergson, Henri, 1998, *Creative Evolution*, tr. Arthur Mitchell, New York: Dover.

———, 1988, *Matter and Memory*, tr. N.M. Paul and W.S. Palmer, Princeton, NJ: Princeton University Press.

Blake, William, 1868, *The Marriage of Heaven and Hell*, London: John Camden Hotten.

Bronkhorst, Johannes, 2007, *Greater Magadha: Studies in the Culture of Early India*, Leiden: Brill.

———, 2011, *Buddhism in the Shadow of Brahmanism*, Leiden: Brill.

De Bolver, Arne, Alex Murray, Joh Roffe and Ashley Woodward (eds), 2012, *Gilbert Simondon: Being and Technology*, Edinburgh, Edinburgh University Press.

Deleuze, Gilles, 1990, *Bergsonism*, New York: Zone Books.

———, 2005, *Cinema 2: The Time-Image*, tr. H. Tomlinson and R. Galeta, New York: Continuum.

Deleuze, Gilles and Felix Guattari, 2009, *Anti-Oedipus: Capitalism and Schizophrenia*, London: Penguin Books.

———, 1986, *Kafka: Towards a Minor Literature*, Minneapolis: University of Minnesota Press.

Doniger, Wendy, 2005, *The Rig Veda*, London: London: Penguin Books.

Freud, Sigmund, 1953-74, "Civilization and Its Discontents", in *The Standard Edition of the Complete Psychological Works of Sigmund Freud*, vol. 21, London: Hogarth Press.

Heidegger, Martin, 1977, "The Age of World Picture", *in The Question Concerning Technology and Other Essays*, tr. William Lovitt, New York: Harper and Row.

Heidegger in *Introduction to Metaphysics*, pp. 199-200, 1959, New Haven, CT: Yale University Press.

Hiltebeitel, Alf, 2007, "Hinduism", in *The Religious Traditions of Asia*, ed. Joseph Kitagawa, London: Routledge.

Jamison, Stephanie W. and Joel P. Brereton (tr.), 2014, *The Rig Veda: The Earliest Religious Poetry of India*, Oxford: Oxford University Press.

Jung, C.G., 1968, *Collected Works of C.G. Jung*, vol. 9, part 2, 2nd edn, Princeton, NJ: Princeton University Press.

Kitagawa, Joseph, 2007, *The Religious Traditions of Asia: Religion, History and Culture*, London: Routledge.

Lacan, Jacques, 2001, *Ecrits: A Selection*, tr. Alan Sheridan, London and New York: Routledge Classics.

Lakshmanjoo, Swami, 2015, *Kashmir Shaivism: The Secret Supreme*, Los Angeles, CA: Universal Shaiva Fellowship.

Olivelle, Patrick, 1998, *The Early Upanishads: Annotated Text and Translation*, Oxford: Oxford University Press.

———, 2008, *Upanishads*, Oxford: Oxford University Press.

Plato, 1996, *Phaedo*, tr. David Gallup, Oxford and New York: Oxford University Press.

Radhakrishnan, S., 1968, *The Principal Upanisads: Edited with Introduction, Text, Translation and Notes*, London: George, Allen and Unwin.

Shastry, Kapali, 1947, *Lights on the Upanishads*, Pondicherry: Sri Aurobindo Library.

Srinivasan, Doris, 1979, "Early Vaiṣṇava Imagery: Caturvyūha and Variant Forms", *Archives of Asian Art*, 32: 39-54.

Stiegler, Bernard, 2009, "The Theater of Individuation: Phase-Shift and Resolution in Simondon and Heidegger", tr. Kristina Lebedeva, *Parrhesia*, 7: 46-57.

———, 2011, "Pharmacology of Desire: Drive-based Capitalism and Libidinal Dis-economy", *New Formations*, 72: 150-61.

Index